Alcibiades and the Socratic Lover-Educator

# ALCIBIADES
## and the Socratic Lover-Educator

Edited by
Marguerite Johnson
and
Harold Tarrant

BLOOMSBURY
LONDON · NEW DELHI · NEW YORK · SYDNEY

Bloomsbury Academic
An imprint of Bloomsbury Publishing Plc

| 50 Bedford Square | 1385 Broadway |
| London | New York |
| WC1B 3DP | NY 10018 |
| UK | USA |

www.bloomsbury.com

**Bloomsbury is a registered trade mark of Bloomsbury Publishing Plc**

First published in 2012 by Bristol Classical Press an imprint of
Bloomsbury Academic
Paperback Edition first published 2013

Editorial matter and arrangement © Marguerite Johnson and
Harold Tarrant 2012

Marguerite Johnson and Harold Tarrant have asserted their right under
the Copyright, Designs and Patents Act, 1988, to be identified as
Editors of this work.

All rights reserved. No part of this publication may be reproduced or
transmitted in any form or by any means, electronic or mechanical,
including photocopying, recording, or any information storage
or retrieval system, without prior permission in writing
from the publishers.

No responsibility for loss caused to any individual or organization acting
on or refraining from action as a result of the material in this
publication can be accepted by Bloomsbury or the author.

**British Library Cataloguing-in-Publication Data**
A catalogue record for this book is available from the British Library.

ISBN: HB: 978-0-7156-4086-9
PB: 978-1-4725-0446-3

**Library of Congress Cataloging-in-Publication Data**
A catalog record for this book is available from the Library of Congress.

Typeset by Ray Davies

# Contents

| | |
|---|---|
| Notes on Contributors | vii |
| Preface | x |
| Introduction | |
|     *Harold Tarrant and Marguerite Johnson* | 1 |
| 1. The role of *Eros* in Improving the Pupil, or What Socrates Learned from Sappho | |
|     *Marguerite Johnson* | 7 |
| 2. Socrates and Platonic Models of Love | |
|     *Dougal Blyth* | 30 |
| 3. The Eye of the Beloved: *Opsis* and *Eros* in Socratic Pedagogy | |
|     *Victoria Wohl* | 45 |
| 4. Plato's Oblique Response to Issues of Socrates' Influence on Alcibiades: An Examination of the *Protagoras* and the *Gorgias* | |
|     *Reuben Ramsey* | 61 |
| 5. Socratic Ignorance, or the Place of the *Alcibiades I* in Plato's Early Works | |
|     *Yuji Kurihara* | 77 |
| 6. Did Alcibiades Learn Justice from the Many? | |
|     *Joe Mintoff* | 90 |
| 7. The Dual-Role Philosophers: An Exploration of a Failed Relationship | |
|     *Anthony Hooper* | 107 |
| 8. Authenticity, Experiment or Development: The *Alcibiades I* on Virtue and Courage | |
|     *Eugenio Benitez* | 119 |
| 9. Revaluing *Megalopsuchia*: Reflections on the *Alcibiades II* | |
|     *Matthew Sharpe* | 134 |
| 10. Improvement by Love: From Aeschines to the Old Academy | |
|     *Harold Tarrant* | 147 |
| 11. Ice-Cold in Alex: Philo's Treatment of the Divine Lover in Hellenistic Pedagogy | |
|     *Fergus J. King* | 164 |
| 12. Proclus' Reading of Plato's *Sôkratikoi Logoi*: Proclus' Observations on Dialectic at *Alcibiades* 112d-114e and Elsewhere | |
|     *Akitsugu Taki* | 180 |

*Contents*

13. Socrates' Divine Sign: From the *Alcibiades* to Olympiodorus
    *François Renaud*    190
14. 'The Individual' in History and History 'in General':
    Alcibiades, Philosophical History and Ideas in Contest
    *Neil Morpeth*    200

Appendix 1. Fourth-Century Politics and the Date of the
    *Alcibiades* I
    *Elizabeth Baynham and Harold Tarrant*    215
Appendix 2. Report on the Working Vocabulary in the Doubtful
    Dialogues
    *Harold Tarrant and Terry Roberts*
    a. The Working Vocabulary of the *Alcibiades*
    b. The Working Vocabulary of the *Theages*    223

Bibliography    237
Index to Platonic Works    251
General Index    252

# Notes on Contributors

Dr Elizabeth Baynham is Senior Lecturer in Classics and Ancient History in the School of Humanities, University of Newcastle, Australia. She is the author of *Alexander the Great, The Unique History of Quintus Curtius* (Ann Arbor, 1998) and co-editor (with A.B. Bosworth) of *Alexander the Great in Fact and Fiction* (Oxford, 2000). Her interests include Greco-Roman historiography and Greek history, especially the era of Alexander and the Diadochoi.

Eugenio Benitez is Associate Professor in Philosophy and Classics at the University of Sydney. He is the author of *Forms in Plato's Philebus* (1989), and editor of volumes on Platonic myths and Plato's aesthetics. In recent years he has been primarily concerned with questions associated with the interpretation of Plato's dialogues.

Dougal Blyth is Senior Lecturer in Classics at the University of Auckland, New Zealand. He has published articles and contributed chapters on Plato, Aristotle, Cicero, Aristophanes and Menander, and was a co-editor of *Power and Pleasure, Virtues and Vices* (Prudentia Supplement, Auckland 2001).

Anthony Hooper was an MPhil candidate at the University of Sydney at the time of writing this paper, and is now a PhD candidate at the same institution, writing his dissertation on immortality in the Presocratics and Plato. He has published articles on myth in Plato in *The European Legacy*, and on Aristophanes' speech in Plato's *Symposium* in *The Classical Quarterly*.

Marguerite Johnson is Senior Lecturer in Classics at the University of Newcastle, Australia. She specialises in Greek and Latin literature, especially the works of Sappho and Catullus. She is the author of *Sappho* (Duckworth, 2007) and co-author of *Sexuality in Greek and Roman Literature and Society: A Sourcebook* (Routledge, 2005). One of her current research interests is myth and fairytale in the ancient world, with particular focus on storytelling in Plato.

Fergus J. King has degrees from St Andrews, Edinburgh, and the University of South Africa. He is Rector of the Parish of the Good Shepherd in the

*Notes on Contributors*

Anglican Diocese of Newcastle and Conjoint Lecturer in Theology at the University of Newcastle, and his current research includes the potential dialogue between Epicureanism and the Fourth Gospel. He is the author of *More Than a Passover: Inculturation in the Supper Narratives of the New Testament* (Peter Lang, 2007), and several articles on New Testament and missiological themes.

Yuji Kurihara received his doctorate in Ancient Philosophy from the University of California, Irvine, and is Associate Professor of Philosophy and Ethics at Tokyo Gakugei University. He has published numerous articles on Plato's epistemology and ethics in Japanese and English.

Joe Mintoff is Senior Lecturer in Philosophy at the University of Newcastle, Australia. His primary research interests are in moral philosophy, specifically the theory of rational choice, the philosophy of Socrates, and ancient approaches to the question of how to live. His articles have appeared in *Australasian Journal of Philosophy, American Philosophical Quarterly, Ethics,* and *Ratio*.

Neil Morpeth is Associate Professor at the University of Newcastle (English Language and Foundation Studies Centre), where he lectures in classical studies and traditions of thought. His published work reflects his wide interests in traditions of thought and their transmission across the ages, and includes *Thucydides' War: Accounting for the Faces of Conflict* (Georg Olms Verlag 2006).

Reuben Ramsey is a PhD candidate at the University of Newcastle, after completing an Honours thesis on Alcibiades. He is currently engaged in an analysis of the vocabulary of three plays by Aeschylus and *Prometheus Bound*, with particular reference to the potential dramatic force of repetition in these plays.

François Renaud is Associate Professor of Philosophy, Université de Moncton, Canada. Trained in both Classics and Philosophy, he has published mostly on Plato, his interpretation, and his Socratic legacy. His publications include *Die Resokratisierung Platons. Die platonische Hermeneutik Hans-Georg Gadamers* (Sankt Augustin 1999), and he has coedited volumes on philosophic commentaries over the ages and Gadamer's response to Plato's *Philebus*. His current projects include a monograph on Plato's *Gorgias*, a co-authored book on *Alcibiades* I, and publications on Cicero's Platonism.

Matthew Sharpe teaches philosophy and psychoanalytic studies at Deakin University. He is the author of several publications addressing modern perspectives on classical philosophy, as well as work on contemporary philosophy.

*Notes on Contributors*

Akitsugu Taki has degrees from Durham University and the University of Tokyo, and is Associate Professor in Ethics and Vice Dean in the Department of Environmental and Social Studies, Josai International University (Chiba, Japan). He has published philological papers on Plato, most recently on a scribe's replacement of Proclus' lemma in his commentary on the *Alcibiades*.

Harold Tarrant is Professor of Classics at the University of Newcastle, Australia. He is the author or co-editor of several books on the Platonic tradition in antiquity, including *Plato's First Interpreters* (2000), *Recollecting Plato's Meno* (2005), and (with Dirk Baltzly) *Interpreting Plato in Antiquity* (2006), all from Duckworth. He has more recently been involved in the production of a new English translation of Proclus' *Commentary on the Timaeus*.

Victoria Wohl is Professor of Classics at the University of Toronto. Her research focuses on the literature and culture of classical Athens, spanning a variety of genres, poetic and prosaic. She is the author of *Intimate Commerce: Exchange, Gender, and Subjectivity in Greek Tragedy* (Texas, 1998), *Love Among the Ruins: The Erotics of Democracy in Classical Athens* (Princeton, 2003), and *Law's Cosmos: Juridical Discourse in Athenian Forensic Oratory* (Cambridge, 2010).

# Preface

The majority of chapters in this volume originated as papers given at a symposium on this topic generously funded by the University of Newcastle's Research Management Committee, and held in Newcastle in December 2008. Two have been written by authors who had expressed an interest in attending but were unable to do so, and a few topics have also changed somewhat. The volume has benefited from further work carried out under the auspices of the Australian Research Council's Discovery scheme (DP09086334), in which Tarrant, Benitez, and Renaud were among five named Investigators. Further funding awarded by the University of Newcastle's Research Management Committee to Tarrant and Johnson for 2011 has also been of great assistance.

Special thanks are due not only to the funding bodies but also to the University of Newcastle's Centre for Literary and Linguistic Computing, particularly to Professor Hugh Craig and Dr Alexis Antonia, for their ongoing advice on matters pertaining to the testing of authorship. Finally, our two Research Assistants, Reuben Ramsey and Terry Roberts, have been of huge assistance in assembling the volume and in collecting and analysing data respectively.

M.J.
H.T.

# Introduction

The ancient world tended to be fascinated by relationships between intellectuals and persons wielding great power. The writings of Themistius mention several relationships between powerful rulers and celebrated minds. These included those that linked the Macedonian monarchs Philip II and Alexander with Aristotle and Xenocrates, but concentrated on those of Roman emperors such as Augustus, Tiberius and Trajan with Arius, Thrasyllus and Dio (e.g. *Or.* 11.173b, 173.3-6D). However, the *Alcibiades*, which is the principal focus of the present volume, shows how relationships between intellectuals and democratic leaders could be just as fascinating. It testifies to this fascination with the mutual attraction of power and intellect when it names (118c) Pythocleides and Anaxagoras as earlier intellectuals who had influenced Pericles, and goes on to mention his on-going studies with Damon, a general intellectual mentor as much as a music teacher (*Laches* 180d). In doing so the work arguably betrays an even greater fascination with the relationship between Alcibiades and Socrates, who could be argued to be the most influential thinker of the entire Western philosophical tradition.

The relationship between a mentor and his able pupil (or pupil-like figure) could be complex and intense. It was not unusual for the former to find the latter attractive, and the Greeks were rather more understanding of any sexual relationships that might develop in such circumstances than most peoples in Europe's past. No doubt it was easy for rumours to arise in any cases where one-on-one instruction occurred without close supervision, and there is speculation about the possibly sexual nature of several close friendships in Platonic dialogues. Friends would watch for telltale blushes that might betray sexual interests, as in Plato's *Lysis* (204b). People's inclination to suspect relationships is illustrated not only by Plato's report of the belief that Parmenides and Zeno were in an erotic relationship (*Parmenides* 127b), but also by a story that emerged in the next century making Socrates not only a pupil of the Presocratic philosopher Archelaus, but also his boyfriend (Diogenes Laertius 2.19). In his own day, however, it could probably be said that Socrates was better known for his strangeness than for his sexual experiments, while Alcibiades is already known for the latter from the first extant Greek comedy, Aristophanes' *Acharnians*.

Charges brought against Socrates, if not in court then at least in the subsequent literature, are that he had been a corrupting influence on two powerful political figures: Critias, leader of the Thirty Tyrants who briefly replaced Athenian democracy in 404 BC, and Alcibiades himself. Such charges had the tendency, countered in Xenophon's *Memorabilia* and Isocrates' *Busiris*, to turn Socrates into their teacher. In Alcibiades' case they developed into a story of a strange sexual encounter. It is that story that fuelled a literature that revolved around their supposed relationship. The *Alcibiades I* is the more substantial dialogue of two in the Platonic corpus that seek to document the relationship, and to provide a kind of paradigm of the education that the right kind of lover can offer the youth who arouses his desire. Other Socratics wrote on this theme, and Plato himself had done so in a more limited way in his *Symposium* and obliquely in other dialogues as well.

The *Alcibiades* probably holds the key to a great many questions concerning which of the rather dubious-looking dialogues in the Platonic corpus really are spurious. It stands on the threshold of what could be regarded as acceptably Platonic theory, but it also has a resemblance to some other dialogues that few think are by Plato. Its place in the growth of the legend concerning the relationship between Socrates and Alcibiades seems to be a pivotal one, and some of its claims about that relationship seem much bolder than anything we might have expected from Plato. Yet even so, Plato often heads off in an unexpected direction, and there is still no agreement about whether this is really a work of Plato's. For some scholars this undecided issue of authorship presents an insuperable obstacle to building upon it for further philosophic purposes, but the work invites us to consider a host of interesting issues, some dry and scholarly, some genuinely philosophic, others almost entertaining. There is no reason to allow the undecided authorship to hinder our attempts to understand the work as fully as possible, both in its own right as a self-standing Socratic dialogue, and against the wider background of dialogues about Socrates.

The relationship between Socrates and Alcibiades described in this work is both erotic (in some rather unusual sense) and at the same time educational. Since such relationships were not unusual in the Greek world, Johnson, with one eye on the *Alcibiades,* takes us first to the world of Sappho, a female whose work likewise combines an erotic dimension with an educational one. She argues that the extent of Sappho's influence over Socrates may be more extensive that scholars usually imagine. Socrates as lover did not exist in a vacuum, and was unlikely to have been as *sui generis* as is often supposed. His attitudes to love are conditioned by the Greek cultural world with which he was familiar, and Sappho offered both an inspiring and a thoughtful paradigm of the loving mentor.

Blyth then looks at three dialogues other than the *Alcibiades* that depict Socrates as something of an expert in love. Being the expert, however, and being a lover in some very special sense, he does not need to be erotically

*Introduction*

disposed to those with whom he talks there. Friendship is rather what motivates him, and not in the *Lysis* alone. While he often adopts what seems to be the pose of the lover, and participates in conversations couched in erotic language, Plato is usually unwilling to represent him in a genuine loving encounter.

Greek theories about the operation of love tend to be closely linked with notions of beauty, particularly visual beauty. Wohl contrasts the operation of love's gaze as it is treated in Xenophon and in the *Alcibiades*, with reference to the Platonic corpus more widely. She explores the visual dynamics of Xenophon's pederastic eros and philosophical pedagogy, drawing some fascinating contrasts with Platonic texts. She concludes with a special emphasis on the Alcibiades of Plato's *Symposium*, who rejects the ordinary understanding of beauty as something fundamentally visual.

Ramsey then adds a rather different dimension by exploring the way that Socrates' lack of success in reforming Alcibiades is treated in two uncontroversial dialogues of Plato, both generally thought to be early. These are the *Protagoras*, which introduces the relationship with Alcibiades at its opening and returns to it with subtle clues from time to time, and the *Gorgias*, where the arguments with Callicles not only make reference to Socrates' 'love' for both Alcibiades and philosophy, but also give us a new perspective to reflect on by seemingly treating Callicles as something of an Alcibiades-type himself. It may be that Plato in his earlier career preferred to treat the figure of Alcibiades and the failure of Socrates to reform him somewhat obliquely.

We then meet three papers that deal with the *Alcibiades* more in its own right, the first two concentrating on dialectical matters, the third on the quasi-erotic relationship. First Kurihara details problems in reconciling the work's concept of knowing one's own ignorance with the way awareness of this ignorance is ordinarily treated in Plato. Since matters of epistemology and self-knowledge lie at the heart of Plato's picture of Socrates, these problems need to be carefully considered by all who would make the *Alcibiades* a genuine dialogue of Plato, particularly a genuine dialogue of a broadly 'Socratic' type.

Mintoff goes on to examine the quality of the dialogue's arguments that we cannot learn justice from the people at large (the many). His essay is essentially a modern assessment of the merits of this thesis of Socrates. He also employs material from the *Protagoras* on what the ordinary people might teach one. He concludes by reaffirming that Alcibiades, even if he learned how to speak Greek from the many, did not get an understanding of justice from that same source.

Hooper highlights Platonic material that points to the possibilities of a relationship that would transcend the traditional division between the lover and the beloved, moving more towards modern ideals of an equal, or at least balanced, relationship in which the separate roles are not so easily discerned. He argues that Socrates in the *Alcibiades* is pursuing this kind of relationship, which will involve mutual caring and mutual benefit, so that the usual distinctions that society made between lover and beloved would not pertain.

The next group of papers compares the dialogue with slightly later material. Benitez reads the ethics of the work against the background of what traditional chronology (following no less an authority than Plutarch) takes to be Plato's last work, the *Laws*. His reading gives some support for Denyer's thesis that the *Alcibiades* is a late dialogue in spite of its form, its preoccupation with Socrates, and its stylistic features.

Sharpe then looks at the *Alcibiades* against the background of the other dialogue in the corpus in which Alcibiades plays the role of principal interlocutor, the *Alcibiades* II. This shorter dialogue is much more regularly, though not invariably, assumed to be by an author other than Plato. Sharpe concentrates on the idea that the dialogue is somehow re-evaluating the man of grand ambitions, and employs the many literary references in the work to explore how this is done. Here tragedy, and particularly Sophocles' *Oedipus the King,* come to the fore.

Tarrant then compares the growth of the legend of the love-match between Socrates and Alcibiades, starting with the writings of the Socratics themselves, and especially Aeschines, in whose pages Socrates had vainly hoped to convert Alcibiades 'by his love alone'. He then moves on to the world of the doubtful dialogues, highlighting the question of how Socrates might have expected Alcibiades to learn from him. Here he considers not only the *Alcibiades* but also another doubtful work, the *Theages*. He attempts to relate the erotic and educational ideology that he finds in these works to that of the Academy towards the close of the fourth century, for there was clearly *some* relationship between the erotic theory of the Socrates-Alcibiades tradition and the Academy under Plato's third successor, Polemo.

The *Alcibiades* actually grew in importance as time went on. Polemo, because Zeno of Citium had studied with him, influenced the Stoic tradition too. The dialogue seems to have been known to Cicero or his source (*de Leg.* 1.58-9, *Tusc.* 1.52), as well as to Plutarch and virtually all subsequent Platonists, promoting regular discussion about the nature of the 'self', attracting regular commentaries among pagan teachers, and much interest from certain Christian authors as well. However, the Christian tradition is influenced by different attitudes to erotic relationships, stemming rather from the Jewish background of their religion.

By a detailed examination of the Jewish apologist Philo of Alexandria, King shows the tensions that existed between Greek, Jewish, and more local traditions. While the kind of education he was promoting was in general more typically Greek, Philo was not noted for the liberalism of his thinking on sexual matters, and much of the Greek erotic ideology was quite foreign to the Jewish tradition. Hence there is a surprising absence,

*Introduction*

in a thinker often considered a kind of early Middle Platonist, of much of the erotic language that one would expect of a Platonist in his time. Philo's position was influential among the Christians, and a representative of the combination of traditions upon which Christianity sought to build.

At this point we move to the Neoplatonic commentators on the *Alcibiades* who worked with a Platonic curriculum in which this dialogue was read first, giving it a formative influence on the pupil's experience of Plato overall. Taki turns to the way in which Proclus approached the Socratic and aporetic elements in the Platonic corpus, and particularly in the *Alcibiades*, upon which he wrote a commentary that has in part survived. Taki discusses how and why Proclus adopts a single approach to many of the dialectical strategies of the Platonic Socrates for which we today would find different names. For him the Socratic strategy is respondent-centred, concentrating on the advances that the interlocutor makes for himself, and he explores the notion that his soul in this process is 'projecting *logoi*'.

Renaud moves on to treat the work's reception in the sole complete extant ancient commentary on it, that of Olympiodorus, concentrating on the commentator's reading of the divine sign that has in the dialogue long prevented Socrates from approaching Alcibiades. In so doing Renaud works through, in a manner that is instructive both for readers of the *Alcibiades* and for those who study the commentaries, a range of issues beginning with the sign, its roles and its supernatural connections, and moving on to the *daimôn-Erôs*, the art of love and Socrates' special expertise in that art.

Morpeth's exploratory essay brings the figure of Alcibiades into modern times, considering the continuing intellectual puzzle presented by Alcibiades as an historical figure and as a trans-historical dramatic character. Alcibiades, whilst very much of his own times, came to represent dreams, ambitions and intellectual currents of thought well beyond his Periclean and post-Periclean worlds. Alcibiades, the historical person, developed into more than the *stratêgos* and political figure originally characterised in Thucydides' worlds at war. For Morpeth, Alcibiades was political electricity, controversy and debate – at once a positive and a negative force in Athenian, Spartan and Peloponnesian society and well beyond.

We conclude with two appendices. Baynham had originally introduced some historical issues at a round table, asking what sort of date in the fourth century would best explain some of the material, such as the reference to Peparethos, the ambitions attributed to Alcibiades, and the warning comments put into the mouths of the royal women of Sparta and Persia. These have since been explored in collaboration with Tarrant, and Appendix 1 brings that to fruition and makes observations about possible historical contexts. These tend, however, to be very far from conclusive.

The results of new vocabulary-based stylometric tests on the *Alcibiades*, other doubtful dialogues, and other Platonic and non-Platonic material, are then presented in Appendix 2a. Tests have been run by Roberts in the context of a research project directed by Tarrant. While it is premature to claim too much on their basis, it can easily be argued that, as far as its working vocabulary is concerned, the dialogue does not look like a typical early dialogue. Rather, on these tests it often looks more like a middle-period dialogue with some special idiosyncrasies. Appendix 2b briefly examines the implications of these tests for the *Theages* too.

Finally, we should like to leave the reader with a quotation from Hermeias' *Commentary on Plato's Phaedrus* (1.1-5), which may itself owe something to the traditions surrounding the relationship of Socrates and Alcibiades, and which illustrates how the legend of the beneficent Socrates on his divine mission ultimately developed:

> Socrates was sent down into generation for the benefit of the human race and of the souls of young persons. As there is much difference between souls in the character and practices, he benefits each differently, the young in one way, sophists in another, stretching his hands out to all and exhorting them to practise philosophy.

It is almost as if the Platonic tradition had countered Christianity with a different figure claiming to be the light, the truth, and the way.

# 1

# The Role of *Eros* in Improving the Pupil, or What Socrates Learned from Sappho[1]

*Marguerite Johnson*

## Introduction

... someone who loves your soul will never leave you ... I am he who will never leave you ... (Socrates to Alcibiades, from *Alc.* 131d)

What did Sappho of Lesbos teach her girls except how to love? (Ovid, *Tristia* 2.365)

What would it mean to call Sappho up from the underworld, the subtext, and put her in the text of Plato? Literally to put her there, to set her down in the middle of the dialogues, conversations among men? How would her presence affect those conversations, scenes of exploration and discovery, aporia and domination? How would she unsettle and destabilise and trouble the fabric of the debates Socrates finds himself in? (duBois 1995, 79)

*Eros* – in theory and, perhaps, in practice[2] – was a central concern of certain pre-Socratics, most obviously Empedocles,[3] and of the Platonic schools from Plato himself on.[4] Indeed, the role of *eros* in improving the pupil – spiritually as well as intellectually – was a *topos* of various philosophical dialogues, including those by persons other than Plato, such as Xenophon (*Symposium*) and Plutarch (*Eroticus*). Yet it may be argued that the inquiry into *eros*, and the employment of *eros* for purposes that may loosely be described as 'educational', had a separate or independent existence, already reflected in poetry, and above all in the poetic 'pedagogies' of Sappho. Taking the latter view as more than idle theorising, I propose to explore the influence of Sappho – duBois' 'underworld' or 'subtext' – on the Platonic Socrates-as-pedagogue, while keeping an eye on the *Alcibiades* I and the undisputed works of Plato that touch on these themes.

How successful Sappho was in utilising the theme of *eros* to improve the 'pupil' is difficult to gauge owing to the paucity of the extant poetry. We can, of course, speculate on this by examining the context of her original performances and considering how her songs may have impacted on her audience. For the purposes of this analysis, however, Socrates is also examined as a kind of pupil of Sappho, in the hope of yielding additional material for an assessment of her success as an instructor in matters erotic.

*Marguerite Johnson*

## Sappho as teacher (Maximus of Tyre on Sappho and Socrates)

The image of Sappho as a teacher has a long and turbulent academic history and, at the risk of reigniting this debate, I wish to review a passage from the *Orations* by Maximus of Tyre (often regarded as a Platonist himself), in which Sappho was presented as an educator along Socratic lines:

> What else was the love of the Lesbian woman – if one may compare older things with newer – except Socrates' art of love? For they seem to me to have practised love each in their own way, she that of women, he that of men. For they both said that they loved many and were captivated by all things beautiful. What Alcibiades and Charmides and Phaedrus were to him, Gyrinna and Atthis and Anactoria were to the Lesbian. And what the rival craftsmen Prodicus and Gorgias and Thrasymachus and Protagoras were to Socrates, Gorgo and Andromeda were to Sappho. Sometimes she upbraids them; sometimes she refutes them and uses irony, just like the words of Socrates. 'Hello to Ion', says Socrates [*Ion* 530a]. 'Fare-you-well to the daughter of Polyanax', says Sappho [155]. Socrates says that he did not approach Alcibiades, though he loves him very much, before he was ready for his words.[5] 'You still seemed to me to be a small and graceful child',[6] says Sappho. He makes fun somewhere of the clothes and way of reclining of a sophist. She: 'And what woman wearing a rustic dress ...' [57]. Eros, says Diotima to Socrates, is not a child but the follower of Aphrodite and her servant [*Symp.* 203c]. And Sappho says somewhere in an ode to Aphrodite, 'And you, lovely servant Eros' [159]. Diotima says that Eros prospers when he has resources but dies when he is without resource [*Symp.* 203e]. She, comprehending this, called [him] 'bittersweet' [130] and 'paingiving' [*algesidôron* 172]. Socrates calls Eros a sophist [*Symp.* 203d]; Sappho, 'tale-weaver' [188].[7] He goes into a bacchic frenzy over Phaedrus under the influence of Eros [*Phdr.* 234d]. Eros shook her heart, 'like the wind attacking the oaks on a mountain' [47]. He is bothered by Xanthippe wailing that he was dying [*Phdr.* 60a], and she at her daughter: 'For it is not right for there to be a lament in the house of the followers of the Muses. These things are not suitable for us.[8]

This long and much-quoted passage has become a historical cornerstone of many studies of Sappho and, in what is arguably the seminal work on the topic of Sappho as schoolmistress, Holt N. Parker (1993; 1996, 183) utilises it in order to illustrate the types of ancient source material accessed by scholars intent on proving that the poet was a teacher of sorts. Careful not to dismiss this passage completely, Parker draws attention to its historical relevance as a piece of biographic text worthy of consideration:

> Maximus' concern here is to show the nobility of love. He no more states that Sappho ran a school than he sets up one for Hesiod, whom he cites for comparison with Socrates immediately before this passage or for Archilochus or Anacreon, whom he quotes immediately afterwards (18.91-m). Further, the important point is missed that not even Socrates ran a 'school'. (Parker 1993; 1996, 155)

## 1. *The Role of* Eros *in Improving the Pupil*

In addition to placing Sappho in a less anachronistic setting, Parker rightly corrects any misconceptions concerning Socrates: neither poet nor philosopher ran schools, neither were educators in the conventional sense that we understand the term today.

In a later article, Parker is much more critical of Maximus as a source for a Sappho-Socrates nexus:[9]

> His quotations, as we have seen, are none too trustworthy and he is a tad uncertain about his sources. More importantly, even a cursory inspection of his oration shows how superficial his comparisons are. It is impossible to determine from his use the context of any of his Sappho quotations; one can scarcely recognise Socrates. ... Now there is nothing 'ironic' about the opening of the *Ion*. The point of comparison is nothing more than the fact that both authors use the word [*khairô*]. Indeed, it looks very much as if Maximus has got Sappho completely turned around, for everywhere else that we find [*khaire polla*] it is used to say 'goodbye', not 'hello'. He misrepresents the *Symposium*, misremembers the *Phaedrus,* and misunderstands [*algesidôron*]. Socrates somewhere criticises someone's dress; so does Sappho. There is something about mourning in Socrates; there is something about mourning in Sappho. The only legitimate thing here is that both use the word [*therapôn*] of Eros. (Parker 2006, 388-90)

This is a sad situation indeed for any hopeful use of Maximus' words as evidence for what was described above as the Sappho-Socrates nexus, although it must be emphasised that Maximus did not set out to argue for a pedagogical influence of Sappho on Socrates (and Parker does not interpret him as doing so). Indeed, Parker makes a valid critique; and if a modern scholar made the casual suggestions of Maximus, she or he would hardly be given the credence granted to one whose words are valorised by reason of their antiquity.

But perhaps Parker is throwing Sappho's baby out with Socrates' bathwater. As mentioned above, Maximus, as Parker understands him, is not suggesting that Sappho was, by default, a 'teacher' of Socrates. Yet by denouncing Maximus' comparisons – for that is indeed what it really boils down to – Parker underplays any Sapphic influence:

> We cannot be sure that he is giving us an accurate account of the context of even Socrates' words, much less that Sappho's words had anything to do with them whatsoever. Sappho tells us that someone female seems a small and ill-favoured child. We know nothing more than that.' (Parker 2006, 390).[10]

Enter Diotima. In the passage from the *Symposium* to which Maximus alludes and on which Parker critiques him (*Symp.* 203e), Diotima 'speaks' of the tenacity of *Eros*:

> ... at the same time on the same day he blossoms and comes alive, when he

is thriving, then sometimes he dies, but is always back again, revived through the very force of his father's nature. (*Symp.* 203e)

These words, ventriloquised by Socrates, are, more or less, as Maximus would have them ('Diotima says that *Eros* prospers when he has resources but dies when he is without resource'). And while Maximus' coalescent reading of *Symposium* 203e and Sappho's 'bittersweet' (*Fr.* 130) and 'pain-giving' *Eros* (*Fr.* 172) is inadequate, as Parker observes,[11] it nevertheless detects a potential Sapphic echo in the *Symposium* by way of a conceptual transference of the meaning of *Eros* from Archaic lyric to Classical philosophy.[12]

There is also the interesting and not inadequate connection Maximus makes between Socrates' 'sophist' and Sappho's 'tale-weaver' as epithets for *Eros*. In the *Symposium*, it is once again Diotima to whom Maximus (indirectly) refers, for it is she whom Socrates quotes. In her story of the birth of *Eros*, Diotima explains that it is the characteristics he inherits from his father, Contrivance (*Poros*), which make him – among other things – a sophist. The immediate context in which the term is used of *Eros* may be seen to be suggestive of a negative quality, or at least a quality that marks *Eros* as a being of duplicitous nature:

... a mighty sorcerer (*goês*), an apothecary (*pharmakeus*) and a sophist (*sophistês*). (*Symp.* 203d)[13]

Yet prior to this line, Socrates is at pains to point out that the machinations of *Eros* are in the pursuit of 'the good (*agathos*) and the beautiful (*kalos*)' (*Symp.* 203d). This qualifying inclusion may be interpreted as a necessary point in establishing *Eros* as a kind of noble or sublime sophist,[14] neither morally good nor bad but rather a magician, a *goês* or *pharmakeus*, who transcends mundane ethical binaries.[15] Herein lies *Eros*' implicit danger as an entity.

As a sophist, or as a precursor to a sophist, Sappho's *Eros* is typically sophistic as *muthoplokos* – 'tale-weaver' (*Fr.* 188), as Maximus maintains. Of course, Sappho's *muthoplokos* is far closer to her *doplokê* ('guile-weaving') – an epithet for Aphrodite in Poem 1 – reminding us that Sappho was as backward-looking to Homer and Hesiod as she was forward-looking to the philosophers and poets of the Classical age. As *muthoplokos*, Sappho's *Eros* is particularly Hesiodic: in the *Theogony*, *Eros* has the power to dominate, indeed subjugate, all the gods – a power interpreted by Jean-Pierre Vernant and Anne Doueihi (1986, 58) as indicative of his ability to induce *thelxis*, that strange state of erotic desire that takes the individual into a temporary realm of altered consciousness (and as such is a process that borders on the magical).[16] As *muthoplokos*, Sappho's *Eros* may well prefigure Plato's more specific claim à la Socrates à la Diotima, of *Eros* as the *goês* and the *pharmakeus* as well as the *sophistês*.

## 1. The Role of Eros in Improving the Pupil

But did Sappho 'teach' Socrates such things, or am I falling into Maximus' trap of comparisons that do little more than make comparisons? Pessimistically, it could be argued that – beyond the connections Maximus makes, which have been discussed somewhat sophistically above – we do not possess enough of Sappho's work to clearly establish how closely her views on *eros* correspond to those of Socrates, let alone to establish a definitive portrait of her as a 'teacher' of Socrates. Optimistically, however, we do have her fragments and a few complete poems (to be analysed at a later juncture herein), just as we have the recorded words of what became the philosophical and literary construct known as Socrates. We have, therefore, a *legacy* and thereby a language that speaks of the role of love in improving the pupil. By 'pupil' I designate those who *heard* Sappho and Socrates; those who heard her sing and the real man speak, and also those who read the recorded words of both. It is in these contemplative moments as audience or reader that their teachings are revealed and one is subject to potential enlightenment. Likewise, it is in these moments of remembering, of recalling their words, perhaps even more than in the original listening, that one is able to meditate *as a student* upon their meaning. And perhaps this is how one should consider Socrates as a pupil of Sappho, for it is in this sense that the Greeks per se understood the pedagogical nature of poetry; regularly treating it, as Mary Whitlock Blundell observes, as 'a source of factual or categorical wisdom' (1991, 12). Furthermore, Blundell notes the Greek emphasis on the importance of emulating and imitating the good sentiments and righteous personae of poetry, which she aligns with 'the practical ethical concerns of Plato's Socrates' (12n.35).

### Socrates as teacher (teaching as embodied performance)

Both educators (and I still use this term with caution) focus on the theme of *eros*. In regard to Socrates' named pupils, Alcibiades, Charmides, Agathon and Phaedrus among others, there are lessons to be learned concerning the nature of *eros* in all its manifestations; Alcibiades in particular must learn from Socrates the intricacies of this force in order to lead a better life and to lead others in the same pursuit. That Alcibiades fails in understanding *eros* and appropriating a good and moral *eros* – what Victoria Wohl defines as 'a legitimate, democratic eros' as opposed to 'an illegitimate, tyrannical eros' (1999, 352) – serves to emphasise its philosophical, moral and educative magnitude in the shaping of a man (according to the Socratic system). As modern readers with historical hindsight, we witness the significance of Socrates' words on the pursuit of a correct *eros* through observing the very ramifications of Alcibiades' 'illegitimate, tyrannical eros', made manifest as *paranomia* ('lawlessness').

But *how* does Socrates teach *eros*? This is a particularly difficult question to answer because Socrates claims consistently *not* to be a teacher at all, and this tricky denial has instigated numerous scholarly meditations on Socrates-the-reluctant-pedagogue.[17] So perhaps a realignment of the way in which we as readers of the Platonic texts regard Socrates as a teacher is in order. Judith Butler's theory of performativity would not go astray here in offering a useful means by which we can out-fox Socrates' denial of the label 'pedagogue' (of *eros*, in this instance). To this end, it could be argued that to teach *eros*, Socrates embodies it – he performs it. With deference to Butler, therefore, Socrates explicates *eros* by repetition of the acts understood by it and reinforced by the cultural constructions of it, Butler's 'process of iterability, a regularised and constrained repetition of norms' (Butler 1993, 95). Socrates as Subject thereby is 'enabled', as Butler would have it, performing *eros* not as a singular 'act' but as a 'ritualised production, a ritual reiterated under and through constraint, under and through the force of prohibition and taboo, with the threat of ostracism and even death controlling and compelling the shape of the production' (Butler 1993, 95).

Oliver Taplin comes close to an application of Butler's theory in his examination of what he identifies as the performative nature of the transfer of wisdom in Greek culture as enacted by poets and philosophers:

> The Greek thinkers in the archaic and classical periods performed their wisdom in different ways and in front of different audiences. As a modern audience that encounters these 'philosophers' only in written works, we tend to disconnect their doctrines from their historical and cultural contexts. By focusing on philosophic 'performances' of wisdom – both oral and written – and by examining the audiences addressed by these thinkers, we can better appreciate their lives and activities and, indeed, their different conceptions of the nature of wisdom. (Taplin 2001, 138)

And on Socrates in particular:

> Sokrates' wisdom was also embodied, for he enacted his wisdom in deeds as well as words: crucial to his performance of wisdom were his extraordinary powers of physical endurance and self-control. (Taplin 2001, 153)[18]

Taplin's work is, in some respects, reminiscent of the ideas espoused by Pierre Hadot on *living* philosophy as opposed to lecturing or writing it:

> Socrates had no system to teach. Throughout, his philosophy was a spiritual exercise, an invitation to a new way of life, active reflection, and living consciousness. (Taplin 1995, 157)

Hadot – like Taplin after him – examines *Symposium* 203c-d in which *Eros* is described and the comparison to Socrates implicit. Here Diotima tells Socrates that *Eros*, owing to his mother, Poverty (*Penia*), is forever poor, far from beautiful, shoeless, homeless and always wanting (among other things). Additionally, like Socrates, *Eros*, when taking after his father, is

## 1. *The Role of* Eros *in Improving the Pupil*

the sorcerer, the apothecary and the sophist.[19] The comparison to Socrates is there and has been discussed by scholars other than Hadot and Taplin, including Catherine Osborne, who has made extensive cross-references between *Eros* and the Platonic Socrates ('Socrates, like Eros, is a liminal figure, always at the door', Osborne 1996, 96). By 'iterating' the very habits of *Eros* as described by Diotima, Socrates performs the essence of *eros* and, in relation to his role as pedagogue, it could be argued that this 'ritualised production' enables him to teach his pupils about the very subject he embodies.[20]

Turning to *Alcibiades*, one may interpret the following passage as an example of a subtler reading of Socrates' performance of *eros*, compared to *Symposium* 203c-d, with a more overt or traditional emphasis on Socrates as pedagogue. Here, Socrates, in exasperation at Alcibiades' stupidity, exclaims:

> ... when his lover [*erastês*] tells him to study and cultivate himself and learn from enquiry so that he can compete with the king, he declares he does not want to and that he is sufficiently content ... (*Alc.* 123e)

Socrates speaks in a hypothetical narrative in this instance, imagining an inexperienced and arrogant Alcibiades meeting with Amestris, Queen of Persia. In the scenario, Alcibiades is allegedly explaining to Amestris his defiance of Socrates, his lover (read 'teacher'), a revelation that would cause her, Socrates posits, to respond in amazement (*thaumasai*). Here Socrates defines himself as *erastês* to Alcibiades' *erômenos*, as an embodiment of *eros* that is inextricably linked to his pedagogy of Alcibiades. This relationship between lover and beloved along with its implicit albeit somewhat coded pedagogy, dependent on Socrates' performance of *eros*, is developed as a theme throughout the dialogue, reaching its dénouement as the text reaches its conclusion:

> **Soc.**: Then will not my *eros* [for you], O excellent one, be just like a stork: after hatching winged *eros* [*erôs hupopteros*] in you [for me and philosophy], it will be nurtured by it [i.e. your *erôs*] in return. (*Alc.* 135e)

David M. Halperin refers to this passage as a 'note of perfect reciprocity' (1986, 69-70),[21] a fitting description of the inherent beauty of the metaphor and its poignant, succinct philosophical sentiment. Herein lies the heart of Socratic erotic pedagogy, namely the sublime concept of 'love and counter-love' (Halperin 1986, 63) – *anterôs* – the teacher's engendering of love in the pupil and the pupil's return of it to the teacher.[22]

The erotic relationship between teacher and pupil in the various texts in which it features as a theme, permeates, moulds and fortifies the education of the pupil while simultaneously enriching the reader (though this does not guarantee success as a pedagogy in every instance). The relationship is particularly evident in the *Symposium* and in the *Phaedrus*, from which comes the following passage:

> **Soc.**: And when life has ended and they become winged and ethereal beings, they have won the first of the three truly Olympian bouts, which brings greater good than either mortal sanity or divine madness is able to provide. (*Phdr.* 256b)

There is, in the depiction of the closing phase of the relationship between the *erastês* and the *erômenos*, the 'Platonic sublimation of the pederastic *erôs*' – a process that 'prepares the soul's return to the immortal realm of being' (Provencal 2005, 119) – an epiphany of the soul of the lover, if you will. This passage also echoes the content of the previously quoted piece from *Alcibiades* I, in which Socrates pictures his love for Alcibiades as a stork that hatches a winged love in his beloved, thereby (hopefully) ensuring the pupil has the potential to achieve the sublime: a heavenly *eros* of reciprocity for one's teacher and for philosophy that may also be taken as a preparatory stage in the soul's journey to the immortal realm (eventually). It is through such mythical discourses as these that Socrates' performativity works – Socrates embodies *eros* by performing the very tale-weaving Sappho ascribes to it. In this sense, Sappho's cultural legacy becomes Butler's cultural constructions (of *eros*, in this instance) that nurture and give meaning to Socrates' performance.

But the philosophical initiation into the mysteries of *eros* and the ultimate sublimation of its earthly embodiment were, in the case of Socrates' Alcibiades, a spectacular disappointment, as Wohl states:

> With his natural talent and prominent political position, Alcibiades could have been Socrates' greatest success, an opportunity to put into practice his theories of good statecraft and to prove that philosophy is better at governing the city than democracy. This tyrant could have been the first philosopher-king. But, of course, this is not how it turned out. Far from being Socrates' most conspicuous success, Alcibiades becomes his most damaging failure ... (Wohl 2002, 158)

In Socrates' defence Wohl suggests that Alcibiades' *paranomia* proved stronger than a first-rate education in wisdom and so triumphed over transcendent *eros* and the imperative to continually strive for self-knowledge. In Socrates' defence of Socrates, if one can so interpret the final lines of *Alcibiades*, he fears the *polis* may prove stronger than him and his pupil:

> I wish that you could achieve this [i.e. a cultivation of justice], but I fear – not because I distrust your ego – but because I see the power of the city, lest it dominate both me and you. (*Alc.* 135e)[23]

The failure of the instructor in *ta erôtika* is not peculiar to the Platonic

## 1. *The Role of* Eros *in Improving the Pupil*

Socrates. Like the evocation of *Eros* the *daimôn* in the speech of Agathon in the *Symposium* and more importantly Socrates' refutation that embraces the concept of striving for what is absent as a key component of the nature of *Eros / eros*, any individual who pursues *eros* is inevitably bound to falter and fail along the way (201a-c) and this is not necessarily a bad thing in the overall journey towards self-knowledge. In this sense, Socrates as a student rather than a teacher fared much better than his own star pupil, Alcibiades. Enter Sappho: Socrates' pedagogue, of sorts.

### Sappho and love's role in improving Socrates

The distinction between *paiderastia* and relationships of the *erastês-erômenos* type is at work, sometimes at subtle levels, in the writings of Plato and his successors. To be the divine lover, Socrates has to shed the ethical limitations of *paiderastia* and become the sublime *erastês*, a Platonic Ideal eventually embodied by Socrates at the end of the *Symposium*. As the *erastês-erômenos* relationship functions at the core of the teacher/student bond in the philosophical treatises of both Plato and the Platonic School, so does it surface in a similar (but not quite the same)[24] form in the work of Sappho in which is revealed her pre-emptive teaching of what Maximus defines (retroactively) as 'the Socratic art of love' (*technê erôtikê*). Like Socrates, Sappho does not teach in any traditional (direct) sense; certainly not in a modern sense, but more in keeping with an understanding of pedagogy in terms of the ancient Greek idea of the (indirect) instructive nature of poetry as previously discussed. And, if the remaining work is anything to go by, she did not formally set out to instruct young women to be wives, nor really how to be women, as one would expect from a female of her prominence and apparent influence. If she taught women anything it was in her role as a poet, as distinct from a teacher; as a poet-teacher as Socrates was a philosopher-teacher. Like Socrates, it was how she lived, what she said, how she enacted her own chosen 'performance' that enabled the transference of her ideas.

In studies by those with an interest in Sappho's pedagogy, whatever that means to individual scholars, Fragment 16 is often cited as an example of her wisdom and her educational value as a poet. In this piece we detect what may be regarded as a revolutionary position, namely the challenge to hegemony in the most subversive of ways, and her preoccupation with the concerns of those who inhabit the closed quarters of the female community. Here her song summons *kallos* ('beauty') and *eros* ('desire') into the lives of her listeners to be embraced imaginatively, intellectually, possibly physically, and with caution (see below) as she extols the pursuit of *kallos*, driven by *eros*. In this monody, Sappho aims to communicate to her audience what, at a superficial level, may be regarded as a relatively straightforward philosophy – the most beautiful on earth is that which one loves:

> Some believe a team of cavalry, others infantry,
> and still others a fleet of ships, to be the most/ beautiful
> thing on the dark earth, but I believe it is
> whatever a person loves. [4]
> ...
> It is very easy to make this
> clear to everyone: the one who by far
> outshone all mankind in beauty,
> Helen, abandoned her high-born husband [8]
>
> and sailed away to Troy with no thought whatever
> for her child or beloved parents,
> but led astray (by *eros*/*Cypris*?) ...
> lightly ... [12]
> ...
> for (this)
> reminded me
> now of Anactoria, who is
> no longer here; [16]
> ...
> I would prefer to gaze upon her
> lovely walk and the glowing sparkle of her
> face than all the chariots of the Lydians and their
> armies. (Sapph., *Fr.* 16.1-20) [20]

For several scholars, the poem prefigures sophistic philosophy.[25] Helene Foley (1998), in her analysis of Sappho and her role in the formation of the philosophies of the *Phaedrus*, discusses the aforementioned scholarship, citing Hermann Fränkel in particular, whose views on the Sapphic-sophist connection are arguably the most influential and detailed. Accordingly, it is timely to quote Fränkel, before we address Foley's reservations on his views:

> The implications of Sappho's astonishing thesis are very far ranging; it contains the potentiality of overthrowing any absolute value. For all values which are to be obtained are subsumed under the conception of the beautiful, so that 'the beautiful' becomes the yardstick for practical activity. According to Sappho, Helen, herself the most beautiful and most desired of women, found life with Paris more beautiful than the life she had previously led; and she thought and behaved as she did because she was seized by love. We do not desire what is in itself beautiful, but we find what we desire beautiful. This anticipates half of the dictum of the sophist Protagoras, according to which man is the measure of all things. Not infrequently, in this age, poetry precedes philosophy and prepares the way for it. (Fränkel 1962, 187)

Fränkel is correct in his view that this type of lyric poetry 'precedes philosophy and prepares the way for it', yet Foley is also correct in her claim that the argument that 'Sappho prefigures sophistry and cultural relativism ... oversimplifies and distorts her poem' (Foley 1998, 60). It does so because it undermines for Foley any potential connection between

## 1. *The Role of* Eros *in Improving the Pupil*

Fragment 16 and the Platonic concept of Ideal Forms. Foley wishes to argue for a stronger connection between Sappho and Plato compared to Sappho and the sophists; for while the tenets of the fragment do not 'deliberately' foreshadow the 'Platonic abstraction of the incorporeal from the corporeal', they take 'a step in that direction by moving the listener beyond beauty in the visual world to beauty in the world of the imagination and to potential poetic permanence' (Foley 1998, 62).[26] In this sense, by citing Helen as the most beautiful in a mortal, corporeal sense, Sappho may be regarded as anticipating the Platonic Theory of Forms: '[Sappho's] lesson is that tangible beauty is to be desired because it is an aspect of a perfect and unattainable beauty ...' (Burnett 1983, 313).

Nevertheless, Fränkel opens up the lyric-philosophical debate, as opposed to narrowing our view of Fragment 16, and in so doing also prefigures some later sophists of his own. Of particular merit is J. Wills' analysis of the fragment, which has potent undercurrents for Platonic alignments to the poem, which Foley has not treated. Building on Fränkel's hypothesis, Wills explores the threatening role of *eros* as a force that underpins the fragment:[27]

> Sappho takes that world and values it precisely for its imperiled atmosphere, as one might love the beauty of the fires that ravin Troy. For her, as for Rilke,
>    das Schöne ist nichts
>    als des Schrecklichen Anfang ...
> Anactoria is, to her, menacingly desirable, 'fair as the moon, clear as the sun, and terrible as an army with banners.' (Wills 1967, 442)[28]

This is a nuanced reading of the fragment and one that is charged with potential Platonic or, more Socratic, points of comparison.

Fragment 16 forges a future correspondence with Socrates' experiences of *kallos* and *eros*, not only in connection with 'pupils'/'lovers'/*erômenoi* such as Phaedrus and Alcibiades, but in a more specific sense. In the sophistry of Diotima in the *Symposium*, for example, the *erastês* who seeks *kallos* is more divine than the possessor of that *kallos* ('since a lover, filled as he is with a god, surpasses his favourite in godliness', *Symp.* 180b). Similarly, Sappho's philosophy in Fragment 16 (verses three and four), which situates the lover-drawn-to-beauty as the certifier of beauty, may be read as prejudicing the lover over the object of the lover's gaze (the possessor of beauty). In this sense the fragment may achieve what Foley has suggested, namely that it prefigures Plato by moving the audience towards an understanding of beauty beyond the mere visual 'to beauty in the world of the imagination and to potential poetic permanence' (Foley 1998, 62).

The comparison between Fragment 16 and Diotima's philosophy in the *Symposium* is one example of how a modern scholar can massage something by Sappho in order to make it resemble something by Plato. Yet the fragment may also be regarded as remaining antithetical to Plato and closer to Gorgias, whose *Encomium of Helen* may be regarded as a far more authentic successor. Like Sappho, Gorgias sets out to praise Helen and her submission to the erotic impulse, regardless of the consequences; perhaps Helen's freedom and indeed inherent danger are embodied in her disassociation from the Delphic maxim. If so – and it is an appealing means to deconstruct her as a preeminent rhetorical figure in Greek thought – we may have detected an influence on the Platonic concept of *eros* as vocalised by Socrates in the very existence of an adversative voice in Sappho that advocates, ultimately, an essentially blind embrace of erotic desire. Accordingly, Sappho, like Helen, who never makes it beyond an understanding of *eros* as something physical, may be regarded as setting a well-known cultural and philosophical precedent against which Socrates can argue. One may destabilise this interpretation by the obvious counter-argument that both Helen and Sappho represent a complete understanding of the Delphic maxim, as both sought out and followed *eros-kallos*, and in this sense demonstrated a profound knowledge of their own selves. This is in keeping with the tenets of the *Phaedrus*, which prejudices the beholder of beauty, and by association the lover, but is not in keeping with the Socratic view as expressed more prominently at *Alcibiades* 133c, namely that self-knowledge must be accompanied by self-restraint or *sôphrosunê* (interestingly, it is in the *Phaedrus* [229e] that Socrates denies comprehension – as it relates to his own self – of the Delphic maxim). It does seem, then, that Socrates appropriates Sappho at certain times when it suits while at other times he moves on from where she left off.[29]

Socrates, whose pedagogy centres on the axiom *gnôthi sauton*, knew himself well enough to know that what he wanted was to follow his beloved. He wanted to follow Alcibiades just as Helen wanted to follow Paris and Sappho wanted to gaze at Anactoria. But his awareness and practice of *sôphrosunê* meant that he waited. He waited because his *daimôn* prevented him from actively and physically seducing the youth (Socrates' *daimôn* in this respect may be said to be representing the philosopher's self-control). When Alcibiades attains manhood and is abandoned by those lovers only interested in his physical beauty, Socrates' *daimôn* quietens its opposition and Socrates seeks out Alcibiades. This scenario of the *Alcibiades* illustrates what is so different between the Socratic and Sapphic arts of love: his restraint (see also *Phdr.* 253c-256e) and her lack of it, or in other words, the precedents she embodies are those against which he can caution.[30]

But, ultimately, Socrates understands the poets, including Sappho, for they demonstrate for him the bewildering and beguiling performance of *ta erôtika*. They give him a voice with which to speak and with which to express the dilemmas and dangers represented by this most profound of primeval forces. And, as mentioned above, they provide him with the

## 1. *The Role of* Eros *in Improving the Pupil*

philosophical opportunities to move on from their lyrical inertia or, more positively, they reflect 'Plato's use of popular or familiar ideas as the departure point for explorations that lead to the production of his own philosophy' (Pender 2007, 1).

As previously mentioned, Sappho's *eros* is the force of Hesiod, a force that is dangerous and unpredictable and ultimately destructive, themes to be observed in the ominous undertones of Fragment 16 as suggested by Wills. Socrates is certainly aware of this – he learned it from the poets, of whom Sappho is a named influence in the *Phaedrus*. Her immediate pedagogy to Socrates in this sense is her continual thematic warnings about this *muthoplokos* (a key component of the lyric inertia mentioned above). To her, *Eros* is a divine force that has the potential to cause *mania* – both of the body and, by implication, the mind:

> Eros the loosener-of-limbs once again shakes me,
> that sweet-bitter, utterly irresistible little beast. (Sappho, *Fr.* 130)

It is such dramatic evocations of the deity/force that seem to be much on Socrates' mind as he discourses on the topic in the *Phaedrus*. Yet one cannot in this instance attribute poetic warnings concerning *Eros* to Sappho alone. In addition to Fragment 130, there is Anacreon's Fragment 413 and Ibycus' Fragment 287C, to name merely two other Archaic examples of the *eros/mania* connection. Indeed, this is a concept as old as Homer[31] – albeit it is Sappho and Anacreon who are named specifically by Socrates in the *Phaedrus* as influences on his views on *eros*.

As the poet who embodies *eros*, and thus teaches it (as suggested by Ovid's words in the line from the *Tristia*), Sappho chronicles, on numerous occasions, its effects on her whole being. This is best illustrated in Fragment 31.1-16:

> He seems to me equal in good fortune to the gods,
> whatever man, who sits on the opposite side to you
> and listens nearby to your
> sweet replies                                                                                 [4]
>
> and desire-inducing laugh: indeed that
> gets my heart pounding in my breast.
> For just gazing at you for a second, it is impossible
> for me even to talk;                                                                          [8]
>
> my tongue is broken, all at once a soft
> flame has stolen beneath my flesh,
> my eyes see nothing at all,
> my ears ring,                                                                                 [12]
>
> sweat pours down me, a tremor
> shakes me, I am more greenish than
> grass, and I believe I am at
> the very point of death.                                                                      [16]

In this seemingly personal account, Sappho performs the very power or energy of the force of *eros*. As Socrates' discussion of *eros* begins with its connection to want or lack in *Symposium* 210e-211b, so too does Sappho sing of unsatisfied desire. The want that is at the very core of this concept of *eros* links it inextricably with *mania*; among those senses that have been extinguished by *eros*, Sappho lists the power of speech – that which makes us human, coherent, eloquent, sane. Likewise, the combination of the two forces emerges repeatedly in the Platonic dialogues, arguably attaining its ultimate expression in Socrates' statement at *Republic* 572e-573b that *eros* and madness join forces in the birth of the tyrant. In contrast, *eros* in the *Phaedrus* is divine madness, that 'which reminds us of that time, before we were embodied, when we followed in the train of a god and caught some glimpse of the beings beyond heaven' (McNeill 2001, 241). Somewhere amid these two extreme views of *eros* Sappho's fragment must sit if we are to judge her as exhibiting any influence on Socrates. As a parent to the tyrant in contrast to the philosopher-king, *eros* is a force to be avoided or, more accurately, stringently confined, along with its co-parent, madness. In Fragment 31, Sappho, it could be argued, exhibited the symptoms of the madness and the tyrannical effects of an unconstrained *eros*, as did her point of comparison in Fragment 16, Helen. Sappho in this sense symbolises to Socrates why one who cares for one's own soul should remain cautious of Earthly Aphrodite and her myth-weaving servant. In this sense, the reading of Socrates' use of Sappho (and other lyric poets) in the *Phaedrus* is one that argues for his 'exploration of how *mania* and reason can be mutually supportive' (Pender 2007, 1).

While a number of poets are named by Plato, particularly in the *Phaedrus*, it is Sappho and also Anacreon who have special appeal to Socrates. In discussing those who have influenced his thoughts on love and erotics, Socrates reveals to Phaedrus their names (and thus begins his counter-argument to Phaedrus' performance of the speech of Lysias, Socrates' rival pedagogue):

> **Soc.**: ... for ancient and wise men and women who have spoken and written about these things will refute me, if I simply yield to gratify you.
> **Phdr.**: Who are these people? Where have you heard anything better than this?
> **Soc.**: At present, I can't really say; but I'm certain I've heard something, somewhere, from someone; perhaps from the beautiful [*kalē*] Sappho or the wise [*sophos*] Anacreon or from some writers. I say this based on what? Somehow full, good sir, is this breast, I feel I have other words – no less inferior – to say beyond those of Lysias. At any rate, I am cognisant of my ignorance and aware I could not formulate such ideas myself. What is left, I think, is that I have been made full – like a vessel – from streams from elsewhere, through my ears. But through my sluggishness I have forgotten where and from whom I heard it. (*Phdr.* 235b-d)

## 1. The Role of Eros *in Improving the Pupil*

Despite scholarly debate about the level of irony present in Socrates' reference to the poets, the text of the *Phaedrus* reveals a genuine engagement with their views on the subjects of *eros, mania* and self-control. Elizabeth Pender (2007) discusses the echoes of both poets in details as minute as the evocation of the landscape in which the dialogue takes place. Similarly, A.W. Nightingale (1995, 158) notes that Socrates' second speech is 'replete with the discourse of lyric poetry', while W.W. Fortenbaugh, writing earlier, argues for discernable influences in both speeches:

> The proper names 'Sappho' and 'Anacreon' have a particular significance and are not a general reference to lyric love poets. These two names are introduced to alert the reader that the poems of Sappho and Anacreon will play a role in Socrates' subsequent speeches. Indeed the primary and so far unnoticed purpose for naming these poets is to anticipate poetic reminiscences occurring in Socrates' two speeches. (Fortenbaugh 1966, 108)

Pender's work is particularly insightful in further exploring a theme raised earlier in this study, that of the pupil as one who hears instructive discourse and the pupil as one who reads it. Socrates is initially vague about his sources ('but I'm certain I've heard something, somewhere, from someone') and then suggests they could be Sappho and Anacreon ('perhaps from the beautiful Sappho or the wise Anacreon or from some writers'). This moment of forgetting and then remembering may be seen as an example of one of the tensions present in the Platonic dialogues in which Plato, the recorder of Socrates' teachings, augments the words of his educator to complete the picture. If this is the case, one may argue that Socrates, who experienced Sappho and Anacreon's songs audibly, can recall the ideas but not the poets; Plato, as one who experienced the ideas as written instruction, can remember the ideas *and* the poets and therefore amend Socrates' anecdote. But perhaps Socrates is being deceptive, remembering the poets all along. Fortenbaugh's previously quoted words suggest this interpretation, and it is important to note in the context of his reading that, despite Socrates' momentary memory lapse, he manages to name two poets but never recalls the prose writers. In this sense, the use of the motif of forgetting and remembering serves to highlight the idea that poetry is the greater vehicle for *paideia*. Accordingly, Socrates is never truly vague on this point; the Archaic poets are so dominant in his thinking that they permeate it; he may not be able to think of specifics (even though I think he can!) because their ideas are ubiquitous.[32]

Moving on from the *Phaedrus*, a case in point is a passage from *Alcibiades* I, which clearly reveals the extent to which Sappho's words infused the thinking of Socrates in the Platonic tradition:

> **Soc.**: So then, nothing of the beautiful [*kalê*], following that inasmuch as it is beautiful [*kalos*], is bad [*kakos*], and nothing that is ugly [*aiskhros*], following inasmuch as it is ugly [*aiskhros*], is good [*agathos*]. (*Alc.* 116a)

*Marguerite Johnson*

> For he who is beautiful [*kalos*] is <beautiful [*kalos*]> as far as that goes, but one who is good [*agathos*] will become beautiful [*kalos*] as a result. (Sappho, *Fr.* 50)

Socrates is insistent with Alcibiades in the passage above, forcing him to engage with this one proposition – amid many, many more in the dialogue – within an overall context of self-knowledge and, therefore, subjective integrity and truth. Linked to these contextual components of the dialectic is the role of erotic pedagogy, as Robert R. Wellman has pointed out: 'The point of the dialogic form epitomising, for Socrates, the educative process is the emotional commitment necessitated when the individual is required, because of Eros, to genuinely agree or disagree with arguments' (1966, 9). Unfortunately, we have no such interpretive context for the fragment from Sappho. Whether she utilised passages such as this for more overtly instructional purposes is impossible to detect; nevertheless, the fragment is similar to the dialectic structure of Socrates' pedagogical method. The use of a circular structure of logic to produce a philosophical premise, evident in both passages, in addition to the more-or-less identical topos asking what *kallos* is, are surely suggestive – in this one specific textual incident – of Socrates' familiarity with the piece from Sappho. Interestingly, Galen, in his comments on these verses by Sappho,[33] associates them with external beauty and the care of one's soul:

> ... many people who are admired for beauty are careless of their souls ... and then are reviled in old age; ... therefore, since we know that the prime of youth is like spring flowers and brings short-lived enjoyment it is better to commend the woman of Lesbos when she says ... (*Adhortatio ad artes addiscendas* 8)

Galen's interpretation of Sappho's verses, quoted above, and indeed the verses per se, are a reminder of a consistent theme in the *Alcibiades* I: Socrates' dedication to loving the inner beauty or soul of Alcibiades even after the blossom of youth fades.[34] As Socrates argues here, the beautiful soul is the good soul, the wise soul (125a, 132a).

## Performing and teaching *eros* ... the hard way

Considering Poem 1, arguably Sappho's most famous composition, one is witness to Sappho as lover, divinely-inspired being, and educator of the dangers of *eros*:

> Seated on your multi-coloured throne, Aphrodite, deathless,
> guile-weaving child of Zeus, I beseech you,
> do not with satiety or pain conquer
> my heart, august one, [4]

## 1. The Role of Eros in Improving the Pupil

but come to me here, if ever at other times as well,
hearing my words from far away,
having left your father's house,
golden you came [8]

having yoked your chariot. Beautiful swift
birds directed you over the black earth,
frequently beating their wings, down from the sky
then through mid air [12]

and quickly they arrived. You, blessed one,
smiling with your deathless face,
asked what I had suffered this time, why
I was calling yet again [16]

and what I wished most to happen to me
in my mad heart. 'Who is it this time that I am to
persuade to take you back into her heart? Who,
Sappho, wrongs you? [20]

'And if she flees now, she will soon be chasing [you].
If she does not accept presents, she will give them.
If she does not love [you] now, soon she will,
even if she is not willing.' [24]

Come to me now, also, and release me from harsh
care. All the things that my heart
desires for me – fulfil. You yourself, be my
ally in this enterprise. [28]

(Sappho, Poem 1)

Sappho's representation – not specifically of the goddess but of her own relationship with the goddess – how she interacts with and experiences the goddess, reflects the Archaic Greek tradition of the poet as divinely-inspired; from Homer on, poets acknowledged the sublime interaction with the gods as a source of artistry – a topic on which Socrates was quite vocal.[35] Sappho takes this further, however, by establishing an intimate relationship with a divine force that extends beyond the boundaries of poetic inspiration and becomes *philia*. Sappho's goddess advises her as well as inspires her, she protects her in the ways of *ta erôtika*, and this bond is a significant expression of what was to become the concept of the educator as divinely inspired, or the educator's connection with the supernatural. In relation to the Platonic Socrates, the manifestation of Sappho's divine *philia* may be regarded as a precursor to Socrates' *daimôn*[36] who, as we have seen in *Alcibiades* I, advises him at first to avoid the youth, then, once the youth has developed, quietly fades into the background, thus allowing Socrates to approach Alcibiades.

While the poem has been the subject of many and varied analyses, it only rarely comes into contact with Socratic views on *eros*[37] and no connections have been made between its ideas and the topic of Socratic pedagogy. Yet, in keeping with the concept of both Sappho and Socrates as teachers by means of performing *eros*, Poem 1 is a potentially fruitful source of exploration. By presenting herself as she does in Poem 1 the poet comes close to what has been previously touched on, namely, Socrates' definition of *eros* as 'want' and, therefore, 'absence'. Captured by *eros*, Sappho's 'lack' or 'want' is so intense that it drives her to engage in an intense prayer – or spell.[38] Her own personal deity, Aphrodite, answers her anxious pleas and promises Sappho that soon the object of desire will return her overtures: she will pursue, she will give presents and she will feel love (*philêsis*) – even in spite of herself (*kôuk etheloisa*). Many scholars, notably feminist scholars, have written on the reciprocity present in Sappho's lyrics addressed to women, yet here there is a strong sense of erotic power dynamics, with Sappho determined to assume the role of the active, dominant partner.

Sappho feels the pain of desire and is told by an omnipotent being that this situation can be reversed – that her 'lack' can be filled by its transfer to the object of desire. In this sense, Sappho as the divinely-inspired educator has performed *eros* that prefigures one manifestation of the Platonic or Socratic *eros*, namely, that to be an instructor in *ta erôtika*, one can perform desire initially – to embody its maddening effects, to demonstrate, if you will – and then pass on the very lesson being taught (via a prayer or a spell in the case of Poem 1). In other words, to be educated in the pain of 'want', the insanity of *eros*, one must be taught to suffer it. This is not to argue that Sappho taught girls, but to reiterate an earlier point: Sappho performed the very conditions about which she, as an inspired poet, was sanctioned to teach. She taught by embodied performance. In this sense, Poem 1 functions as pedagogy in the same way as Fragment 31 does: the poet situates herself as the object or victim of *eros* in order to teach its effects. But Poem 1 also goes further. The transfer of *eros* to an unnamed object – the unwilling woman in question – works, educationally speaking, like a science experiment: Sappho as devotee of Aphrodite or burgeoning sorceress (or both), performs a religious ritual or brilliant spell (or both) before her audience, the outcome of which, the metamorphosis of an indifferent woman into a love-sick pawn, is tantalisingly withheld but guaranteed nonetheless. Sappho's *eros* is not only *muthoplokos* as the very syntax and poetic qualities of Poem 1 attest but also a forerunner to Diotima's mighty sorcerer, apothecary and sophist. Sappho's message to the audience of this monody can be summed up by Ovid's words – 'What did Sappho teach her girls except how to love?' (*Tr.* 2.365) – for to teach *eros* is to transfer the pain it brings onto one's pupils. Surely, this is pedagogical *thelxis*.

Socrates himself is no stranger to a little magic as demonstrated in the *Charmides* where he attempts to perform a spell on the youthful Char-

## 1. *The Role of* Eros *in Improving the Pupil*

mides in order to attract the youth's attention. Socrates offers a cure for Charmides' headache by performing *pharmakeia* as prescribed by Zalmoxis (156e). In this alleged cure for the soul – for the body cannot be healed without the healing of the soul – Socrates discusses the need for incantations as well as a magically-charged object, in this instance a leaf (155e). The performance is part of Socratic pedagogy; Socrates, whose topic in the dialogue is *sôphrosunê*, demonstrates this very quality by performing both his desire for Charmides (by magic tricks) and his restraint (by keeping the fire that burns inside him [155d] under control). Similarly, in a lesson that proves harder for the pupil than it does for the instructor, Socrates' *eros* for Alcibiades becomes an educational topic in *Alcibiades*. At the heart of the dialogue is the theme of erotic pedagogy as noted by Wellman (see above); Socrates admits his *eros* for Alcibiades – he proclaims it in the opening line (103a1) – and as the work progresses, Socrates teaches Alcibiades *ta erôtika* by means of spell-binding discourse and dialectic that entrance the student to such an extent that he increasingly strives to please his teacher with a passion that embraces the erotic and that inevitably leads to the ultimate expression of the reciprocity of *eros* in the work, the image of the stork and the egg (*Alc.* 135e). In the *Symposium* there is a similar performance of *eros* for instructive purposes that is characterised by the transfer of the condition from the teacher to the pupil in a way similar to Sappho's description of promised metamorphosis in Poem 1. When it comes to the speech of Alcibiades we learn, following his arrogant declamation to Socrates, that he is aware of his love for him (218c) and his equally conceited offer to satisfy Socrates' desire (218d). Socrates rejects him with his well known 'gold for bronze' metaphor (219a). The desire that Socrates has harboured, the 'lack' that he has embodied, is then transferred to his pupil as Alcibiades articulates:

> He takes in youths by pretending to be their lover (*erastês*) but then he swaps the roles and becomes their beloved (*erômenos*) instead. So I warn you, Agathon; do not be utterly deceived by him. Come to learn (*gnonta*) from our sufferings and beware. You do not have to be the proverbial fool, suffering yourself just to learn (*gnônai*) it. (*Symp.* 222b)

Alcibiades finally experiences the 'lack' or desire and so finally knows of the *eros* that Socrates embodies. The lesson is hard but effective.

## Conclusion

> But whether the mother of the theory was a Mantinean or a Lesbian, it is at any rate quite clear that Socrates' discussions of Love are not unique to him and do not begin with him either. (Max. Tyr. 18.7)

These lines from Maximus, on the originator of Socrates' second speech in the *Phaedrus*, further suggest Sappho to the readers of the Platonic dialogues. This association between Diotima and Sappho has been suggested in several instances herein, and noteworthy is the idea of Yves Battistini (1995) that these women were, ultimately, one and the same. This will surely remain a hypothesis, yet it is, nevertheless, pleasant to desire its possibility.

Throughout this essay, the terms 'teacher' and 'pupil' have been used cautiously and incautiously in an attempt to capture and convey the specific and – to modern eyes – unusual pedagogy of Sappho and Socrates. Teaching for them was, ultimately, a performance. When it came to teaching *eros*, the process was not only dramatic, highly personal and ego-driven, but also magical, taking students – and themselves – into *thelxis*. Teaching was seduction and transference of states of being. It was cruel at times but always poetic. If Sappho taught Socrates anything, it was through her yearning, her flushing and fainting, her desire for women long gone and her longing for punishment of others at hand. Socrates listened to her performances, transported to him via the voices of others, and so, I suggest, imitated her ways; he balanced a leaf on Charmides' head, he wandered shoeless and unkempt, he chased Alcibiades and at times gave up the chase. He performed Sappho.

## Notes

1. For Harold Tarrant: mentor, colleague, friend. Translations of Sappho, Plato and Ovid are my own; Maximus of Tyre is translated by Parker 2006 with slight alterations; Galen is translated by Hardie 2005.

2. Among the famous suspected relationships are one between Archelaus and Socrates (Diogenes Laertius 2.18) and another between Parmenides and Zeno (Pl. *Parm.* 127b).

3. The concern with *Eros* is most obvious at a cosmic level, so that Plato in the *Sophist* (242c-243a) suggests that several had told myths to us, as if we were children, with some postulating three basic realities of which two are sometimes drawn together in love and marriage, producing offspring that they nourish; Empedocles' rather different theory is alluded to at 242e-243a, being contrasted with that of Heraclitus, which is likewise thought of as involving both love and hostility.

4. Regarding the erotic ideals of the Academy under Polemo, see Tarrant's contribution to this volume.

5. Parker (2006) rightly suggests Maximus' reference is to *Alcibiades* 103a.

6. Maximus has written *chariessa* (graceful) instead of *kacharis* (graceless).

7. For which Maximus is the only source extant, as he is for some of the other quotations of Sappho.

8. Max. Tyr. 18.9, 230.11-232.15 Hobein, 160.234-162.268 Trapp, 232.203-234.235 Koniaris; see Parker 2006: 389.

9. Admittedly, in his 1993 article, Parker notes that the comparison is broad and likely ironic; contra, Foley 1998, 39-41.

10. Foley 1998, 40 makes the valid point that although Maximus is not the subtlest reader of Plato, he would have had access to works by Sappho that are no

*1. The Role of Eros in Improving the Pupil*

longer available to us – works to which Socrates and Plato would have also had access.

11. Although I am not convinced that Maximus misinterprets *algesidôron*, as Parker would have it.

12. On the connections between the Sapphic *eros* and the later, philosophical interpretations, see duBois 1995, 77-97; Foley 1998, 39-70; Greene 2009, 147-61.

13. The use of the term *goês* is complex in Platonic texts as Plato does not always use it in a negative way whereas, culturally speaking, in non-Platonic texts it is regularly used as a term of derision and suspicion. The *Republic* and *Laws* contain condemnatory references to the *goês* and to *goêteia*; see, for example, *Laws* 909, 932e-933e; *Rep.* 598d, 602d. The complexity in the Platonic texts is partly the result of the comparison of Socrates and the *goês*; see, for example, *Meno* 80b and related instances where Socrates is described as weaving enchantments (*Symp.* 215c). Knowledge is called a *pharmakon* at *Republic* 595b; in the *Timaeus* artificial cures (*pharmaka*) are opposed to natural methods of curing. See also *Charmides* for the magician Socrates. For further discussion on these terms in Plato, see Belfiore and Gellrich. See also Irigaray. As with the contradictory uses of these words, Plato's use of the word 'sophist' is also problematic; whereas the application of 'sophist' to *Eros* above is somewhat ambivalent, but positively coloured (perhaps) by the broader context in which it is placed, it garners an unambiguous (i.e. positive) meaning when applied to Diotima at *Symp.*208.

14. On the concept of qualifying the Platonic construct of 'sophist', see Taylor 2006.

15. This reading is indebted to C.C.W. Taylor's ideas on Socrates-as-*goês*, one of his many (dis)guises in Plato: '... what kind of *goês* was Socrates in Plato's depiction? Not a charlatan or illusionist, since the latter creates false beliefs, whereas Socrates' characteristic skill lies in getting rid of them. I should like to suggest, following a suggestion of Alexander Nehamas, that Plato intends to depict Socrates as a *goês* in the sense of magician, of someone possessed of unaccountable powers. Though he disclaims expertise in matters of good and bad, he systematically claims not merely to reveal inconsistencies in the thinking of his interlocutors, but to free them from false beliefs' (Taylor 2006, 167). Socrates as an earthly embodiment of *Eros* is thereby naturally suggested in my line of thought, an idea as old as Maximus himself and a comparison made by several scholars of more modern ages: see, for example, Maximus 18 (more obliquely than overtly); see also Friedlander 1945, 342: 'may it be remembered that Diotima's Eros has many traits of Socrates, and that Socrates is Eros' appearance on earth'; more recently, Osborne 1996, 94-95. Osborne reminds us that the observation was also made by Ficino in *Symposium Commentary*, Oratio 7.

16. See Segal 1974; 1996.

17. See especially, Nehamas 1992 and Tarrant in this volume (148): 'The idea that a worthy lover can *improve* the beloved is particularly associated with Pausanias' seemingly rather conventional speech in the *Symposium*, but it is seldom made much of by Plato's Socrates.'

18. Taplin prefigures this analysis of Socrates by a discussion of the early sages and their performance of wisdom; citing Solon, who through utterance and action, convinced the Athenians to continue war with Megara over Salamis by pretending to be mad: '... he feigned madness, rushed into the Agora with a garland on his head, and recited a poem that he had written on Salamis, which called for war' (Taplin 2001, 141). Did the performance educate (read manipulate) the Athenians? Taplin continues: '... the Athenians were duly roused to anger, and proceeded to

## Marguerite Johnson

recapture Salamis' (2001, 142). On Heracleitus, Taplin writes: 'Herakleitos did not simply document his research: he was "doing things" with his words. Using an oracular form and voice, Herakleitos makes paradoxical and enigmatic pronouncements. He says in fragment 93 that "the lord whose oracle is in Delphi neither speaks nor conceals, but offers a 'sign'". Since Herakleitos himself uses language in precisely this way, we may infer that he was deliberately adopting Delphic discourse. He did this, no doubt, because the riddling discourse of the oracle was well suited to conveying his central claim: that unity consists of coexisting opposites' (2001, 145). The example of Heracleitus is particularly useful in relation to Socrates' embodiment or performance of *eros*; as Heracleitus performs a 'ritualised production' (Butler 1993, 95) of his philosophy of unity and coexisting opposites via the discourse of the Delphic oracle, so Socrates performs his understanding of *eros/Eros* in all its multiplicities by embodying different facets of it. An effective example of Socratic performance of the essential philosopher is provided by Taplin in his analysis of *Symp.* 220c-d (162-3).

19. See n. 13.

20. On other examples of Socrates as living or embodying *Eros*, see Hadot 1995, 161-3.

21. I note Halperin's treatment of the passage in my translation in terms of his textual inclusions.

22. A concept also expressed in the Platonic construct of the gaze and the mirroring of it in the beloved's eyes; see Victoria Wohl's contribution to this volume.

23. A (somewhat) equivalent passage is to be found in the *Symposium*, where Alcibiades admits: 'I know perfectly well that I cannot disprove him when he tells me what I should do; yet, the very instant I leave him, I return to my old ways and indulge my desire to please the crowd' (216b).

24. I do not subscribe to the all too common notion that Sappho engaged in relationships with younger women; there is little if any evidence in what remains of her work to support this theory. For this reason, I avoid applying the concept (and the words) *erastês-erômenos* to her relationships. Maximus' *technê erôtikê* is a preferred term as it can be used without age distinctions (although this is not to argue that Maximus himself understood her relations with women to be without the generational gaps that defined those of Socrates). As to Ovid's words from *Tristia* 2.365, I take *puella* as a standard word from the Latin erotic vocabulary.

25. See Fränkel 1962; Wills 1967; Race 1989-90.

26. See also Greene: '... the power of Poem 16 derives from its ability to invoke beauty with incredibly vivid specificity while at the same time making us keenly aware of beauty in its paradigmatic form. Specificity and generality are held in a delicate balance in the poem, yet Sappho shows that the lover's encounter with beauty in the object of desire necessarily entails an encounter with the very nature of beauty itself since "the lover responds not just to the beloved but to beauty in the beloved"' (Greene 2009, 153-4; the quotation is from Foley 1998, 61).

27. Wills' point is supported by Sappho's inclusion of the metaphor of Helen in the fragment; Helen as an icon of one who followed erotic desire becomes a symbol in antiquity of the potential disasters of *eros/Eros*. Catullus understood this, as exemplified by the final stanza of his *Poem* 51; see Johnson 1999.

28. Interestingly, Wills argues that 'Sappho goes beyond Protagoras in her vision of a beautiful and destructive anarchy' (1967, 441).

29. See Tarrant 2007, 4, who notes the pedagogical imperative for Alcibiades, as reason for the inclusion of the maxim. See also Foucault's reading of *Alcibiades*

## 1. The Role of Eros in Improving the Pupil

and *Apology* in relation to the maxim and the related Platonic concept of care of the self in connection with Socratic pedagogy (1986, 43-6).

30. See Rowe and his argument on the non-philosophical *eros* of Sappho and other lyric poets; on Socrates' use of Sappho and Anacreon in the *Phaedrus*, for example: 'love poets give us better arguments in favour of the non-lover than Lysias could ever muster' (1986, 151).

31. For this rich tradition, see Calame 1999. Clearly Socrates knew of Ibycus, as demonstrated at *Phdr.* 242c.

32. Further, see Pender 2007, 10 on Socrates' metaphor of his ears being filled by the streams of others: 'Such a pointed poetic image, full of irony from a character readily identifiable as determinedly prosaic, punctures the sense that the reference to the poets is casual.'

33. It is to Galen we owe the preservation of the verses; he refers to Sappho's *Poem* 58 on making the most of one's youth.

34. Sappho sings of the inevitable fading of youthful bloom in *Poem* 58, but does not extend the image to include beauty of the soul.

35. On the topic of Socrates' views on poets, poetic inspiration and interpretation of poetry – both by the poet and by the listener – see Ledbetter 2003. On the vexed question of Socratic versus Platonic views on the value of the poets, see also Ledbetter.

36. A comparison already noted by Bagg 1964, 73.

37. For these, see n. 11 above.

38. On the magical and incantatory characteristics of the poem, see Segal 1974; 1996; also Cameron 1939 and Petropoulos 1993.

2

# Socrates and Platonic Models of Love

*Dougal Blyth*

### Introduction

In this chapter I shall argue that in none of the three main Platonic dialogues in which *erôs* is thematised, the *Lysis*, *Symposium* and *Phaedrus*, is Socrates depicted as being really a lover, an *erastês*, of anyone, as far as his mode of philosophic interaction goes.[1] I shall pursue this claim by treating each dialogue in turn, and evaluating the dramatic depiction of Socrates in relation to the account of love (or, in the case of the *Lysis*, friendship)[2] that Socrates in each dialogue presents.

Models of philosophical love are proposed in both the *Symposium* and *Phaedrus*, while in each of the *Lysis, Symposium* and *Phaedrus* Socrates himself claims to be an expert in love, a claim I take seriously. But I will argue that the love in which Socrates is an expert is primarily that experienced by others, and is his own love only in a derivative way, and only insofar as he loves the truth, which on Plato's developed account famously turns out to be transcendent. Socrates does on occasion playact the role of a lover in both the *Symposium* and the *Phaedrus*, and his interest in speeches in the latter dialogue, insofar as they lead to philosophy, at least, is depicted as erotic. Nevertheless Socrates is not there portrayed as himself erotically inclined to others, even as a means to philosophy, as I shall show.

### *Lysis*

The opening of the *Lysis* presents the potential for an erotic response by Socrates: he meets some youths, *neaniskoi*, including Hippothales and Ctesippus, outside the city walls (203a and following, although possibly these young men are older than the normal age of *erômenoi*, objects of pederastic *erôs*). Socrates is invited into a private wrestling school where he is told there are many other youths, specifically called *kaloi*, suggesting their sexual attractiveness (203b8). The teacher of the school, Miccus, is said to be well-disposed to Socrates (204a5), so he would perhaps present no obstacle to a seduction. The invitation to enter is then repeated (204a8-9). Clearly Plato means here to measure Socrates against the model of a lover of young men.

## 2. Socrates and Platonic Models of Love

Socrates' response is, nevertheless, to turn away from any immediate erotic reaction, toward discussion: he asks which of the boys within is *kalos* (204b1-2), deflecting attention to the erotic responses of his interlocutors.[3] He hears of the way Hippothales pursues his love for Lysis (204b-e) and then criticises this (205a-206b). Thus Socrates acts here not as one motivated as a seducer of boys, but as a student and a director of others' *erôs*.

Socrates' erotic expertise first appears in his recognition that Hippothales is in love. Here Socrates makes the bold claim that he can recognise both a lover and his *erômenos* (204c1-2).[4] His expertise extends further to directing Hippothales' behaviour as a lover (cf. 206c4-7), although instead of advising Hippothales on how to treat Lysis, Socrates himself enters the 'erotic arena' of the wrestling school to demonstrate it in person (206c-207b). The presence of Hippothales as audience to the conversation that ensues then stands guarantee that Socrates could not here intend really to make *himself* the lover, philosophical or not, of Lysis.

The first substantial result of the conversation with just Lysis is Socrates' persuasion of him that his happiness depends on gaining knowledge (207d-210d), signalled explicitly to the reader as a lesson for Hippothales (210e).[5] Lysis, by contrast with his companion Menexenus, is depicted as intelligent and also motivated to understand, both here and later in the conversation, at 213d2-e1, where Socrates remarks on his philosophical potential (213d6).

When Menexenus returns, Socrates tells his story about wanting a friend (211d-212a) which sets the theme of the rest of the dialogue. In some contexts this story could be seen as a seduction monologue, and so we should perhaps recognise here again an invitation to evaluate Socrates' motives. The questions Socrates then raises as to how to specify which party is a friend might remind us of the practical problem for a boy beset with suitors, that of identifying which is a true friend; while again just such a topic, between an older man and a boy, would provide an opening for a lover to prove himself a genuine friend. Moreover the dialectic liberties Socrates has already taken with Lysis' naivety (cf. e.g. 209c-210a),[6] along with the manipulations of the term *philos* at 212a-213d,[7] point to the problem of deceptive persuasion in such cases. But Socrates does not discuss with the boys his own virtues or usefulness, and regularly prevents them from uncritically adopting any of the lines of thought he introduces.

I turn now to what I take to be the final theory of friendship (221d-222d) in order to interpret this depiction of Socrates in its terms. My interpretive approach is the following: since the dialogue ends dramatically in *aporia*, Plato must have intended either to leave open the questions raised about friendship, or to provide the means to recognise a theory that he expected the reflective reader to arrive at.[8] In the latter case, if we can identify a theory that both follows from clear indications in the text and solves its problems, we have good reason to identify it as what was intended.[9]

To achieve this, we must first unravel the ultimate confusion. This is not as difficult as it might seem, since there are just two specific elements to the confusion, which can be corrected relatively straightforwardly. The agreements prior to this point can be summarised as follows: the cause of friendship is a desire (221d3), of a kind that is intrinsically value-neutral (221b5, d1-2), but since the friend, as its object, is good either as means or end, there must be some final such 'friend' (i.e. object of *philia*) as a source of value (220d8-e4),[10] and what desires must be naturally related (*oikeion*) to its friend (221d6-e5) because it lacks it.[11]

Socrates then confuses the issue by the manner in which he combines two further points. First, he gets the boys to agree that what is *oikeion* cannot be what is similar, since it was previously agreed that friends cannot be similar (222b3-c3). Secondly, he asks whether good is naturally related (*oikeion*) to everything and bad to nothing, or each of good, bad and neutral to its own kind (c3-7), to which the boys answer the latter (222c7-d1). Socrates points out that this answer threatens to contradict the previous results, that friendship cannot occur between those who are similar, or both good (222d1-8). Thus on the assumption that the *oikeion* is reducible to the similar, the whole theory is now incorrectly taken to have been refuted (222e1-7). But that was not the assumption the boys adopted.

So let us take the alternative account of natural relatedness Socrates first offered at 222c3-5, and which the boys themselves preferred. Given that the bad is naturally unrelated to anything else (cf. 214c7-d3)[12] we are left with the claim that the good is naturally related to itself and to the neutral. But the good is presumably also similar to itself; thus friendship occurs in the case where what desires, and so is neutral, is naturally suited to a related good. Since in this case there is no assimilation of natural relatedness to similarity (222b3-c1), the result allows for a consistent account of the subject and object of *philia*, friendship.

A complete theory of *philia* in the dialogue's terms would also have to explain precisely the connections of the former term to desire (*epithumia*) and love (*erôs*). Yet these are nowhere in the dialogue made quite clear, beyond the statement that desire is the cause of friendship.[13] Previously Socrates has restricted the sense of desire here by excluding any that might be intrinsically good or bad (221b5-6), but he does not specify whether he thinks the latter kinds actually occur, so it is unclear whether he means that the whole genus of desire in every case, or just one species, is the cause of friendship.

Again, it is unclear whether, in the various places where these terms are linked with *love*,[14] the latter (which is presumably understood as a state of desire) is identified with all of the relevant kind of desire, and so with friendship as a whole, or is, perhaps, assumed to be a subdivision within it.[15] The earlier proposals regarding friendship[16] signify that Socrates allows this to have non-human objects. In that case we might think

## 2. Socrates and Platonic Models of Love

that he allows for a similar extension of love (*erôs*) also.[17] But, in the absence of definition of these terms, none of this can be resolved by reference to the text of the *Lysis*.[18]

This returns us to relevant conventional assumptions about what friendship, desire and love each are, in relation to one another. Normally an ancient Greek would assume, I suppose, that love (*erôs*) is differentiated from at least some other desires and friendships by its intensity, its sexual-romantic mode,[19] and the exclusively human form of its object. But given Plato's extensions of the senses of both friendship and love mentioned above, let us retain as conventional differentia of *erôs* only the first two criteria, intensity and sexual romanticism. My general claim is that these are not depicted by Plato as really characterising Socrates' interests in any other people, and nothing has come to light to contradict this in what I have so far discussed of the *Lysis*.

I turn now to attempt a positive characterisation of Socrates' relationship with Lysis. *Philia* may be reciprocal, as the relationship between Lysis and Menexenus shows (221e6); possibly, then, other forms of desire might also be so. Indeed, reciprocity might occur at the level of the genus, desire, between instances of different species. This is presumably typical of the standard model of the asymmetrical pederastic relationship in ancient sources. Such a model is assumed initially by Hippothales and Ctesippus, and Socrates can be taken as appealing to it at 222a6-7. In combination with the theory of the subject and object of love implied in the *Lysis*, this involves *erôs* as such only on the part of the lover, and a non-erotic response of friendship from a beloved who is naturally related to the lover. Note that, in conjunction with the implied theory such reciprocated desire must imply that people be individually complex, each involving separately both a neutral (i.e. desiring) and good (i.e. beneficial) part, the latter as the object of desire in another, who desires in return.

Relating this to the dialogue's characters, we see, first, that Lysis seems to have been impressed by Socrates (cf. 222a4), and clearly has an *erôs* (in an extended sense) aroused for understanding (cf. 211a7-8, b4-5 vis-à-vis 207d-210e, 213d2-7) – appropriately, since he recognises he lacks it. Secondly, Socrates must seem to him to promise understanding, but he is not himself a 'first friend'. In terms of the theory, Socrates would have to function similarly to the way a doctor does in relation to health, not himself necessarily possessing it, but being a means to it. He thus functions not as a final friend, but as an instrumental beloved who himself gains a *philos* in exchange for arousing (and perhaps facilitating) Lysis' *erôs* for knowledge.

Socrates' own desire for Lysis is suggested by his speech about desire for friends (211d-212a). Yet this is not erotic desire, but *philia* for Lysis' *philosophia* (cf. 213d7) and is what makes him useful to, and in that sense good for, Lysis; taken on its own (or in relation to himself) Socrates' desire for *philoi*, would be of neutral value, on the given theory. Conversely,

33

*Dougal Blyth*

Lysis' philosophical potential counts as a good for Socrates, as the specifically related object of the latter's desire for a particular kind of friend, but intrinsically neutral (i.e. in relation to Lysis himself), albeit directed to the related potential good of his own knowledge.

All of this is left implicit in the questions about what ends *philia*, or generally desire, can be satisfied by, and what nature those ends have, both in and beyond human beings. More precisely, there are two major philosophical questions left open by the dialogue (as the means to answering the covering question as to what a friend is). The first is, given the demonstration that there must be one or more final causes of friendships, what such causes might be. The second and related question is whether people of different natures are dedicated to different ultimate ends (note the contrast in character and ability between Lysis and Menexenus, despite their quick assumption that they are naturally related, 221e5-7). Moreover, with the second question also corresponds that as to what kinds of people are naturally related to one another and how. This leads to further questions about the nature of the soul and its pathology, and the natures of the virtues and other values.

What I have provided is meant to be no more than a sketch of a possible solution to the text's interpretive problems, so as to show that such a solution would explain what it means to say Socrates is portrayed not as a philosophical lover, but as a would-be friend. He is not portrayed as himself in love with Lysis' soul, but befriending him, i.e. responding, as one who is naturally related, to Lysis' awakening philosophical interest (see especially 213d6-214a2, 218c4-8 and 222b3-c3, where Socrates controls the development of the conversation to this effect). Note also that at 223a1-2 Socrates is clearly not preoccupied erotically with Lysis, since he then intends to talk to Hippothales or Ctesippus again, possibly about something different.

No doubt more could be said in relation to the detail of the text about how Socrates has modelled, for Hippothales' benefit, a lover talking to his beloved, but perhaps it is sufficient here to say that, to the extent that Socrates has gone beyond that task, he has performed as the friend and beloved of the neophyte philosophical lover, Lysis; while to the extent that he hasn't, he has directed Hippothales toward the tasks, first, of himself acquiring wisdom if he wishes to benefit a boy he loves, and, then, of arousing Lysis' desire for that knowledge in the way Socrates has modelled.

## *Symposium*

I turn now to the *Symposium*, where I will first consider the dramatised relationship between Socrates and Agathon, as to its erotic potential. While already an adult, the host Agathon is the youngest and most beautiful of those present (213c4-5), and he invites Socrates to share his couch and praises his wisdom (175c6-d2), which is suggestive of the role of

## 2. Socrates and Platonic Models of Love

an *erômenos*. Socrates compliments him repeatedly,[20] although clearly ironically, and teases (194c1-d4) and criticises him (198d3-199a5, 199d-201c) (with reference to the latter recall Socrates' advice to Hippothales in the *Lysis* at 205d-206b not to praise the boy one pursues but to humble him). Again, when Alcibiades arrives, he mimics suspicion that Socrates is pursuing Agathon (213c2-5), which Socrates and Agathon playfully acknowledge subsequently (222c-223b).

But there are contrary indications. Socrates initially displays a very unerotic rudeness to his host in bringing his own guest,[21] whom he sends on ahead, himself arriving late (174e-175c), and moreover he clearly acknowledges Pausanias as Agathon's genuine lover (177d8-e1). Again, the dialectical criticisms of Agathon's ideas mentioned above seem more severe than a lover should risk, and Alcibiades' warning at the end of his speech clearly denies that Socrates is really a lover of any young man he initially appears to pursue (222b3-4).

I will discuss the latter point further, but first we should consider the relationship between Socrates and Alcibiades. When Alcibiades enters and pretends to jealousy of Agathon, Socrates admits to having been Alcibiades' lover (213c7-d4), as at *Protagoras* 309a1-b7. Alcibiades claims that Socrates is jealous if he praises anyone else (214d6-8), while later Socrates claims Alcibiades is jealous of Agathon (222d1-2). There seems no doubt that in the *Protagoras* and *Symposium* Plato depicts Socrates as having previously pursued Alcibiades in something like the way a lover does his beloved, but at an age when other youths no longer attract lovers. Nevertheless the role-playing in the *Symposium* itself, when Alcibiades is already in his thirties, and admits to having left Socrates' company for politics (216a6-c3), cannot be considered evidence of any continuing erotic relationship.

Our best evidence for Plato's views of the earlier relationship is Alcibiades' speech. He describes Socrates as 'casting spells' like Marsyas by his discourse (215c1-d6), something a seducer might do, and reducing Alcibiades' own self-esteem by his talk (215e5-216c3), once again in accordance with the lesson Socrates himself gives in the *Lysis* on how a lover should speak to his *erômenos*. Alcibiades explicitly states that Socrates 'is erotically disposed' to beautiful youths (*erôtikôs diakeitai*, 216d2), but then he seems to contradict this, saying that really he is self-controlled, disinterested, and despises beauty as much as wealth and status,[22] implying the 'erotic disposition' is ironic. Alcibiades tells us Socrates is not really a lover and instead causes the youths to fall in love with him.[23]

While this seems like a pretty clear explosion of the myth of the erotic Socrates, Alcibiades may be somewhat mistaken in some respects, something he himself admits as a possibility before speaking (214e10-215a3). His current drunkenness might be taken as an image of his general lack of clear understanding. Since he admits he has misunderstood Socrates in the past, why should that not still be the case? Along with Socrates' apparent erotic disposition, which Alcibiades clearly thinks is ironic, he mentions Socrates' confession of ignorance (216d3-4), with the implication that this too is insincere. Presumably Alcibiades is thinking of the divinities he thought he perceived in Socrates' soul, like the statues inside a Silenus figure, which would have to be items of moral knowledge.[24] But if Alcibiades is mistaken,[25] perhaps Socrates, unlike Silenus, does not himself possess divinities within his own soul apart from his interlocutors. Socrates himself then would not be uniquely beautiful, or an ultimate object of *erôs*, contrary to the assumptions of Apollodorus, Aristodemus, and Alcibiades. Socrates might rather be a means, like the doctor, as the *Lysis* seems to suggest.

If we turn to Diotima's theory of love, and consider it in relation to Socrates personally, we gain confirmation and an explanation of this proposal. Beauty itself is not the kind of thing found ultimately within a person; rather it is transcendent (211a-212a). Admittedly the complete initiate in the highest mysteries of love is truly virtuous (212a3-5), but Diotima does not say that the divine forms of the virtues are themselves located literally within any human soul, as Alcibiades seemed to think.[26]

To become virtuous the lover begins by loving beautiful bodies, followed by souls and then customs, laws, and forms of knowledge, before discovering beauty itself (210a-e), but for this a guide helps.[27] Diotima instructs Socrates in this theory, but there is no evidence she guides him in practice, since 209e5-210a1 indicates he has not been initiated yet even into the preliminaries that she has, by that point, told him about. Again, at 210a1-2 she declares that she doesn't know if he can master the final rites. In this way the dialogue draws attention to the question of Socrates' own status in relation to these stages of progression.

In answer we need only note that the older Socrates who recounts Diotima's teaching does in the dialogue himself claim expertise in love, as in the *Lysis* and *Phaedrus*;[28] it is thus difficult to escape the implication that he is portrayed as having in the interval completed the final rites of *erôs*.[29] It must follow that Socrates in the flesh is no longer himself a lover at the stage of loving boys for their bodies or their souls (as described at 209b4-c7, 210a4-c6). According to Diotima that is the status of someone whose talk about virtue is merely on the path by which he himself is presently being brought to higher loves he does not yet experience, including ultimately the vision of beauty. She explicitly states that the lover of beauty itself will not be moved as before by the beauty of bodies.[30] Nor does it seem that the complete initiate would still be moved erotically by beauty of soul, or, similarly, by the other intermediate objects such as customs, laws and the various forms of knowledge (211d8-e4), for the following reasons:[31] Diotima distinguishes beauty itself as quite unique in its desirability by comparison with all other things called beautiful (210e6-b5), including explicitly any speech or knowledge (211a7; cf. Blondell 2006, 155) while just before this she explicitly denies that someone even loving

## 2. Socrates and Platonic Models of Love

the beauty of knowledge would still love the beauty of a 'single custom' (or 'practice', *epitêdeuma ti*, 210d2-3). This suggests that each erotic stage here extinguishes the preceding one (contra Sheffield 2006, 172-4). Thus if Socrates is the complete initiate he would not really be erotically disposed to young men's souls. Moreover, in any case, if he is an expert, it seems reasonable to identify Socrates in the role of the guide to love for others, rather than himself an inexperienced lover on the way to the truth.

### *Phaedrus*

One problem that remains is whether expertise in love is consistent with Socrates' claim to ignorance as reported by Alcibiades, which I have defended as not ironic.[32] Although I don't have room to deal with this at length, I think the *Phaedrus* gives us grounds to defend their consistency (cf. Rowe 1986, 9). In brief, according to Socrates here, in human embodiment our souls have no direct knowledge of the forms, but merely a recollection of a pre-natal experience.[33] Even the account of knowledge by collection and division seems to be a superhuman task,[34] and Socrates makes no claim to have mastered it, albeit he calls himself a lover (*erastês*) of collections and divisions themselves (266b2-3). On the other hand his claim here to expertise in *erôs* (257a7-8) gains credibility from the profundity of the vision of *erôs* and its ultimate object, again primarily the form of beauty, that Socrates' great speech contains, as well as from his quite distinctive way of responding to Phaedrus' aesthetic *erôs* for rhetoric.

With reference to the *Phaedrus*,[35] I will discuss first the initial depiction of Socrates' interests (227a-230e). Phaedrus is already known to him (228a5), but seems to assume that Socrates shares his enthusiasm for rhetoric, in particular about love (227c3-5).[36] Socrates seems particularly interested in the influence on him of Lysias (227b6-11, 228a6-b1). It turns out Phaedrus holds a copy of a new speech by Lysias, and Socrates says he would walk as far as Megara to hear this (227d3-5, 230d6-e1), and calls himself 'in love with speeches' (228c2). Nevertheless he assumes primarily that it is Phaedrus who is in love with this speech (228a-c), and perhaps he is actually concerned at the effect Phaedrus' enthusiasm has on his soul. Ultimately their conversation leads to a message to Lysias that the ability to write speeches without knowledge, and without the ability to explain the subject in person, is second-rate (278b8-e4). No doubt Socrates is interested in speeches in the sense of philosophical conversation, but clearly not in conventional rhetoric for its own sake. This can be explained by reference to his subsequent rejection of sophistic speculative reinterpretation of myths (229e4-230a6). Here, as Griswold argues (1986, 2-9, 36-44, and *passim*), Socrates claims he has no leisure for a pursuit unrelated to self-knowledge, and so presumably his interest in Phaedrus and rhetoric is here related somehow to that pursuit.

Given Socrates' interest in Phaedrus himself, let us turn to the question

*Dougal Blyth*

whether the *Phaedrus* portrays Socrates in the role of a lover. When he hears of the bizarre topic of Lysias' speech, persuasion of a boy to sexually gratify a non-lover, he initially depicts himself as sexually attracted to boys (227c9-d1). Then after hearing Phaedrus' speech Socrates says he is aroused primarily by Phaedrus' own enthusiasm for it, assuming Phaedrus to be an expert (234d1-6). This might seem to represent an *erôs* for Phaedrus, but Socrates turns the focus instead back to the speech and Phaedrus' own aesthetic *erôs*. Socrates distinguishes the object of Phaedrus' enthusiasm and purported expertise as the rhetorical form of the speech, not the content (234e5-235a2) but then criticises the speech on this very basis (235a2-8). Again, this might seem like a lover's humbling of his beloved, but Socrates then claims inspiration to make a speech rhetorically better than Lysias' (235c5-d3), which rather puts him in the role of a rival to Lysias as Phaedrus' beloved. This reverses the interlocutor's roles as in the *Lysis* (where it turned out, on my account above, that Lysis was found to be a lover, in that case of truth).

In what follows both Phaedrus and Socrates alternately play-act the role of lover while the other plays the beloved (cf. Griswold 1986, 29-30). Phaedrus first plays the lover (235d-237a): he is aroused by Socrates' promise to make a speech (235d4-e1), but Socrates toys with him gaining concessions as to his rhetorical task, like an *erômenos* eliciting gifts from his lover before satisfying him (235e5-236a6). Socrates then teases Phaedrus (236b5-8, d4-8), who demands Socrates satisfy him, like an aroused lover promised sexual gratification (236c1-8, d6-7), even threatening, first, to use force (236d1-3), and then to withdraw his own gifts, i.e. subsequent speeches of his own (236e1-3). Moreover, it is Phaedrus who points out that the two of them are alone in a beautiful and erotically charged location (236c8).

Socrates now portrays himself as ashamed to satisfy Phaedrus' desire (237a4-5), in this case for an immoral speech, as an *erômenos* might feel at allowing sexual gratification. Nevertheless he then begins the speech, albeit with his head covered for shame. Thereafter he cuts it short before he reaches the immoral part of the case, that a boy should allow a non-lover sexual gratification (241d2-7, cf. e2-7), and starts to escape across the river (242a1-2).

When he returns at the behest of his *daimonion*, before giving the great speech in praise of love that is his recantation, Socrates adopts the opposite role, that of the lover speaking to his beloved, and invites Phaedrus to play the role of the *erômenos* (243e4-6), as audience of the speech. I conclude that, as with the previous play-acting of the reverse roles and Socrates' original ironic self-presentation as a lover of speeches, this too is no sincere depiction of Socrates as a lover of Phaedrus.[37] The dialogue shows he is rather a friend seeking to alleviate the limitations of Phaedrus' amoral enthusiasm for rhetoric.

I propose that the recantation is portrayed as Socrates' attempt to

## 2. Socrates and Platonic Models of Love

convert Phaedrus to a passion for the content rather than the form of speeches, and thus to a concern for their morality and ultimately for philosophy. Nevertheless it is depicted as a failure: Phaedrus' immediate response at the end of the great speech (257c1-4) shows he is still only interested in engaging Socrates in a competition with Lysias in persuasive power (contra Gooch 1992, 310). Despite Socrates' efforts, Phaedrus is still preoccupied with rhetorical form.

Phaedrus is, all the same, clearly concerned about the value of speeches, as his report of a politician's criticism of Lysias shows (257c4-7). Socrates thereupon seeks to reassure Phaedrus' aesthetic passion so as again to attempt to relate it to philosophy, first by arguing that politicians themselves strive to produce written speeches as decrees (257d-258c), and then by introducing the question of how to distinguish good speeches from bad ones (258d4-11, 259e1-2). This takes up the rest of the dialogue, and ties philosophy to rhetorical form instead of content,[38] since, on Socrates' account, it turns out to be a key ingredient in 'true' rhetorical expertise.

So as to gain Phaedrus' confidence in order to influence him in this way, Socrates must take on a persona of shared enthusiasm for epideictic rhetoric, as a form of beauty. Given his attitude in the *Gorgias*, we should doubt this enthusiasm is meant to be seen as genuine. That Socrates makes repeated references to external inspiration, implying that he is acting out of character, seems to confirm this.[39] But I think it would be wrong to call Socrates here insincere: his behaviour seems rather to be the result of deliberate investment in psychic identification with Phaedrus' passion. Socrates' repeated references to the rural context seem to enable him to pursue that passion beyond the limitations of Phaedrus' conception of the beautiful. We could imagine Socrates' aim to be merely to convert Phaedrus to philosophy (cf. 257b3-6, 278b-279b), but his insistence that what he discusses must be relevant to self-knowledge (229e4-230a6) suggests that he is depicted as himself benefiting from the conversation. Perhaps by revising the object of the *erôs* he adopts from Phaedrus he purifies his own capacity for *erôs* and so revives his dialectical ability (cf. 230d5-e4).

This has relevance to the questions we were left with by the *Symposium*. Perhaps we should say that the master of the art of love, although disdaining all phenomenal beauty as merely an ephemeral image by contrast with the form itself, nevertheless does return in practice to engage in loving such images, by means of a deliberate act of psychic identification with the perspective of a neophyte such as Phaedrus.[40] Perhaps by internally experiencing the intended revision of the neophyte's awareness of the true object of *erôs* Socrates recovers, or enacts, the self-knowledge he here makes his priority, and this self-knowledge, that is, his knowledge of *erôs* and, perhaps, of his own ignorance too, is what gives him his dialectical ability. It makes sense here to conceive of self-knowledge not as an acquired state, but a form of activity enabled by Socrates' interaction with Phaedrus' aesthetic *erôs*, given that the soul itself is defined in this dialogue by self-movement (*Phdr.* 245e7-246a1), i.e. a form of activity.

Socrates' great speech in the *Phaedrus* (243e-257b) gives us a more detailed account of the relationship between a philosophical lover and beloved than the other dialogues. It describes the ultimate causes of love, the complex interactions of the parts within the lover's soul, and their distinct motives, and the experience and behaviour of both lover and beloved. Yet for current purposes I need mention only a few central features. A true lover is overwhelmed on meeting his beloved because the latter's beauty reminds him of the transcendent form of beauty his disembodied soul once saw (249d5-8, 250b-251a), and the lover cultivates the *erômenos* as a fellow devotee of the same god in whose train both disembodied souls once followed, sharing the god's characteristics, and so the lover worships his beloved as an icon of that god (252d-253c). The boy, without understanding, falls in love in return with his lover (255c-256a). Within the lover an intra-psychic struggle occurs between the intellect, affected as above, and the appetite for sex (254a-e). When the intellect wins, ideally they form a chaste philosophical relationship, or otherwise one devoted to status, involving only occasional capitulation to sexual desire (256a-e, cf. 252e1-5). In either case the relationship is permanent.

Now, in brief, none of this is foreshadowed in the relationship between Socrates and Phaedrus.[41] First, there is no indication that there was any subsequent monogamous but chaste erotic relationship between the two of them (although admittedly the historical Phaedrus soon after the dramatic date went into exile); secondly, there is no indication that on meeting Phaedrus Socrates was thunderstruck with any kind of recognition of either his beauty or psychic kinship (in fact his interest in rhetoric seems a far cry from Socrates' interest in dialectical philosophy, notwithstanding the initial ambiguity regarding their mutual enthusiasm for speeches (*logoi*); thirdly, there is no indication of Phaedrus being affected by a 'counter-*erôs*' and falling for Socrates in any particular way, and in fact he seems completely uninspired by Socrates' great speech, indicating quite a contrast in character and interests; and finally, nor is there any evidence, beyond the play-acting between the two of them, of any erotic struggle within the soul of Socrates to maintain his own self-control in the presence of his beloved, by contrast with his claimed effort to control himself when he meets Charmides (*Charm.* 155c-e), and perhaps when alone with Alcibiades, assuming he was even tempted then (*Symp.* 219b-d) – whereas if he wasn't, then all the less is he portrayed as any kind of lover.

## Conclusion

These three uncontestedly Platonic dialogues, the *Lysis*, *Symposium* and *Phaedrus*, are the most obviously erotic, portraying Socrates as speaking about *erôs*, and most explicitly raising by their dramatic and other literary

## 2. Socrates and Platonic Models of Love

features the question of whether Socrates was in fact a lover of boys. It seems that in none of them is the right answer 'yes', even when we distinguish the model of the philosophical lover of souls from that of the debased lover of bodies. If anything, Plato seems to make efforts to show that Socrates adopted this pose deliberately and ironically in order to avail himself of an acceptable social model of interaction as a cover for his protreptic and pedagogical interest in aristocratic young men of philosophical potential. This is not to say that he sought to hide his real intentions, as a philosophical seducer might, but just that, on Plato's depiction, he sometimes used this model as an ironically managed bridge between the ordinary pederastic social expectations of socially elevated Athenians and the peculiar characteristics of the dialectically driven relationship he had with his philosophical friends.

It is the failure to understand precisely this, the dialectical nature of the philosophical relationship Socrates cultivated, that leads Alcibiades at the end of his speech in the *Symposium* both almost to forget Socrates' arguments (221d-222a), and then to misrepresent Socrates as having deceived the boys he has pursued: himself, Charmides and Euthydemus among others (222a7-b4). But this list must be compared and contrasted with the list at *Apology* 33d-34a, Critoboulus, Aeschines, Epigenes, Theodotus, Theages, Plato and Apollodorus: neither these men nor their relatives complained of such deception by Socrates.

Finally on the *Alcibiades* I, by way of compensation for taking this topic up here, I must admit that what I have said cannot help decide the question of its authenticity. Socrates' self-presentation there in the role of a lover of Alcibiades' soul is consistent with the latter's reported experience of him in the *Symposium*, and intelligible in terms of the 'bridging' use of the model of pederasty I have ascribed to Socrates.[42]

I don't see any need to extrapolate in any case to Socrates' engagement in any of the practices implied by the accounts of *erôs* given by his speeches in the *Symposium* and the *Phaedrus*. The speech in the *Symposium* focuses on the role of an incomplete lover on his way to the vision of beauty, which Socrates, as a professed expert in love, must be understood to have already attained, and in which case he has relinquished the real love of mere images of beauty. That in *Phaedrus* is designed to answer the preceding two speeches and encourage the already erotically disposed Phaedrus in the belief that there is a greater beauty than the aesthetic beauty of rhetoric for him to love, and that the pursuit of this involves philosophy. In both cases, and generally, Socrates merely makes use of the pre-existing Athenian preoccupation with *erôs* to advance the case for philosophy. In brief, as Alcibiades reveals, Socrates' 'erotic disposition' is ironic (216e4-5: *eironeuomenos de kai paizôn panta ton bion pros tous anthropous diatelei*).

*Dougal Blyth*

## Notes

1. Contrast the claims made, e.g. by Penner and Rowe 2005, 269, at their L 10, that Socrates is portrayed in the dialogues as engaged in a 'romantic relationship with [Alcibiades]'; by G. Scott 2000, 59, 73, 79, who claims that in *Lys.* Socrates is depicted as a real lover of Lysis; and by Rowe 1998, 6, asserting that in *Symp.* Socrates is presented as a 'philosophical lover', who is perpetually on the lookout for beautiful young men with whom to talk'. Blondell 2006, 162-74 argues that evidence locates Socrates on each of the different steps of the *Symposium*'s ladder of love, implying that he is portrayed in various places as really a lover of young men, body and soul (see esp. her pp. 162-8, and 176); ultimately her point is more complex, but in brief her evidence reduces to *Charm.* 154b-155d, *Alc.* I and passages in *Symp.* On each of these see further below.

2. Because the distinction between *erôs* and *philia* is important in my account of the *Lysis* I will generally stick to translating the latter as friendship, and *philos* (along with *philon*) as friend, although the latter might in some contexts be more precisely, if not succinctly, rendered 'object of *philia*'.

3. I think G. Scott 2000, 60 misunderstands this when he claims (focusing only on Socrates' earlier questions) that he 'is evidently more interested in seeing what is going on inside the Palaestra than in talking to [Hippothales and Ctesippus]'.

4. Presumably he recognises the beloved by the lover's reaction to his name (cf. Euripides *Hippolytus* 310) or presence. Cf. Penner and Rowe 2005, 4-5 n. 7, downplaying the significance of this.

5. In addition to teaching Hippothales how to speak to one he loves, this is presumably meant also as a lesson to Hippothales that he too needs to acquire knowledge, in order to be in a position to promise it to his beloved.

6. For analysis of the peculiarities, tied to their own interpretation, see, e.g., Penner and Rowe 2005, 25-38; cf., briefly, Price 1989, 3.

7. Penner and Rowe 2005, 51-63 make an interesting attempt to show that Socrates' aim is not just to deceive Menexenus. I mean only to say here that Plato clearly wishes to raise that *suspicion* in the reader's mind, if only initially, whatever the conclusion he hopes the reader will finally arrive at.

8. Contrast Penner and Rowe 2005, 195-230 for defence of a different method, interpreting the *Lysis* in the light of positions found in, and questions raised by, other dialogues.

9. This is not to assert that Plato recommends such a theory as known truth, or even his own committed belief, but to say that in such a case the theory would be something he proposes as worthy of further investigation, which would either have to go beyond the circumstances and characterisations of the dialogue in the search for truth, or perhaps be related back to those characters in terms of the theory's suitability to their stage of education.

10. Cf. 219c5-220b8 where the theory of the 'first friend' as the source of value is initially established, leading immediately into the problem that the previous model of friendship presupposed that any friend was only good as a means to remove an evil; at 220d8-e4 the first-friend theory is restated in the teeth of this problem, which is only thereupon resolved by introducing the principle that neutral desire, not evil, is the cause of friendship. Cf. also Penner and Rowe 2005, 128-33 and 257-60 on the problem whether and in what sense Socrates still thinks of other things that are only valuable for the sake of the first friend as themselves still friends.

11. *Oikeion* is often translated here and at *Symp.* 193d2, 205e6, cf. 192c1, as

## 2. Socrates and Platonic Models of Love

'[one's] own', 'what belongs [to one]', or 'what is akin'. As Price 1989, 8 notes, the former can also translate *philon* (particularly in poetry). Someone is *oikeios* to another if he belongs to the same household (*oikos*); this includes both natural relations (kin) and conventional relations (slaves), but a Greek would easily overlook slaves (despite their often being called *oikeioi* as such); a wife is conventionally related to her husband by marriage, but naturally as his reproductive partner (a relationship known in Greek as *ta philtata*).

12. Admittedly at 214c7-d3 bad people are agreed to be dissimilar, not naturally unrelated, to anyone (on the ground that they have no stable identity), but it will follow that they cannot be naturally related to anyone, insofar as relationships are as such determinate, and so require determinate terms.

13. Most explicitly at 221d2-4. The conception of being responsible for something here is probably best understood as that of being necessary and sufficient for it; being necessary accords with the normal meaning of *aitios*: a form or genus is an *aition* in this sense, and it is the basis of the 'Academic' principle of causation first expressed theoretically here at 221c3-5, while clearly the relevant kind of desire is understood as sufficient for friendship at 221b7-c1, and apparently also in the second half of 221d2-4.

14. I.e. *erôs*, esp. at *Lys.* 221b7-c1, 221e3-5, 221e7-222a4; cf. 211d7-e7.

15. Jenks 2005, 66 concludes very quickly that, in the *Lysis*, '*philia* ... includes *erôs* as well as familial bonds of care and affection', which is generally reasonable, but he does not investigate all relevant passages.

16. *Lys.* 212d5-e6, 217a4-b4, and 218e2-219a6.

17. Compare the enlarged sense of love (*erôs*) extending beyond human objects at *Symp.* 204d-205d.

18. See Hyland 1968 for an interesting argument that across a variety of dialogues Plato repeatedly treats *erôs* as a rational subdivision of desire, and, moreover, *philia* as a yet more rational subdivision of the latter. But he does not note that *Symp.* 207a6-b6 extends *erôs* to irrational animals; again, at *Lys.* 221b7-c1, *philia* must be no less broad than *erôs* (and Hyland, p. 43, revises his claim as that the highest kind of *erôs* is a form of *philia*). Ludwig 2002, 213 with n. 135 follows Price 1989, 8, in claiming that the *Lysis* equates *philia* and *erôs*; this is based particularly on Price's appeal to 221e5-222a3, but that passage is not at all dispositive.

19. Cf. Rowe 1998, 5: 'the core meaning [of the word *erôs*] in the *Symposium* is inseparable from *sexual desire*' (his emphasis); and Santas 1988, 70. Sheffield 2006, 2 n. 2, who denies this, appeals to Ludwig 2002, 7-13, but at p. 378 (cf. pp. 212-16) he allows that *erôs* involves two key components, the need to possess and a response to beauty; in the case of human objects this certainly amounts to sexual desire, and any explanation of *erôs* that does not account for that necessarily fails. Even for Plato, as Roochnik 1987, 120 notes with reference to *Symp.* 210a4-8, it must begin with physical desire.

20. *Symp.* 175d7-e6, 194a8-b5, 198a3-d3, 199c3-6, 201d8-e3.

21. This is noted by Blondell 2006, 148.

22. *Symp.* 216c-e, 218c-219e, 222b3-4.

23. *Symp.* 216e2-217a2, 217e6-218b4, 219d3-7, 219e-221d, 222a1-7.

24. *Symp.* 215a6-b3, 216d-217a, esp. 216d4-7.

25. Cf. Reeve 2006, 124-33; Sheffield 2006, 204; Blondell 2006, 158 with bibliography, n. 44.

26. Blondell 2006, 156-7 gives the impression of following Alcibiades in this error, although possibly she is redeemed on p. 158.

27. *Symp.* 210a6-7, 210e2-3, 211c1.
28. *Symp.* 177d7-8, cf. 193e4-5, 198d1-2; cf. *Lys.* 204c1-2, 206c4-7 and *Phdr.* 257a7-8.
29. Cf. Blondell 2006, 156-61 for an extended defence of this claim, and p. 156 n. 34 for further bibliography.
30. *Symp.* 210b5-6, 210c5-6, 211d3-8.
31. Here I disagree with Price 1989, 43-5.
32. Cf. Reeve 2006, 133-6; Roochnik 1987.
33. *Phdr.* 249c1-6, 250a-d, 254b5-7.
34. *Phdr.* 265c-266c, 273e1-8, cf. 249C6-8
35. Generally here my ideas about the *Phaedrus* owe more to reflection on Griswold 1986 and Ferrari 1987 than can be acknowledged in the notes below, even where I do not follow them.
36. Phaedrus is probably meant to infer this merely from his knowledge of Socrates' willing engagement in erotic speeches as depicted in the *Symposium*. The dramatic date of the *Phaedrus* is likely to be shortly before mid-415 BC when Phaedrus was exiled: see Rowe 2005, xii with n. 3 (= xxv), following Nails 2003, App.1; cf. Nussbaum 1986, 212 with n. 24; the dramatic date of the *Symposium* is the day after the end of the Lenaia of early 416 (173a5-6 with Athenaeus 217b).
37. Thus I disagree here both with Nussbaum 1986, 200-33, esp. 205-13, cf. 229, who claims the dialogue depicts Socrates and Phaedrus as (truly) lover and beloved, and Gooch 1992, who argues that Nussbaum is wrong to claim they are already lovers before the great speech, but nevertheless Phaedrus is converted by it (see following).
38. It also ties rhetorical form to philosophical content, insofar as a hypothetically complete knowledge of the comprehensive collection and division of all there is (*Phdr.* 273e1-4, cf. 262b-266d), and in particular such knowledge of the human soul (*Phdr.* 269d-272b), must be included within the 'true' art of rhetoric.
39. *Phdr.* 230b-c, 235c-d, 237a, 238c-d, 242b-d, 243e-244a, 257a, 258e-259d, 279b. On the significance of the environmental references see Ferrari 1987, ch. 1, esp. 21-5; and *passim*.
40. Cf. Sheffield 2006, 179-80, although p. 182 (on the continuing lower loves of the guide in *Symp.*) seems to me confused, unless it were reinterpreted in accordance with what I think the *Phaedrus* adds to the picture here.
41. Cf. more briefly, Griswold 1986, 152.
42. Thus I reject the assumption of Gordon 2003, esp. 28, that Socrates is depicted as really loving Alcibiades' soul in *Alc.* Her main evidence for this is just that he recognises the power of Alcibiades' assets, as she lists them, which does not amount to the same thing.

3

# The Eye of the Beloved: *Opsis* and *Eros* in Socratic Pedagogy

## *Victoria Wohl*

Beauty is in the eye of the beholder. Or is it? This was a live question in antiquity and one with significant philosophical ramifications. Both Plato and Xenophon align vision, *eros* and philosophy, but they start with different models of vision and reach different understandings of both *eros* and philosophy. In Plato's *Alcibiades* I the paradigm of self-knowledge is an eye seeing itself in the eye of the other and a lover seeing his soul in the soul of a beloved. The dynamics of this optical paradigm, with its narcissistic gaze and mirroring love, are developed further in Plato's *Symposium*, where the lover's eye becomes the metaphor for philosophical *theôria*. Xenophon inverts this visual dynamic: shifting the focus onto the object, he imagines the philosopher not as a lover but as a beautiful beloved. The way Xenophon develops his optical paradigm highlights his philosophical and pedagogical differences from Plato. It also helps to illuminate the role of Alcibiades within Platonic philosophy. Alcibiades in the *Symposium* resists the optical model he is advised to adopt in the *Alcibiades*; instead, he looks at Socrates with an eye more Xenophontic than Platonic. As a result, his loving gaze allows us to behold the true beauty of the philosopher, a strange but wondrous sight.[1]

The optical passage of *Alcibiades* comes within a discussion of care of the self. Socrates and Alcibiades have agreed that caring for oneself is a prerequisite for all other activities, but we can't care for ourselves if we don't know what a self is and so the ethical project of self-care requires a prior epistemological project of defining the self (128a-129a).[2] The self is not one's possessions or body, Socrates shows, but one's soul: to know yourself (as the Delphic oracle commands) is thus to know your own soul (130e7-8). This raises a new question – 'how might we best know the soul?' – to which the answer is the optical *paradeigma*.

> Soc.: Now, look. If the Delphic oracle spoke to our eye, as if to a man, with the advice 'See yourself,' how would we understand that advice? Doesn't it mean to look at that in which the eye that was looking was going to see itself?
> Alc.: Obviously.
> Soc.: Do we know what actual thing we can look at to see both the thing and ourselves at the same time?

45

Alc.: Clearly it's a mirror or something like that, Socrates.
Soc.: You're right. And isn't there also something like that in the eye in which we see?
Alc.: Yes.
Soc.: Have you noticed that the face of the person looking at the eye appears in the pupil of the person directly facing him, as in a mirror? This is called the *korê* and is a double (*eidôlon*) of the person seeing.
Alc.: That's true.
Soc.: Then an eye, gazing at another eye and looking into that part of it which is best and with which it sees, would see itself.
Alc.: It seems so.
Soc.: And if it should look at another part of the human body or any other thing except that to which it happens to be similar it will not see itself.
Alc.: Right.
Soc.: And if an eye is going to see itself it must look into an eye, and specifically into that part of an eye in which the excellence of the eye resides. And that, I suppose, is the pupil.
Alc.: That's so.
Soc.: Well then, dear Alcibiades, if the soul, too, is going to know itself, it must look into another soul, and especially into that part of it in which the soul's excellence, wisdom, resides, and that part which happens to be similar to itself?
Alc.: I suppose so, Socrates.
Soc.: Can we speak of any part of the soul more divine than this, which is the locus of knowledge and wisdom?
Alc.: We cannot.
Soc.: Since this part of it is like the god, and someone looking into this part and coming to know all that is divine, both the god and wisdom, in this way might best know himself?
Alc.: So it seems. (Pl. *Alc.* 132d5-133c7)

This optical schema offers a paradigm for a life of philosophical self-scrutiny. If (as many scholars believe) this dialogue was the traditional starting point for a course of Platonic philosophy, the optical *paradeigma* introduces many key themes of the programme to come: the priority of the soul over the body, the importance of knowing and working on yourself, the divinity of the intellect. The passage also implicitly aligns this philosophical program with a pederastic erotics. Nicholas Denyer, in his commentary on this passage, remarks that 'glaringly absent is explicit mention of how erotic are looks from, or into, someone's eyes'.[3] But if this erotics is not explicitly elaborated, it is implicit in the passage. The dialogue as a whole is framed by the *eros* between Socrates and Alcibiades: it opens with the question of why Socrates has become Alcibiades' lover only now, after his youthful beauty has begun to fade and his other lovers have abandoned him. This initial question is answered in the section leading up to the optical passage: it is because Socrates loves Alcibiades' self – that is, his soul – not his body that he has stuck around when the others have left (131c6-d6). The observation that the soul is the self is thus offered as a key not only to self-knowledge but also to true love: Socrates

## 3. The Eye of the Beloved

is Alcibiades' only real *erastês* (131e10-132a2). The paradigmatic eye is a lover's eye and that into which it gazes is the eye of its beloved. In the context of the dialogue's erotic scenario, then, the optical paradigm becomes paradigmatic for a mode of philosophical *eros*.

This *eros* is structured by a fundamental narcissism. For the viewer-lover does not, in fact, see the divinity of the other soul; he merely sees – and is encouraged to see – his own divinity reflected there. When he looks into the eye of his lover, he sees not the other but only himself. The movement of the argument in this passage is revelatory. In answer to Socrates' question about how an eye might 'see itself,' Alcibiades had originally proposed a mirror and, in fact, Socrates' question seems to call for this answer: he asked, 'Do we know what actual thing (*ti tôn ontôn*) we can look at to see both the thing (*ekeino*) and ourselves at the same time?' (132e1-2). The mirror is both a reflection of the viewer and also an object in its own right, a precious one in the ancient world and often highly ornamented.[4] Socrates accepts Alcibiades' suggestion but immediately supersedes it: 'You're right. And isn't there also something like that in the eye in which we see?' (132e5-6). The mirror is dropped, as it were, in favour of the eye. With the mirror, one sees both the object and oneself. We might think of the ancient trope of the friend as a mirror of the self: looking into his face, we see, as Aristotle puts it, another self (*heteros egô*), a reflection that is both us (*egô*) and other (*heteros*).[5] But with the eye of the other, one doesn't see the other – one doesn't even really see the eye. All one sees is oneself. The other is reduced to his own pupil (*opsis*) and that pupil to a mere puppet or statue (*korê*) of the viewer. Lacking even the autonomy of a mirror, the other becomes a mere *eidôlon* or double of the self. And that self, in this narcissistic fantasy, is simply divine: both *korê* and *eidôlon* can refer to statues of the gods.[6]

The philosopher-lover gazes into the eyes of his beloved and sees himself as a god. Self-knowledge becomes not only solipsistic but even onanistic. The other becomes irrelevant: his autonomy and alterity, his actual otherness, is elided both as a precondition of this mirroring – for we are told that the eye can only see itself in what is like itself (*homoion*, 133a11) – and as the goal of this same mirroring, which is, after all, *self*-knowledge. The other disappears in the philosopher's loving self-regard. If this is problematic as a model for *eros*, it is no less so as a model for philosophy. Andrea Nightingale has shown how Plato adopts the metaphor of *theôria*, the journey to see a foreign spectacle, to figure philosophical contemplation as an encounter with otherness, the end result of which is *thauma*, wonder.[7] But in this passage, the only *thauma* is the wonderful vision of one's own wonderful self.[8]

The erotic and visual dynamics of this scene set the stage for the more developed theory of *eros* proposed in Diotima's speech in the *Symposium*. There, as in the *Alcibiades*, the emphasis falls on the lover not the beloved: the lover is more divine than the beloved (*theioteran gar erastês paidikôn*,

180b3), and the god Eros himself is a lover not a beloved (203c3-4, 204c2-6). Far from a subject of philosophical *eros*, the *erômenos* is not even its object: what the lover wants is not the beloved in and for himself, but immortality and eternal possession of the good (204d1-206a13), which he achieves through procreation, spiritual or physical. The beautiful beloved goes from object to instrument, for the lover can only procreate in beauty (206c4-5): the beloved's beauty becomes merely a vehicle for the lover's self-reproduction. Similarly, in the ascent passage, the love of a single beautiful body is superseded by the love of beauty in all bodies, then the love of beauty in the soul and in institutions, and finally, the vision of absolute Beauty, the Form of the Beautiful, which is unique and autonomous, eternally the same, homogenous in all its parts and forms: *auto kath'hauto meth'hautou monoeides* (211b1). This absolute beauty is intellectual not corporeal: touching it, the perfected lover gives birth not to images, *eidôla*, of the truth but to truth itself (212a4-5). Like the philosopher ascending from the cave in *Republic* 7, leaving behind the *eidôla* of the physical world for the true light of the Sun, the lover leaves behind the *eidôla* of human beauty for the vision of abstract and immortal beauty. In the process, he abandons his former beloved: when he comes to see the general nature of Beauty, 'his zeal for a single individual slackens and he considers it something worthless and contemptible' (210b4-6). Thus there is good reason to concur with Gregory Vlastos' famous claim that Plato's erotic theory places no value on the love of another whole and unique individual. As Vlastos puts it: 'Since persons in their concreteness are thinking, feeling, wishing, hoping, fearing beings, to think of love for them as love for objectifications of excellence is to fail to make the thought of them as *subjects* central to what is felt for them in love.'[9]

This 'failure', as Vlastos puts it, has its foundations in the optical paradigm of the *Alcibiades*. There solipsistic self-knowledge seems to elide the beloved, who far from being an autonomous ('thinking, feeling, wishing, hoping, fearing') subject, becomes a mere *eidôlon* of a higher truth. Aligning the viewer-lover with the search for wisdom and the beloved with a repudiated materiality, it seems to imagine philosophy – and love – as a narcissistic project in which the philosopher can know and the lover love only what reflects himself.[10]

Elsewhere Plato seems to offer a more reciprocal model of optical desire, one that grants more autonomy and agency to the beloved. The central myth of the *Phaedrus*, in particular, seems to privilege the beloved, whose beauty is the source of an emanation that nourishes and improves not only his lover but also himself (255c-3). Amidst a flood of mutual desire and an orgy of swelling 'wings' the beloved too becomes a lover (255d3), a reversal likewise hinted at in the ornithological metaphor for reciprocal *eros* at the end of the *Alcibiades* (135d7-e3).[11] But even in the *Phaedrus*' fantasy of mutual desire, *anterôs* is a mirroring *eidôlon* (*eidôlon erôtos anterôta ekhôn*, 255d8-e1): for the beloved, an *eidôlon* of his own beauty flowing

## 3. The Eye of the Beloved

back to him; for the lover, a recollection and imitation of the divine beauty he had experienced in his initiation. Each thus thinks he loves the other, but 'he doesn't realise that he is seeing himself in his lover as in a mirror' (*hôsper de en katoptrôi en tôi erônti heauton horôn lelêthen*, 255d5-6).[12] In this respect, the *eros* of the *Phaedrus* is not so different from that of the *Alcibiades*. This Platonic conception of *eros* as self-reflection is not the only possibility, however. We find an alternate construction of the pederastic relationship – and an alternate optical paradigm – when we turn to Xenophon. Xenophon shifts the balance of erotic power and the centre of philosophical gravity away from the lover and onto the beloved, with important implications for his imagination of both *eros* and philosophy.

One might expect to find little *theôria*, erotic or otherwise, in the relentlessly practical philosophy of Xenophon. Indeed, Xenophon can be downright anti-theoretical. In the *Memorabilia*, Xenophon's Socrates tells his followers to learn only enough geometry to measure their land and not to worry about complicated diagrams that will do them little good and distract from more useful pursuits (*Mem.* 4.7.2-3); likewise, they should learn astronomy and mathematics only as far as is useful and avoid the 'empty business' (*tên mataion pragmateian*, 4.7.8) of abstract knowledge. The same pragmatism informs the *Memorabilia* as a whole, which glosses *gnôthi seauton* as knowing your own strengths and weaknesses (4.2.25) and measures the value of Socratic wisdom in terms of its utility for an ethical life as an Athenian *kalos k'agathos*. In a text that eschews the metaphysical for the physical, the unseen marks the edge of Xenophon's epistemological ambition: Socrates must labour to prove the existence and benefit of things one cannot see (like the gods or the soul) by pointing to their visible effects (e.g. 4.3.14). The metaphysical is brought within the realm of the physical world and subjected to its standards of utility and visibility – a trajectory directly opposite to that of Platonic philosophy.[13]

But the antitheoretical is itself a theoretical position, and Xenophon too builds on an implicit optical paradigm, with its own theoretical implications. Xenophon, like Plato, aligns vision, *eros*, and philosophy, but he works with a different model of vision – an intromissive not extramissive model – and as a result conceptualises both *eros* and philosophy in a very different way from Plato. For him, *eros* is not a lover seeking to see, know, and reproduce himself but a beloved impressing himself on the eye and soul of his lover: this visual impression is in turn the paradigm for Xenophon's philosophical pedagogy, a pedagogy based on the vision of the beloved and beautiful Socrates.

Early in Book I of the *Memorabilia*, Xenophon recounts an anecdote about the power of a kiss. Socrates, he begins, advised staying away from sexual relations with the beautiful, since once one touches them it is difficult to maintain one's self-control (1.3.8). When he found out that Critoboulus had kissed the handsome young son of Alcibiades he launched into a polemic against kissing. Kissing the beautiful is as risky as turning somersaults among knives or jumping into fire (1.3.9). It turns a free man into a slave, involving him in extravagant expenditure on harmful pleasures, with no spare time to care for anything noble or good (1.3.11). 'By Heracles,' exclaims Xenophon, who was himself present at the discussion, 'that's a terrible power you ascribe to a kiss!' Socrates explains by comparing the deadly kiss to a spider bite: a tiny spider, not even the size of a half-obol, can drive a grown man mad with pain merely by touching him with his mouth (1.3.12). When Xenophon objects to the analogy on the ground that 'spiders inject something through their bite', Socrates responds that the beast called 'youth and beauty' is in fact much more dangerous than a spider 'because the latter injects something through physical contact, whereas the former, without a touch, if one just looks at him, injects something even from a distance that drives one mad. So I advise you, Xenophon,' he concludes, 'whenever you see someone beautiful, flee at full speed; and you, Critoboulus, I advise to spend a year in exile, which may be just enough time to recover from your bite' (1.3.13).

This anecdote is significant in a number of ways. Its importance is marked by its cast of characters. First, this is the only time the author appears as a character in his own text, and he plays the role not of ardent acolyte but of defender of the kiss. Secondly, the kisser Critoboulus is one of Xenophon's favourite characters: the son of Socrates' loyal friend Crito, he features a number of times in the *Memorabilia* in contexts discussing *eros* or beauty; he is also a guest in Xenophon's *Symposium* and the primary interlocutor in his *Oeconomicus*. Finally, the youth he kisses is the son of Alcibiades himself. This anecdote comes in the part of the *Memorabilia* where Xenophon is defending Socrates against the charge of corruption of the youth, specifically Critias and Alcibiades. In this apologetic context, the choice of these particular boys – the son of Socrates' most loyal supporter and the son of his most conspicuous pedagogical failure – is hardly accidental. Indeed, the whole scene serves an apologetic purpose: it is offered as proof of Socrates' remarkable *enkrateia*: 'he was so manifestly secure against such temptations that he could more easily refrain from beautiful boys in the bloom of youth than most people could from those who were ugly and past their prime' (1.3.14). Far from corrupting the youth, Socrates resisted their attractions and even taught them to resist one another.[14]

While the perils of the kiss situate this episode within the defence of Socrates, its visual dynamics place it within an ethics of viewing well analysed by Simon Goldhill (1998) in his discussion of a scene in *Memorabilia* 3 that bears close resemblance to this kiss episode. Socrates goes to see the *hetaira* Theodote, whose beauty prompts a dialogue on the utility and danger of viewing (3.11). Goldhill shows how this dialogue constructs viewing as an ethical act that can be measured – as all things are in Xenophon's world – by its civic usefulness: will looking at this object in this way make you a better citizen? By that criterion, sex appeal is ethically

## 3. The Eye of the Beloved

perilous. Theodote's beauty is compared to a web in which she catches men (3.11.6); it arouses a desire that undermines the masculine self-control of those who look at her. Socrates, of course, is the exception; his extraordinary *enkrateia* causes a paradoxical inversion, as Goldhill (1998, 122) notes: 'in his demonstration of his mastery over the subjections of desire he himself becomes the object of desire'. Thus the scene ends with the beautiful courtesan trying to seduce the homely philosopher. This same point is illustrated in the episode of the kiss, which (like the Theodote episode) shows Socrates' mastery over the desirable object of erotic spectation and thus turns him into the desirable object of ethical spectation, the model of the enkratic man.

What is the optical logic at work in these anecdotes and how do they operate within the larger visual dynamics of Xenophon's pederastic *eros* and philosophical pedagogy? The kiss episode imagines the sight of the beloved object acting physically upon the viewer. The beloved projects himself bodily into the bloodstream of the lover through his vision. Vision thus becomes a kind of touch, even a penetration, a bite. This odd notion draws on a theory of optical intromission (formulated first by the atomists) that imagined vision originating not in the eye of the beholder, but in the object, which was thought to emit a physical simulacrum (*eidôlon*), particles in the shape of the object that then struck the eye of the viewer. By contrast, the optical paradigm in Plato's *Alcibiades* presupposes a theory of extramission in which vision is explained as an emanation from the eye of the viewer that presses upon the object. According to this logic, the *korê* – the reflection in the other's pupil – is not just a *trompe l'oeil* but the literal physical presence of the viewer in the eye of the other. Both theories, intromissive and extramissive, imagine vision as tactile, but the touch moves in opposite directions: in Plato, the viewer projects himself onto the object; in Xenophon the object projects himself onto – or, as the spider metaphor implies, injects himself into – the viewer.[15]

The different model of vision implies a different model of *eros*. I suggested that the optics of *eros* in the *Alcibiades* and Diotima's speech in the *Symposium* emphasise the viewer/lover at the expense of the viewed/beloved; the philosopher is an erotic *theôrist* who sees in the eyes of his beloved his own divine excellence; his gaze renders the other transparent, a cypher for the absolute beauty that lies beyond him. The optics of extramission jibe with this reading: vision is the projection of the lover onto the beloved so that what he sees when he looks at him is, quite literally, himself: the *korê* in the other's eye is not a reflection of him but is literally him. Xenophon's intromissive model, by contrast, locates agency on the side of the *erômenos*. It is he, the beautiful object, who reaches out optically to the viewer and grabs him, kisses, bites him. His beauty, like Theodote's, captures and entraps. Its touch also transforms: like the tiny spider's bite, it can drive the viewer mad or, if he is prudent, drive him into flight or exile. The best the lover can do in the face of his

## Victoria Wohl

power is to practise *enkrateia*, as Socrates does. But Socrates' resistance is exceptional and the kiss of the spider boy suggests the passivity, optical and erotic, of the lover and his vulnerability to the infectious sight of his beloved.

The erotic possibilities of this optical model are played out in Xenophon's *Symposium*. That text opens with the threat of the spider's bite: the spectacle of the beautiful boy Autolycus, whose pancratic victory is the occasion for the party. The vision is described in epiphanic terms: like a light appearing in the dark, the boy 'draws every eye to himself' and makes every viewer 'suffer something in his soul' (*epaskhe ti tên psukhên*, 1.9). As in the intromissive theory of optics, the vision acts upon the viewer and the object of the gaze has sovereignty over its subject: anyone who saw Autolycus would say that 'beauty is something royal' (*basilikon ti kallos einai*, 1.8). This object not only touches the viewer but transforms him in its own image: 'all those who are possessed by the gods seem worthy spectacles (*axiotheatoi*), but while those who are possessed by other gods become more grim to look at and more fearsome in their voices and vehement in their bearing, those who are possessed by chaste love are more affable in their expression and gentler in their voice and noble in their gestures' (1.10). The spectacle of the beautiful boy acts upon his lover and makes him a spectacle in turn: this is what happened to Autolycus' lover Callias, Xenophon later comments: his love made him *axiotheatos* to all those initiated into the mysteries of this god (1.10).[16]

In Athenian pederasty, the adult *erastês* educates his young *erômenos* and moulds him in his own image; this is also the pattern in Platonic pedagogy, where a good lover makes his *erômenos* over into a lover of the good. But here the influence is reversed: it is the *erômenos* who moulds his *erastês* and turns *him* into an *erômenos*, an object worth looking at and desiring. *Eros* here is not only transformative but transitive. Thus Callias loves Autolycus but Socrates loves Callias: singing the young man's praises, he describes himself as a 'co-lover (*sunerastês*) with the city of those who are good in nature and desire *aretê*' (8.41). Autolycus' beauty has indeed rendered his lover *axiotheatos*: a worthy spectacle for Socrates, for the city, and for the reader of this text, which stages the happy vision of philosophers in love.

Critoboulus, whom Socrates warned against the spider bite of the beautiful in *Memorabilia*, plays a key role in this text, too, but here he himself is doing the biting. The symposiasts go around the table each telling what he takes most pride in. Critoboulus prides himself on his beauty and describes the 'sovereign power' (as he says, *tên basileôs arkhên*, 4.11) of the beautiful. They improve their lovers by merely sitting there (4.13), 'breathing something into them' that makes them more noble and daring (4.15). Socrates himself has experienced this inspiration: when he rubbed bare arms with Critoboulus, he says, he thought he had been bitten by a wild beast and for five days he felt a stinging in his arm and his heart

## 3. The Eye of the Beloved

(4.28). Rather than running away himself (his advice to Critoboulus in *Memorabilia*) Socrates now jokingly begs Critoboulus to stay away from him and not touch him, at least not until his beard is fully grown (4.28).

As in the *Memorabilia*, the context here is apologetic – the handsome young Autolycus is the son of Lycus, one of Socrates' historical accusers – and Socrates once more displays his tremendous *enkrateia* and provides proof against the charge of corruption (4.24, 4.26).[17] Again here we see the autonomy and agency of the beloved and the sting or bite he inflicts on his lover. And again the bite of love is transformative and transitive. Critoboulus tells us that he knows the power of beauty not from his own effect on others (which Socrates himself has attested) but from the effect of his beloved on himself: if you all suffer the same thing looking at me as I do when looking at Cleinias, he says, then beauty really is a powerful force (4.11). He too has been set ablaze by a kiss (4.25), he confesses, and would gladly be blind to everything else if only he can gaze upon Cleinias (4.12).

> Socrates said, 'Won't you stop always going on about Cleinias?' And Critoboulus replied 'Do you think he is any less on my mind if I don't say his name? Don't you realise that I hold such a clear image (*eidôlon*) of him in my soul, that if I were a sculptor or painter I could draw his likeness no less from his *eidôlon* than from looking at him face to face?' Socrates responded, 'If you have such an accurate image, then why do you drive me crazy always bringing him where you will be able to see him?' 'Because the sight of him has the power to delight, Socrates, but the sight of the *eidôlon* does not provide pleasure but only instils longing (*pothos*).' (Xen. *Symp.* 4.21-22)

This passage encapsulates Xenophon's optics of *eros* and makes a vivid contrast to the optical *paradeigma* in Plato's *Alcibiades*. The passage builds on the intromissive theory of sight and pushes it to its logical extreme: the viewer takes an *eidôlon* of the object into himself and holds it in his soul. Compare this to the Platonic scene, in which the viewer projects an *eidôlon* of himself into the eye of the other. Plato's viewer-lover looks at the beloved and sees only himself; Xenophon's, by contrast, does not even need to look at the beloved since his image is always before his eyes, as it were. If, as Jean-Pierre Vernant argues (1991, 167-8), an *eidôlon* is a double, then in Xenophon's *Symposium* it is the beloved who reproduces himself in Beauty, not the lover as in Plato's *Symposium*.

But that spectral double does not replace the original object. In Platonic optics, the beautiful beloved is a cypher standing in for an absolute beauty that is distinct from him. He is in this sense himself always an *eidôlon*, a false image of a true beauty that exists elsewhere. For Xenophon, too, the *eidôlon* is insufficient, but instead of drawing the eye up to the abstract Form of the Beautiful, it draws the soul back toward the real, physical being of the beloved. *Pothos*, the longing that comes with lack or absence, leads from the visual image to the thing in itself: the beautiful beloved is his own Form. *Pothos* asserts the autonomy and alterity of the other: the other is a separate person, with a real existence outside of the viewer's mind's eye; he cannot be enfolded into the viewer's own self-projection nor disappear in the viewer's dominating gaze. This means that Xenophon's *eros* is always a relationship between two, not the solipsistic self-mirroring of a single self-absorbed viewer.

Back at Xenophon's *Symposium*, Critoboulus makes an explicit claim for the pedagogical value of his beauty: he compares its effect to that of Socrates' words (4.18) and argues that he is more persuasive merely by sitting there and being looked at than Socrates is by speaking. He even stages a beauty contest between them, in which he wins the prize, a kiss from a young dancing boy. This is all in jest and the tone is light, but the comparison between Critoboulus' looks and Socrates' words invites us to think about the philosophical implications of this erotic model. What would it mean to imagine the philosopher not as a lover (as Plato does) but as a beloved? To answer this question we can return to the *Memorabilia*. That text gives us a vision of the philosopher to fall in love with. It offers not so much the teachings of Socrates – neither dogma nor dialectic – but the life of Socrates: what he did, what he said, his piety and self-control and good-sense. Xenophon's Socrates does not present an intellectual method so much as an ethical model, a model to look at and to imitate.[18]

The text's mimetic design is illustrated by the career of Alcibiades, who (along with Critias) is Exhibit A in Xenophon's defence of Socrates. To those who accuse Socrates of making Alcibiades violent and lawless, Xenophon responds that Alcibiades was good while he was with Socrates, and only went bad after he stopped associating with him. Like Plato's Alcibiades, Xenophon's is enormously ambitious and uses Socrates as a means to fulfilling his ambitions. 'Would one say,' Xenophon asks, 'that Alcibiades and Critias desired the lifestyle of Socrates and his *sôphrosunê*, and for this reason reached for his company, or because they thought that if they associated with him they would become most skilled in speech and action?' (1.2.16). Xenophon poses these as alternatives: either they desire (*epithumêsante*) to be like Socrates or they merely want to learn his tricks: a passionate mimesis is set against the kind of training one might seek from a sophist. Alcibiades is clearly in it for the tricks, and his failure is represented as a failure of imitation: 'I believe,' Xenophon says, 'that if a god granted them [Alcibiades and Critias] the opportunity to live their entire life as they saw Socrates living or else to die, they would prefer to die' (1.2.16).[19]

Philosophical learning is thus for Xenophon a matter of mimesis. 'It seems to me astonishing that anyone could believe that Socrates corrupted the youth,' says Xenophon, 'since he was most in control of his desires and appetite of all men. How could he, being the sort of man he was, make others impious or lawless or greedy or akratic or soft?' (1.2.1-2). Socrates' own life is his lesson, a lesson one learns by associating with him and watching him. Mimesis seems to happen by a process of osmosis based on

## 3. The Eye of the Beloved

physical intimacy: you learn Socratic philosophy by being with Socrates; 'being with' leads to 'being like'. This is why Alcibiades and Critias were better while they were with Socrates but deteriorated after they left him: association with the good *is* the practice of virtue (*tên men tôn khrêstôn homilian askêsin ousan tês aretês*) and association with the bad is its dissolution (1.2.20). How, then, can Socrates be blamed for corrupting Alcibiades when he turned bad only after leaving his company, and how can he have made Alcibiades bad when there was no badness in his own nature (1.2.28)?

One becomes like Socrates by being with him and absorbing his goodness by association. Plato floats a similar theory on occasion: in the *Theages*, Aristides claims never to have learned anything from Socrates, but to have improved when he was with him – even if he was just in the same house, but even more when he was in the same room, and above all when he sat next to him and touched him (130d1-e4). In Plato's *Symposium*, however, Socrates rejects this idea: when Agathon calls him to come sit next to him so that by touching him he can gain the fruits of his wisdom, Socrates replies that it would be very nice if wisdom could flow from one person to another when you touched one another, like water flowing from a full vessel to an empty one (175d3-e2), but alas it does not work that way.

In Plato, one cannot gain wisdom from merely 'being with' the wise. In Xenophon, by contrast, such pedagogy by proximity does seem to be possible. 'Socrates never promised to be a teacher of *kalok'agathia* (the condition of being both beautiful and good). However, by being visibly (*phaneros*) *kalosk'agathos* himself, he made those who spent time with him hope to become the same by imitating him (*mimoumenous ekeinon*)' (*Mem.* 1.2.3). During his life Socrates was 'always visible' (*en tôi phanerôi*, 1.1.10) in the gymnasia or agora, available as a manifest model of philosophical *kalok'agathia*. Now that he is dead, mimesis must proceed via *anamnêsis* (remembrance). 'Nothing was more beneficial than being with Socrates and spending time with him anywhere and in any business; even remembering him when he is not present (*to ekeinou memnêsthai mê parontos*) affords no little benefit to those who were accustomed to be with him and to accept him' (4.1.1). Thus the whole *Memorabilia* becomes a sort of distance learning programme, a mnemotic mimesis of Socrates' presence in his absence.

Xenophon's own text is therefore a practical enactment of his optical theory. It offers Socrates as a beautiful object to look at and to emulate, even to love. Through a process of textual intromission, Socrates works on the viewer like the biting vision of a beautiful boy: the sight of him injects something into us, something that instead of making us mad inspires us to self-improvement. Philosophy, like *eros*, is intromissive, transformative, and transitive: love of wisdom and of the wise transforms lovers into love objects for other lovers. 'Because I am erotic,' says Socrates, 'when I desire men, in loving them, I am entirely and terribly eager to be loved in return by them, and in longing for them to be longed for in return and wanting to be with them to have them want to be with me' (2.6.28; cf. 3.11.18). The end of desire is to become desired. This is the process of mimesis: the lover imitates the beloved and himself thereby becomes worthy of love. This mimesis aims at identity but also preserves difference: what the viewer desires in the object is precisely what makes him different, and instead of remaking that other in his own likeness – as in the extramissive logic of the *Alcibiades* – he transforms himself in emulation of the other. We can then imagine philosophy as a process of intellectual intromission: the beautiful beloved literally presses himself upon the amorous student's eye and reshapes the student in his own image. Xenophon's *Memorabilia* is successful if the reader comes away with an *eidôlon* of Socrates in his soul so clear that, as Critoboulus said of his beloved, 'if I were a sculptor or painter I could draw his likeness no less from his *eidôlon* than from looking at him face to face' (*Symp.* 4.21). Philosophy is not, then, a matter of seeing, knowing, and reproducing the self, but of seeing, loving, and imitating the other.

There is an irony to all of this, though. Xenophon, I have suggested, preserves the autonomy or otherness of the beloved in a way that Plato does not. But while Xenophon sets up Socrates as an object of desire and emulation, he does so in part by stripping him of his otherness, what Plato refers to – and celebrates – as his *atopia* (unusualness) (*Symp.* 215a2, 221d2). Xenophon's Socrates is a good Athenian gentleman: he obeys the laws and worships the gods the city worships; he teaches his followers to run a profitable estate and respect their parents.[20] This is in sharp contrast to Plato's Socrates. A barefoot weirdo who stands outside by himself while the others are drinking, he is described in the *Symposium* as completely unique: like no one else (*mêdeni anthrôpôn homoion*, 221c4-5), he can be compared to no human being, dead or living. His *atopia* makes him an object not of mimesis – we couldn't really be like him even if we wanted to – but of *thauma*: to gaze upon Socrates (as Plato's texts allow us to do) is to marvel at his singularity.

The specific gaze that shows us this extraordinary vision is Alcibiades'. It is Alcibiades who in Plato's *Symposium* looks at Socrates and sees in the paunchy, snub-nosed philosopher an object of beauty and desire. This is to say that, despite the teaching of the dialogue bearing his name, Alcibiades looks on Socrates with a gaze more Xenophontic than Platonic. Indeed, Alcibiades describes himself in the *Symposium* as like a man suffering from a snakebite: he can describe his experience only to others who have also been bitten. 'I have been struck in my heart or soul or whatever it is called,' he says, 'bitten by the words of philosophy, which are more vicious than any snake' (218a2-5). The biting metaphor here is aural not visual and herpetological not arachnid, but the effect is the same: Socrates words have touched him, entered his bloodstream and possessed him, made him

## 3. The Eye of the Beloved

feel shame and an impulse to work on his soul (215d6-216c3). His only recourse against this powerful beloved is to do what Socrates had advised Critoboulus in the *Memorabilia*: turn tail and run away. When Alcibiades takes up the position of lover (217c7-8), his desirous gaze transforms Socrates into an *erômenos*: he tells of his failed attempt to seduce the always enkratic philosopher and concludes that the older man pretends to be an *erastês* but is actually the *erômenos* (222b3-4). The power that Xenophon ascribes to the beloved – the power to inspire and infect and transform his lover – had no place in Diotima's model of *eros*; instead, it is discovered through Alcibiades' love for Socrates.

Alcibiades famously compares Socrates to a hollow statuette of Silenus with an *agalma*, an image of the god, inside (*Symp.* 221d7-222a6). He looks like an ugly Silenus, but the point of the comparison is rather the magical power of his words. In Xenophon's *Symposium*, too, Socrates is compared to a Silenus (5.7). There, as we might expect, the comparison makes a point about the utility of beauty: Socrates claims that his splayed nostrils and bulging eyes are actually more beautiful because they are more useful for smelling and seeing (as, he adds, are his thick lips for kissing, 5.7). In Plato, again as we would expect, the comparison plays into the distinction between physical and spiritual beauty, the denigration of the corporeal and the superiority of Ouranian over Pandemic *eros*. But when Alcibiades looks at his beloved Socrates, his eye is drawn not upward to the Form of the Beautiful but inward to the little *agalma* within Socrates.

This brings us back to the optical paradigm of the *Alcibiades*. There the lover looks into the soul of his beloved and sees a sacred statue, a *korê*, but the god it represents, as we have seen, is just himself. Alcibiades in the *Symposium* fails to enact the narcissistic self-regard Socrates recommends in the *Alcibiades*; instead, when he looks at the other he sees a divine image not of himself, not of the Forms, but of Socrates, in all his particularity.[21] Later he describes opening up the hollow Silenus to find inside the marvellous treasure of Socrates' *sôphrosunê* (216d6-7) and the wisdom of his words (222a1-6), an inner *agalma* (*ta entos agalmata*) that is in itself – and not in anything it might reflect – 'divine and golden and perfectly beautiful and wonderful' (*theia kai khrusa einai kai pankala kai thaumasta*, 216e6-217a1). If in the end Alcibiades never fully takes that divine *agalma* into his own heart (as Critoboulus does the image of his beloved Cleinias), neither does he superimpose his own image over it: the little image he sees in Socrates is not merely his own double (*eidôlon*) but the *agalma* of an other who is wondrous precisely because he is other.[22] And if we readers of Plato's *Symposium* retain an *eidôlon* of Socrates in our souls, it is because we catch an eye disease (as Plato says in the *Phaedrus*, 255d5) from Alcibiades and see through his eyes the infectious image that has struck him with its strangeness.[23]

Perhaps, then, Alcibiades plays such a central role in Plato's *Symposium* – and in Platonic philosophy in general – not because he follows the

## Victoria Wohl

optical paradigm of the *Alcibiades* but precisely because he rejects it. By refusing to turn Socrates into a mirror for his own self-regard (an ironic refusal for a man famed for his narcissism) he allows us to see Socrates as a unique and desirable object. Alcibiades thus brings to Plato's *Symposium* the visual logic of Xenophon's erotic schema, in which the vision of the beautiful beloved is infectious and transformative precisely because it cannot be assimilated to or replaced by an *eidôlon* of the self. Xenophon, ironically, fails to preserve that powerful alterity in regard to the one object that matters most, Socrates; that Plato succeeds is thanks in part to the loving eye of the beautiful *erômenos*, Alcibiades.

## Notes

1. I defer to others in this volume on the question of the dialogue's authenticity. If the dialogue was not written by Plato himself, it was regarded already in antiquity as a quintessential distillation of his views. See Pradeau 1999, 22-9. My paper makes no claim to be an exhaustive study of *eros* and *opsis* in Plato, which would surely need to examine the *Timaeus*, *Theaetetus*, *Phaedo* and (in more depth than I can here) *Phaedrus*.

2. On self-knowledge in the dialogue, see Annas 1985; Goldin 1993; Pradeau 1999, 47-53, 70-81.

3. Denyer 2001, 229 ad 132c9-133c17, with other examples of the trope.

4. On mirrors in ancient thought, see McCarty 1989; Frontisi-Ducroux and Vernant 1997, 112-75; Bartsch 2006, 15-56 (esp. 41-56 on this passage).

5. *MM* 1213a15-27, quoted by Denyer 2001, 233-4 ad 133b7-8. Cf. Pradeau 1999, 76.

6. Vernant 1991, 151-92 traces the development of images in Greek thought from re-presentations of the gods to illusory representations; see further Steiner 2001, 4-78. The precise referents of the optical diction in this passage (*opsis*, *korê*) are disputed: see especially Brunschwig 1973.

7. Nightingale 2004, esp. 94-138; and cf. 35: 'the gaze of the *theôros* is characterised by alterity'. This *theôria*, as Nightingale shows, is also erotic: philosophers are 'lovers of the sight of truth' (*tês alêtheias philotheamonas*, *Rep*.475e4) and gazing upon the Forms stokes their passion (116).

8. Contrast Halperin 1986 who reads the passage as 'the clearest exemplification' (69) of the reciprocity and equality of Platonic *eros*. That equality is achieved, however, by the elimination of difference between lover and beloved, as both become lovers, each using the other as a means toward philosophical development: thus 'one's lover becomes in all literalness another self, an alter ego' (70). Pradeau's reading of the passage seems to me to offer the most compelling case for its reciprocity: he proposes that what one looks at in the eye of the other is precisely the capacity (both one's own and the other's) for self-improvement via reflection: 1999, 72-80.

9. Vlastos 1973, 32. Cf. Nussbaum 1986, 165-99. A strong argument against the Vlastos-Nussbaum position is mounted by Sheffield 2006, ch. 5, who argues that Socrates' account of *eros* is not incompatible with love for individual others, even if that is not its ultimate end; see also Halperin 1985, 182-7; Halperin 1986; Price 1989, 45-54, 97-102; Gill 1990. My thinking on this question has been informed by Kaja Silverman's (Lacanian-inspired) notion of the erotic gaze as an 'active gift of love' that idealises the other while preserving his or her otherness (1996, 39-81).

## 3. The Eye of the Beloved

10. Perhaps in this model of *eros* Plato is building on the logic of Athenian pederasty, which generally emphasised sameness over difference: it is both homosexual and, within Socrates' close circle of companions, homosocial, and one of its goals as a cultural practice is to make the young beloved more like his older lover. Likewise, the distribution of active and passive roles – *erastês* as viewer and *erômenos* as visual object – may adopt the logic of pederasty. Contrast Halperin 1986 who proposes that in stressing the *anterôs* of the beloved (in the *Phaedrus*, in particular), Plato radically reverses the pederastic norm.

11. Halperin 1986; Nussbaum 1986, 213-23; Ferrari 1987, 167-75, 182-4; Price 1989, 84-102, 215-22; Nightingale 2004, 160-6.

12. Griswold 1986, 119, 126-29; Ferrari 1987, 161-2; Steiner 2001, 203-4. Griswold 1986, 128: 'When all is said and done, what the lover really wants is himself as he would like to be: himself fulfilled, whole, perfected, godlike.' As he notes, though, this self-love is not necessarily selfish: it can entail a desire to improve the beloved.

13. Compare Socrates' discussion with the artisans at *Mem.* 3.10: his dialogue with the painter shows that the character of the soul is imitable (1-5); that with the sculptor that experiences of the soul can be represented in corporeal form (7-9); and the discussion with the armourer that the most beautiful breastplate is the best fitting (10-15). The spiritual is rendered both visible and useful. On this episode see Goldhill 1998, 112. This pragmatic orientation is in keeping with Gray's (1998, 105-22) understanding of the *Memorabilia* as an innovative elaboration on *khreiai*, the pithy sayings of wise men.

14. On the central role of *enkrateia* in Xenophon's Socratic philosophy, see Dorion 2003a; Morrison 2008, 18-27. Pangle 1994 stresses the defensive nature of Xenophon's portrait of Socrates in the *Memorabilia*; cf. Morrison 1994 and the helpful discussion of Dorion 2003b, lxv-lxx.

15. For a convenient synopsis of these two optical theories and further references, see Bartsch 2006, 59-67. In his wider corpus, Plato combines intromissive and extramissive optical models, sometimes within a single passage: Frontisi-Ducroux and Vernant 1997, 139-40; Nightingale 2004, 10-11. The optical metaphor in *Phaedrus*, for example, seems to operate within an intramissive logic, as *himeros* (there derived from *rheô*, 251c5-d1) flows from the beloved through the eyes of the lover and into his soul (251b1-7). But inasmuch as the source of this flood, the boy's beauty, is an effect of the lover's worship of his particular god, in whose memory he chose this beloved and in whose likeness he moulds him (252d5-53c2), that intramissive dynamic presupposes a prior extramissive movement: the beloved injects into the lover a beauty that the lover had projected onto him. Later variations on these optical models are well studied by Goldhill 2001; Bartsch 2006.

16. In this regard, Xenophon's theory of optics perhaps resembles Aristotle's, on which see Johansen 1998, 37: 'In perception the sense-object acts on the sense-faculty so as to make the sense-faculty actually like it.' I discuss the philosophical significance of this symposium's erotic spectacles in Wohl 2004.

17. Huss 1999, 399-406; Danzig 2005.

18. For Xenophon's 'art of imitation' and one example of Socrates' mimetic pedagogy in *Memorabilia*, see Rossetti 2008.

19. O'Connor 1994, 158. Compare *Alc.* 105a3-6: 'if a god should ask, "Alcibiades, would you rather live with what you have or die if you cannot possess more?" Alcibiades would choose to die.' The point there, however, is not to encourage mimesis of Socrates but to change Alcibiades' definition of happiness.

20. Xenophon's Socrates' conventionality is fitting if, as Gray 1998, 159-92 proposes, the *Memorabilia* builds upon and 'Socratises' traditional wisdom literature. On the conventional religiosity of Xenophon's Socrates see Calvo-Martínez 2008.

21. Nussbaum 1986, 187-91 stresses the uniqueness of Alcibiades' love for Socrates. See further Sheffield 2006, ch. 6, and on Socrates' appeal, O'Connor 1994. For contrasting views of Socrates as *erômenos*, see Brekman 1982, 431-43, 454-6; Halperin 1986, 68-72.

22. At *Phdr.* 251a6-252d7 the beloved is likewise an *agalma*, an image of divine beauty, but it is clear that this image is one of the lover's own manufacture (*hoion agalma tektainetai*, 242d7): Griswold 1986, 127; Ferrari 1987, 171-2; Reeve 2006.

23. See Halperin 1992 on the *eros* aroused by Plato's texts; cf. Halperin 1986, 78-9.

4

# Plato's Oblique Response to Issues of Socrates' Influence on Alcibiades: An Examination of the *Protagoras* and the *Gorgias*[1]

*Reuben Ramsey*

Plutarch (*Alcibiades* 1.2) opines that Alcibiades' fame owes a great deal to his friendship with Socrates. While it is certainly true that the greater part of the early literary representations of him appear in the Socratic writers, it is just as likely that Alcibiades is, after all, famous for being Alcibiades. The survey of responses to his career and relationship with Socrates makes it clear that it was not because of his friendship with Socrates that the Socratics preserved Alcibiades' memory but because of the necessity of explaining away his later career. Alcibiades was a known associate of Socrates and a skilled exponent of the sort of Sophistic techniques with which Socrates, rightly or wrongly, was associated. He was also, because of his personal attributes and his impact on the recent history of Athens, an outstanding and controversial figure in his own right, even decades after his death. The Socratics, especially Plato, may have preferred Alcibiades to disappear from the tradition but Alcibiades' reputation was such that this was impossible. Alcibiades was a central element in the accusations that Socrates was a corrupting influence on the young men he associated with.[2] He was therefore also a central element in any attempted defence of Socrates.

The writings of the earliest Socratics exist only in fragments, in titles, or not at all. Of the early Socratic authors, Antisthenes, Phaedo, Euclides, Aeschines, Plato and Xenophon all either wrote Socratic dialogues entitled *Alcibiades* or made significant reference to him in their works.[3] With the exception of Aeschines, Xenophon and Plato, their surviving writings are too fragmentary to shed much light on the treatment of Alcibiades in the early Socratic tradition. These three authors respond to the Alcibiades issue in different ways. Both Aeschines and Xenophon treat him as a specific case the Socratics had to answer.

In defending Socrates, Xenophon acknowledges that Alcibiades, along with his older contemporary Critias, was a significant factor in the origin of the charge that Socrates corrupted the young. In the *Memorabilia* he confronts these issues directly and rationally. He focuses his defence on Socrates' demonstrated goodness of character and habits and contrasts these with the ambitious nature of both Alcibiades and Critias. The two are linked in Xenophon's defence of Socrates in the *Memorabilia* to the extent that Xenophon refers to them using dual forms wherever possible.[4]

Aeschines' response to the same issues is not so much a defence of Socrates' involvement with Alcibiades as an attempt to explain Socrates' failure to influence Alcibiades for the better, characterising it as a failure of desire.[5] Aeschines, unlike Plato or Xenophon, does not seek to absolve Socrates of all blame for Alcibiades' later career. He imputes to Socrates a kind of arrogance in supposing that he had been given some sort of divine dispensation to help Alcibiades.

## Alcibiades in Plato

Plato, on the other hand, uses Alcibiades symbolically, as representative of the qualities and character of a class of younger men with whom Socrates had important dealings. In the dialogues securely attributed to him, Plato does not, outside the *Symposium*, directly confront the issues surrounding Alcibiades and their negative reflection on Socrates.[6] Elsewhere, in two important dialogues, the *Protagoras* and the *Gorgias*, Plato uses an oblique strategy, which aims to dissociate Socrates from the Sophists and other potentially negative influences, to characterise Alcibiades as corrupt by nature and therefore immune to Socrates' positive influence and to portray him as representative of a type, i.e. as representative of aspects of character which are to be regarded as being held in common with an important cross-section of his generation.

## Importance of the frame in Plato

It is worthwhile at this point to make a few comments regarding the use of dramatic 'frames', including short introductory scenes, in Plato's dialogues (cf. Thesleff 1982). Frames in Plato are used toward a number of important functions which have a bearing on the reading of the dialogue as a whole. They set the dramatic context of time and place; they also enhance the dramatic impact of dialogue form. In addition, the frames have a deeper, thematic application. Gagarin (1977) gives a detailed account of the significance of the frame of the *Symposium* in which he describes how the portrayal of the (uncharacteristically) washed, combed and besandalled Socrates typifies the object of *desire* and the great importance of this depiction of Socrates to the dialogue as a whole. The first frame of the *Protagoras* is designed to bring Alcibiades to our attention in the context of the dialogue. In the following discussion it will be argued that this connection highlights the relationship between Socrates and Alcibiades precisely because it is one of the important background issues

*4. Plato's Oblique Response to Issues of Socrates' Influence on Alcibiades*

of the dialogue. Similarly, the second frame, featuring Socrates and Hippocrates, serves to distance Socrates from the practising Sophists. Both elements are important to Plato's vindication of Socrates for his relationship with Alcibiades. The frame to the *Gorgias*, though less clearly delineated,[7] is likewise significant in this regard. It is only a very slight frame, showing Socrates, in company with Chaerephon, meeting Callicles at the entrance of Callicles' home, where the celebrated Gorgias has just completed a display of his talents and has opened the floor to all questions (447a, c). The very first words, spoken by Callicles, set the tone for the rest of the dialogue: 'This is the way they say one ought to take part in war and battle, Socrates.' Indeed, the *Gorgias* consists of a succession of three verbal battles, with Socrates fighting for the precedence of the good over the merely advantageous. In the light of the remarks made by Callicles (486a-b), foreshadowing Socrates' death years later, it may be said that Socrates' life and philosophic mission are at stake.

## The *Protagoras*

Plato's *Protagoras* contains what can be regarded as an effective vindication of Socrates, his methods and his influence on others. In framing this apology, Plato does not directly confront accusations deriving from the career of Alcibiades but seeks rather to distance Socrates from the Sophists, and from Alcibiades, and to portray Socrates' influence as positive, with the blame for Alcibiades' later career deflected onto other intellectuals. In the *Protagoras* there are eleven separate references to Alcibiades who is, after all, only a subsidiary figure.[8] There are also certain clear links between remarks made by Socrates and the reported deeds of Alcibiades as a political figure.

### *Analysis of the* Protagoras *frames*

The very first address of the *Protagoras* is significant in relation to Alcibiades' importance to the dialogue (309a1-2). It has Socrates hunting, not Alcibiades himself, but his 'ripeness'. Denyer (2008, 65) says the periphrastic reference to Alcibiades 'elevates him and his beauty to epic grandeur'. The oblique nature of the reference suggests further that it is not Alcibiades *per se* who has aroused Socrates' interest, but certain desirable qualities that he may or may not possess.[9] Alcibiades continues to be the subject of conversation (309b3): 'Were you really with him? And how was he disposed toward you?' The secondary question may imply that Alcibiades' affections have been somewhat hot and cold, or that Socrates' pursuit of him is still in its early stages. There are already, in the reference to Alcibiades' on-coming manhood (309a3-5) and the fickleness of his affections, several subtle suggestions of a distance between them. These are developed when, after asserting that Alcibiades seemed quite well disposed toward him, that day not the least, and had in fact spoken repeatedly in Socrates' favour (309b5-6),[10] Socrates widens the suggestion of distance between them with a statement that is very out of character for a supposedly ardent lover:

'While he was there I paid him no attention and even forgot him altogether!'

There follows a longish, gossipy passage of question and answer, in which it is revealed that the more beautiful, because most wise, person who has displaced Alcibiades in Socrates' affections is none other than the wisest of them all, if you really believe the wisest to be ... Protagoras (309c1-309d1). This ironic barb is almost characteristic of the one-line sting of stage comedy and the entire passage, with its chatty, slightly salacious tone, has something of the fast-paced bantering nature of comic dialogue.

At the end of the first frame we have both Alcibiades and Protagoras flagged for our attention, the former for whom Socrates' avid interest is called into question, the latter for whom he expresses ironical admiration. Neither of them seems to come off particularly well.

The conversation turns quite naturally to how Socrates and Protagoras came to meet, which introduces the second frame, featuring Socrates and his young acquaintance, Hippocrates (310a). Hippocrates has visited Socrates in the early hours, all afire to meet Protagoras, who alone is wise (310d6), and to pay him all his fortune and those of his friends as well (310e2) in order to attain to his wisdom. In painting Socrates' reaction to this, Plato takes the opportunity to distance him from Sophists as a class. At 313c5f., Socrates is made to describe Sophists as 'a kind of merchant or peddler of provisions on which the soul is nourished,' if indeed their wares are actually nourishing and not poisonous (313c4-e1). He embarrasses Hippocrates by manoeuvring him into an admission that he might become a Sophist (312a1-7), and persuades him what a dangerous thing it is to give over care of one's soul to a teacher about whom one knows nothing (313a1-c3). Eventually (314b6-7), it is decided that the two will go together to Callias' house to investigate matters further.

The twin frames dissociate Socrates from Alcibiades, from Protagoras (though with some grudging admiration) and from the Sophists as a class. The central dialogue, the first thesis of which is 'can virtue be taught?', develops the ideas laid down in the frames. In the course of the discussions, Plato continues to focus on Socrates' essential difference from the Sophists and characterises Alcibiades, from Socrates' point of view at least, as a suspect character.

## *The main dialogue of the* Protagoras

Socrates and Hippocrates arrive at the home of Callias and, once it is determined that they are not additional Sophists, they are admitted

## 4. Plato's Oblique Response to Issues of Socrates' Influence on Alcibiades

(314c-e2). Present are three of the leading Sophists of the time (Hippias, Prodicus and Protagoras) and a cross-section of wealthy and influential Athenians, along with assorted foreigners. Alcibiades arrives in company with Critias shortly thereafter (316a4). It is, dramatically speaking, quite natural that his arrival should be pointed out, not as one might suppose because of his relationship with Socrates, but simply because he was mentioned at the beginning of the dialogue in connection with the events being narrated.

After an initial skirmish (316b1-317c5), Socrates' cross-examination of Protagoras begins after all present have been called together (318a1). Alcibiades is mentioned in passing (317d10-e2) as having, along with Callias, gotten Prodicus, the expert in the use of words, up from his couch.

At 318e5-319a2, Protagoras gives, at his second attempt, his famous definition of the aim of Sophistic teaching: sound deliberation concerning domestic affairs and those of the city, and how to be most effective in deed and word.

Socrates asks whether Protagoras is claiming to be able to make men good citizens and whether he is talking about the art of politics, to which Protagoras readily assents (319a3-7). Socrates then questions whether he really has developed a method of teaching these things (319a8-9). Protagoras does not get an opportunity to detail his method because the question is lost in the ensuing discussion about whether virtue can be taught at all. Both Protagoras' claims, to have developed a specific teaching and to be able to make men better citizens, are in sharp contrast with what is known about Socrates from the traditions about him, especially those derived from Plato.

At 320a2-320b1 Alcibiades' disreputable character is baldly attested in a surprising way when Socrates suddenly adduces him as evidence for this thesis that virtue cannot be taught. Socrates singles Alcibiades out in a way that draws attention to his particular presence (320a3), informing Protagoras and the assembly (in front of Alcibiades himself) that Pericles was afraid that Alcibiades would corrupt his own younger brother, Cleinias.

In these passages the careful dissociation of Socrates from both Protagoras and Alcibiades that was begun in the framing sequences is developed with the introduction of an important difference between Socrates and Protagoras and an explicit reference to Alcibiades as being of questionable character who, far from being a victim of corrupting influences, is himself a corrupting influence on others. The distinctions drawn between Socrates and the Sophists, as represented by Protagoras, serve to distance Socrates from the perceived negative effects of a Sophistic education and attribute them to others, particularly Protagoras, but it is also interesting that Alcibiades keeps close company with the miscreant Critias. The isolation of Alcibiades builds a kind of dramatic anticipation. Anything that is said from now on by Socrates or Protagoras can legitimately be taken as having a bearing on the figure of Alcibiades. At the very least we may read further statements in the light of Alcibiades' acknowledged presence.

What follows are Protagoras' mythological parable, which is designed to show, not only that virtue can be taught, but that education is in fact necessary to its attainment (320c8-328d2), and Socrates' digression on a poem by Simonides (342a6-347a5).

These two passages are bracketed by references to Alcibiades. We have noted the way in which Socrates has been made to isolate him as a suspect character before Protagoras' long *mythos* begins. Shortly before Socrates' digression on Simonides, Alcibiades is made to address Callias quite brusquely in criticism of Protagoras and in favour of Socrates (336b7-d5), one of the occasions on which Alcibiades spoke in Socrates' favour mentioned in the first frame. Again, after Socrates' discussion of Simonides' poem, it is Alcibiades (and no other) who rudely cuts off a long-winded prepared speech by the pompous Hippias (347b3). A short while later he again presumes to criticise Protagoras himself (348b2-8).

In light of the way in which Alcibiades is portrayed in this dialogue, the implication of Protagoras' speech is that if Alcibiades has failed to attain to virtue it is the fault either of himself or of his mentors. All humans share a sense of justice and shame (322c7-d2), and 'he who cannot share in shame and justice must die as a sickness to the city' (322d4-5). Because all humans received a share in virtue everyone is potentially an adviser (322e2-323a3). Further, virtue is teachable (323c5-e3) and all children are taught virtue by their parents from an early age (325c5-6) while teachers, lawmakers, elders and poets continue the process (325c6-326c3). Protagoras professes to be a teacher of this virtue (328b1-2), Socrates does not. At 333d4-8 Plato introduces another important distinction between Protagoras and Socrates where he has Protagoras maintain, under pressure of Socrates' dialectic, that people can show good judgement in acting unjustly *if* the results are advantageous, a position that has clear relevance to Alcibiades' later career.

These distinctions made, it remains to be shown what kind of example Socrates would have set and what kind of things one may have learned from him. In a literary digression on a poem by Simonides (342a6-347a5), Socrates describes the actions of a 'good and noble man' when estranged from his close relations (345e6-346b5). This behaviour is contrasted with that of 'scoundrels' (346a3). This passage is a development in the construction of the thesis, derived from Simonides' poem, that becoming good is difficult but being (i.e. remaining) good is impossible (344e5-6) and that no one errs knowingly (345d9-e4), and is worth quoting in full:

(Simonides) believed a good and noble man often has to force himself (*hauton epanagkazein*) to become a friend to someone and to love and praise them, as often happens to a man alienated from his mother or father, or from his country or from something else of the kind. Scoundrels, on the other hand,

## 4. Plato's Oblique Response to Issues of Socrates' Influence on Alcibiades

when something of the same kind happens, see and blame and point out and condemn the wickedness of their parents or of their country as if they are pleased to do so, in order that, where they themselves have failed, others may not call them out or reproach them for their failings; so they blame them all the more and willingly add to unavoidable enmity. Good men, however, hide their hurt and force themselves to give praise (*epikruptesthai te kai epainein anagkazesthai*) and, should they be angered when treated unjustly by their parents or their country, they soothe themselves and reconcile themselves to it (*autous heautous paramytheisthai kai diallattesthai*), forcing themselves (*prosanagkazontas heautous*) to love and praise their own people. (*Protagoras* 345e5-346b5)

The repeated use of reflexive pronouns and the middle voice emphasises the importance of the self-control practised by noble men and their responsibility for their own behaviour. Their good behaviour comes from within, through the practice of self-restraint and self-guidance. Where Protagoras believes that virtue is teachable and that he can teach it, Socrates, through the medium of Simonides' poem, is made to emphasise the necessity of *self*-control. As Socrates considers the poem 'well and rightly composed' (339b6-8) it is likely he also approves of its contents and the passage becomes both representative of Socrates' own good character and a depiction of the good influence he would likely have on his associates.

We have seen Plato's efforts to dissociate Socrates from the Sophists and to bring the figure of Alcibiades into focus as a questionable character, but as yet we have no evidence that these constructions are directly, rather than merely symbolically, related to the career of Alcibiades, or that they are in any way an attempted vindication of Socrates' influence on him.

There is, however, a correspondence between Socrates' comments about the distinctive behaviour of the good and noble man (at 345e5-346b5, quoted above) and the speech to the Spartans attributed to Alcibiades by Thucydides in Book 6 (89-92), which would seem to indicate that Plato is in fact responding to the known details of Alcibiades' later career, when he was indeed 'alienated from his country'.

According to Socrates' interpretation of Simonides, the scoundrel accusingly points out his country's trouble so people won't blame them for their own failings (346a3-7). In Thucydides' version of Alcibiades' speech to the Spartans, the whole of 6.89 represents Alcibiades' defence of his career at Athens, his role in the internal politics of the city and in what we would nowadays refer to as 'foreign relations'. Alcibiades must respond to the slanders against him (6.89.1; 6.90.1) so the Spartans will not disregard him because of their suspicion (6.89.1). As he seeks to render himself attractive to the Spartans, Alcibiades criticises the Athenians on several points. At 6.89.5 he speaks of their tendency toward excess and accuses 'the mob' of being easily led toward base behaviour. At 6.89.6 he criticises democracy, the signal feature of the Athenian way of life: 'Since we who think a little knew democracy (sc. for what it is?), myself no less than anyone, in so much as I could heap abuse on it'.[11] Nothing more need be said of his reference to democracy as 'acknowledged folly' (6.89.6). Although most of the explicit charges made by Alcibiades are against his political enemies, ('others' who lead the mob toward 'wickedness', 6.89.5; those who drove him out, 6.92.2) the context of his assertions and the forum in which they are made have the character of a vicious and self-serving attack on his own people.

Next, scoundrels will 'blame (their people) all the more and willingly add to unavoidable injury' (346a7-b1). In Thucydides' account, Alcibiades goes on to describe the relentless ambition of the Athenians: it is their intention (according to his own view of the matter) to gain control over Sicily, Italy and Carthage; this going well, they will move against the Peloponnese with the intention of gaining control over the whole of Greece (6.90.2-3). This, in all probability, bears a close resemblance to Alcibiades' own grand scheme in which the conquest of Sicily, for which he had argued so forcefully (6.16-18), was a crucial first step.[12] By attributing his own plans to the Athenians as a foregone conclusion, Alcibiades is carefully and calculatedly playing on Spartan prejudices about the Athenians' meddling imperialism. In attempting to secure for himself a place among the Spartans, as one who is useful to them because he well knows the Athenians and their plans (6.91.1) he greatly harms the interests of his city. Alcibiades, already estranged from his city, goes on to add further to this pre-existing estrangement, or, as Plato's Socrates has it, 'willingly adds to unavoidable enmity' by recommending to the Spartans that they at once send help to the Syracusans and set about the fortification of Decelea (6.91.4 and 6.91.6).

Finally (346b1-5) the attitude of the good and noble man when he feels he has been unjustly treated by his parents or his city is described: the good man reconciles himself to it and forces himself to praise them. This is precisely the opposite of the position demonstrated by Alcibiades at 6.92, where Thucydides has him assert that those who are forced by their friends to become enemies are the most bellicose (6.92.3). Alcibiades, far from accepting the judgement of his city, does not consider himself a patriot when he is unjustly treated but only when secure in his citizen rights. Rather than submit to the injustice of being driven out, he, as a true patriot, will do everything in his power to get his city back (6.92.4). In this there is something of an acknowledgement of the harm he is doing to his homeland and he seeks to justify it with the same bald assumption (that his interests are identical with those of Athens) that underpins his speech to the Athenians at Thucydides 6.16-18.

We have then an important section of a speech wherein Socrates, following Simonides, whose views he approves, lays down the appropriate pattern of behaviour for a good and noble man in a speech which seemingly parallels, almost point-by-point, a single famous account of one of Alcibiades' speeches. Moreover, the episode to which Plato seems to be

## 4. Plato's Oblique Response to Issues of Socrates' Influence on Alcibiades

referring, Alcibiades' betrayal of Athens in favour of the Spartans and his own best interests, is an outstanding instance of the behaviour for which Alcibiades became notorious and which would have formed a key element in the charges that Socrates had a corrupting influence on the young men with whom he associated.

In the *Protagoras* Plato has distanced Socrates from the sophists, whose teachings may or may not be poisonous (Socrates famously has no teachings) and who claim, through Plato's representation of Protagoras, to be able to make men good citizens (Socrates makes no such claim). Alcibiades, on the other hand, has been carefully singled out in the dialogue and characterised as a potentially harmful influence. The description of the behaviour of the good and noble man is delivered in a context that features a prominent Alcibiades and contrasts vividly with the known details of Alcibiades' future career.

As noted above these two significant passages are bracketed by references to Alcibiades. Alcibiades' challenging remarks to Callias, Hippias and Protagoras are not appropriate to a young man addressing his elders and further emphasise the less desirable aspects of his character. We are presented with a series of almost comedic images portraying Alcibiades as a tyro disrespectfully tweaking the beards of his elders. His attitude to Socrates is, however, quite different. He almost seems to be courting him.[13]

These are clear indications that Plato's *Protagoras* contains a carefully constructed response to the issues surrounding Alcibiades' career and Socrates' presumed influence on him in which the treatment of Alcibiades is both symbolic and particular. The established link between Protagoras' thought and expediency, the implied and explicit attacks on Alcibiades' character and the depiction of Socrates as, potentially at least, a good moral influence who 'proves' that no one does wrong knowingly demonstrates that Alcibiades and others like him are the victims of imperfect knowledge. These considerations in conjunction with the facts that (a) Socrates apparently possesses a sound knowledge and believes it is not teachable, (b) Protagoras merely claims to have such knowledge and believes it is teachable, and (c) Alcibiades associates with teachers other than Socrates, together form a reasoned vindication of Socrates' philosophy and influence.

In attempting to show that Socrates' remarks have a bearing on the figure of Alcibiades and his future career as known to Plato and his readers, especially through the writings of Thucydides, it is significant that Alcibiades is not the only malefactor among the associates of Socrates. Among those present at Callias' house in the *Protagoras* are no less than six Athenians, including Alcibiades and Critias, who will later be implicated in the affair of the profanation of the mysteries.[14] As Socrates is present only incidentally (in order, as we are told in the second frame, to vet Protagoras as a suitable teacher of wisdom for Hippocrates), the implication is that these people, or rather, this *type* of person, is to be associated with the Sophists rather than with Socrates. The various statements made by Protagoras and Socrates may therefore be regarded as significant for these other persons also.

Critias in particular is linked with Alcibiades in this dialogue. We have already noted that these two are closely associated in Xenophon's defence of Socrates in the *Memorabilia*. In the *Protagoras* they enter Callias' house together not far behind Socrates himself, at 316a3-5, and their consecutive speeches (336b7-d5 and 336d6-e4) reinforce the connection. This close association with Critias contributes to the symbolic characterisation of Alcibiades as representative of a type. Critias, like Alcibiades, figured prominently among his peers, was implicated in the profanation of the mysteries and had a chequered political career; he would become a leading member of the infamous Thirty who governed Athens after her defeat in the Peloponnesian War.[15] Alcibiades, however, was a special case. His relationship with Socrates, whatever its nature, was famous in antiquity. He was a prominent figure in his generation, a significant proportion of whom, in their eagerness to achieve greatness, were a compelling force behind the successes of the Sophists and, arguably, the downfall of Athens. These factors, along with his outstanding personal characteristics, make him useful as a symbolic representative of those of his class and aspirations and therefore likely to be chosen as a key reference point for any attempted vindication of Socrates.

## The *Gorgias*

The linking of Alcibiades and Critias in the *Protagoras* develops the symbolic potential of both characters, while downplaying, to a certain extent, the significance of Alcibiades as an individual. This is the case even if one takes into account the apparent references to the growing literary tradition surrounding him. Something of a similar sort occurs also in the *Gorgias*, where Callicles, who is referentially associated with the background figure of Alcibiades, makes several statements that bear a close relation to positions adopted by Alcibiades in the other of his two important speeches in Thucydides, that to the Athenians in favour of the Sicilian expedition (6.16-18).[16]

In the *Gorgias*, Callicles is representative of the same political aspirations as are associated with both Alcibiades and Critias by Xenophon in the *Memorabilia*. Although he is, perhaps, not quite of a class with them in terms of wealth or social status, he is of sufficient standing to play host to Gorgias (447b7-8), and the ideas he expresses would not seem out of place coming from either Critias or Alcibiades. Callicles, who praises the one who can oppose his own will to law and custom, is characterised, like the Alcibiades and Critias of Xenophon's *Memorabilia*, as one who respects the value of learning only for its potential practical applications, focusing on the ability to confound audiences and persuade them to his own ends.[17]

## 4. Plato's Oblique Response to Issues of Socrates' Influence on Alcibiades

Whether or not Callicles is a historical person, it is helpful to regard him as representative of his generation and to use him, with caution, to gain insight into other individuals.[18] He is certainly one of the strongest of Socrates' interlocutors and although by the end of the dialogue he may be seen to have been refuted, he remains unconvinced.

In Socrates' first remarks after Callicles takes up the argument (481c5-482c3), Alcibiades is mentioned as one of Socrates' two lovers (481d3-4), the other being Philosophy, which is much less fickle than Alcibiades who is always 'saying different things at different times' (482a5-7). In this same passage Socrates accuses Callicles of demagoguery (481d5-e5): he is unable to contradict either of his own two lovers, Demos the son of Pyrilampes and the Athenian *dêmos*; he is continually 'shifting up and down' (481d7-e1) and 'saying what (they) want to hear' (481e3; 481e5-482a2). Though these accusations do not exactly describe the methods of Alcibiades, who was more inclined to have the *dêmos* change its mind to please him, his character as a successful manipulator of the fears and desires of the people would be familiar to anyone who had read Thucydides' account of his career. These characterisations are recalled to the reader by his close association with this passage. Callicles is subtly portrayed as having more in common with the changeable Alcibiades than with the constant temper of philosophy.[19]

These preliminaries lead up to Callicles' general statement of his philosophical position. There are similarities between his remarks and positions we may fairly attribute to Alcibiades, especially in the light of his portrait in Thucydides. After accusing Socrates of acting like a 'young hot head' (482c4) and of being himself a demagogue (482c5), he goes on to assert (482e5-6) that law and nature are for the most part in opposition to each other, a commonplace in Sophistic circles.[20] Although no such statements are categorically attributed to Alcibiades, these beliefs are strongly reminiscent of the position he expounds to the Athenians at Thucydides 6.16.4. After asserting that he himself deserves to rule and that his great deeds are a benefit to himself and the city (6.16.1-3), Alcibiades declares it to be no injustice (*oude ... adikon*) that a man who thinks highly of himself should not be equal with others (*mê ison einai*). The same sentiments are expressed at 483d2-6 where Callicles adduces evidence from nature that it is just for the better and more powerful man to take a greater share than the inferior and less powerful. That the weaker blame and attack such behaviour (483c1), as asserted by Callicles, is reflected in the fact that Alcibiades, in the opening remarks of his speech (6.16.1-6), is forced to justify himself and his actions to the Athenians. Callicles' complaint on this point (483c1-8), that the weak call the attempt to have more than another (*pleon echein* = *mê ison einai*) unjust (*adikon*) and shameful precisely because they are too weak to take more for themselves, would not seem out of place coming from Alcibiades after his exile.

Again, at 484a2-b1, Callicles seems to be speaking in a way that is reminiscent of Alcibiades in his speech to the Athenians in Thucydides. Where Callicles speaks of a man of sufficient spirit who will shake up and tear apart all institutions that are contrary to nature and become the master, Alcibiades matter-of-factly informs the proudly democratic Athenian assembly that he deserves to rule, adducing his strengths and achievements as evidence. The reference to lion cubs that precedes this passage (483e4-484a2) strongly recalls Aristophanes' famous remark about Alcibiades at *Frogs*, 1431-2 and serves to further emphasise the significance of this passage in relation to Alcibiades' career in particular.[21]

There are further passing references seemingly designed to draw our attention to Alcibiades, which increase the likelihood that this is Plato's intention. At 484c5-d2 Callicles criticises philosophy as a fine thing in moderation, if pursued at an appropriate time of life, but potentially a man's undoing even if he is (like Alcibiades) 'altogether favoured by nature' (484c8). He goes on to criticise 'men who speak falteringly (*psellizomenon*) and play childish games' (485a6-b2). *Psellizô* recalls Alcibiades' famous lisp, mocked by Aristophanes at *Wasps* 44-5, as well as his habit, later recorded by Plutarch (*Alcibiades* 10), of halting in his speech as if searching for the best word or argument for the circumstances. The playing of childish games recalls Alcibiades' reckless and lawless behaviour as described by Thucydides at 6.15, and by Plutarch centuries later with a wealth of anecdotal evidence. The reference to childish speech and manners is extended up to 485c2 in a passage that recalls Alcibiades' childish lisping more strongly than it does the awkwardness of a sheltered philosopher who finds himself speaking in a public forum.

Callicles, who is by now fairly well associated in the reader's mind with the background figure of Alcibiades, ends his speech, along with affirmations of goodwill, with a warning to Socrates. Plato has him prophetically foreshadow exactly the circumstances of Socrates' death at the hands of the Athenians (486a7-b4). This can hardly be expected to escape the notice of Plato's audience. The facts that (a) Alcibiades was doubtless in the minds of the jurors who sentenced Socrates for corrupting the youth and that (b) Alcibiades has been so carefully associated with this passage make it difficult not to interpret the battle between Callicles and Socrates as an attempted defence of Socrates, his methods and his influence. Where Callicles is portrayed as ambitious and unscrupulous, Socrates makes an impassioned defence of reasoned self-control as the foundation of a good life.

Socrates develops his thesis thus (506c5- 507d6): positing that the good and the pleasant are not the same and that the pleasant is done for the sake of the good and that goodness is found in good order (506c6-e2), Socrates goes on to show that the well-ordered soul is self-controlled and the self-controlled soul is good (506e4-507a2); also just; also pious; also brave; in short, completely good and blessed and happy besides (507b1-c5). Each of us must therefore flee from a lack of self-discipline if we are to truly attain to the good (507c8-d6). Concealed beneath this straight-

## 4. Plato's Oblique Response to Issues of Socrates' Influence on Alcibiades

forward piece of moral philosophy is a clear criticism of the careers of people like Alcibiades and, if we accept his contextual association with this dialogue as significant, of Alcibiades himself.[22] The larger part of the dialogue, which begins with an inquiry into the nature and value of persuasion, portrays Socrates' 'battle' with Callicles, where we see him defending this thesis, that to do what is unjust is more shameful than to suffer it and that the self-controlled man is the best and happiest. Each of the developments in his argument, the nature of persuasion (or 'flattery'), the value of a public as opposed to a private life, justice versus injustice and the necessity of self-control, bears directly on the career of Alcibiades.

The last reference to Alcibiades (519a8) is in a speech in which Socrates speaks of people who thoughtlessly gratify their desires and then, when their lack of self-control comes back to them, blame not those who had actually been the cause of the trouble but those with whom they were associating at the time, who may have advised them somewhat, meanwhile praising those who were really responsible (518c5-e1). Socrates accuses Callicles (518e1-519a4) of behaving in much the same way, in praising the politicians who, without self-control or a sense of justice, filled the city with 'harbours, dockyards, walls, tribute and other such nonsense' (519a1-4). But when the results of these excesses come home to the Athenians they will praise these men (Plato again cites Themistocles, Cimon and Pericles at 519a5-6) while blaming their present counsellors, 'You,' says Socrates, 'if you are not careful, and my friend Alcibiades ... (who are) not to blame for their woes but perhaps share in the blame' (519a7-b2). While Socrates' prediction does not describe Alcibiades' eventual treatment at the hands of the Athenians, his mention in this passage effectively characterises him as one of a class of unscrupulous demagogues, of whom Callicles is the chief representative in this dialogue.

These references draw our attention to Alcibiades in the context of one of Socrates' greatest battles, and a crucial one in terms of his relationships with the young men of Athens. If the debate between Callicles and Socrates is read in the context of Alcibiades and his later career, a reading that is encouraged by the text, then we have a picture of Socrates doing his very best to set a younger friend on what he sees as the right path. Socrates does not fail to convince because his influence is not good; it is much better and more noble than the impatient and ambitious Callicles has time for. He fails because the younger man in question simply refuses to be convinced. Though it is not Alcibiades but Callicles whom Socrates fails to convince, Callicles, like Alcibiades, represents an important cross-section of the young men of Athens whose ambition was fired by the heyday experiences of Athens at the peak of her power and inflamed by the rhetoric of orators.

If it could ever be proved conclusively that Callicles was a symbolic figment of Plato's literary art, the question would be closed and we would be free to draw our conclusions about Alcibiades as directed by the text. If, however, it were proved beyond doubt that the Callicles of the *Gorgias* was a historical individual, we are still free to regard him as somehow emblematic of type, and we are still invited by the text to juxtapose him in our understanding with Alcibiades and draw our conclusions accordingly. Even without the references to Alcibiades in the text we could assume his sympathy with the views expressed by Callicles, particularly in the light of the speeches attributed to him by Thucydides, and feel justified in making cautious use of Callicles to flesh out our understanding of Alcibiades in his milieu. With such clear indications as we have from the text, we can feel some confidence in concluding that this dialogue presents an image of the character and inclinations of the Alcibiades-type. If Plato did not intend for us to understand Alcibiades and his relationship with Socrates by means of this dialogue, he at least intended us to have him in mind as a signal example of the self-seeking individual, utterly lacking in self-control, against whose world view Socrates argues forcefully.

The image we are left with is that of a generation which has been spoiled by the excesses of empire and demagoguery (519a1-4). They are inconstant, being swayed by the moods of the *dêmos* and their own caprice (481d5-482a2). They are prepared to act unjustly for the sake of advantage (482c5-486d1) and interested in philosophy only for its practical, political applications (484c5-d2), for this is the consensus of Callicles and his 'comrades in wisdom' (487b6-d2); they are contemptuous of self-control (491e2). These characteristics make them arrogant and impatient and, consequently, unteachable (505d4-e3). As described above, each of these characterisations, excepting only the last, is accompanied by references to Alcibiades, either by name or by inference.

## Conclusion

The oblique approach to the issues surrounding Alcibiades and Socrates' relationship to him here described allows Plato to understate the importance of Alcibiades, to make the issues surrounding Socrates' alleged negative influence on the young more about the young in general than Alcibiades in particular: Alcibiades is altogether too potent a symbol of malfeasance and too strongly associated with Socrates to be dealt with directly. Plato, by making Alcibiades a subsidiary figure, is able in effect to criticise Alcibiades with reference to an important cross section of his generation and to criticise that generation with reference to Alcibiades.

While both works contain important philosophy, in both we see Plato writing not purely as a philosopher but also as a controversialist, albeit, perhaps, unwillingly.

Given Plato's treatment of Alcibiades and the issues surrounding him in these securely attributed dialogues, the variant approach preserved in the *Alcibiades* raises certain questions. We may fairly ask why Plato would suddenly acknowledge Socrates as an ardent lover of Alcibiades, as

## 4. *Plato's Oblique Response to Issues of Socrates' Influence on Alcibiades*

per tradition, where previously he had played down the erotic aspects of their relationship and subtly undermined them. One may also ask why Plato would choose to portray Socrates in an active teaching role while elsewhere this aspect of his relationship with Alcibiades has been skilfully depicted as one of influence rather than of education.

## Notes

1. This chapter is the product of some preliminary researches into the treatment of Alcibiades by the early Socratics, particularly Plato. I am indebted to my supervisor, Prof. Harold Tarrant, for his unstinting generosity, helpfulness and sound advice, and to the reasoned judgement of an anonymous reviewer. Line numbers for the *Protagoras* and the *Gorgias* are taken from the 1977 printing of the Oxford edition of Plato's *Works* (vol. 3). All translations are my own.

2. Cf. Xen. *Mem.* 1.2.12.

3. Kahn 1996, 5-20; Guthrie 1971, 308, remarks that Antisthenes made attacks against the demagogues, particularly Alcibiades.

4. Xen. *Mem.* 1.2.12-49.

5. The fragments of Aeschines are those in Giannantoni 1990.

6. In the *Symposium* Socrates is *not* attracted to Alcibiades, and Plato, through the mouth of 'Alcibiades' himself, fully exonerates Socrates from his failure to win Alcibiades over to a life of philosophy. See M. Gagarin, 'Socrates' "Hybris" and Alcibiades' Failure', *Phoenix* 31.1 (1977): 22-37.

7. There is a very brief 'frame' introduction, terminating at 447c9. Thesleff has long postulated a scene-change at this point, a change that has been obscured, according to him, by conversion from reported to dramatic form (Thesleff 1982, 86 = 2009, 234); see now Thesleff 2007 and Thesleff 2003.

8. The references are: first frame, 309a2, 309b2 (309b6 where he is referred to by patronymic only); Alcibiades enters with Critias, 316a4; associated with Prodicus, 317e1; his corrupting influence, 320a4 and 320a6; his defence of Socrates, 336b7; again associated with Critias, 336e1; insolent behaviour (toward Hippias), 347b3; and toward Protagoras (again in favour of Socrates), 348b2 and 348c2.

9. Cf. *Tht.* 150c, where Socrates must test promising people to see whether they are pregnant with a fertile truth or a mere phantom. The nature of the qualities that Socrates finds desirable is soon to be made clear.

10. On these occasions, however, Alcibiades has shown himself something of a boor (336b7 and 348b2, below).

11. This is a somewhat obscure statement and the sense of '*hosôi kai loidorêsaimi*' is not clear. At any rate, it is hardly a ringing endorsement of the institutions of his native city.

12. It is doubtful whether his views were shared by the Athenians in general, much less by the other Athenian generals, and it is doubtful whether they would or could have carried them out as envisioned by Alcibiades. Cf. Bloedow 1973, particularly his discussion of Alcibiades in Sparta. Cf. Plutarch (*Alcibiades* 17.2-3): 'He conceived the expedition to Sicily as a beginning for what he was planning, not, like the others, as an end in itself.'

13. See especially 336b7-d5 and 348b2-8. The suggestions are subtle but, I believe, unmistakable and agree with the depiction of Alcibiades as ardently in pursuit of Socrates in Plato's *Symposium* (217bff.). That Alcibiades' pursuit of

Socrates is motivated by a selfish desire to attain to his skills in debating (as stated by Xen. *Mem.* 2.1.15) is indicated in this dialogue by Critias' remark (336e1-2) that Alcibiades always wants to be on the winning side.

14. Alcibiades, Eryximachus, Phaedrus, Critias, Adeimantus (Scambonides) and Charmides. These are derived from a list compiled by Debra Nails 2002, 18. Nails notes (315) that four of the company present at Plato's *Symposium* would 'within months' be among those accused of sacrilegious crimes in 415 (Alcibiades, Eryximachus, Phaedrus and the 4th?) without noting those present in the *Protagoras*.

15. Plutarch tells us (*Alcibiades* 33) that it was Critias who engineered the return of Alcibiades from exile in 411.

16. Alcibiades is mentioned by name only three times in the *Gorgias*: 481d3; 482a6 (as '*ho Kleinieios*'); 519a8. He is, as discussed below, referenced obliquely at key points throughout the dialogue.

17. Cf. de Romilly 1992, especially 156f., and Guthrie 1971, 301, who attributes to Critias precisely the views articulated by Callicles.

18. Cooper 1977, 791, says of Callicles that he was '... apparently a real person though we hear nothing of him outside this dialogue'. Taylor (Oxford Classical Dictionary Online) says simply his 'historicity is disputed'. Nails 2002, 75-7 accepts his historicity.

19. The authorship of the *Alcibiades* notwithstanding, it may be relevant that in that dialogue Socrates fears above all that Alcibiades might come to be a '*dêmos*-lover' (*dêmerastês*, the only occurrence of this word in Plato) and thereby become corrupted (132a, cf. 135e).

20. While Alcibiades is always portrayed by Plato as being respectful of Socrates, he also has Callicles make professions of goodwill toward him even while criticising him (e.g. at 486a3-4).

21. *Frogs* was produced in 405 BC while Athens was debating over the recall of Alcibiades and the remark is made in that context. That one should tolerate the lion is Aeschylus' verdict. Euripides, who condemns Alcibiades (1427-9) because he was quick to help himself and slow to help Athens, is rejected by Dionysus as a suitable poetic saviour for Athens. The metaphor of Alcibiades as lion is preserved also in an anecdote related by Plutarch (*Alcibiades* 2) wherein Alcibiades, accused of biting like a girl in a wrestling match, counters with, 'No, like a lion.'

22. This passage is shortly followed by an extended attack on four of the leading politicians of Athens, and particularly Pericles, the guardian in whom Alcibiades takes such pride at *Alc.* 1.104b, who, according to the Socrates of the *Gorgias*, failed to make either the city or its individuals better (*Grg.* 515d-516a; cf. *Alc.* 1.118d-119a).

5

# Socratic Ignorance, or the Place of the *Alcibiades I* in Plato's Early Works

*Yuji Kurihara*

## Introduction

There is no doubt that the main theme of the *Alcibiades* consists in self-knowledge, as is taken for granted by Julia Annas (1985). In this dialogue, Socrates, in trying to persuade Alcibiades that he ought to know himself before seeking to advise the Athenians, discusses the nature of self-knowledge. For this reason, in the first half of the dialogue (109d-110d, 113b-e, esp. 116d-118c), Socrates stresses the importance of the so-called 'Socratic ignorance' that helps the possessor acquire her self-knowledge. Interestingly enough, this special type of ignorance is expressed in two ways:

(i) One *knows* that one does not know. (117c2-3, 3-4, 117d4-5, 117e9-118a1)
(ii) One *thinks* that one does not know. (106e1-2, 109e7, 110a1, 2, 110c9, 117b11-12, 117e1)

On the face of it, the difference between (i) and (ii) may not be significant for our understanding of the notion of Socratic ignorance; but once we begin to look into Plato's early works more carefully, we notice that he has Socrates use only (ii), but never (i), in emphasising the crucial role of Socratic ignorance. This textual fact, it seems to me, has been neglected by most Platonic scholars including Leonardo Tarán, who makes reference to 'Socrates' profession of ignorance, his often repeated assertion that he only *knows* that he does not know' (my emphasis).[1] Since Plato often stresses the distinction between knowledge and belief, most obviously in *Meno, Republic* V-VII, *Theaetetus*, and elsewhere, we must not disregard the fact that Socratic ignorance is expressed in these different ways in the *Alcibiades*. For, in this detail, we may find a subtle hint that this work is spurious. That is, we may be led to conclude that the author, who has been careless enough to ignore the philosophical implications of the distinction in question, cannot be Plato; for Plato is one of the most philosophically cautious writers.

To begin with, I consider the function and the meaning of Socratic ignorance in the early dialogues, arguing that Plato is aware of the above distinction. Then, turning to the *Alcibiades*, I discuss 116e-118c where we encounter the two different expressions of Socratic ignorance in relation to 'the most contemptible stupidity' (*hê eponeidistos amathia* 118a4-5), that is, thinking one knows what one does not know, referred to as 'double ignorance' below. By analysing this passage in detail, I shall try to show that the author misconceives the nature of Socratic ignorance. On this basis I shall suggest that the *Alcibiades* might be spurious.

## 1. Socratic ignorance in Plato's early works

### 1.1. Socratic ignorance in the Apology.

At *Apology* 20c-23c Socrates explains why he has been called 'wise'. In his view, he is wise because of 'human wisdom' (20d8). Specifically, what kind of wisdom is it? It is true belief that he *thinks* he does not know, as indeed he does not know; this true belief is contrasted with false belief possessed by the politicians, poets, and craftsmen who *think* they know what they do not know.

> **T1** (*Ap.* 21d3-6): Neither of us really knows what is fine and good (*kalon k'agathon*), but this man [the politician] *thinks* he knows something when he does not, whereas I, as I do not know, *do not think* I do either.[2]

The type of false belief the politician possesses can be called 'double ignorance' in the sense that it is ignorance of *single* ignorance of what is fine and good. On the other hand, Socrates possesses a different type of *belief* that can be called 'Socratic ignorance'. I want to make the following three observations on single, double, and Socratic ignorance in the *Apology*.

First, single ignorance is contrasted with knowledge of what is fine and good, which no one except the god is supposed to possess. As Brickhouse and Smith claim (1994, 30-8), this type of knowledge is wisdom that makes the possessor 'wise' (*sophos*). In this respect, wisdom (*sophia*) is distinct from other types of knowledge such as craft or art (*technê*). In the case of craft, even if craftsmen know about their specific subjects, we do not call them 'wise' but 'experts' or 'wise with respect to each subject'. So even experts cannot be 'wise' without qualification.

Secondly, double ignorance is concerned not directly with what is fine and good but with the possessor himself. For, as is stated at 21c7-8, Socrates tried to show the politician that he thought he was wise (*sophos*), but in fact was not, so that he turned out to be ignorant of what kind of person he was. Hence the distinction between Socratic and double ignorance lies in the fact that the former is characterised as *true belief* of what kind of person the possessor is, and the latter as *false belief*, self-ignorance. Thus, precisely, Socratic ignorance cannot be self-knowledge, according to Plato's constant distinction between knowledge and belief, but is a kind of

## 5. Socratic Ignorance, or the Place of the Alcibiades I in Plato's Early Works

self-awareness that makes the possessor believe truly what kind of person he is.[3]

Thirdly, inasmuch as double ignorance is characterised as self-ignorance, it keeps influencing almost all beliefs (and so actions) that the possessor has in his private and public (or political) life. For, whatever I do in my life must be regarded by me as something *good for me*. Even if I do something bad for me, it is taken and chosen as better than other things. In choosing an action, I must be thinking of 'myself' as some sort of person; otherwise, I could not decide what is best for 'me'. My self-image is logically prior to my decision to do something. Besides, in Plato's teleological scheme, something good for me is determined in relation to the ultimate good for me, that is, happiness. Double ignorance makes my happiness unnoticed by me, while Socratic ignorance influences my whole life by always directing my attention to what I am and what my happiness consists in. This is how our philosophical inquiry and life begins: starting from Socratic ignorance.

In this way, the *Apology* makes it clear what double and Socratic ignorance are and how each of them influences the possessor's whole life. These features can be seen in other early dialogues.[4]

### 1.2. Socratic and double ignorance in the aporetic dialogues

Let us here try to formulate how Socrates' interlocutors come to acquire Socratic ignorance in the 'aporetic' dialogues such as the *Charmides*, *Laches*, and *Euthyphro*.[5] This description, of course, a description that has become almost a group title, comes from the fact that all of them end in *aporia*, an impasse, with regard to inquiry into the definition of virtue. They share almost the same framework within which Socrates cross-examines his interlocutors' belief that they know what they do not know. The recurrent steps are as follows:

1. Socrates' interlocutor (= X) thinks of himself or is thought of as being, say, temperate.[6]
2. If X is temperate, X must know what temperance is.[7]
3. If X knows what temperance is, X can define it by stating what it is.[8]
4. But X cannot define temperance.[9]
5. Thus, X does not know what temperance is (from [3] & [4]).
6. Thus, X is not temperate (from [2] & [5]).
7. Thus, X comes to believe truly that X is not temperate or that X does not know what temperance is (from [1] & [6]).[10]

As regards Plato's view of Socratic and double ignorance, I here make two observations about this general framework. First, as is clear from (1) and (2), double ignorance primarily concerns the possessor's belief that he is a virtuous person. Even if it is said that he believes that he knows what he does not know, this belief is derived from his belief that he is virtuous. So double ignorance is characterised primarily as a false belief about what kind of person the possessor is, and, derivatively, as a false belief that he knows what he does not know.[11]

Secondly, Socrates' method of refutation or cross-examination, *elenchus*, leads the interlocutor to believe that he is not virtuous or that he does not know what he does not know. This is how the interlocutor comes to possess Socratic ignorance. This effect of Socratic *elenchus* has much to do with Socrates' tenet: 'Care for your soul' (cf. *Ap.* 29d-30c). As a result of the failure of their inquiry, the interlocutor, following Socrates, begins to care for his soul (cf. *La.* 199e14-201c5, *Charm.* 176a6-b4). Conversely, this indicates that double ignorance does not exist independently of another sort of mental condition called 'thoughtlessness' (*ameleia*) as contrasted with 'care' (*epimeleia*). In a Platonic context thoughtlessness is not merely the lack of caring for the soul, but has some positive content in the sense that the person is involved in activities concerning body, money, or honour, etc. (cf. *Ap.* 29d7-e3, 30a5-b6) and is disposed to direct himself to them. In the case of Socrates' interlocutors, thoughtlessness, as an activity and a disposition directed elsewhere, directs itself to honour.

### 1.3. Socratic and double ignorance in the Meno

In response to Meno, who doubts the possibility of inquiry (80d-e), Socrates offers his theory that learning, or inquiry, is nothing but recollection (*anamnêsis*), and aims to show that inquiry as such is possible for us (81a-82a). To illustrate his theory, Socrates appeals to a paradigmatic example: that a boy should solve a geometry problem that he has not been taught how to figure out (82a-86c). Socrates stresses that the boy himself solves the problem by recollecting the answer that was already latent inside his soul. I do not wish to discuss the illustration as a whole but focus on the following passage:

> T2 (*Men.* 84a3-b5): There now, Meno, do you notice what progress this boy has already made in his recollection? At first he *did not know* what is the line that forms the figure of eight feet, and he *does not know* even now: but at any rate he *thought he knew* then, and confidently answered *as if he knew*, and was aware of no difficulty; whereas now he feels the difficulty he is in, and besides not knowing *does not think he knows.* – That is true. – And is he not better off in respect of the matter which he did not know? – I think that too is so. (tr. W.R.M. Lamb)

In T2, Socrates distinguishes clearly between single and double ignorance. As regards single ignorance, he emphasises that the boy does not know the correct answer to the original question, so he remains the same as before. As for double ignorance, however, the boy is better off in that he is immune to it. How is it so?

*5. Socratic Ignorance, or the Place of the* Alcibiades I *in Plato's Early Works*

Single ignorance concerns a particular answer to a particular question. At first, the boy presented a false answer; in this sense, at that time he possessed single ignorance as false belief. Double ignorance, on the other hand, consists in the false belief that one knows the correct answer that one actually does not know. So the boy possessed double ignorance as well, and, more importantly, because of this he answered falsely without hesitation. Double ignorance is the false belief that actualises single ignorance.

Double ignorance can be explained differently. As is stated in T2, the boy thought he knew and confidently answered as if he knew (*hôs eidôs* 84a7), which expresses his double ignorance. Since the phrase '*hôs eidôs*' also means 'as if he were the one who knows', double ignorance is taken to be self-ignorance of what kind of person one thinks one is (cf. 84b11, c5). Despite the fact that the boy was not one who knows the answer, he thought of himself as such a person. Now, however, he comes to think that he is not one who knows the answer, so he possesses Socratic ignorance of himself.[12]

In T2, Plato thinks of the transition from double to Socratic ignorance as a great progress in recollection, despite the fact that the correct answer is not still available to the boy. Why is he better off with respect to the matter that he did not know? This can be answered by the need for a transition prior to recollection. Without this transition, the boy never begins to inquire into the true answer, and will remain ignorant of it. It is not until he comes to think about himself *truly,* because of his attainment of Socratic ignorance, that he 'yearns to know' the true answer (cf. 84c6). Hence the boy is making progress towards recollection in being ready for inquiry.[13]

### *1.4. Socratic ignorance in the* Charmides?

I have thus far tried to provide textual evidence that in the early works (including the *Meno*) Plato depicts Socratic ignorance exclusively as a condition in which one *thinks* truly that one doesn't know what one doesn't know. Plato has no need to state that one *knows* that one doesn't know what one doesn't know. There might be someone, however, who objects that the *Charmides* actually deals with *knowledge of* knowledge and *ignorance*, that is, the knowledge of what one knows and does not know.[14]

> T3 (*Charm.* 167a1-8): 'Then only the temperate man will know himself and will be able to examine what he knows and does not know, and in the same way he will be able to inspect other people to see when a man does in fact know what he knows and thinks he knows, and when again he does not know what he thinks he knows, and no one else will be able to do this. And being temperate and temperance and knowing oneself amount to this, to *knowing what one knows and does not know*. Or isn't this what you say?' – 'Of course', he (Critias) said.

*Prima facie*, T3 includes a mention of Socratic ignorance as 'knowing what one does not know'. Careful examination, however, will lead us to understand this first impression is wrong. First, even if Socrates refers to knowledge of ignorance in T3, his aim lies in restating Critias' conception of temperance rather than disclosing his own, as is clear from 'Or isn't this what you say?' (167a5-7). We must be extremely careful about attributing this notion to Plato as well as to Socrates. Secondly, just prior to this passage, Plato has Socrates confess his ignorance of temperance as knowing oneself (cf. *dia to mê autos eidenai* 165b8-c1) and his 'fear of unconsciously thinking I know something when I do not' (*phoboumenos mê pote lathô oiomenos men ti eidenai, eidôs de mê* 166d1-2). By this, obviously, Plato intends to make a clear contrast between Socrates, who possesses Socratic ignorance and attempts a further inquiry into temperance, and Critias, who thinks he knows what it is. If in fact Socrates is ignorant of temperance, he is not temperate, according to the general framework of the Socratic *elenchus*, as we saw above. Then, even if this definition of temperance were correct, it would not necessarily follow that he *knows* of himself what he does not know. Thirdly, we made it clear above that Socratic ignorance has to do with the self above all, but the discussion immediately following T3, 169c-171c, will show that the knowledge of knowledge and ignorance in question is concerned with other people's sciences or crafts only, but not with the possessor himself (and virtue) at all. Besides, it turns out that the temperate person with this knowledge cannot even know *what* other people know and do not know, but only *that* they know and do not know (cf. 170d1-10). This result also indicates that Plato is not concerned with Socratic ignorance in this passage.[15]

For these reasons, contrary to its apparent impression, I conclude that we cannot make use of the *Charmides* to argue that Plato characterises Socratic ignorance as *knowing* one does not know. In his early works, therefore, Plato seems aware of the distinction between believing and knowing one does not know, taking Socratic ignorance for true belief of the self.[16]

## 2. Socratic ignorance in the *Alcibiades I*

Let us now turn to the *Alcibiades*, in the first half of which we encounter the issue of Socratic ignorance. The passage I want to focus on is 116e-118c where Socrates aims to reveal that Alcibiades suffers from double ignorance as contrasted with Socratic ignorance. This passage begins with Alcibiades' confession of what he experiences now:

> **T4** (*Alc.* 116e1-4): By the gods, Socrates, I don't know what I'm saying myself, and I seem just like someone in a strange state. As you question me, at one time things seem one way, but at another time they seem different.

Up until this stage Socrates had been examining whether Alcibiades

*5. Socratic Ignorance, or the Place of the* Alcibiades I *in Plato's Early Works*

knows what is just (*ta dikaia*) and what is unjust (*ta adika*), before rising up to advise the Athenians, and is led to the conclusion that he does not know. As a result of the argument, as shown in T4, Alcibiades finds himself in a strange state (*to pathêma*, 111e5; cf. *pathos, peponthas*, 118b4, 8) in which he unwillingly gives opposite answers about the same things. Calling this strange state 'wandering' (*planâsthai*, 117a10, 11, b3, 7, c3, 7, d1, 4, 118a13; cf. 112d8),[17] Socrates goes on to clarify what gives rise to this state. Roughly speaking, his argument consists of three steps:

1. If S knows X, S is not confused about it. So, by contraposition, if S is confused about X, S does not know it (116e-117a4).
2. When S does not know X, if S *thinks/knows* S does not know it, S is not confused about it, but S hands it over to one who knows it (117a5-d6).
3. When S does not know X, if S *thinks* S knows it, S is confused about it and makes mistakes (117d7-118a6).

And finally Socrates applies (3) to Alcibiades' current state saying:

> **T5** (*Alc.* 118a15-b2): But if you are confused, isn't it clear from what came before that not only are you ignorant of the greatest things (*ta megista*) [sc. what's just and admirable (*kala*) and what's good (*agatha*) and what's advantageous], but not knowing them you think that you do know?

Obviously, this passage as a whole is a reminiscence of the passage from the *Apology* (20c-23c) quoted as T1 above. T5, for example, makes a contrast between single ignorance of 'what's admirable and good' (cf. *kalon k'agathon, Ap.* 21d4) and of 'the greatest things' (cf. *ta megista, Ap.* 22d7) and double ignorance that is characteristic of the politicians, poets, and craftsmen in the *Apology*. Furthermore, it seems plausible that the intensive study of 'wandering' in this passage was provoked by reflection on the meaning of Socrates' 'wanderings' (*tên emên planên, Ap.* 22a6-7) that he undertook in order to examine the meaning of the Delphic oracle.[18] So if the author intends to remind us of the *Apology*, we can evaluate whether he or she really understands the crucial distinction between single, double, and Socratic ignorance, together with the concept of wandering.

First of all, as was already pointed out in the Introduction, in talking about Socratic ignorance, the author is indifferent to the distinction between knowing and thinking. As to how to go up to the sky, for example, Socrates confirms that Alcibiades is not confused, because he does not *think* (*oiei*) that he understands this when he does not understand it (117b11-12). Soon after that, Socrates generalises this point, saying that when Alcibiades does not understand something, but *recognises* (*gignôskeis*) that he does not understand it, he is not confused about that sort of thing (117c2-3). And Socrates provides two examples of craft,

83

cookery and helmsmanship, which he discusses in terms of *knowing* (*oistha*, 117c4), and concludes:

> **T6** (*Alc.* 117d4-5): So you aren't confused about the things you don't know (*mê oistha*), so long as you *know* (*eidêis*) that you don't know (*ouk oistha*) them.[19]

As we saw in Section 1, Plato never adopts 'knowing' (*eidenai*) for Socratic ignorance, but always stresses the contrast between true and false *belief* of the self, so it must be doubted why the author keeps using 'knowing' here. To look into the transition from (2) to (3) above, for example, what we can get by contraposition of (2) is that: When S does not know X,

2′. If S is confused about X, S does not *think/know* S does not know it.

If the consequent of (2′) means that S thinks (falsely) S knows X, this accords with what Plato holds in the early works and what the author of this passage writes, then it can be concluded that:

4. S is confused about X if, and only if, S thinks falsely S knows it. (T5)

In the case of 'knowing', however, the consequent of (2′) is misleading. If its double negation is changed into simple affirmation in exactly the same way that we get (4) above, it is simply wrong to say that S knows S knows X. Accordingly, using 'knowing' instead of 'thinking', the author proves to be too careless about the philosophical and logical implications of this passage to be identified with Plato.

Aside from this formal problem, let us now try to elucidate what kind of knowledge the author has in mind. In using 'knowing' for Socratic ignorance, the author clearly thinks of some second-order knowledge that concerns not only first-order knowledge/ignorance of something, but also the *self* of the possessor reflexively. Is this then the same as the Socratic ignorance found in the *Apology*?

After his wanderings or persistent investigations (*exetasis*, cf. 22e7) among quasi-wise people, Plato's Socrates comes to accept that the oracle is irrefutable and that he is 'wise' by the standards of human wisdom (*hê anthrôpinê sophia* 23a6-7). This human wisdom must be identical to Socratic ignorance, judging from the fact that Socrates does not distinguish them in that context. So we are inclined to claim that Socratic ignorance can be depicted in terms of wisdom or knowledge. The author of *Alcibiades* 116e-118c too, I suspect, had thought so – without cautious examination of the nature of human wisdom. It should be noted, however, that Socrates' human wisdom is neither the divine wisdom (*sophia*), which only the god possesses, nor a craft or science (*technê*), which the experts use, but *phronêsis* (*to phronimôs echein*, 22a6) that enables one to continue

## 5. Socratic Ignorance, or the Place of the Alcibiades I in Plato's Early Works

further inquiry, due to one's true belief regarding the self. This type of practical wisdom constantly prompts us to desire to know the truth, which makes our whole life philosophical.[20] Only where philosophy is concerned, it seems, does Plato tend to relate true belief to knowledge.[21]

On the other hand, the Socrates of *Alcibiades* 116-18 regards Socratic ignorance as quite a different type of knowledge. He has Alcibiades admit that the one who *knows* that he does not know will not err precisely because he hands the matter over to the expert who knows it. Here Socratic ignorance is characterised as a type of knowledge of handing over (*paradidonai*, 117e2; *epitrepein*, 117c7, d2, e5) to the experts that enables the possessor to live without making mistakes.[22] This, however, is a negative type of knowledge, and does not assist the possessor to reconsider the good of her whole life, but rather keeps her thoughtless regarding her happiness. So this type of knowledge in the *Alcibiades* is something very different from Socrates' *phronêsis* that motivates and inspires the possessor to live a philosophical life.

In addition, holding that double ignorance is 'the cause of bad things' (118a4), Socrates here takes living without making mistakes to be a happy life void of bad things. This, I believe, cannot be identical with the philosophically happy life that the Socrates of the *Apology* has in mind in examining others. These passages are written in line with two completely different conceptions of human happiness.

This leads us to consider the philosophical meaning of 'wandering' in this passage. Socrates accounts for Alcibiades' state of wandering in terms of double ignorance, which is plainly the main aim here. In the *Apology*, by contrast, talking about his 'wanderings' (*tên emên planên*, 22a6-7), Socrates appeals to his Socratic ignorance in that he keeps examining quasi-wise people, thinking he does not know what is good and fine. For him, his wanderings are nothing but philosophical activities aimed at seeking for the truth. This is how Socratic ignorance as wandering must be positively located between double ignorance of the self and simple knowledge of the greatest things. If Plato's Socrates emphasises the positive aspect of wandering this way, then we must conclude that the author of our passage misunderstands the important role of wandering in philosophy.[23]

## Conclusion

I have tried to distinguish the *Alcibiades* from Plato's early works, focusing on textual evidence that indicates that its author does not make a distinction between thinking and knowing with respect to Socratic ignorance. To be sure, this evidence is slight, but it is the more important, I believe, because the form and the content of this dialogue are very similar to those of Plato's early works. The *Alcibiades*' focus, as often in the aporetic dialogues, is on the crucial role of 'caring for the self', but this is not derived from any attempt to inquire into the definition of virtue. Instead of the 'What is F-ness?' (*ti estin;*) question, Socrates asks whether Alcibiades knows what things are just (*ta dikaia*), what things are good (*ta agatha*), what things are admirable (*ta kala*), etc. in terms of the plurals.[24] This also gives rise to some difficulty in placing this dialogue among the early canonical (or at least aporetic) dialogues.[25]

Moreover, regardless of philological or historical reasons, the fact that the author overlooks the philosophical implications of Socratic ignorance and of wandering provides a sufficient reason to doubt of another possibility: that Plato wrote it at some time in the later period.[26] It is hard to imagine that Plato has discarded his views on Socratic ignorance by then.[27]

It is true that the issue of the authenticity of this work will remain undecided (perhaps forever!), but just as Socrates succeeds in making Alcibiades repeatedly wonder (*thaumazein*, 103a1, 104c4, d4), and wander, about how to live, so the *Alcibiades* keeps compelling us to reconsider the structure of the Platonic corpus as a whole, while reflecting upon our life at the same time. It is because this dialogue is as enigmatic to us as the Delphic oracle was to Socrates (*ainittetai*, *Ap*. 21b4); as a matter of fact, it is just such an enigma that prompts us to engage in philosophy.

## Notes

1. Tarán 1985, 85. Cf. Mackenzie 1988, 332: 'his knowing that he knows nothing'; 334: 'The *Apology* is about Socrates' knowledge of ignorance', etc.

2. In this paper I use translations from Cooper 1997 unless otherwise noted, except for the *Alcibiades I*, for which I rely on Johnson 2003.

3. Cf. Mackenzie 1988, 333-7. Fine 2008, 59-66, discusses the meaning of *sunoida emautôi* in the *Apology*, but pays little attention to the relation between Socratic ignorance and self-awareness.

4. It is often pointed out that even in the *Apology* Socrates lays claim to some knowledge or wisdom (21b4-5, d6-8, 22c9-d2, 23b1-4; cf. 29b6-7). See below, with Mackenzie 1988, 331; Fine 2008.

5. I do not include the *Lysis* in this group, in spite of its similar appearance. For, first, there is no question about '*philia*' as expressed by abstract noun in the *Lysis*, but '*philon*' is discussed, which would suggest that this dialogue was written with quite a different intention from the aporetic dialogues. Secondly, Plato does not seem to treat friendship as a virtue in his dialogues, which distinguishes the *Lysis* from the aporetic dialogues. Following Vlastos 1991, 46-7, I believe that the *Lysis* is one of the transitional dialogues of Plato's earlier period. I also believe that Plato wrote this dialogue to consider what makes virtue virtue.

6. Cf. *Charm*. 157d6-8: [Critias] said: 'Then you must know that not only does [Charmides] have the reputation of being the most temperate young man of the day, but that he is second to none in everything else appropriate to his age'; *La*. 193e2-3: 'In deeds I think anyone would say that we [sc. Laches and Socrates] partook of courage, ...'.

7. Cf. *Charm*. 158e7-159a3: 'Now it is clear that if temperance is present in you, you have some opinion about it. Because it is necessary, I suppose, that if it really

## 5. Socratic Ignorance, or the Place of the Alcibiades I in Plato's Early Works

resides in you, it provides a sense of its presence, by means of which you would form an opinion not only that you have it but of what sort it is.'

8. Cf. *Charm*. 159a6-7: 'Well, then, since you know how to speak Greek ...I suppose you could express this impression of yours in just the way it strikes you?'; *La*. 190c4-7: Soc.: We say then, Laches, that we know what [virtue] is. – La.: Yes, we do say so. – Soc.: And what we know, we must, I suppose, be able to state. – La.: Of course; *Euthphr*. 5c8-d7: So tell me now, by Zeus, what you just now mentioned you clearly knew: what kind of thing do you say that godliness and ungodliness are, both as regards murder and other things; ... Tell me then, what is piety, and what impiety, do you say?

9. Cf. *Charm*. 175c8-d2: But in spite of the fact that the inquiry has shown us to be both complacent and easy, it is not a whit more capable of discovering the truth; *La*. 194a6-b4: La.: I am ready not to give up, Socrates, although I am not really accustomed to arguments of this kind. But an absolute desire for victory has seized me with respect to our conversation, and I am really getting annoyed at being unable to express what I think in this fashion. I still think I know what courage is, but I can't understand how it has escaped me just now so that I can't pin it down in words and say what it is; *La*. 200e2-5: Soc.: If in the conversations we have just had I had seemed to be knowing and the other two had not, then it would be right to issue a special invitation to me to perform this task; but as the matter stands, we were all in the same difficulty; *Euthphr*. 15c8-12: Soc.: Either we were wrong when we agreed before, or if we were right then, we are wrong now. ... So we must investigate again from the beginning what piety is.

10. Cf. *Charm*. 176a6-b1: And Charmides said: 'But good heavens, Socrates, I don't know whether I have [temperance] or whether I don't – because how would I know the nature of a thing when neither you nor Critias is able to discover it, as you say?'; *La*. 200a4-8: Ni.: That's a fine attitude of yours, Laches, to think it no longer to be of any importance that you yourself were just now shown to be a person who knows nothing about courage. What interests you is whether I will turn out to be a person of the same kind. Apparently it will make no difference to you to be ignorant of those things which a man of any pretensions ought to know, so long as you include me in your ignorance. On the other hand, Euthyphro would not admit that he was ignorant of what piety is, but wanted to avoid talking with Socrates; *Euthphr*. 15e7-8: Some other time, Socrates, for I am in a hurry now, and it is time for me to go.

11. This accords with the fact that in the *Apology* Socrates examines those who are ignorant of what they are.

12. We can account for the distinction between single and double ignorance in terms of two types of false belief. For single ignorance is the false belief as a false answer to a particular question, whereas double ignorance is the false belief that one is the person who knows the answer to the question. So Socratic ignorance in this case is characterised as the true belief that one is the person who doesn't know the answer to the question.

13. Needless to say, the boy's recollection is merely *an illustrative example* to show that it is possible for us to inquire into more important matters such as virtue. So we must know that in this example double ignorance is not necessarily concerned with 'oneself' without qualification but 'oneself' in respect of a particular question and answer. However, Plato has in mind that this example can be used to explain the possibility of inquiry into virtue, in which case, as was seen in the *Apology* and other dialogues, double ignorance is regarded as self-ignorance without qualification. On the other hand, Socratic ignorance as an important stage of recollection leads us to self-realisation without qualification. By characterising

one making progress in inquiry as 'better off', Socrates must have in mind the close connection between philosophical inquiry and human happiness; cf. *Men.* 86b6-c2.

14. See, for example, Tuckey 1968, 39-40.

15. I take it that Plato urges the reader not to misunderstand the nature of Socratic ignorance, daring to discuss a similar but in fact completely different type of knowledge in the *Charmides*.

16. There are some other important passages in the Platonic corpus in which Socratic ignorance is depicted as true belief of the self. For example: *Lys.* 218a6-b1: There remain only those who have this bad thing, ignorance, but have not yet been made ignorant and stupid by it. They are conscious of not knowing what they don't know (*eti hêgoumenoi mê eidenai ha mê isasin*); *Tht.* 210c2-4: And if you remain barren, your companions will find you gentler and less tiresome; you will be modest and not think you know what you don't know (*sôphronôs ouk oiomenos eidenai ha mê oistha*); *Soph.* 230d2-4: ... [the man of cross-examination] removes the opinions that interfere with learning, and exhibits [the soul] cleansed, believing that it knows only those things that it does know, and nothing more (*tauta hêgoumenon haper oiden eidenai mona, pleiô de mê*); see also *Phdr.* 235c6-8: I know well that I have thought of none of these ideas from myself – I am aware of my own ignorance (*suneidôs emautôi amathian*) (my translation); cf. Fine 2008, 60-1, n. 23.

17. Johnson 2003, 24, n. 30 points out that the literal meaning of *planâsthai* is closer to 'wander', translating it 'confused'. Compared with the rest of the Platonic corpus, our passage is very special in that this notion is intensively discussed.

18. Furthermore, both passages name double ignorance 'the most contemptible stupidity' (*hê eponeidistos amathia, Alc.* 118a4-5 and *Ap.* 29b1-2).

19. Cf. 117e9-118a2: 'Since it is neither those who know nor those who don't know but know (*eidotes*) that they do not know, are any others left, save those who don't know but think that they do?'

20. This is what Plato sheds light on in discussing Socratic ignorance in the *Lysis* (217a3-218c2).

21. See, e.g., *Men.* 98b1-5 where Socrates says, 'Indeed, I too speak as one who does not have knowledge but is guessing. However, I certainly do not think I am guessing that right opinion is a different thing from knowledge. If I claim to *know* anything else – and I would make that claim about few things – I would put this down as one of the things I *know*'. Socrates has the right to claim this, insofar as this belief contributes to his philosophical life. In correspondence Harold Tarrant suggested to me the importance of this passage for my theme.

22. This is the issue with which Socrates and his interlocutors are concerned in the opening passages in the *Laches* and the *Protagoras* (esp. 312b-314c).

23. There is another impressive passage in Plato's canonical dialogues where Socrates stresses his wandering situation. At the very end of the *Hippias Minor*, referring back to 372d8-e1 ('I go back and forth (*planômai*) about all this – plainly because I don't know'), Socrates confesses: 'on these matters I waver back and forth and never believe the same thing. And it's not surprising at all that I or any other ordinary person should waver (*planâsthai*). But if you wise men (*hoi sophoi*) are going to do it (*planêsesthe*), too – that means something terrible for us, if we can't stop our wavering (*planês*) even after we've put ourselves in your company'. Here too, Plato's Socrates takes his wandering to be based on his Socratic ignorance in contrast to the 'wise' men's double ignorance.

24. For references to knowledge of ethical values in terms of the plural, see, e.g., *Gorg.* 460a-c; *Rep.* 506a, 520c; *Phdr.* 277d-278e. For the 'what is F-ness?' question in the *Alc.*, see 127e9.

*5. Socratic Ignorance, or the Place of the* Alcibiades I *in Plato's Early Works*

25. Cf. Smith 2004, 105: 'Those who regard it as authentic almost universally regard the *Alcibiades* I as an early Platonic dialogue'.

26. Denyer 2001, 11-12 guesses that Plato wrote the *Alcibiades* at some time in the early 350s. Aside from the authenticity, it may be possible to say that it was written after the *Republic*, judging from the fact that the treatments of doing one's own (*ta hautôn prattein*, 127c) and of the notion of friendship (126b-127d) clearly presuppose those of the *Republic*.

27. See n. 16 above.

6

# Did Alcibiades Learn Justice from the Many?

*Joe Mintoff*

Can virtue be taught by the many? Socrates insists that the perfection of our souls is of supreme importance (*Ap.* 29d-30a, *Cr.* 47d-48a, *Gorg.* 477e), he defines virtue as that which will make our souls good if it comes to be present (*Gorg.* 506d, cf. *Rep.* 353b), and he claims that, if we do not already possess virtue, then we should seek some teacher of it (*La.* 200d-201a, *Euthd.* 282a-b). We shall assume that he is basically right: that if our ultimate aim is to *live well*, if this requires us to know how to do so, and if we are unsure whether we already possess this know-how, then we should in the first instance seek some teacher in good living.[1] Who should it be? Not the many, according to Socrates.[2] As a general rule, and especially on matters of virtue, he asserts that we should be guided by the one with expert knowledge (assuming he exists) rather than the many, who lack such knowledge (*Ap.* 25b, *Cr.* 47b-d, *La.* 184d-5a, *Gorg.* 459a). Unlike other interlocutors in other dialogues, Alcibiades disagrees. Having suggested that he has learnt *justice* from people in general, he meets Socrates' stock assertion that '[w]hen you give the credit to "people in general", you're falling back on teachers who are no good' (*Alc.* 110e2-3), and he responds with the thought that the many can teach lots of different things. If we aim to live well, this issue is of vital importance. Together with the Great Speech in the *Protagoras*, the ensuing discussion in the *Alcibiades* is the most extensive treatment in the Socratic dialogues of the competence (or otherwise) of the general public to teach virtue. Accordingly, we shall approach the issue of whether the general public can teach virtue by examining Socrates' arguments, in particular, that the Greek public did *not* teach Alcibiades justice.

I

Socrates' first argument is quite brief – 'they can't even teach you what moves to make or not make in [draughts]. And yet that's a trivial matter, I suppose, compared with justice' (*Alc.* 110e5-6) – and they very soon move on from it.[3] However, in his commentary on the *Alcibiades*, Proclus takes more time to examine how best to formulate this argument and others, and, since we too are primarily interested in seeing what truth there is in

## 6. Did Alcibiades Learn Justice from the Many?

Socrates' claims, we shall follow him and consider it and those other arguments in more detail. In this case, Proclus adds the unstated major premise, and also disambiguates two senses in which some matter might be trivial:

> **T1** The many are unable to teach one how to play draughts, a matter of less significance [and – to match the major premise – of less difficulty to understand] than what is just.

> **T2** Those who cannot teach what is of less significance cannot be good teachers of what is more significant; and those who cannot judge correctly matters easy to know cannot teach what is more difficult and harder to understand. (Proc. *in Alc.* 254 [O'Neill 1965, 166])

Now, as Proclus realises, **T2** is false: 'Hippocrates was capable of teaching the art of medicine but not of building, although the latter is less important [and presumably less difficult] than medicine' (Proc. *in Alc.* 254 [O'Neill 1965, 166]). He thinks, however, that a fairer examination of the argument reveals that the reference to draughts is meant to be not only to what is less important than justice, but also to what is more engaging and more familiar to the many. The plausible thought is that if someone cannot do what is trivial *and familiar*, then they certainly will be unable to do what is serious *and unfamiliar*. Proclus suggests modifying the major premise accordingly, and, if so, we also need to modify the minor to match:

> **T1\*** The many are unable to teach one how to play draughts, *even though they engage in it and are familiar with it*, a matter of less significance [and of less difficulty to understand] than what is just, *a matter in which they have less experience and with which they are less familiar*.

> **T2\*** Those who cannot teach what is of less significance, *in which they engage and with which they are familiar*, cannot be good teachers of what is more significant, *in which they have less experience and with which they are less familiar*; and, *under the same conditions*, those who cannot judge correctly matters easy to know cannot teach what is more difficult and harder to understand. (Proc. *in Alc.* 254-5 [O'Neill 1965, 166])

Proclus now finds **T2\*** indubitable, as it may be, but in this case **T1\*** is false: the many have more experience of and are more familiar with matters of justice than matters of draughts. Earlier in their conversation, Socrates had reminded Alcibiades of those occasions when, as a boy playing some game or other, he had loudly and confidently accused a playmate of cheating, and Socrates eventually gets him to admit that he cannot recall any time at which he thought he did *not* know about justice and injustice (*Alc.* 110b1-c11). Thoughts about justice start early, and are apt to be held with great engagement. Justice *is* more serious than draughts, but Socrates' first argument fails to show that the many are no teachers of it.

Alcibiades has his own response to Socrates: 'they [i.e. the many] can teach a lot of things that are more important than [draughts] ... for example, I learned to speak Greek from them; I couldn't tell you who my teacher was, but I give credit to the very people you say are no good at teaching' (*Alc.* 110e11-111a3). The way he describes it, Alcibiades learnt Greek from someone in particular from the many. No doubt he actually learnt Greek in the course of his interactions with numerous people from the many, but in any case he clearly supposes that *each* person in general would make a good teacher of Greek, and he therefore suggests that *each* would also make a good teacher of justice.[4]

Now Socrates agrees – surprisingly as we shall see – that the many *are* good teachers of Greek, but he argues that this case differs from that of justice. He supposes that understanding Greek consists simply in having the vocabulary to be able to say what wood and stone and such things are (*Alc.* 111c4-5), though we might suppose that it also involves being able to say what sentences are grammatical or not.[5] Socrates is happy to admit that the many know such things:

> **A1⁻** People in general agree about *what wood or stone is, and similarly for all such cases* (e.g. men, horses) – since they give the same answers if you ask them and they reach for the same things when they want to get some wood or stone or suchlike (*Alc.* 111b11-c5), as they do when they want grammatical sentences.[6]
>
> **A1** Indeed, people in general agree with each other on these things, as we said, and also with themselves when acting privately. (*Alc.* 111c7-8)[7]
>
> **A2** But if people in general agree with each other on some subject, and with themselves when acting privately, then it is likely that they would make good teachers of such things. (*Alc.* 111c7-12)

Things are different with justice. Just as Socrates supposes that knowing Greek involves knowing what *men* (and lots of other things) are like, he assumes that knowing justice consists in knowing what *just and unjust* men are like. And on this issue there is violent disagreement:

> **D1** People in general neither agree among themselves or with each other about *just and unjust people and actions.* (*Alc.* 111e12-112a3)
>
> **D1⁺** Indeed, people in general disagree a huge amount about just and unjust people and actions, so much so that they sometimes fight battles and lose their lives over it – as the conflicts between the Achaeans and Trojans, and the Athenians and Spartans, attest. (*Alc.* 112a6-c7)
>
> **D2** But if people in general disagree about some subject, and especially if

## 6. Did Alcibiades Learn Justice from the Many?

they disagree so much that they resort to such extreme measures, then they do not understand such things (*Alc.* 111b6, 112d1-4), and so they would not make good teachers of them. (*Alc.* 111a11-b1)

In other dialogues, Socrates argues that teachers of *athletics* are few rather than many, and so teachers of virtue must also be few rather than many (*Cr.* 47b-d, *La.* 184d-185a), but the fact that the teachers of Greek are many shows that this inference is weak. It is not the fact that people are *many* that disqualifies them as teachers, but rather the fact that they *disagree*, and this is a better reason to conclude that Alcibiades did not learn justice from them.

Alcibiades has no further response, but he is reluctant to admit that he is unlikely to know anything about justice (*Alc.* 112d11). In the remainder of the paper, we shall pursue at length how he might have responded, to thoroughly examine whether we too should admit that we have not learned justice from the many.

## II

The place to start is with Socrates' crucial admission that the many are good teachers of Greek, to see if Alcibiades could have made more of it.

Premise **A1**, concerning people's agreement about Greek, delivers immediate profit. Socrates clearly supposes that people *agree with each other* on some subject when they have the same *beliefs* on that subject, since he supposes that this agreement is evinced by their assertions and their actions, and so – by extension – that a person *agrees with themselves* when they have the same beliefs at one time as they do at another, so that they do not assert one thing at one time and something different at another. Alcibiades, for example, is eventually made to see that he does not agree with himself: 'I swear by the gods, Socrates, I have no idea what I mean – I must be in some absolutely bizarre condition! When you ask me questions, first I think one thing, and then I think something else' (*Alc.* 116e3-5). Now Socrates admits that people agree with themselves about *what men are like* (meaning, recall, that they are consistent in the things they identify as men), though not about *what just men are like*. However, given that people are so often reduced to contradiction under cross-examination by him when asked to generalise about what the *just (or pious, or courageous, etc.) man* is like, Socrates should also admit that they would likewise be reduced to contradiction were they asked to generalise about what *men* are like – though they may be better at identifying men than identifying just men, that is unlikely to mean they are any better at (say) *explicitly defining* what it is to be a man. The implication is that, sometimes, a person agrees with themselves on some subject even though they cannot readily define their terms without contradiction, but this is still enough for them to understand that subject. This is so with Greek, and it *might* also be so with justice.[8]

Premise **A2**, which takes agreement to imply knowledge, causes complications however. As Proclus puts it: 'not in every case are those who agree with each other on any subject knowledgeable about the topic on which they have agreement. For at the present time the many agree that gods do not exist, but this has happened to them through lack of knowledge' (Proc. *in Alc.* 264 [O'Neill 1965, 173]). In other contexts, Socrates himself seems to concur, claiming that even if the many all agree with Polus that the unjust man can be happy, this is no refutation of his contrary opinion (*Gorg.* 473d). It seems that people in general could all agree on some matter, but still be mistaken, and so be poor teachers of it. Socrates' response is to cross-examine Polus and eventually to reduce him to contradiction, thus showing that he disagrees with himself (*Gorg.* 474b-480a). Proclus' response is to claim, more generally, that all those with false moral beliefs disagree with themselves, as we can see by observing the evil man: 'on account of his rational nature he must in some way see the truth, but on account of the emotions and imaginings implicated in matter he must be distracted towards ignorance and personal conflict; this is shown by his repentance once the emotions have abated' (Proc. *in Alc.* 264 [O'Neill 1965, 173]).[9] Accordingly, the fact that the many mistakenly believe there are no gods does not impugn (A2), since they do not agree with themselves in private. There are two problems with this explanation, however. First, our rational nature does not always mean we will in some way see the truth – there are plenty of intelligent and unrepentant atheists these days, and plenty of people with false moral beliefs who are also intelligent and unrepentant (pick a good moral philosopher with whom you disagree), and if repentance shows that one saw the truth all along, lack of repentance suggests that one did not. Secondly, even if in some way we see the truth, that does not always mean we disagree with ourselves – perhaps if we were to think rationally then we *would* believe that gods exist, perhaps we have thought about it and *suspect* that gods exist, but such hypotheticals and suspicions do not make for belief (if, when asked, we do not assent that gods exist, and do not act accordingly), and without such a belief our godless ways exhibit no internal inconsistency. There *are* cases in which those who agree with each other and with themselves in private lack knowledge. This is so of unrepentant atheists, and nothing so far precludes it also being so of speaking Greek.

It is still possible to make something of Proclus' discussion, however. Let us say that a person *judges consistently* on some subject when the judgements they would make at one time *about cases* are consistent with those they would make at other times. In these terms, **A2** implies the claim:

> **A2.0** If people judge consistently on some subject, and if people agree with each other on those judgements, then it is likely that they would make good teachers of such things.

## 6. Did Alcibiades Learn Justice from the Many?

The judgements of the godless masses are a good objection to **A2.0**. Proclus is wrong to think, in our terms, that if a person judges consistently then they judge correctly. Elsewhere, however, he makes more helpful comments. He claims that speaking Greek has more than one aspect. Obviously, one is observing the Greek usage of names (e.g. that this thing is called 'man'), which he agrees the many are teachers of in virtue of the fact that they correctly exhibit customary Greek usage. But there is also what he refers to as 'assign[ing] the legitimate uses of terms that are naturally appropriate to their subjects' (Proc. *in Alc.* 259 [O'Neill 1965, 169]), knowledge of which is characteristic of 'the philosopher and the man who has examined the nature of things' (Proc. *in Alc.* 259 [O'Neill 1965, 170]). The problem with the judgements of the godless masses, we might suggest, is not that they disagree with themselves, but rather that they have not properly examined the nature of what they talk about.

In particular, they have not considered matters in the careful and systematic way philosophers do. Such critical reflection involves the attempt to articulate general truths underlying the judgement of cases, an openness to their being examined in the cauldron of critical discussion, and, with luck, the success of their passing all the requisite tests. Let us say, therefore, that a person *generalises consistently* on some subject when they critically reflect on the matter and make *generalisations* consistent with all their (post hoc) judgements about cases.[10] In these terms, it seems plausible to suppose that:

> **A2.1** If people judge *and generalise* consistently on some subject, and if people agree with each other on those judgements *and generalisations*, then it is *justified to believe* that they would make good teachers of such things.

We seek a teacher. Now, if *one* other person generalises consistently, then *they* are justified in believing their conclusions, but it doesn't follow that *we* should believe them – there are intelligent and well-informed people these days who spend lots of their time reflecting on the gods' existence, many of them come to their own more-or-less consistent conclusions, but they are *different* conclusions, and they can't all be right. However, if *every* other person generalises consistently, and they *all* come to the same conclusions, then we would be perfectly justified in believing them – if *all* discussants of such matters (theologians *and* reflective atheists) were eventually to converge on significant theological issues, if they *all* eventually came to the same conclusions, then surely we would have very good reason to take them as teachers on those matters. Now the godless masses are no objection to **A2.1**. First, it is very unlikely they met the first condition: few such people in Proclus' day are likely to have reflected very much concerning the gods' existence, let alone to have consistently generalised on the basis of their religious intuitions. Secondly, even if each of them did generalise consistently for themselves, it is unlikely they would satisfy the second condition: right now, theologians disagree amongst themselves and with reflective atheists, and this is good reason for supposing that, right now, this is what would happen to the public in general were they to become more reflective about such matters. Thirdly, if the godless masses ever were to meet both of these conditions, then Proclus would simply be wrong, and we would have perfectly good reason to think that the gods do not exist, and that we might be able to learn something on the matter from the many. The problem with **A2.1**, however, is that few people reflect much on theology, and even fewer on linguistics, and so it does not help us explain why people are likely to be good teachers of Greek.

We can fix this problem. Socrates' well-known discussion with Meno's slave boy shows how, if we couch it in the terms we have introduced, the slave boy judges consistently in geometry: asked on one occasion whether a specific four-unit square contains four specific two-unit squares, he replies that it does (*Meno* 83b), and no doubt he would have made the same judgement if asked at any other time. Initially, however, he does *not* generalise consistently: he was originally asked how to double the area of a square of two-unit width, and confidently answered that the width of the required square is four units (*Meno* 82e), but, initially unbeknownst to him, this is inconsistent with the judgements he is disposed to make. Eventually, he *does* generalise consistently: Socrates directs him to think about the matter, he asks him questions which lead him to make specific judgements about specific geometrical claims, from which the slave boy comes to see the correct general answer for himself, and confidently agrees with the generalisation that 'the diagonal of the given square produces the double-sized figure' (*Meno* 84d-85b). In between, it was always going to happen. For, *even as he gives his mistaken answer*, the slave boy nevertheless *would* generalise consistently: the geometrical judgements he is unavoidably disposed to make very tightly constrain the generalisations to be made about how to double the area of a square, which means that, after some bumbling around and some assistance from Socrates, the slave boy *would* eventually see the general answer for himself.[11] As would anyone else. The moral Socrates draws is that our immortal souls have over countless ages learnt everything there is, and that 'we need not be surprised if it can recall the knowledge of virtue or anything else which, as we see, it once possessed' (*Meno* 81c). By contrast, the only moral we draw is the more modest one that in *some* subjects (e.g. geometry) we can expect that people can judge consistently and *would* generalise consistently, even if their first reflections are likely to be incoherent, and even before we have asked them questions and gotten them to reflect on those matters.

As in geometry, so with Greek. Let us say that a person *would generalise consistently* on some subject when, if they *were* to critically reflect on the matter and make generalisations, then those generalisations *would* (at least eventually) be consistent with all their judgements about cases.

## 6. Did Alcibiades Learn Justice from the Many?

Accordingly, our own explanation of why the many are teachers of Greek is that:

> **A1.2** As we saw, people in general judge consistently and agree with each other about what wood and stone is, and similarly for all such cases; but, further, *they would generalise consistently and in agreement with each other about such matters.*

> **A2.2** But if people judge and *would* generalise consistently on some subject, and if people agree with each other on those judgements and *would* do so on those generalisations, then it is justified to believe that they would make good teachers of such things.

This presumes that linguistic judgements are just as constraining as geometric ones.[12] As we noted, people are unlikely to be any better at explicitly defining what it is to be a *man* than they are at defining what it is to be a *just man*, at least in the short term. But, in the much longer term, we may believe that if they seriously thought about the matter, then (perhaps with guidance) people *would* eventually arrive at some definition (perhaps not a very pretty one) which is consistent with all their specific linguistic judgements (perhaps after relabelling a few cases). And if so, we will believe that their present linguistic judgements reflect a presently-unarticulated understanding of speaking Greek, and that this understanding is what makes them good teachers.

And as with Greek, *perhaps* with justice as well. We should be fair, however. We need to remember that the fact that people would in the short term be reduced to contradiction if asked to generalise about justice does *not* show that they lack understanding of justice, any more than the incoherent first response of Meno's slave showed that he lacked knowledge of geometry. We need to ask whether, given their pre-reflective intuitive judgements and notwithstanding their poor initial efforts at generalising them, people nevertheless do exhibit some hitherto-unarticulated understanding of justice. We end this section by briefly describing two strategies Alcibiades might have used to argue so.[13]

He might have argued that people know justice by nature. Responding to Socratic doubts about whether virtue can be taught *at all* (and, by implication, doubts about whether *sophists* can teach it), Protagoras relates a myth with the following literal content (*Prot.* 320c-323a). We humans are weak creatures. But we do possess technical know-how for various specific needs (e.g. to promote health), which we should not be surprised to find distributed unequally, since any specific need requires only a small number of practitioners. This know-how is taught at specialist institutions. In addition, humans possess at least minimal social know-how – presumably consisting in such things as: don't lie, don't steal, keep promises, respect neighbours, etc. – which we can expect to be distributed (almost) universally, since society will exist at all only if (nearly) all possess such know-how and are disposed to exercise it.[14] *This* know-how is taught by all-and-sundry, from nursemaids to school teachers to legislators, both privately and publicly. Protagoras rounds off his speech with Alcibiades' very analogy: 'as it is you are spoilt, Socrates, in that all are teachers of virtue to the best of their ability, and so you think that no one is. In the same way if you asked who teaches the Greek language you would not find anyone' (*Prot.* 327e). We can expect people to know justice, on this suggestion, since we can expect them to have been taught the social rules which in general are necessary for the preservation of society (among which are linguistic rules), and these essential rules are simply what justice consists in. People will judge cases uniformly, and would generalise uniformly from them, since they have been taught the same rules.

Alcibiades might have argued that people know justice by convention. Proclus again: 'those who give the many the credit for being teachers of what is just, as of speaking Greek, seem to me to state clearly that *they consider what is just to be so by agreement*, like names' (Proc. *in Alc.* 259 [O'Neill 1965, 170], emphasis added).[15] It is possible to take the analogy between language and justice further than the fact that both are necessary for society: it might be a law of nature that people have some *language* or other [similarly: some *concept of justice* or other], but it is a matter of convention which particular one they have; however – in turn – given that they have one rather than another, it will be a no-less-binding law that those people *talk* [similarly: *act*] in some ways rather than others. Given the way they live, some things are simply not stones, and other things are simply not right. We can expect people to know justice, on this suggestion, since we can expect people to have been taught particular social rules or others by society, and, *in that society*, such rules are simply what justice consists in (since, in that way of life, these particular social rules have at least as much normative force as their particular linguistic rules). People in general will judge moral cases uniformly, and would generalise uniformly from them, just as we have seen they would with their language.

### III

All this still leaves us with Socrates' objection that the many *disagree* so much about justice that they would not make good teachers of it, an objection to which Alcibiades had no response.

In relation to premise **D1**, however, we need to ask: how much do people *really* disagree about justice? We have in passing distinguished between two different levels of knowledge. On the one hand, there is the judge's ability to say the right thing about particular cases – the many agree about what stone is like because they pick out the same things as stones, we saw, and similarly they will be able to judge justice if they can pick the just men and actions from the unjust. On the other hand, there is the generaliser's ability to correctly enunciate general principles – the moralist will enjoin

## 6. Did Alcibiades Learn Justice from the Many?

us *not to lie, to keep our promises*, etc., they will typically have some advice about what these rules imply in particular cases, and they will occasionally have some justification of these rules in terms of yet more general principles.[16] Now it is perfectly possible for agreement to occur at one level and disagreement at another, and this raises the question of what factors are most relevant in determining whether a given person is a teacher. For example, Euthyphro and Socrates agree that the gods also have disputes amongst themselves (*Euthph*. 7b), again over what's just and unjust (*Euthph*. 7d), and to such an extent that they too are led to make war on one another (*Euthph*. 8a). This obviously causes problems for Euthyphro's earlier claim that the holy is what is agreeable to the gods, and the unholy what is disagreeable (*Euthph*. 7a), but this is not our current concern. Rather, of interest right now is Euthyphro's response that the gods will at least all agree that whoever kills someone unjustly should pay the penalty (*Euthph*. 8b), and Socrates' admission that the same applies to men as well (*Euthph*. 8c). In these cases, at least, there is agreement on principles but disagreement on cases – 'So at least they're not disputing whether the wrongdoer must pay the penalty; but perhaps what they dispute is who the wrongdoer is, or what he did, or when' (*Euthph*. 8d) – and, if this is so, this very agreement on moral principles suggests that people might actually know something about justice, notwithstanding rhetoric about how very violent their disagreement about cases might be. The fact that people disagree about which men are just does not imply that they disagree about the relevant moral principles, and that *might* be enough to make them teachers of justice.

Therefore, in relation to premise **D2**, we should ask: *does* disagreement always imply ignorance? The short answer is that it appears not.

Proclus fears that *philosophers* contradict this premise. He considers the following difficulty: 'If disagreement is evidence of ignorance, we shall state that the philosophers too are ignorant, for they also disagree with each other and reject each other's hypotheses, some advocating one system, some another' (Proc. *in Alc*. 267 [O'Neill 1965, 175]). This is a problem, presumably, because philosophers are commonly supposed to be the knowledgeable. He responds, rightly, by pointing out that disagreement within some group might manifest in two ways: it might be that everyone in that group is ignorant, or alternatively that some are knowledgeable (and agree with one another) and some ignorant. And he claims that in the second case the knowledgeable subgroup differs from their ignorant complement in the fact that the former agree with themselves and with each other, and the latter agree in neither way. The response to the difficulty therefore seems to be that, even though philosophers in general disagree, there is nevertheless a knowledgeable sub-group of so-called *genuine* philosophers (Proc. *in Alc*. 268 [O'Neill 1965, 175-6]). This is true enough. But Proclus' proposal for distinguishing the genuine philosophers from the rest won't quite work – as we have seen, there might be some like-minded clique amongst the godless philosophers who are unrepentant in their atheism, but who are ignorant for all that, and who do not differ in these respects from the wise. And, more to the point, his response is in fact an admission that philosophers in general *are* ignorant – the fact that philosophers *in general* disagree while some philosophical *sub-group* is knowledgeable obviously does not falsify the claim that disagreement amongst a group is evidence that *the very same group* is ignorant, and so this premise convicts philosophers of ignorance no less than the many.

Times have changed, and these days we are more likely to have the thought that *recognised experts* contradict premise **D2**. Like Proclus, Terrance McConnell is also troubled by the fact that philosophers disagree amongst themselves, but his response is different: 'Physicians sometimes disagree amongst themselves regarding diagnostic judgements; legal scholars frequently disagree about what the correct legal decision is in a complicated case; and physicists take radically different positions on fundamental issues in their discipline' (McConnell 1984, 207), yet this does not lead us to doubt the expertise of any of them. Now, if we identify the subject of their disagreement narrowly as *this patient's diagnosis*, then it is indeed unclear whether these physicians are to be relied upon concerning *that* matter. However, there is a perfectly legitimate sense in which their disagreement is also a *medical* one, yet that would not stop us going to *them* were we to want medical treatment. And if physicians and lawyers can disagree and yet still count as experts, why not philosophers?

One answer is that true experts *cannot* disagree: disputing philosophers are not experts, and nor are disputing doctors, in the strict sense. Socrates has very high standards: when he refers to doctors, for example, he refers in the strict sense to medical practitioners who always fully cure their patients (*Euthd.* 280a; cf. *Rep.* 342b). He would obviously deny that those McConnell mentions really are doctors. Our own standards are not so high: we ordinarily have no problem referring to the imperfect specimens we deal with as doctors, and so we must mean something different by the term. Hippocrates of old was a doctor in this sense, as is the average physician nowadays, even though they differ greatly in their ability to promote health. On this matter, the ordinary sense is the right one: for if Socrates accepts that the many know what wood and stone are like, because they say the same things and seek the same objects, he should also accept that they know what doctors are like, for exactly the same reason – they all assert that *doctors* are the just people you should go to when you are sick, and they behave accordingly. Hippocrates was the one to see if you were sick in ancient times (but not nowadays), just as the general practitioner is today. Generalising, a practitioner is someone with sufficient ability to do something that we ought to seek them if we aim to have it done (and don't care who does it). In particular, the teachers of a given subject will by definition be those we ought to seek if we aim to learn it (cf. *Alc.* 111d2).

## 6. Did Alcibiades Learn Justice from the Many?

The correct answer to the question above about physicians and philosophers is that true experts *can* disagree, but that philosophers disagree too much even by ordinary standards. Now, two experts can disagree *about (some) particular cases* and still be experts, but only if they basically agree about their most general principles – if, for example, two physicians disagree about a patient's treatment, and we find out that one is a western physician while the other practises Hippocratic medicine, then we *would* think that one or the other was not really an expert. When an act-utilitarian and a deontologist disagree about crucial cases, for example, they are in exactly the same situation, they disagree because they hold different fundamental moral theories, and we should say exactly the same thing, that one or other is *not* an expert. Further, two experts can even disagree about some very general principle in their discipline and still be experts, but only if they basically agree on many other general issues – for example, two astronomers might disagree about the extent and duration of the universe, but that is only against a background of widespread agreement on many other fundamental matters, and if we suddenly discovered that one of them endorsed the *Ptolemaic* picture of the universe, then we would have no hesitation in saying that *he* is no expert. The same applies to act-utilitarians and deontologists: their disagreement is as basic as the one between a Ptolemaic and a modern astronomer, and we must treat their claims to expertise in the same way. In sum, the most relevant factor in determining whether a person is an expert is their knowledge of the most general principles. Doctors are experts in medicine (unlike philosophers in ethics), and so Alcibiades could have stated that disagreement is *not always* evidence of ignorance.

Further revisions in Socrates' premises are therefore necessary. Let us say that people *pretty much* agree with each other on some subject when their beliefs on that subject agree at least as much as the beliefs of commonly recognised experts (e.g. doctors, etc.) in *their* subjects – *pace* Socrates, experts properly so-called can disagree with each other. Obviously this could and should be specified further, but it is specific enough to allow us to conclude that Greek speakers pretty much agree about language, though philosophers do not about ethics. Similarly, let us say that a person *pretty much* judges (or generalises) consistently when the consistency of their judgements (and generalisations) is at least as great as the consistency which commonly recognised experts exhibit in *their* subjects – which, *pace* Socrates again, need not be complete, if they are at all critically reflective about their inevitably imperfect disciplines. Things are the other way around in this case, in that the average philosopher pretty much *generalises* consistently (which is to say that they are good at crafting internally coherent ethical theories), unlike the average Greek speaker (who rarely bothers to theorise at all about language). Small disagreements are *no* evidence of ignorance; and, correspondingly, we must now suppose that agreement does not have to be complete before it is evidence of knowledge:

**A2\*** If people judge and would generalise *pretty much* consistently on some subject, and if people *pretty much* agree with each other on those judgements and would do so on those generalisations, then it is justified to believe that they would make good teachers of such things.

**D2\*** If some group of people *do not pretty much agree* with each other about some subject, then it is not justified to believe that they would make good teachers of such things; similarly, *if some individual does not pretty much agree with themselves on some subject, then it is not justified to believe that they would make a good teacher of such things.*

These principles are not the ones Socrates enunciated, but nevertheless they are the logical upshot of his initial admission that the many are teachers of speaking Greek. Since there is universal agreement that the imperfect and sometime-disagreeing practitioners we deal with are experts properly so-called, then, surprisingly, his admission indirectly implies that *near-universal* agreement is necessary and sufficient for justifiably being thought to be a good teacher.

So back to premise **D1**. Our question in relation to this premise is now: do the beliefs of people in general about justice agree at least as much as the beliefs of commonly recognised experts (e.g. doctors, etc.) in *their* subjects? Now we described above two strategies Alcibiades might have used to argue that people in general exhibit some hitherto-unarticulated understanding of justice, and if so then (like other knowledgeable groups) they would presumably also exhibit the level of agreement typical of experts. Therefore let us assume – so that Alcibiades' view will receive its best hearing – that Protagoras is right that each society will teach everyone the social rules in general necessary for the preservation of any society, and that the conventionalist is right that the particular social rules taught in any society are *in that society* simply what justice consists in.

Even so, it doesn't follow that people in general *will* agree to the requisite level. First, even if we can expect all to be minimally competent in social know-how, Protagoras himself claims that some will possess this know-how to a greater degree than others (depending on their natural talent for such things), and will do so to such an extent that we should seek *them* rather than the others if we wish to acquire this know-how (*Prot.* 326e-328a). This is at least possible, and if true it would in our terms imply that people will disagree with each other about justice (since if one person possesses greater know-how than another then they must differ in their know-how, and in turn in their judgements), and will do so to such an extent that those people with lesser social know-how will *not* count as teachers (applying our definition, above).[17] Secondly, even if justice is simply relative to the rules taught in any given society, the conventionalist's reliance on the analogy between language and justice itself suggests that agreement will not always occur. For, as with language, it is possible that there are different *moral dialects* within any given society concerning

## 6. Did Alcibiades Learn Justice from the Many?

those matters which go further than those strictly speaking necessary for its continued survival, and also possible that the differences between them are greater than any to be found amongst recognised experts. Either way, it doesn't follow that people in general are teachers of justice.

Furthermore, in societies like our own, it is likely that people in general will *not* agree to the requisite level. For example, all societies will teach that *killing is unjust*. However, it is probably only necessary (strictly speaking) for societies to teach that killing (say) *productive and law-abiding members of society* is unjust, and this means that different societies could teach different things about killing *others*, such as foetuses and infants, sinners and criminals, the aged and infirm, not to mention animals and slaves. Let us say that a society is *liberal* to the extent to which the many have an equal right to the most extensive liberty compatible with a similar liberty for others (Rawls 1972, 60), and therefore to the extent to which we can expect the greatest variation in ways of thought and living (*Rep.* 557b); and that a society is *traditionalist* to the extent to which the universal teaching of social rules extends beyond those that are strictly-speaking necessary for the continued survival of any society, and is therefore one in which people will have fewer liberties than members of liberal societies. Now, given that societies are left to their own ways of life and constrained only by the need to co-exist peacefully, different societies *do* take different approaches on these further matters: liberal societies leave people comparatively free to choose (e.g. in relation to abortion and euthanasia); traditionalist societies make more specific demands, frequently different in different traditions. Similarly, given extensive liberty of thought and action constrained only by an equal liberty for others, different social groups (and individuals) *within a liberal society* will most likely believe different things on these matters: liberals that people have comparatively extensive rights to choose for themselves; traditionalists that duties are more important, though (again) different duties depending on the tradition of which they are a part. In short, different moral dialects are not only possible in a liberal society, but likely. We should therefore expect that:

> **D1\*** People in general *in a liberal society* do not pretty much agree with each other about just and unjust men and actions, *nor on how they would generalise from those judgements*.

This is what we see in present-day liberal societies. People in such societies do not seem to agree sufficiently in their judgements – witness the familiar disagreements in our own society about matters such as abortion, capital punishment, and euthanasia, and note that many more people agree on whether the relevant moral sentences are *grammatical* than agree on whether they are *true*. More importantly, it is unlikely that they would sufficiently agree in any generalisations they made from those judgements – recall the above-mentioned disagreements between philosophers, some of which concern exactly the same matters, and note that if *trained theorisers* in ethics cannot meet the requisite level of agreement, then we can hardly expect that *people in general* would do so. If you let people believe what they like about justice, then they are bound to disagree.

So Socrates was pretty much right. Though they taught him how to speak Greek, Alcibiades did *not* learn justice from the many.

## Notes

1. Socrates variously characterises what is of supreme importance: (i) doing well, or happiness (*Euthd.* 278e, 282a), which he argues is identical to knowledge (*Euthd.* 281e); (ii) perfecting our selves (*Alc.* 124b), or, what is the same thing, perfecting our souls (*Alc.* 130c); and (iii) living well (*Cr.* 48b; *Gorg.* 512e), which he supposes amounts to living honourably and justly (*Cr.* 48b; *Ap.* 28b). If we suppose that living well is the basic notion and that it consists most generally in being guided by virtue, then we can explain the supreme importance of doing well (since anyone who lives well will do well), and of perfecting our selves (since this will consist in acquiring virtue).

2. By the many, or people in general, we mean those people who are minimally competent in practical matters. When it comes to Greek, the many consist of those who would be described as Greek speakers. When it comes to justice, the many consists of nearly all adults, if, as Protagoras suggests at *Prot.* 327e, we can expect the average adult to be minimally competent at interacting with others.

3. The translation has 'knucklebones', but this has been changed throughout to 'draughts' to match the translation of Proclus' commentary.

4. This is not the only way the many might have knowledge of justice. Alcibiades might alternatively have suggested that he could rely on what the majority of them believe, or more generally on what some social decision process led them to endorse, about justice. See Denyer 2001, 119, 122, who seems to attribute this view to Alcibiades. Thus Aristotle: '[t]he many, no one of whom taken singly is a sound man, may yet be better than the few, not individually but collectively. ... Just as in mass they become [when brought together] as it were one man with many pairs of feet and hands and many senses, so also do they become one in regard to character and intelligence' (*Pol.* 3.11.1281b1-6). This is an interesting idea, but we cannot pursue it in this paper. Two critical comments will have to suffice. First, majority opinion about how to live well taken from amongst a set of individual opinions – even individually coherent opinions – need not itself be coherent. Secondly, even if majority opinion were coherent, the conflicting opinions of the many will exhibit not only random error (which majority voting would indeed counteract), but perhaps also some systematic error (which it would not).

5. Proclus also supposes that one aspect of knowing Greek involves accuracy in the use and pronunciation of the language, but claims that this is characteristic of the few who know grammar rather than the many (Proc. *in Alc.* 259 [O'Neill 1965, 170]). He must be supposing that this knowledge consists in knowledge of explicit grammatical rules (which the many may indeed lack), rather than knowledge of how to speak grammatically (which the many will presumably possess). But if people in general count as knowing vocabulary because they can pick out stones

from non-stones, then they will also count as knowing grammar if they can pick out grammatical sentences from others.

6. Admittedly, there might be one or two exceptions. But such linguistic deviants would not makes us, or Socrates, retract the view that people in general know Greek, and so we should interpret the claim that people in general agree about stones (etc.) as the claim that nearly all people agree.

7. In addition to people's agreeing with each other, and with themselves acting privately, Socrates adds a further agreement 'But don't they also agree in public? Cities don't disagree with each other and use different words for the same thing, do they?' (*Alc.* 111c8-10). We shall not pursue the matter. First, this further point deserves a more complex treatment: given that Socrates is about to highlight the disagreements over justice in part by reference to the Trojan war (*Alc.* 112b2-9), then the correct answer to his rhetorical question might be that cities do sometimes use different words for the same thing, or that in this type of case saying different things does not count as a disagreement (see also Denyer 2001, 124, on 111c3-4). Secondly, it seems simply to reiterate the first point at a higher level: just as each individual within some polis agrees with themselves (i.e. what they say at one time is the same as what they say at another) and with all others in the polis, so too the polis considered as a whole agrees with itself (i.e. what one individual in the polis says is the same as what any other says) and *with all other poleis*.

8. Proclus comes to Socrates' aid on this point: 'You see how Socrates has entrusted the names given to classes to the knowledge of the many, but what can and cannot race, and what is healthy or not is discerned by suitability only and is hard to ascertain since it is more remote than objects of sense and requires skilled knowledge' (Proc. *in Alc.* 267 [O'Neill, 1965, 175]), commenting on *Alc.* 111d6-e7). To discern a man is merely a matter of sense-perception, but to discern a just man is more complex and presumably requires theorising. See McDowell 1985, however, for a view that assimilates moral judgement to sense perception.

9. Vlastos argues that Socrates implicitly shares the general claim. He argues that Socrates' elenctic practice reveals a belief in the assumption that '[w]hoever has a false moral belief will always have at the same time true beliefs entailing the negation of that false belief' (Vlastos 1994, 25), which obviously implies that any consistent set of moral beliefs will contain only true beliefs (26). This is in part why Socrates can be so confident that he will be able to refute interlocutors with (what he takes to be) false moral beliefs.

10. The parenthetical qualification is meant to allow for the possibility of mutual adjustment between general principles and case judgements. If a person generalises consistently on some subject then they will have reached what is sometimes called narrow reflective equilibrium, and, if those reflections are also consistent with reflections in other subjects, then they will have achieved wide reflective equilibrium. For details, see Rawls 1951 and Daniels 1979.

11. This is not to say that, right at the start, the slave boy believes the correct generalisation, or even the specific judgements Socrates will induce him to make later. We should say that he does not believe the correct answer, because he asserts a different one when first asked and would act accordingly. And we *might* say that he does not believe the specific judgements, if we are impressed by the fact that the slave boy has probably never before thought anything about such matters. On this issue, see Vlastos 1994, 23 and Beversluis 2000, 53-5.

12. Though perhaps for different reasons. Presumably behind the geometric constraints lie geometric truths, and behind the linguistic constraints lie the

conventions of speakers about usage. However, whatever the truth-makers for the relevant constraints, it is the constraint itself which explains – if it is true – why people *would* generalise consistently in the relevant area. Thanks to a reader for raising this issue.

13. Here is a contemporary understanding of morality that adopts strategies akin to both: 'Some moral injunctions and prohibitions [the ones we will in a moment call 'natural'] are explained and justified, when challenged, by reference to the unvarying dispositions and needs of normal human beings, living anywhere in any normal society: for example, the requirement not to cause suffering when this can be avoided. On the other hand, some injunctions and prohibitions [the 'conventional'], as in duties arising from kinship, duties of politeness, of many kinds of loyalty, are in fact traced back, when challenged, to a particular way of life in which these duties are essential elements' (Hampshire 1989, 138). Hampshire too draws the analogy between different languages and different conceptions of the good life (156).

14. See Taylor 1991, 86-7, on *Prot.* 322d1-5, for discussion of the need for the parenthetical qualifications.

15. Denyer suggests that Alcibiades' view depends on a belief that there is more than just an analogy between language and values, in particular that 'one's native language indicates a lot about the sort of person one is ... not only sharing the speech of that group [i.e. one's own ethnic group], but also or instead sharing its manners, customs, values and political allegiance' (Denyer 2001, 121).

16. As the limiting case, there is also the theorist's ability to correctly enunciate fundamental principles – the philosopher, for example, might propose that justice consists in those rules necessary for the preservation of society, and that all other principles are to be justified on the basis of this single one. Note that, if the moralist does not care to provide any further justification of his moral rules, then for him they will count as fundamental principles.

17. Protagoras seems to have a broader understanding of what it is to be a teacher. As we have seen, he thinks that the many can teach virtue 'to the best of their ability' (*Prot.* 327e), but that he himself is rather better at doing so and well worth the fee he charges (*Prot.* 328a). Perhaps, in our terms, we should distinguish between those who *can teach* something from those who *are teachers of* it – thus, it seems natural to say that while I can teach my son mathematics, that does not make me a mathematics teacher. Perhaps, therefore, Alcibiades could respond that even if the many are not teachers of justice, nevertheless they can teach justice, and that is all he ever claimed. Still, if we seek to learn something as important as justice, then we will want teachers of justice rather than merely those who can teach it. On this point, see Taylor 1991, 83.

# 7

# The Dual-Role Philosophers: An Exploration of a Failed Relationship[1]

*Anthony Hooper*

## I

Many commentators have seen the relationship between Socrates and Alcibiades as evidence that Aristophanes' caricature was fundamentally correct: Socrates truly was a man suspended in the air with the clouds, far beyond mortal concerns.[2] Socrates, on this reading, is not truly a lover, and if he is, he is merely a lover of the supersensible and perfect 'forms', and not of other people. But in the *Alcibiades* we have a portrayal of Socrates' first discussions with the famous Athenian, where he is seemingly intent on making Alcibiades a better man. It is difficult to reconcile this image with the previous account.

In the *Alcibiades* Socrates says to Alcibiades, 'You know, what I've said about the need for education applies to me as well as to you – we're in the same condition' (*Alc.* 124b-c).[3] If Socrates were truly wiser than all other people, if not wholly self-sufficient, it seems strange that he would compare himself so closely to a student who, as fertile a ground as he is for education, is all but ignorant of any divine matters, and whose only concern is for the fame that comes from the admiration of the mob. So was Socrates' remark about his own condition another example of his famous irony? I believe that it was not, and that such comments are indicative of what has come to be called 'erotic reciprocity,' which some philosophers have seen as the core of Plato's account of *eros*.[4]

In this paper I will argue that Socrates is trying to involve Alcibiades in what I will call a 'dual-role' relationship, in which both parties act as both a lover and a beloved.[5] In such a relationship, I will contend, the two lovers will construct a social space in which they will be most able to satisfy their desire to possess the good. I do not believe that Socrates' actions in the *Alcibiades* can be understood without an awareness of these ideas, so I will first expand on these concepts by turning to the *Phaedrus*, in which Plato gives them their clearest formulation, and then give a reading of the *Alcibiades* through this framework, and finally turn to the *Symposium* to show why Socrates' efforts failed.

Anthony Hooper

## II

All lovers, Socrates tells us, desire to possess the good forever (*Symp.* 206a), and overcoming our ignorant belief that we possess the good when we do not is the first step we must take in order to possess the good life. But there are two further facts lovers must be aware of and avoid if they are to have any hopes of becoming truly good. First, we have to appreciate that we can also be ignorant of the true nature of the good, which, as for the first three speakers in the *Symposium*, can lead us to pursue a deficient form of the good, and will ultimately lead us into contradiction.[6] Secondly, we must be aware of the nature of humanity, which, like for Eros himself, is one of becoming, rather than Being. Unlike the gods who are unchanging in their eternal knowledge of the forms, we mortals must appreciate that everything we come to possess ultimately will slip from our grasp, whether it is the pretty flower that loses its vibrancy, or some knowledge which we will come to forget. We are, therefore, in a dangerous position in that we may fall back into a deficient understanding of either our own possession of the good, or the means or even end of our satisfaction, at any time. To truly possess the good, then, it is simply not enough that we come to understand things about ourselves, about the world, or even about the good; it is equally important that we live in a context in which our knowledge can be easily and quickly replenished. The immortality mortals strive for, then, is not that of the gods, but one in which we are continually reminded of the nature of the good, and our deficiency in it.

Philosophers are those people who are not content simply to reproduce a deficient state of the good for themselves, nor continually to possess a deficient understanding of the good; they are those people who, as Socrates tells us in the *Republic*, desire to know the truth (*Rep.* 6.501d), and to replace their poverty with plenty in the ultimate hope of resembling the divine.[7] In this process we strive, not simply to remain deficiently good, but to attain knowledge of what is truly good, and perform acts of virtue based on this understanding. In the following discussion I will argue that Plato puts forward the model of the dual-role relationship, in which both parties assume the role of lover *and* beloved, as the means by which we are to attain immortality. That is, it provides for us the context in which we will be continually stimulated towards an increasingly adequate way of being, for both others and ourselves.

In his palinode in the *Phaedrus* Socrates explains that a dual-role relationship occurs between two people who share a similar nature, and so are able (after a certain period of time) to see in the other an image of themselves as they hope to be, i.e. as they are ideally.[8] But it would be wrong to think that this relationship is motivated merely by cold, rational self-interest, as it was for the non-lover and the beloved in Lysias' speech in the *Phaedrus* (230e-234c). We are not drawn to the other by our own knowledge of utility, but through a feeling of erotic desire. We are at-

## 7. The Dual-Role Philosophers

tracted to them because through them we catch a glimpse of the divine (*Phdr.* 253a). But this relationship is not for everyone. It cannot exist, Socrates implies, between people whose reaction to the beautiful is to satisfy their lust by seeking sexual pleasure (*Phdr.* 250e-251a). A more moderate and productive temperament is required, so the relationship exists between two people who 'devote their life to Love through philosophical discussions' (*Phdr.* 257b).[9] The lovers who enter this relationship are those who are inspired to create *logoi* (i.e. speeches and discussions), not just of the beautiful, but of virtue, the good, and also the divine (*Phdr.* 253b-c).[10]

But it is necessary for Plato to pull down the standard hierarchical relationship typical of the times in which he wrote, in which one member is active, and the other member is passive. Each party here will be an erotic lover of the good, and each will also be the beloved of the other, but *in neither* role will they be merely passive. David Halperin (1986, 68) argues that, 'the genius of Plato's analysis is that it eliminated passivity altogether: according to Socrates both members become active, desiring lovers; neither remains solely the passive object of desire'. As a lover each party will strive towards the good, and as a beloved each will have a duty to care for the other, and aid them in their own journey. As suggested by Andrea Nye (1990, 148), what Plato is detailing here is the attempt of two (or more) parties to create a social space in which each look upon both themselves and the other in a particular way; and in which each party has a particular role, and there are certain duties attached to these roles. It is important to note that this is not a relationship in which we are primarily concerned about our own self-interest; instead, it is fundamentally built around the idea of care. In the *Phaedrus* we are told that the good lover is one who 'makes every effort to draw [his beloved] into being totally like himself and the god to whom he is devoted' (*Phdr.* 253b-c). It is a relationship, Socrates tells us, which is free of envy, jealousy, mean-spiritedness, and single-minded self-interest.

Within this context the correct action of the lover is to give beautiful speeches in praise of their beloved as an image of the divine, and also virtue, the beautiful and the good in general (*Phdr.* 253a). The role of the beloved is to criticise and to probe these *logoi*, debate with the other, and in doing so to nurture their own understanding of these principles. It is not simply something that it is nice to do; it is indeed the correct, and expected, action of the beloved that they are impelled to do, not by the other, but through their own concern for the other. As Nye argues (1990, 143), in the best relationship we do not simply help the other insofar as it aids our self-interest, we are committed to developing an entire range of habits and practical skills to make the relationship as productive as it can be. And, because this will now be a reciprocal relationship, both parties are equally committed both to producing speeches, and to debating with the other (*Phdr.* 256a-b, 257b). I will now briefly explore the benefits of this relationship.

First, it is beneficial because it is built around the production of *logoi*, a process that in recent studies has been given a high priority.[11] In the course of our lives we at times become aware of our own ignorance, and we are sometimes faced with such overwhelming evidence that our understanding of the good is deficient that even a cretin will be led to change their mind. But to rely on these events alone is a risky business, as they may not, and usually do not, occur too often. The benefit of the dual-role relationship is that it provides lovers with a stable method of learning about what is good insofar as both parties are committed to challenging the other.[12] As Radcliffe Edmonds points out (2000, 271), the ideal of Socratic dialectic is one in which both parties question the other, a situation in which Socrates seldom finds himself in Plato's dialogues. Through such discussions we are able to utilise not only our own experience of the good but also the experiences that the other has had too, and so are given insight into a new and different way of looking at the world. In this way we are able to build upon the knowledge of the other, like two people adding more and more pieces to a block tower. But as with the block tower, the higher we build it the more unstable it becomes; as our ideas become more complex and abstract they become harder to conceptualise, and it is easier to forget the connections we have previously made. But the benefit of this relationship is that it puts us in the best position to build our understanding back up. I will now discuss why this is so.

In the *Laws* we are told that 'when one thing is put in motion by another, it is never thereby endowed with the power of independent self-movement' (*Laws* 10.898b), which is an important lesson for the lover to learn. No matter how much our beloved teaches us, we can only truly possess the good when we actively take it upon ourselves to strive for the divine. The second way in which this relationship is beneficial, then, is that we have before us a reminder of this necessity. The other is not simply a pretty face or a fine orator through whom we catch glimpses of the divine; here we identify the other as someone who is pursuing divinity, and so is an image, not just of the divine, but also of mortality: they are not someone who simply possesses the good, they are someone who, like us, must strive for it.[13] Thirdly, this relationship is beneficial to us because each party is the beloved of the other. Traditionally in Athens the beloved was supposed to be passive, staring straight ahead while the lover gratifies himself, gaining the benefit of any knowledge or social standing the lover bequeaths to them in exchange. But in this relationship the beloved's role is transformed into an active one based on care. In the *Timaeus* we are told that 'to care for anything is to provide for it the nourishment and the motions that are proper to it' (*Tim.* 90c-d, cf. *Laws* 10.903b). Edmonds (2000, 270) makes the claim that, in a dual-role relationship, as a beloved we act as a midwife to the other, helping them bring to term the beautiful speeches inside them. We have seen that this is done through engaging in dialectic, so as a beloved it is our role to engage in philosophical discussions with the other, and actively to probe and challenge their opinions. Halperin (1986, 75) argues:

> Because both the lover and the beloved, aroused alike by their visions of an identical beauty emanating (apparently) from each other and driven by the intensity of their separate desires to new labours of visionary creativity, make *simultaneous* and *reciprocal*, though *independent*, progress towards the contemplation of the forms.

Halperin is right to suggest that the progress that we make has to be considered our own (as we learnt from the *Laws*), but we must be careful not to think that the other plays a passive role in our attempt to possess the good life. I wish to make the stronger claim that only in the dual-role relationship, when one has assumed the responsibility of being an active lover and beloved, and only when we nourish the practices and habits that attend these roles, can we possibly hope to reach the highest mysteries of *eros*.[14] In this relationship, as Nye argues (1990, 143), we come to see that rigorous erotic development is something that can only be considered in a communal context, where the 'for the sake of' the self cannot be separated from the 'for the sake of' the other. As Socrates says in the *Phaedrus*, in this relationship the two partners become the best of friends, and will help each other even after their passion for each other has died (*Phdr.* 256C-d).

What Plato has outlined here is the basis for a community composed of two parties who are both committed to possessing the good life, and who develop this relationship, for their own sake, but equally for the sake of the other. Only in such a relationship can we really ever hope to possess the good and the divine in any meaningful way, as only in such a relationship can we avoid the two types of ignorance I outlined previously. With this discussion in place I now want to turn to two cases of Socrates' interactions with Alcibiades, and attempt to show that Socrates is trying to begin a dual-role relationship with Alcibiades.[15] I will start this examination with the *Alcibiades*, and I will then turn to the final speech in the *Symposium*.

### III

In the *Alcibiades* Socrates asks a question that, though offered merely as an example of something Alcibiades does not know, and is never directly addressed again, strikes at the heart of the intended relationship between the two. The question he asks is 'Do you know the means by which you will ascend to the heavens?' (*Alc.* 117b). This question may have more significance than at first appears, as Plato often uses the idea of 'ascent' as a metaphor for education, and the celestial sphere is painted as the realm of the gods, 'reality', and, importantly, the Good. Taken literally, the ascent would be beyond the bounds of even Alcibiades' ambitions, but taken metaphorically it would mirror the ultimate desire of the Platonic philosopher. Philosophic love must have that ultimate desire, and philosophy must lead to the means of ascent.

Several commentators have argued that Socrates, by the end of his relationship with Alcibiades, swapped roles from lover to beloved because he is either self-sufficient, or at least because he has ascended beyond mortal concerns.[16] But I will argue that this is not the case, and that Socrates' commitment to creating a dual-role relationship rather than a reverse-role one is hinted at when he says: 'let's discuss together how we can become as good as possible' (*Alc.* 124b-c). I shall argue that the reason why Socrates suggests this is because he thinks they are ultimately in the same condition. Plato's Socrates is not a godlike figure; he is, as several commentators have pointed out, a needy figure:[17] he is a lover of wisdom – a philosopher – and we love only what we lack (*Symp.* 200a). Socrates is attempting to bring Alcibiades into a dual-role relationship, not only because he cares for Alcibiades, and sees him as a promising (and beautiful) student, but for his own sake as well.[18] But though Socrates is intent on making Alcibiades a philosopher, he is aware that a mind untrained in rational discourse will not be able to leap immediately into discussion of abstract ideas like the Good, or divinity. So Socrates attempts to teach Alcibiades by appealing to his passions, specifically to his desire for fame and honour, and so to catch him up in the 'Bacchic frenzy of philosophy' (*Symp.* 218b). He offers three arguments to show how philosophy, represented by Socrates himself,[19] is 'worth the world' to Alcibiades (*Alc.* 105e).[20]

First, Socrates takes exception to Alcibiades measuring his own abilities as a leader against amateur statesmen; that is, the people at large who pretend to know the way a city is run (*Alc.* 119b-e). Obviously the professional statesman will have an easy victory over such people, so Socrates appeals to Alcibiades' competitive nature here, and taunts him for stooping to compete with the ignorant.[21] Alcibiades has set himself a ridiculously simple goal: to out-fox the witless, and to gain the love of the impressionable. But Socrates will show Alcibiades that he is deluding himself if he thinks he can be so easily satisfied. Socrates begins his argument by pointing out that Alcibiades is ignorant of what 'justice' is.[22] All good statesmen know about justice, so it is only natural that Alcibiades should desire knowledge of it. Socrates then goes through a progression of arguments to show that:

1. The just is admirable (115a).
2. The admirable is good (115e).
3. The good is advantageous (116c).
4. Therefore, the just is advantageous (116d).

To know the just is the same as understanding the good, so what Socrates is doing is showing Alcibiades the necessity of learning the good. But we

## 7. The Dual-Role Philosophers

can also see that Socrates does not end with equating the just with the good, but by equating it with advantage. If Alcibiades, ironically, cannot see that the Good is good in itself, then at least he can be pointed aright by showing him that knowing the good is to his benefit.

Secondly, Socrates attempts to turn Alcibiades' gaze inwards, so that he sees the need to attend to his own soul. A good statesman, Alcibiades agrees, is someone who teaches the citizens virtue, but Socrates tells us that we cannot teach something unless we know it ourselves. So in a famous (but textually problematic) passage concluding at 133c Socrates gives the following argument:

i. To be a good statesman we must understand ourselves (128e).
ii. To have self-knowledge we must understand our own souls (130e).
iii. To know our soul we must look at that region in which the soul is good (133b).
iv. The good part of the soul is divine (133c).
v. Therefore to be a good statesman we must have an awareness of the divine (133e).

In these first two arguments Socrates is trying to help Alcibiades revise the trajectory of his striving away from the masses and towards the heavens, and by doing so he hopes to halt the eternal cycle of desire and temporary satisfaction that hinders Alcibiades' ascent. But fixing one's gaze on the heavens does not help one ascend to them. Socrates also has to show Alcibiades the necessity of striving if he hopes to ascend himself.

It is here that Alcibiades shows his need for education most clearly. In the midst of their dialectic Alcibiades insists that Socrates do all the talking himself (*Alc.* 106b, 114e), rather than demanding of him to answer questions or make speeches. But at several points here Socrates explicitly shows Alcibiades that he is merely the questioner, and that it is Alcibiades who is giving the answers (*Alc.* 113a-c). In this way Socrates teaches Alcibiades an important lesson: that the advances in the conversation come from Alcibiades himself, and that learning is more efficient when one's beliefs are questioned, rather than listening to the speeches of others.[23] Coupled with this is Socrates' assertion that education comes with training, like that of an athlete (*Alc.* 119c). It is important to note that Socrates does not recommend merely listening to him, which is ultimately a passive process in which we acknowledge and understand the work of others, rather than coming to our own appreciation of the topic.[24] For an athlete training does not simply imply making oneself faster and stronger; in training the athlete develops certain techniques. It is not good enough that they become strong and win a single race; if they truly want to be the best they must commit themselves to a whole lifestyle. The training of lovers is similar, in that it is not good enough to know the good; rather, they must habituate themselves to a whole list of activities that allow them to remain knowledgeable. That is, Alcibiades must learn how to become an effective lover, and a caring beloved.

We can see how Socrates, through attempting to impress these three points on Alcibiades, hopes to turn him into a philosophical lover, as only from this point will he be able to enter into a dual-role relationship with Athens' future leader. I now wish to turn to the *Symposium* to show further evidence that Socrates is attempting to enter a dual-role relationship, and also to suggest why exactly Alcibiades failed to become a philosopher.

## IV

Socrates' commitment to creating a dual-role relationship is shown again in the *Symposium*, in a passage reminiscent of the one in the *Alcibiades*, in which the younger Alcibiades had told Socrates: 'Now it's your turn to consider what you think best for you and me,' to which Socrates had replied, 'You're right about that ... In the future, let's consider things together. We'll always do what seems the best to the two of us' (*Symp.* 219a-b). This passage is demonstrative of a dual-role relationship in a far stronger way, because here Socrates does not simply want to do what *is* best for them (which could involve one being ignorant of this good), but he instead suggests that they do what they *together* have come to decide is best for them. So, though it may seem clouded by Alcibiades' drunken ravings, I believe that this speech gives important insights into Socrates' relationship with Alcibiades. I now want to consider why Alcibiades failed to enter a dual-role relationship with Socrates.

From the very start we can see that some of Socrates' lessons have sunk in (though maybe not in the way that Socrates' would have liked). Alcibiades has been made to admit – and the point has obviously sunk in, considering Alcibiades' outburst – that '[his] life ... was not better than the most miserable slave's' (*Symp.* 215e-216a). Socrates first lesson was therefore understood (though we couldn't really say it was *learnt*, given the tone of the speech), as Alcibiades has been made aware that the good can come only through philosophy. We also see that he understood his second lesson, as he recounts that he was made to admit that his primary responsibility is to attend to his personal shortcomings (*Symp.* 216a),[25] that is, to his own soul. But it becomes obvious that Alcibiades was unable to *learn* these lessons because of his failure to appreciate the necessity of striving, and this is most obviously shown in his comparison of Socrates to a statue of Silenus (*Symp.* 215b).

First, the comparison is indicative of his misunderstanding of the human condition. Alcibiades sees Socrates as all poverty on the outside, but all wealth on the inside. As Mary Nichols argues (2004, 202), what Alcibiades misunderstands is that humans occupy an intermediary position between ignorance and wisdom, and because he does not understand the idea of such a middle ground the idea of striving is a foreign one. In

## 7. The Dual-Role Philosophers

discussion with Socrates, Alcibiades was able to see beautiful and godlike things (*Symp*. 216e-217a), but he couldn't understand that this new vision came about because of his own development, despite the lengths Socrates took to show him just this. He mistook the environment that allowed him to have this experience for the experience itself,[26] so he confused his own creation for something that Socrates had given, or at least shown, him. That is why he thinks it prudent to set up an exchange: Socrates' wisdom for the use of his body.

Alcibiades' second fault is that he equates possession with satisfaction. This is to be expected considering Alcibiades' ignorance of intermediary states, as satisfaction is an all-or-nothing feeling: one is either satisfied, or one is not. Socrates rejects this deal; first because it shows that, even though he has progressed to the point where he values wisdom, he still overvalues the beauty of bodies (as pointed out by Socrates in his remark that Alcibiades is attempting to exchange bronze for gold). Secondly, and most importantly, Socrates rejects the deal because he thinks that it is a bad deal for *Alcibiades*: possessing wisdom, after all, isn't as simple a cracking open a statue of Silenus.[27] Alcibiades' third fault, then, is that he sees no difference between wealth and resource: he does not see that a man with a truck full of gold is not really rich when his truck is dangling over a precipice. If Socrates simply told Alcibiades what he knew of the good, nothing helpful would come of this.[28] Indeed, this temporary satisfaction of his desire for wisdom would actually stifle Alcibiades' ascent, and it would ultimately leave him even more resentful of Socrates when this new knowledge passed away.

Because of these faults Alcibiades only succeeded in learning the negative lesson that he was ignorant of the good, while being unable to learn the positive lesson that wisdom only comes to those who strive for it. Because of this he assumed that Socrates was unjust,[29] in that Socrates showed him he was ignorant, dangled the promise of wisdom in front of him, and then abandoned him to his present state. So Socrates ultimately failed to kick-start Alcibiades' ascent to the heavens, and was therefore unable to enter a dual-role relationship with him.

### V

It is clear, I believe, that Socrates is a lover, and he has seen in Alcibiades a kindred soul whom he wants as a companion in his ascent towards the heavens. Though many of the claims I have made here are certainly contentious, and although I have not had time to expand on them in sufficient detail, I hope that the alternative reading of Plato's theory of love that I have suggested here seems at least plausible. To conclude this paper, however, I wish to shift the emphasis of the discussion slightly, and say a few words about how the conclusions I have advanced here may influence the dating of the *Alcibiades* I.

*Anthony Hooper*

*Prima facie*, this dialogue appears quite similar to Plato's earlier, *aporetic* dialogues, as here too Socrates steers the conversation predominantly by asking questions of his interlocutor, rather than by offering expansive epistemological, metaphysical and ethical doctrines, as he does in his Middle and Later period. In this paper, however, I have taken great pains to show the continuity in the doctrines advanced in the *Alcibiades* particularly with the *Symposium*, *Republic* and *Phaedrus*, but also with the *Theaetetus*, and even the *Laws*. Consider, for example, Socrates' assertions here about the necessity of looking to the health of our souls before we act in the world, and his claim that the soul is raised towards divinity in its attempt to know itself. Such a view appears to be uncannily similar to assertions Plato only starts making in his Middle writings, beginning with the *Phaedo*, then developing in the *Symposium*, and other dialogues from this period. Moreover, Socrates' assertion at 133a that our vision of our own soul is mediated through our experience of viewing the souls of others is a doctrine that Plato only begins advancing in a dialogue as late as the *Phaedrus*. Similar claims could be made about the role of education advanced in the *Alcibiades*, as well as Socrates' assertions as to how interlocutors in search of wisdom should relate to one another, and their relationship with these later dialogues. It will be sufficient to say, for now, that there are significant parallels in the advice that Socrates gives to his new-found friend in the *Alcibiades*, not only with the picture painted by Alcibiades of their later discussion in the *Symposium*, but also in Socrates' interactions with several interlocutors in the Middle and Late period dialogues. Such doctrinal similarities should not be ignored in our attempts to find a context for this dialogue.

## Notes

1. All quotes from Plato in this paper come from the respective translations in John Cooper's *Plato: Complete Works* (1997); minor modifications may have been made for specific purposes.

2. See Jonathan Lear 1998; Martha Nussbaum 1996; Dominic Scott 2000; Gregory Vlastos 1981.

3. Further evidence that Socrates believes that both he and Alcibiades share a similar state is found later in the dialogue (*Alc.* 127e) when Socrates claims that, if Alcibiades answers the questions posed to him, both of their states can be improved.

4. See especially David Halperin 1986; Radcliffe Edmonds 2000.

5. This term is intended to suggest something slightly different from the concept of *anterôs* or reciprocated love (*Phdr.* 255e), which very much subordinates the love of the beloved to that of the lover.

6. For an elaboration of how each speaker ends up contradicting themselves see Stanley Rosen 1999.

7. Plato writes in the *Theaetetus*: 'But it is not possible, Theodorus, that evil should be destroyed – for there must always be something opposed to the good; nor is it possible that it should have its seat in heaven. But it must inevitably haunt

## 7. The Dual-Role Philosophers

human life, and prowl about this earth. That is why man should make all haste to escape from earth to heaven; and escape means becoming as like God as possible; and a man becomes like God when he becomes just and pure, with understanding.' (176a-b).

8. In the *Phaedrus* Socrates argues that lovers are predisposed to be attracted to those who share their nature (*Phdr.* 252c-253c). Mythologically, Socrates' explanation for this is that the lover and their beloved, before their souls have become embodied, were in the chorus of the same god as they journeyed around the heavens. To de-mythologise this claim somewhat, Socrates seems to be suggesting that people are attracted to those who embody the same goods as they themselves value. Lovers of honour (the attendants of Ares) prize those who reflect honour most clearly, and the same is true for lovers of rule (the attendants of Hera), lovers of wisdom (the attendants of Zeus), and all other lovers. Because they share this nature, Socrates argues that the beautiful beloved acts as a living image of what the lover themselves would be ideally (cf. *Alc.* 133a-c).

9. This point is reiterated in the *Symposium* when Diotima talks of the man who 'instantly teems with ideas and arguments about virtue' (*Symp.* 209c) in the presence of beauty, and at the end of the ascent passage where we are told that throughout their ascent the lover has 'given birth to many gloriously beautiful ideas and theories in unstinting love of wisdom' (*Symp.* 210d).

10. Robert Zaslavsky 1981, 1, argues that 'philosophy is not simply truth achieved, but a way to achieve truth'. The philosopher is interested in creating *logoi*, to enter into philosophical discussions as a method of possessing the good through production of speeches. As Socrates says in the *Republic* (7.532d-e), it is dialectic that will take us to the end of our journey, and help us possess what we desire.

11. Most notably by Richard Hunter 2004; Charles Kahn 1999; C.D.C. Reeve 2009; Frisbee Sheffield 2006.

12. Martha Nussbaum 1996 also sees stability as one of the benefits of Socratic *eros*, though for her it is *eros* itself, rather than our ascent, which becomes less turbulent. *Eros*, however, is by definition a passionate desire, and as we attain the higher mysteries of *eros* it still pursues the good with as much vigour as it did beautiful bodies at the beginning of our ascent.

13. Andrea Nye 1990, 146, argues that because of this we are able to love someone, not for what they are, but for what they will become.

14. It should be noted that, particularly at the start of such a relationship, some amount of asymmetry between the lovers will be present. Were a philosopher successful in catching a prospective lover in the Bacchic frenzy of philosophy, the first party would have a clearer vision of the divine, and a greater ability to raise themselves higher. And even though the asymmetry between the lovers may lessen, it is inevitable that one lover will have raised themselves closer to wisdom, and become more proficient in the rites of philosophy, than the other.

15. In the *Republic* (1.338a-b) Thrasymachus accuses Socrates of wishing to learn from everyone but to teach no one. By arguing that Socrates is attempting to enter a dual role relationship with Alcibiades, I will attempt to show that Thrasymachus' claim is invalid.

16. See Bloom 2001; Belfiore 1980; Lear 1999.

17. See Allen 1991; Bury 1909; Gould 1963; Sheffield 2006.

18. It should also be noted that, at 105d-e, Socrates explicitly declares that he is hoping to exert great influence (specifically his divinely approved influence) over Alcibiades. However, Socrates' desire is not indicative of a cynical grab for power;

instead, it is for the real power that is power to achieve the good, as outlined in the *Gorgias* (466b-468e).

19. It is important to note, however, that Socrates has not transcended the need for philosophical striving here, as he too is pursuing wisdom.

20. Socrates himself sees no completely insurmountable tension between a political life and a philosophical life. Not only does Socrates famously suggest in the *Republic* that the best rulers are philosophers, in the *Alcibiades* Socrates tells Alcibiades: 'Get into training first, my dear friend, and learn what you need to know *before* you enter politics' (*Alc.* 132b, my emphasis). Socrates sees this as something to do *before* entering politics, rather than *instead* of entering politics. At several points in the dialogues, however, Socrates does suggest to his interlocutors that philosophy is a primarily private enterprise (*Ap.* 31c, *Prot.* 312a-b), and because philosophical training takes a lifetime, in suggesting that one trains in philosophy before entering politics, he is claiming that one ought to focus on private philosophical discussions, rather than a public, political life.

21. Alcibiades' love of competition is one of the characteristics that Plutarch focuses on in his biography of the Athenian general's career in his *Greek Lives*.

22. The relationship between knowledge of justice and the job of the statesman is shown in the *Republic* (1.332e) where Socrates argues that justice is best applied in the context of making war and building alliances.

23. Socrates claims (*Rep.* 1.330c) that we care most about what we produce ourselves, and so it is important to make Alcibiades aware that he himself is producing his understanding of the good so that he will care about this understanding by nurturing it, and replacing it if it passes away.

24. Socrates' criticism of education as studying is shown at *Republic* 7.517c where he says: 'Education isn't what some people declare it to be, namely, putting knowledge into souls that lack it, like putting sight into blind eyes'.

25. Though it is important to note that Alcibiades still sees a tension between philosophy and politics, as he believes that Socrates taught him that '[his] political career is a waste of time' (*Symp.* 216a).

26. Halperin 2005 argues the stronger point that Alcibiades confused the object of his desire, of which he is reminded in Socrates' presence, for Socrates himself. Either way the result is the same.

27. As Robert Scott Stewart 1989, 265, argues, 'it is Plato's view that the simple possession of truth without the knowledge of that truth has either a negative value or no value at all'.

28. R.E. Allen 1991, 104, noted that Socrates was critical of Alcibiades' love because he knew that it was not a productive *eros*, and so was not really love at all.

29. The idea that Socrates treated Alcibiades unjustly is forwarded by Roger Duncan 1977.

# 8

# Authenticity, Experiment or Development: The *Alcibiades I* on Virtue and Courage

*Eugenio Benitez*

### I. The strangeness of the *Alcibiades*

It has become customary to begin any discussion of the *Alcibiades* with a review of its puzzling features.[1] Any way you look at it, the *Alcibiades* is a strange dialogue. Stylistically it is peculiar, not only because it contains some unique terms,[2] but also because it contains similarities to early, middle and even late dialogues. These similarities are distributed to different parts of the dialogue, prompting some scholars to maintain that the *Alcibiades* was written piecemeal, perhaps by different authors (cf. Clark 1955). On most accounts of the *Alcibiades*, however, it resembles, or seems to have been written to resemble, an early Socratic dialogue.[3] But this too is odd, since stylometric studies tend to place it at least among the middle dialogues, and in many cases after the *Republic*.[4] A relatively late dating also fits with the conjectures of many scholars on the basis of anachronisms, allusions and other considerations.[5]

The *Alcibiades* is also peculiar as a drama. For one thing, it contains only two characters. In this it resembles the minority of Platonic dialogues, including only *Ion*, *Hippias Minor*, *Hippias Major* (if that dialogue is authentically Platonic), *Euthyphro*, *Crito*, and *Phaedrus*. Of these the *Crito* and *Phaedrus* are obviously exceptional, the former being historic, the latter being an intimate dialogue on an intimate theme.[6] All the rest, except for the *Alcibiades*, are comic dialogues, or have significant comic elements, resembling mime in structure and form, and on that basis might be thought to be fairly early works in the original genre of Socratic dialogue.[7] Perhaps the *Alcibiades* is to be treated, as Joyal suggests (2003, 2), as an example of the *special* genre of the 'Alcibiades dialogue', but if true, that would be clear evidence of its dramatic peculiarity. If, on the other hand, the author of the *Alcibiades* was attempting to write something that resembled more closely the *Ion*, the two *Hippias* dialogues, or the *Euthyphro*, it will be peculiar for ways in which it is distinctively *un*-Socratic, such as its apparent allusions to mature Platonic doctrines.

The dialectical development of the *Alcibiades* is also odd. As many have noticed, its arguments are exceedingly simple, neat, and self-contained.[8] This seems particularly true of the dialogue from its beginning up until

*Eugenio Benitez*

119a, where there is a machine-like production of eight separate dialectical arguments of similar length and complexity. Indeed, this mechanical quality led Taylor to describe the *Alcibiades* as an excellent manual, and for that very reason not by Plato.[9] I like to think this simplicity hides much greater depth and subtlety of purpose, but in so thinking I may be, like Iamblichus, according the dialogue too much respect.[10]

Finally, one might say that the *Alcibiades* is doctrinally odd. While resembling a Socratic dialogue in many ways, it seems to go beyond them in suggesting a view about the self itself,[11] and a view about parts of the soul,[12] that go beyond the ethics of Socratic dialogues, which have little or no metaphysical commitment and treat the soul as simple and indivisible.

Faced with such peculiarity, it is not surprising that much of the extant scholarly literature on the *Alcibiades* concerns the question of authenticity. Despite its Neoplatonic credentials,[13] doubts were sure to arise. Even had Schleiermacher and subsequent athetisers not added the *Alcibiades* to their list of *spuria*, the most recent stylometric tests would have provoked scepticism (See, e.g., Brandwood 1990). Nevertheless, so long as its fate in the Platonic corpus remains nicely balanced, the *Alcibiades* I provides us with some interesting opportunities. For the moment, we are free to investigate what it means for our interpretation of Plato in the light of the authenticity or otherwise of the *Alcibiades*.[14]

## II. The available options

What are the options that such an investigation might lead to? First, we might find that significant, established features of our interpretation of Plato would be threatened by the inclusion of the *Alcibiades* among the genuine works. One option, if that were the case, would be to reject it on the grounds of general inconsistency with Plato. Nicholas Smith has recently explored this option. Smith asserts that the past century of scholarship has produced a 'secure understanding' about a number of issues in Plato's 'canonical dialogues'.[15] He discusses nine ways in which the *Alcibiades* threatens the secure understanding.[16] Briefly, Smith maintains that in the *Alcibiades* (but not elsewhere) Socrates:

(a) puts his *daimonion* to the test,
(b) calls his *daimonion* [a] god (*ho theos*),
(c) accepts non-committal answers from his interlocutor,
(d) fails to distinguish between public and private persuasion,
(e) assumes that death is an evil,
(f) maintains that one who recognises his own ignorance will not err,
(g) maintains that virtue is teachable,
(h) acknowledges the existence of a personal self, and
(i) partitions the soul.

## 8. Authenticity, Experiment or Development

If the *Alcibiades* threatens the secure understanding of Plato on all these matters, that may be because it is the work of an 'imitator',[17] or because it is, to use Smith's unfortunate terms, a 'clumsy forgery' or a 'fake'.[18] It is not clear to me that any of these terms are helpful. They suggest that the author, whoever it may be, simply wants to mimic Plato's style and approach to philosophy, or even intentionally pass off the work as genuine. But such an imitator, forger or faker would be careful to avoid the kind of sore-thumb strangeness the *Alcibiades* so plainly exhibits. Had the dialogue exhibited only the facile dialectic and thinly drawn characters that Taylor (1926, 522) described when he judged against its authenticity, it might be an imitation, forgery or fake. As it is, whoever wrote the *Alcibiades* seems to have a significant knowledge of Platonic philosophy and its development from Socratic philosophy. In that case, the way in which the *Alcibiades* threatens the secure understanding of Plato is, on the face of it, just as strange for an imitator, forger or faker as it is for Plato. Of course, even though that will mean that the same strange things need to be explained in each case, the content of the explanation may differ if the author is supposed to be Plato or, say, an Academic writer. But given that a considerable amount of explanation is needed either way, we might as well first seek what sort of explanation is available if Plato is the author, and turn to the other explanatory task only if we fail.

A second option, one that is consistent with trying to explain, or in this case explain away, the lack of fit of the *Alcibiades* with Plato's other dialogues, is to treat it as singular; as an experiment of sorts. This is not as unlikely as it might at first appear. Other dialogues, such as the *Menexenus* and the *Cratylus*, have been difficult for Plato scholars to place because of their unique topics and structure. One objection to this option involves pointing out that the *Alcibiades*, unlike the *Menexenus* and *Cratylus*, overlaps with many of the philosophical themes of other Socratic dialogues. Its singularity, if you want to call it that, results from its distinctiveness on familiar topics, rather than distinctiveness full stop. Although I think this objection sufficient to recommend other options first, I don't think it is sufficient to defeat the notion of the *Alcibiades* as experiment. A useful comparison for sustaining the experiment option might be made with the *Philebus*. There we have a dialogue on familiar Platonic themes (the good life), which raises familiar Platonic problems (one and many, participation, predication), and which addresses these themes and problems by means of a metaphysical hypothesis unparalleled in the dialogues, the so-called 'fourfold classification'[19] of all things into limited, unlimited, mixed, and cause (23b-31b). Scholars have tried, without any sign of consensus, to fit this metaphysics to that of other dialogues,[20] or to unwritten doctrines of Plato.[21] Indeed, one has gone so far as to suggest that the metaphysical section of the *Philebus* is developed experimentally, without any consideration of doctrine, simply for the purpose of furthering the ethical discussion.[22] If the *Philebus* could directly contradict the doctrine of other Platonic dialogues merely for the sake of the experimental development of an ethical view, then surely the *Alcibiades* could do the same. In fact, this option might best explain the curious passage about the self itself. Nevertheless, I think the experiment option is not the most attractive one.

In this paper I want to consider a third option for explaining the peculiar features of the *Alcibiades*, namely that the dialogue belongs to a transitional period in Plato's career. I should point out that I am not in general an advocate of the developmental hypothesis about Plato's thought. Nor am I committed to arguing for the authenticity of the *Alcibiades*. Nevertheless, it seems to me that certain features of doctrine in the *Alcibiades* can be reasonably well explained by means of a developmental hypothesis, and I hope that by laying out this option I may at least add to a more careful consideration of the issues that matter about the dialogue. To clarify how, I first want to return to the inconsistencies discussed by Nicholas Smith.

Smith assumes that if the *Alcibiades* is authentic, then it should be consistent with the 'canonical dialogues' of Plato. What he means by a 'canonical dialogue' seems simply to be a dialogue whose authenticity has never been seriously questioned. The dialogues Smith uses for comparison in discussing his nine inconsistencies, however, include only: *Euthyphro, Apology, Republic I, Hippias Minor, Protagoras, Gorgias, Meno, Symposium,* and *Phaedrus*. Several comments need to be made about this selective comparison set, for it is obvious that these are not the only canonical dialogues, and different comparisons could be made to show different things.

The first point that needs to be noted is that, had the full set of canonical works been considered, all sorts of remarkable inconsistencies between them would appear, many of which are as singular as the inconsistencies with the *Alcibiades*. On some points of comparison we would find only one dialogue that threatens an otherwise secure interpretation. A good example is Socrates' espousal of hedonism in the *Protagoras* (351cff.), which is unparalleled in the dialogues of Plato. On this point of comparison, the degree of inconsistency of the *Protagoras* is as great as anything in the *Alcibiades*. Since the *Protagoras* is a canonical work, however, other explanations must be adduced. Thus, the appearance of an inconsistency with an otherwise secure interpretation is by itself no indicator of inauthenticity. But what about *nine* inconsistencies? Wouldn't that be too many? That brings me to the second point.

Had Smith considered all the canonical works, he might have found that the *Alcibiades* is not so singular as it appears. Other dialogues are inconsistent with the comparison set on the same points that the *Alcibiades* is. For example, the *Crito* appears to be inconsistent with (b) and quite possibly (a) as well. At the very end of the *Crito*, after Socrates describes a voice he hears ringing in his ears, dissuading him from fleeing

## 8. Authenticity, Experiment or Development

death (and here compare *Apology* 40a-c), he says he should stay and suffer the death penalty, 'since god points the way' (*epeidê tautêi ho theos*, 54e1-2). It seems plausible that the god Socrates refers to is his *daimonion*.[23] Yet if so, then that contradicts (b), and the fact that he tests the decision to stay, in his deliberations with Crito, seems to contradict (a) as well. This example is debatable, of course, but it opens a can of worms on the 'secure interpretation' of Plato, which might eat away at all nine inconsistencies in the same manner.

There is a third, more serious, issue with the selective comparison set. It is evident in regard to the ninth inconsistency (i), about partitioning the soul, that the *Alcibiades* is not at all inconsistent with canonical works generally; at most it is inconsistent with canonical works written, say, before the *Republic*. Quite obviously Socrates 'partitions the soul' in the *Republic* and *Phaedrus* and other canonical dialogues. Here we begin to see that, although Smith's comparison set includes middle dialogues, his points of comparison are thoroughly Socratic; he is testing the credentials of the *Alcibiades* as an early Socratic dialogue.

Here is where I see an opening for the third interpretive option. Why should we make the assumption that an authentic *Alcibiades* should be like Plato's *early* Socratic dialogues? The stylometric measures are all against placing it among the early group. And whatever its date of composition, its differences from early Socratic dialogues give us reason to suspect that the author is attempting something different. Moreover, we know that Plato *did* write 'Socratic' dialogues that are in many ways remarkably un-Socratic. It was precisely the un-Socratic elements of the middle dialogues that led to the developmental hypothesis in the first place. Plato even wrote *later* Socratic dialogues, which are in some ways like but in other ways very much unlike the early dialogues – the *Theaetetus* and the *Philebus*, for example. All these dialogues are more sophisticated than the *Alcibiades*, and the late ones show an engagement with the history of philosophy and with the Academy that the *Alcibiades* does not.[24] Nevertheless, despite the apparently simple drama of the *Alcibiades*, there is evidence of doctrinal sophistication, including, perhaps, reference to the Forms and a tripartite soul. Why not, then, consider the possibility that the *Alcibiades* is a transitional dialogue, like the *Protagoras*, *Gorgias*, and *Meno*, all of which contain singular inconsistencies with early Socratic dialogues?[25]

I want to examine the possibility of transitional development as an explanation for some of the overall peculiarity of the *Alcibiades*. It is not possible to provide a thorough examination on all the points of comparison here, so I will focus on one specific issue, namely the account of courage. This focus is related to Smith's point (e) above, about whether death is an evil. As he says (2004, 104):

> [O]ne of the most notorious views Plato gives to Socrates concerns the unity of the virtues, from which it follows that if one is courageous, for example,

he will also be pious, just, temperate and wise. But if that is true, then precisely because the courageous man would be in every way the virtuous man, death would surely be no harm to him ...

I think there is evidence that the account of courage in the *Alcibiades* shows signs of transition from the Socratic view that all virtue is one thing to the later Platonic view that the virtues are distinct from each other, and that courage is particularly different. The account of courage in the *Alcibiades* seems to fit well with a developmental account of virtue in Plato. I will begin by outlining briefly the developmental account.[26] After that I hope to show that the position of the *Alcibiades* on courage looks away from Socratic views, towards more Platonic ones. If the *Alcibiades* fits well enough on this point, then perhaps it would do so on the others. In that case, the hypothesis that the *Alcibiades* is a transitional dialogue ought to be investigated before declaring it spurious on grounds of inconsistency with canonical works.

## III. Development in Plato's account of virtue

As we have already noted, one of the most striking assertions to be found in Plato's early dialogues is the assertion of the unity of virtue, or more specifically, the claim that all the parts of virtue are to be understood as forms of knowledge. In connection with this assertion we find in the early dialogues the intellectualist idea that what it is to be brave or temperate or just is simply the possession of a certain kind of knowledge. There are no emotional or non-cognitive elements in virtue. In the *Charmides*, for example, it is suggested that temperance is 'doing one's own' (161b6) and this is then interpreted as 'knowing oneself' (164e7). In the *Laches* an initial non-cognitive account of courage is rejected in favour of one that describes it as 'wise endurance' (192d) and 'knowledge of the proper objects of fear and confidence' (199d-e). As Irwin has remarked (1995, 40), in neither the *Charmides* nor the *Laches* does anyone dispute the identification of courage or temperance with 'some kind of knowledge'.

It is not until the *Protagoras*, however, that the unity of virtue thesis is explicitly stated and defended. Of particular interest for our purposes is the discussion near the end of the dialogue, where Protagoras admits that four of the virtues (justice, piety, wisdom and temperance) seem to be pretty much the same, but courage and wisdom are distinct. He says:

> My view is that all these are parts of virtue, and that four of them resemble each other fairly closely, but courage is very different from all the rest. The proof of what I say is that you can find many men who are quite unjust, unholy, intemperate, and ignorant, yet outstandingly courageous. (349d-e, tr. Guthrie)

It is tempting to think that Protagoras' resistance on this point shows that

## 8. Authenticity, Experiment or Development

courage is the most difficult of the cardinal virtues to fit into the unity thesis. Nevertheless, Socrates denies Protagoras' claim and spends the rest of the dialogue providing a sophisticated argument to show how *all* the parts of virtue, including courage, are knowledge of the same kind, namely knowledge of the measure of pleasure and pain.

If courage was the last and most difficult virtue to assimilate with the others, in the middle dialogues it is soon separated from them. In the *Republic* Socrates explicitly distinguishes the soul into parts and treats separate virtues as related in different ways to different parts of the soul. Wisdom is specifically associated with the rational part. Courage is specifically associated with the spirited part, and temperance is specifically associated with the appetitive part. Justice turns out to be a result of a specific relation and specific action of each of the parts. In Irwin's view, the *Republic* 'presents a sharp and radical criticism' of the intellectualism of the early dialogues, for now 'elementary moral education ... is intended to fix the right non-cognitive responses in people... The pleasures and pains of young people are to be formed so that they go in the direction reason will approve when it comes along' (Irwin 1995, 223; cf. *Rep.* IV. 401-2).

In particular there seems to have been a change in the understanding of courage. In the *Republic*, courage 'is no longer identified with knowledge of good and evil; instead it is identified with a condition of the spirited part, which holds tenaciously ... to the right beliefs about what should be done' (Irwin 1995, 224; cf. *Rep.* IV.429b). Thus, the *Republic* treats courage non-cognitively, in a way that implies it must be non-identical to the other virtues.

This does not imply that courage is no virtue at all. Indeed, the *Republic* still implies that courage is tied to the other virtues, since it (along with temperance and wisdom) is necessary for justice in the soul.[27] Nevertheless, the change to the account of courage in the *Republic* allows us to envisage a secondary, non-cognitive form of virtue. I do not mean the 'slavish' virtue described in *Phaedo* 68c-69e, which is adopted by people only for the sake of its consequences, but the 'demotic' or 'popular' virtue of the well-trained auxiliaries of *Kallipolis*. The auxiliaries don't choose virtue simply for its consequences; virtue makes a difference to them for its own sake. They just don't fully understand why. From the *Meno* onwards, Plato seems to think that so long as a person has the right beliefs, his actions may be no less virtuous (98b-d). Thus, courage is possible without wisdom.

In the late dialogues we find even stronger and more explicit separation of the virtues than we see in *Republic*. In the *Statesman*, for example, the Eleatic Stranger turns a critical eye to the claim that 'all the parts of virtue are dear to each other' (*panta ... allêlois ta ge tês aretês moira ... philia*, 306b13-c1). To illustrate the 'natural difference' (*diaphoran tois sungenesin*, 306c5) between the virtues, the Stranger picks courage (*andreia*, 306a12ff.) and temperance (*sôphrosunê*, 306b3ff.). He explicitly describes these two virtues not only as other (*heteron*, 306b3), but as hateful (*ech-*

*thran*, 306b10) and opposite (*enantian*, 306b10) to one another. Moreover, people who have one of these virtues tend *not* to have the other. Temperate people tend to be cowardly, they move to action too slowly and without enough spirit; courageous people, on the other hand, tend to be intemperate, and are moved too quickly and with too much emotion (308a-b).

Shortly after this passage, of course, the Stranger points out that what good character requires most is a community and an upbringing that weaves together the natural dispositions of courage and temperance (309b). In that case, it may be that we have to distinguish natural dispositions to virtue from the finished article. But the language of the *Statesman* in 306-7 strongly suggests that Plato is now at least willing to acquiesce in conventional usage, and allow the terms 'courage' and 'temperance' a wider range than he previously had. It is hard to imagine the Socrates of the *Laches* or *Protagoras* ever allowing the assertion that courage and temperance are opposites to stand.

In the *Laws* as well the virtues are not treated as one. In particular, courage is separated from the rest of virtue and assigned a lesser status. In Book I the Athenian Stranger criticises the Spartans for zealously pursuing courage to the exclusion of other virtues. He says that courage is of all the four cardinal virtues the least in importance (630c-631a).

The development of Plato's views about the unity of virtue and particularly the relation of courage to the other virtues, then, provides us with a point of comparison for the *Alcibiades*. What is the perspective on virtue there? Does it resemble the early Socratic dialogues, or does it show the more sophisticated view about the relation of different virtues to different parts of the soul found in the *Republic*? I think the position of the *Alcibiades* on virtue and on courage sits easily in between the early and the late dialogues, with some distinct affinities for the position in the *Republic*. Let us examine the evidence.

## IV. Virtue and courage in the *Alcibiades*

I will first survey the general account of virtue in the *Alcibiades*, overlooking, for the moment, what it has to say about courage. It will be clear from this survey why the *Alcibiades* is so often treated as (an imitation of) an early Socratic dialogue. From the beginning and for nearly half its length (103-18), the overall emphasis of its arguments is the absolute necessity of knowledge for the excellent use of power. First, we discover that obtaining one's ends requires understanding what one really wants (103a-106b).[28] Then Socrates suggests that understanding is necessary in order to communicate well about anything (106b-107c). He then exploits analogies with the technical arts (*technai*) – shipbuilding, medicine, strategy, and music – to show that expertise and expert knowledge are required for excellence (*aretê*) of all sorts (107c-108d), and particularly for justice (108d-112d). From this point on, the focus is gradually directed to the

## 8. Authenticity, Experiment or Development

answerer himself (112e-113c), namely Alcibiades, with the aim of showing him that he does not understand the real relation between advantage and justice, because he does not really know what he thinks he knows (113c-118c). In general the point of view about virtue, justice and knowledge expressed throughout the first half of the dialogue is Socratic. At the end of the dialogue, too, we find characteristically Socratic identifications: (a) the identification of temperance with self-knowledge (131b), (b) the identification of self-knowledge with wisdom (133c) and (c) the identification of wisdom with justice (134c).

All these things give the *Alcibiades* its unmistakable Socratic flavour.[29] But what, then, of the discussions of war and courage? I think that here there is a considerable difference from the early Socratic dialogues. Remarkably, when it comes to discussion of warfare, Socrates treats all of the cognitive issues – deliberations about with whom to go to war (107d4-5), when to go to war (107e2-3), and the conduct of war (108d10) – under the heading of justice, rather than courage. Clearly this is counterintuitive. When Socrates asks Alcibiades for the virtue associated with all of these cognitive issues, Alcibiades cannot answer. He has to be coaxed in the direction of justice, and even then it is Socrates who finally says:

> What, then, is that 'better', about which I asked, in going to war or not going to war with those against whom we ought or ought not, and when we ought or ought not to go to war? Is it not identical with justice? (109c9-11, tr. Jowett)

It seems very odd that courage is not mentioned at all in this discussion. In the *Laches*, when Nicias defined courage as knowledge of the fearful and hopeful (196d1-2, 199a10-b1), Socrates showed that his definition implied knowledge of what should be feared and what should not, and how to conduct himself accordingly (199e).[30] If Plato still considered courage to be a form of knowledge, one would expect it to be discussed in all these contexts of martial deliberation in the *Alcibiades*. It is not until 115b, however, that Socrates even mentions courage. There he says that 'the attempt to save those whom we ought to save ... is courage' (*tên epicheirêsin tou sôsai hous edei, touto d' estin andreia*, 115b6-7). Note that here there is no necessity of knowledge; rather, courage is implied simply in right action in wartime.

Interestingly, Socrates goes on to speak in a restricted way about *this* courage, referring only to the willingness to save whom we ought to save in battle (*kata tên andreian ... kalon einai tên boêtheian*, 115c7). Again, this is strikingly different from the *Laches*, in which Socrates refused to treat brave behaviour in war as distinct from brave behaviour in the face of poverty, disease, or other unfortunate circumstances (*Laches* 191c-e). It is not so different, however, from what we would expect if there were a demotic form of courage, to which citizens could be habituated, without fully understanding the reasons for their actions, as in the *Republic* and the *Laws*. Such courage would be a restricted and dependent good. Valuable though it may be, it would not be the greatest good or the most valuable thing.

The dialectic that ensues is designed to show Alcibiades precisely this. For *he* thinks that courage is the greatest good (115e6-7), but he does not fully understand either courage or the rest of virtue. The exchanges on this point are worth quoting in full:

> Soc.: And the greatest goods you would be most ready to choose, and would least like to be deprived of them?
> Alc.: Certainly.
> Soc.: What would you say of courage? At what price would you be willing to be deprived of courage?
> Alc.: I would rather die than be a coward.
> Soc.: Then you think that cowardice is the worst of evils?
> Alc.: I do.
> Soc.: As bad as death, I suppose?
> Alc.: Yes.
> Soc.: And life and courage are the extreme opposites of death and cowardice?
> Alc.: Yes.
> Soc.: And they are what you would most desire to have, and their opposites you would least desire?
> Alc.: Yes.
> Soc.: Is this because you think life and courage the best, and death and cowardice the worst?
> Alc.: It is.
> Soc.: Then you number courage among the chief goods, and death among the chief evils?
> Alc.: Yes.
> Soc.: And you termed the rescue of a friend in battle honourable, because courage, which is a good, is shown in the action?
> Alc.: I did.
> Soc.: But evil because death ensues, which is an evil?
> Alc.: Yes.
> Soc.: Then you ought to describe any such action as follows: If you call it evil in respect of the evil which is the result, you ought also to call it good in respect of the good which is the result?
> Alc.: Yes.
> Soc.: Is it then honourable in so far as it is good, and dishonourable in so far as it is evil?
> Alc.: Yes.
> Soc.: Then when you say that coming to the help of a friend in battle is honourable and yet evil, that is equivalent to saying that it is good and yet evil. (115d1-116a8, tr. Jowett)

Notice that, *pace* Smith, Socrates does not assume that death is an evil. The entire argument is *ad hominem*, based upon Alcibiades' assertions and aimed at bringing him face to face with contradiction. The reason why

## 8. Authenticity, Experiment or Development

Alcibiades is contradicted is because he does not know how to measure the value of things, and cannot see that neither is courage an unqualified good, nor is death an unqualified evil.

It is instructive to compare this argument with the final argument about the unity of virtue in the *Protagoras*. For Alcibiades is having difficulty in measuring one good (courage) against another (life), since the one good may involve the sacrifice of the other. Socrates emphasises the apparent conflict – 'when you say that coming to the help of a friend in battle is honourable and yet evil, that is equivalent to saying that it is good and yet evil' (116a6-8) – and points out that Alcibiades himself is conflicted (117a8-11). In just the same way the *Protagoras* emphasises the conflict of *akrasia*:

> You say that a man often recognises evil actions as evil, yet commits them, under no compulsion, because he is led on and distracted by pleasure, and on the other hand that, recognising the good, he refrains from following it because he is overcome by the pleasures of the moment. The absurdity of this will become evident if we stop using all these names together – pleasant, painful, good, and evil – and since they have turned out to be only two, call them by only two names – first of all good and evil, and only at a different stage pleasure and pain. Having agreed on this, suppose we now say that a man does evil though he recognises it as evil. Why? Because he is overcome. By what? We can no longer say by pleasure, because it has changed its name to good. Overcome, we say. By what, we are asked. By the good, I suppose we shall say. I fear that if our questioner is ill-mannered, he will laugh and retort, What ridiculous nonsense, for a man to do evil, knowing it is evil and that he ought not to do it, because he is overcome by good. (355a6-355d3, tr. Guthrie)

In the *Protagoras*, however, this conflict is to be resolved by means of the art of *measurement*. It is intriguing what happens in the *Alcibiades*. Alcibiades' conflict over the choice of courage or life is not immediately resolved. After the discussion of living honourably and well, there is a long interlude emphasising the deplorable extent of Alcibiades' ignorance. After that, however, the dialogue returns to the question of what overcomes conflict, and what produces concord and agreement. Here we see that the conflict within Alcibiades is not to be resolved so simply as in the *Protagoras*, by an art of measurement, but analogously, by a geometrically proportionate rule. At 126c Socrates compares what produces agreement in cities with what produces agreement about numbers. In the case of numbers it is the art of measurement. 'But what is the *other* agreement of which you speak,' Socrates asks at 126d8-10, 'and about what? What art can give *that* agreement? And does that which gives it to the state give it also to the individual, so as to make him *consistent with himself* and with another?' ('I suppose so,' answers Alcibiades). The inclusion of the phrase 'consistent with himself' is important to us here, since the conflict experienced by Alcibiades over the choice of courage or life was not resolved. The agreement and the art that produces it here cannot be arithmetical, because the parties to be reconciled are not commensurate, as the discussion of differences between men and women, men's business and women's business, is supposed to show.[31] But it can be proportional, when each of the parties 'does its own work', and the art that is concerned with this proportional concord, is justice.

Thus, justice is a superior virtue to courage; it is in fact the greatest good, and ignorance of it the greatest evil that can befall a man. Only justice can bring about the reconciliation of incommensurate things, through proportionality rather than strict rationality. Only justice can resolve the conflict Alcibiades feels in his soul between the value of courage and the value of life. If this is correct, however, then the account of virtue and courage in the *Alcibiades* has shifted significantly away from the unity of the virtues in early Socratic dialogues, away from the unifying art of measurement in the *Protagoras*, and towards the more complex view associated with the theory of a tripartite soul composed of incommensurate parts in *Republic* IV.

## V. Conclusion

I think I have shown that the *Alcibiades* implies a different position about the unity of virtue, and a different understanding of what courage is than is found in the early Socratic dialogues. It would be misleading, however, to say that the *Alcibiades* directly contradicts the secure interpretation of Plato on these issues. On the contrary, the perspective on virtue in the *Alcibiades* puts it in between Socratic and Platonic dialogues. It shows evidence of a development in which courage is regarded as still a virtue, but as a non-cognitive one. And it shows evidence of treating justice as the supreme virtue, with courage dependent on justice for its proper exercise. All of this is consistent with the view about courage and the tripartite soul found in the *Republic*.

What would be the point of an imitator, perhaps one writing from a later vantage point around the time of Plato's death or somewhat after, making a dialogue that looked transitional like this? It would seem most peculiar of all to blend some Socratic with some Platonic features about virtue, when the more fully developed account of virtue was available. Perhaps the stylometric tests will eventually show us that the *Alcibiades* was not written by Plato, but on the basis of the available doctrinal evidence, I still see no good reason to deem it spurious.

## Notes

1. See Smith 2004, 93. See also the introduction in Denyer 2001. The recent tradition of pointing out peculiarities of the *Alcibiades* (as opposed to just features that indicate inauthenticity, like anachronisms or stylistic anomalies) may be traced to Friedländer 1964, 11, who calls the *Alc.* 'the strangest case.' Smith 2004, 94 n.6, provides a good review of the literature since that time.

## 8. Authenticity, Experiment or Development

2. See, for example, the term *enoptron* ('mirror'; 133c9,14), which occurs in no other dialogue of Plato, yet appears as a key term in the most original, enduring and distinctive analogy of the *Alc.*, that between the mirror of the eye (the pupil) and the mirror of the soul (the intellect). *Katoptron* is the only term used for mirror (elsewhere) in Plato; it also occurs in the *Alc.* at 132e2, 133a2, c8. Or again, see the unparalleled use of *ho theos* in the *Alc.*, referring to Socrates' divine sign, or the peculiar (and disputed) phrase *auto t'auto*, 129b1.

3. Smith 2004, 105 says: 'Those who regard it as authentic almost universally regard the *Alcibiades* I as an early Platonic dialogue.'

4. See Ledger 1989, 144; Nails 1994, 62-7.

5. See the introductory discussion in Denyer 2001, especially 'the date and motive of the *Alcibiades*' (11-14), and also 'the authenticity of the *Alcibiades*' (14-26).

6. The *Alcibiades* is also an intimate dialogue on an intimate theme, but there is no space to consider a comparison with the *Phaedrus* on these grounds here.

7. The appearance of dialogues with more characters and more complex conversation seems (plausibly) to have been a development.

8. See Jowett 1982, vol. 2, 462, who speaks of the 'thin and superficial' treatment of character in the *Alc.*, and the 'few not very conclusive words of Socrates'. Schleiermacher also spoke about the dispersed simple arguments of the *Alc.* (cited in Denyer 2001, 14-15).

9. Taylor 1926, 522 describes the *Alcibiades* as an 'unskilled' and 'colourless' textbook, adding that because Plato was averse to writing manuals, it probably was not written by him.

10. Iamblichus says that the *Alcibiades* contains all the Platonic wisdom 'like a seed' (Dillon 1973, 72). But it is possible in general, and common in later Neoplatonism, to see the seeds of things in a work when they are not really there at all.

11. See *auto t'auto*, 129b1, and compare R.E. Allen's comment (1962, 187-90). Allen establishes that the phrase is substantive, not pronominal, but his claim that the phrase means 'the self itself' has been doubted. Goldin 1993, 5-19, claims to have undermined Allen's view, but I find his argument (essentially that the self referred to must be Alcibiades' self) unconvincing. Moreover, even if the self referred to is Alcibiades' self, sometimes a character in a Platonic dialogue himself represents, or stands for, a form. Plausibly, Lysis stands for the *prôton philon* of the *Lys.*, Charmides for the form of temperance in the *Charm.*, Laches for the form of courage in the *La.*, and so on (cf. Teloh 1986, 25-38).

12. See 133b, and comment by Smith 2004, 105.

13. The authenticity of the *Alc.* was never doubted in antiquity. This, by itself, is no more significant than the fact that in antiquity neither the *Hipparchus* (dubious: see either Aelian *VH* 8.2 or Athen. 11.506c) nor the *Theages* (both now considered spurious) were doubted. But the *Alc.* enjoyed greater authority than these. No less a figure than Proclus wrote a commentary on it (see Westerink 1954), and it became the starting point for study of Plato (see Diogenes Laertius 3.62; Albinus, *Intr.* 149.35-7; and see the comments by D'Ancona 2005, 13-14).

14. What it means for our interpretation of Plato is the important issue, as Smith, Denyer and Joyal have pointed out, not the authenticity or inauthenticity per se. See Smith 2004, 95-6; Denyer 2001, 25-6; and Joyal 2003, 4-5. Of these, Smith's discussion is by far the most thorough.

15. Smith 2004: 'secure understanding' (96); 'canonical dialogues' (104, 106).

16. See Smith 2004, 100-5. Many of these apparent incongruities require further discussion. My discussion here touches on (e) since that is related to Plato's views about the unity of virtue and especially the status of courage.

*Eugenio Benitez*

17. See Denyer 2001, who uses 'imitator' throughout his introduction.

18. See Smith 2004, 97. It should be clear that Smith uses the terms 'forgery' and 'fake' in reference to spurious Platonic dialogues in general, not to the *Alc.* in particular. But Smith does not go out of his way to separate the *Alc.*, which he does believe to be spurious (96 n. 8, 100 n. 12), from the other *spuria* in terms of the intention of the author. My own view is that even the *spuria* in general should not be characterised as forgeries or fakes, but my objections here pertain only to characterising the *Alc.* in that way.

19. The phrase is Hackforth's (1945, 37).

20. See Benitez 1989 for a discussion of various interpretations.

21. See Sayre 1983 for a discussion of the view that the *Phlb.* represents esoteric Platonism.

22. See Shiner 1974. Shiner explains the Four-Fold Classification as a misdirected meta-ethical argument (48). In his view, Plato's only aim in *Phlb.*23b-31b is to offer a general explanation of the origin of good and evil. But because Plato does not distinguish between moral and metaphysical goodness he mistakenly casts the argument in the form of a metaphysical theory. The four-fold classification, on this view, is designed to serve only a limited end, one that is more appropriately described as meta-ethical than as metaphysical. Others who appear to share this view include Davis 1979 and Hackforth 1945, 50, who warns 'if the metaphysical doctrine thus lacks completeness, we should again remember that it is not introduced for its own sake, but for an ethical purpose'.

23. If it were any other god who pointed the way to Socrates in particular matters, then that in itself would require as much explanation as the use of *ho theos* in the *Alc.*

24. For discussion of how the later dialogues, including in particular the *Tht.* and *Phlb.*, reveal a new-found concern in Plato (and the Academy) over the work of Presocratic philosophers, see McCabe 2000.

25. I have already mentioned Socrates' hedonism in the *Prot.* In the *Gorg.* there is Socrates' unparalleled statement that he is the only real statesman in Athens (521d), and in the *Men.* (81a-86b) we have Socrates' appeal to recollection, which involves a positive belief in the immortality of the soul, something Socrates in the *Ap.* denied.

26. Readers wanting to get a thorough discussion of the development of Plato's ethics should consult Irwin 1995. Although not entirely uncontroversial, I think it comes as close to being an orthodox account of development as any. It is thorough and clear, and notes of disagreements with other developmental views are ample. I have relied on Irwin to some extent in recounting the developmental story here, though I have tried always to support my assertions directly from passages in Plato.

27. Irwin 1995, 229: 'temperance and bravery are not separable from justice, for the concord and friendship required by temperance and bravery are possible only if the different parts of the soul perform their proper function, as they do in a just soul'.

28. Since the distinction between what one wishes and what one really wants is thematic in the *Gorg.* (466b-468e), it is clear that I am not simply importing that distinction into the discussion of *Alc.* 103-6. Compare the discussion at 113-16, and, even more explicitly at 134e, where Socrates says, 'For if a man, my dear Alcibiades, has the power to do what he likes but has no understanding, what is likely to be the result, either to him as an individual or to the state? For example, if he be sick and is able to do what he likes, not having the mind of a physician – having moreover tyrannical power, and no one daring to reprove him – what will happen to him? Will he not be likely to have his constitution ruined?' (tr. Jowett).

## 8. Authenticity, Experiment or Development

29. It might be objected that I have left out an important difference between the *Alc.* and early Socratic dialogues, namely that while they maintain that virtue is not teachable, the *Alc.* holds that it is. This was Smith's point (g) above. I think Smith overstates his point. He says: 'At 119a1-6, Socrates claims that Zeno of Elea was such an excellent teacher that Pythodorus ... and Callias ...*became wise* as a result of their associations with Zeno' (Smith 2004, 105, my emphasis). But Socrates actually only asserts that Pythodorus and Callias grew wiser (*sophôteros*, 119a3) through association with Zeno, though they paid him 'to become wise and famous' (*sophos te kai ellogimos gegonen*, 119a6). Quite apart from the transparent irony in the use of positive and comparative forms of *sophos* here, there is no implication whatsoever that Zeno succeeded in teaching these men virtue. Moreover, the thrust of the whole dialectic from 109d-110d seems to be that there are no teachers of virtue. Though the question is asked 'When and how is justice learned?' it receives no positive answer. We find instead that it is *not* from others, *nor* by one's own nature or ingenuity. This line of reasoning is the familiar one from the *Men.*, that at least there are no teachers of virtue. And this is made even more explicit in 110e-112d, where we find that people in general do not understand justice, and that therefore there are no teachers of it. [Cf. on this point the discussion by Mintoff in the present volume – eds.]

30. Although Nicias' definition is subsequently refuted, it is refuted only on his premise that courage is merely a part of virtue, not the whole of virtue. As many commentators have noted, someone like Socrates, who maintains the unity of the virtues, would not have to give up the view that courage is knowledge of what one should fear and what one should not fear, etc.

31. See 127a6: some things are peculiar to men and some peculiar to women, emphasised by the *men/de* contrast.

# 9

# Revaluing *Megalopsuchia*: Reflections on the *Alcibiades II*

## Matthew Sharpe

### Introduction: on the status of the *Alcibiades II*

It is perhaps unsurprising that there is very little critical philosophical literature on the Platonic *Alcibiades* II, the dialogue which in the ancient world bore the subtitle *On Prayer*. The dialogue today is almost unanimously held to have been written not by Plato, but by a later, perhaps inferior, imitator. Because of Alcibiades' fame, and known association with Socrates, this relationship seems to have been a favourite theme for many different dramatists, 'so that at least five or six dialogues bearing this name passed current in antiquity' (Jowett I, 3). The dialogue is not mentioned, nor attributed to Plato, by Aristotle. It is moreover a short piece, some thirteen Stephanus pages only. Undoubtedly, it contains some flawed or partial argumentation. Its content confirms, and may perhaps have been inspired by, Xenophon's remarks concerning Socrates' public religiosity in the *Memorabilia* I (Xen. Mem. 1.1.2). There is also a significant dating error, which situates the dialogue impossibly in 399 BC, after the death of Alcibiades in exile (141d). Stylometric considerations have also been adduced in favour of considering the dialogue as the product of a later writer. Benjamin Jowett was as direct as he is heavy-handed in his assessment of the text:

> The dialogue is poor and weak; and there is a certain abruptness or *agroikia* about the conversation which is very un-Platonic ... the characters are ill-drawn. Socrates assumes the 'superior person' and preaches too much, while Alcibiades is stupid and heavy-in-hand. (Jowett II, 44)

For these and like reasons, much of the work that has been devoted to the text is of a philological kind, bearing on the question of its authenticity. Recently, however, this trend has begun to change. Christopher Bruell devotes a chapter of his book *On the Socratic Education* to the *Alcibiades* II. Jacob Howland has written an extended piece on the text in *Interpretation* (1990, 18.1: 63-90). As Howland observes, whether the dialogue was written by the historical individual Plato or not, there is no doubt that the text reflects his influence, and raises many questions which go to the heart

## 9. Revaluing Megalopsuchia

of Plato's authentic philosophical *oeuvre*. '[T]he speeches and deeds of Alcibiades [in the *Alcibiades* II] are clearly situated within, and so should be interpreted in the light of, the dramatic constellation of the Platonic dialogues' (Howland 1990, 64). These questions concern the nature of Socratic philosophising, and so of philosophy *per se*, in its tense relationship with the religious opinions and political ideals of non-philosophical, political life. In this way, we can endorse Jowett's observation that, despite the dialogue's many alleged flaws, it is a dialogue that raises questions of continuing interest for modern readers, or for anyone engaged in the singularly unusual (*atopos*) business of philosophical education (Jowett II, 4).

Even if we disregard the philological evidence, there is good reason for Platonic commentators to be uncomfortable concerning the *Alcibiades* II, and to question its author's motives. First of all, given the acknowledged Platonic intention to defend his teacher against the charges of impiety and corrupting the youth laid against him by the city of Athens, the dialogue is deeply troubling. Its action ends with Socrates accepting a votive crown proffered by Alcibiades (151a-b).[1] This action takes place perhaps on the very steps of the temple to which Alcibiades had been on his way to gift it to the gods, Socrates having just persuaded Alcibiades that he should not practise the city's traditional religious observances but keep silence, pending his philosophical education (150c).

More than this, on a first reading, the *Alcibiades* II can seem in large measure to repeat closely the first *Alcibiades*, whose authenticity is now generally accepted. In both dialogues, Socrates accosts an initially reticent young Alcibiades. Following an extended exchange, Alcibiades is turned around to becoming Socrates' willing student. Both dialogues are punctuated by two extended Socratic speeches, each of which belongs to a clear dramatic phase.[2] In the first half of either text, Socrates shows that Alcibiades is in fact ignorant, either concerning justice (*Alcibiades* I, 118d) or the good for which we should pray (*Alcibiades* II, 148a-b), where he had taken himself previously to have no need of education.

Then, in the second halves of the two dialogues, Socrates convinces Alcibiades that he, and so philosophy, will be necessary should Alcibiades achieve all that his vaulting political ambition or *eros* implies. In both dialogues, this *eros* is identified by Socrates in similar terms: Alcibiades desires the rule of Athens, and as much of the known Hellenic and barbarian world as he can win (*Alc.* I, 105b; *Alc.* II, 141a-b). Even the speeches in each of the dialogues' second halves have significant parallels, with Socrates – again somewhat controversially – praising the virtues and wisdom of the Spartans as the paradigms for Alcibiades' renewed political education (*Alc.* I 122e-123d; *Alc.* II 148d-149d).

In both dialogues, finally, Socrates succeeds in redirecting Alcibiades' restless psyche away, at least momentarily, from his quest for political rule and the adoration of the many. In the *Alcibiades* I, Alcibiades is goaded towards knowledge of the self (*Alc.* I, 127e-135e). In the *Alcibiades*

II he is moved towards reflection upon the noble and the base (150e). This terminus is the noble justification for Socrates' seemingly bold and open rejection of traditional civic piety in the latter text. Alcibiades admits that he had been about to pray at the temple for tyrannical rule. Socrates' advice that he should not pray, in this manner, is hence salutary. It responds to the concern that, until we know the truly good, we may always be prone to ask for (and be granted) such bad things as might offend the gods, and be truly self-destructive (150c). Only a divine being could know the good for which it is worthy to pray.

At the same time, these apparent similarities between the *Alcibiades* I and *Alcibiades* II (which point if not to a single author then a single philosophic lineage and set of concerns) should not blind us to differences between the two texts. Indeed, the later text,[3] whoever its author may be, throws a peculiar light or shade upon its predecessor, in a way that can make us reflect upon the limitations of Socrates' educative endeavours, and its efficacy with political men of the type represented so dramatically by Alcibiades. For it is not wholly amusing to say that the *Alcibiades* II is the darker son or brother to the first and more famous *Alcibiades* dialogue. The *Alcibiades* I shows Socrates' initial philosophical seduction of Alcibiades in his twentieth year or so, just as his first beard was sprouting, and the youth was about to begin his infamous political career. By contrast, the *Alcibiades* II, set at some point evidently quite soon after this initial conquest, intimates the imminent, tragic failure of Socrates' attempts to turn Alcibiades' soul away from the course it was to set into sacrilege and dishonour, treason and debauchery, and the crippling of Athens.

For all these reasons, a study of the *Alcibiades* II recommends itself to the student of Platonic philosophy.

## Blindness, madness and tragedy in *Alcibiades* II

So what then, more exactly, can we say concerning the meaning and the action of *Alcibiades* II? The dialectical conversion of Alcibiades to the recognition of his need for self-knowledge in the *Alcibiades* I culminates in a famous erotic image: that of two eyes gazing into each other, each seeing itself framed in the other's translucent surface (132d-133b). Such, Socrates appears to imply, is the best image of the aim of philosophic education. The student learns self-knowledge by espying, in the soul of the teacher, the noble goods to which he should aspire, 'which most resemble the divine' (133c). By contrast, the *Alcibiades* II is from the start filled with details that suggest Alcibiades' failure to have followed up on his promise to undertake this Socratic education since their first meeting. When Socrates first accosts him (for it is clear that Alcibiades has not been with his would-be teacher and lover), we are told that he seems to Socrates to have 'downcast eyes' (*phainêi ge toi eskuthrôpakenai te kai eis gên blepein*,

## 9. Revaluing Megalopsuchia

138a). The principal example of sickness to which Socrates recurs, as he tries to delineate the species of illness, is *opthalmia*, a disease of the eyes (140b1). Soon after, we learn that Alcibiades has not renounced or in any way qualified his tyrannical desire to rule all of Greece and the barbarians since first meeting Socrates. Indeed, here in contrast to *Alcibiades I* – wherein the youth had not protested when Socrates proposed he would rather die than be deprived of his desire for universal political acclaim (*Alc.* I, 105a) – Alcibiades soon admits that he would never sacrifice his life, 'for then what use could I make of them [my lordship and rule]?' (*pôs gar an, mêthen ge ti mellôn autois chrêsesthai*, 141c). In terms of Plato's characteristic ranking of the order of human desires, from the base and bodily, via political honour rooted in *thumos*, to the most elevated, philosophic desire (*Rep.* IV, 435d-441b), Alcibiades appears subsequent to meeting Socrates to have gone backwards or rather downwards.

The entire *Alcibiades* II is filled with an atmosphere of darkness and tragic foreboding. From its beginning, the exchange between Socrates and Alcibiades concerns less the possibility of self-knowledge than its limits, or what stands opposed to it: namely, ignorance, madness and illness (138c-e). Interestingly, this focus upon madness or *aphrosune* is read by some commentators as a sure sign that the dialogue is a later text, directed against the Cynics. This is because the Cynics regarded all forms of ignorance as species of madness. In the *Alcibiades* II, though, madness is aligned with knowingly or consciously willing harm upon oneself and what one cares for, against the type of folly (such as that attributed to the democratic many) that asks for evil things out of ignorance concerning the good (Hutchinson 1997b, 596-7).

However that may be, the context of the dialogue, and what the readership would have known concerning the near-Olympian *hubris* and *paranomia* that were to characterise Alcibiades' political career, would surely provide their own sufficient justification for raising this topic. Alcibiades is the only character in the *Symposium* whom Socrates decries as mad, asking protection from Agathon lest Alcibiades beat him up (*Symp.* 213D1) – as Plutarch tells us Alcibiades once beat up his childhood teacher (Plutarch, *Alc.* 7.1). More than this, the *Phaedrus* names philosophy itself as a species of divine, specifically erotic, madness alongside the prophetic, ritual, and poetic *maniai* (*Phdr.* 244b-245b, 265a-e). Madness is hence far from a concern external to Plato's thought and *oeuvre*.

The dialogue is also full of references to, and examples taken from, Greek tragedy, which place the concern with *aphrosune* in wider political and philosophical settings. Socrates' first example of someone who has been drawn, as Alcibiades might, to pray for great evils is the Oedipus of *Oedipus at Colonus*, whose curses brought down disaster upon his entire house (138b-138c). In the central exchange of the text, the cases of Orestes and Alcmaeon, both matricides, are considered (143d). Socrates' next 'counter-factual' functions ostensibly to show Alcibiades that ignorance concerning the means or object of an action can be beneficent when the end chosen is evil. In this case the hypothesis is that Alcibiades might consider killing his adoptive father, Pericles, in order to fulfil his political desire (143e-144c). The prospect of parricide against the leading politician of the city clearly evokes Oedipus' famous, unwitting deeds. The dialogue closes with Socrates likening himself to both Kreon and Teiresias in Euripides' *Phoenician Women* (151b). Teiresias has appeared to the King in a laurel crown, which Kreon takes as an auspicious omen of victory. Just so, the crowned Socrates 'wishes for noble victory over your [Alcibiades'] lovers' (*kai bouloimên an kallinikos genesthai tôn sôn erastôn*, 151c). Yet in the *Phoenician Women*, Teiresias in fact comes as the herald of a sea of troubles, and for Kreon himself: namely, the news that if Thebes is to be saved, his own son Menoeceus must die to repay the ancestral debt incurred by the crime of Cadmus, the city's founding father, against Ares (Howland 1990, 66). Read in context, the *Alcibiades* II thus finishes with a prediction that Socrates' failure to conquer Alcibiades' many other admirers – and principally the many in the Assembly who would soon adoringly be eating from his hand – will lead to a sea of troubles for Socrates.

In this light, even the 'uncharacteristic' historical error in the text of the *Alcibiades* II becomes poetically or politically suggestive.[4] One example Socrates introduces of someone who has, like Alcibiades, desired tyranny as the greatest good, only to end badly, is that of the murderer of Archelaus of Macedonia. The tyrannicide, Archelaus' beloved – just as according to tradition Alcibiades was Socrates' beloved (*Alc.* I 103a; *Prot.* 309a; *Symp.* 213d) – was himself slain only days later (141d). But the date of these events was 399 BC. This was after Alcibiades' death. By the same token, it was in this year that Socrates was put to death by Athens, and Xenophon confirms that this was partly because of his association in the public mind with Alcibiades' impiety and *hubris* (Xen. Mem. 1.2).

## A central note on the literary character of the Platonic dialogues

How we interpret any Platonic dialogue depends on how we conceive of these highly peculiar pieces of literature and philosophy. As we have already been suggesting, the fact that these dialogues contain what is today called philosophical argumentation in no way means that they contain only such argumentation. Nor does it mean that all the author of these texts intended to convey is reducible to the content, or outcomes, of the *elenchi* or *diaereses*. Of course, this does not mean that the work of hermeneutics or philology should wholly trump philosophy, as we respond to and weigh Plato's thought. It does however mean that if we are to weigh Plato's philosophical thought concerning the subjects raised by the dialogues, or even discover what that thought is, we need to pass by way of

## 9. *Revaluing* Megalopsuchia

philology. As the *Seventh Letter* confirms, he does not convey the full content of this thought directly in his writings (*Ep.* VII, 342c-e). Amongst other things, Plato's well publicised attack on poetry in the *Republic* in no way prevented him from ceaselessly citing and recasting the works of the tragedians and epic poets 'in order to vary [them] into the infinite and impossible – namely into all of his own masks and multiplicities', to quote Nietzsche (*Beyond Good and Evil*, 190).

This esotericism is also not unrelated to how he conceives of philosophy as an activity or way of life. The dialogues, or at least a significant proportion of them, seem to have been produced by Plato, or in some cases by his followers, largely for the audience outside the academy as well as for teaching within it. They are as it were the political or external face of Plato's philosophical activity: the face this activity shows to the city, in order to entice the philosophically minded, and show the benefit or nobility of philosophy to others. As such, they are as much what could be termed meta-philosophical as philosophical texts. Dialogues like the *Parmenides*, *Sophist* and *Theaetetus* are more directly philosophical or conceptual in our modern sense than others. The shorter, aporetic dialogues reflect upon philosophy's place in the field of human endeavours and, in particular, to its relation to the differing conceptions of the good life held by others. What is it to do philosophy? What are its motives, its justification, and its good? Why are some people drawn, even today, to devote their lives to it, despite continuing wider incredulity? Does philosophy have a place within the city? Or is it always in a comic or tragic disjunction with the majority of people, who understand neither it, nor its good?

### Considerations concerning '*megalopsuchia*'

This excursus has not then been wholly inessential to our reading of the *Alcibiades* II. For its primary philosophical interest, we would suggest, lies at the level of this Platonic metaphilosophy or philosophy about philosophy. In particular, the dialogue has interesting things to say concerning at least three Platonic questions. There is first of all the 'aesthetic' question concerning the relationship of philosophy with tragedy, a question which has been raised powerfully by Martha Nussbaum in *The Fragility of Goodness*. Secondly, there is the 'ethical' or perhaps 'psychological' question of the nature of the desire or drive (*eros*) to do philosophy, and its relationship – emblematised by Socrates' infatuation with Alcibiades – with the political desire for tyranny. Thirdly, or above all, there is the 'political' question of what Socrates' encounter, and failure, with the tyrannical young Alcibiades indicates concerning Socratic philosophy's politics, or its relationship with non-philosophic, political life.

What I am going to argue can be summarised by considering one final, stylistic peculiarity of the *Alcibiades* II. This peculiarity too has led commentators to believe that the Cynics must have been the target of the author of the text. It is that, when Socrates lists the different species of *aphrosune* at 140c-d, he lists the *megalopsuchos* or 'great-souled' men alongside the vain (*êlithios*), stupid (*embrontêtos*), the good hearted (*euêthês*), the naïve (*akakos*) or dumb (*eneos*). *Megalopsuchia*, it is noted, was for Cynicism that philosophic state of soul which enabled a person to take calmly all of life's misfortunes. However, before that, as Aristotle's *Nichomachean Ethics* attests, *megalopsuchia* was the name given to the highest exemplar of political, versus philosophical, virtue: indeed the very ornament (*kosmos*) of all the other civic virtues. In general, Hutchinson notes, the *Alcibiades* II's evidently deflationary use of the term *megalopsuchia* is the only such instance in all Greek literature (Hutchinson 1997b, 597). Far from being evidence that this dialogue is an allegorical set piece for a later thinker to refute the Cynics, I want now to argue that it shows the author's intention as being to highlight that political, as opposed to philosophical, desire is inevitably wedded to the causes of tragedy in political life.

There is no question that both Plato and Socrates, and very many philosophers since, have been fascinated by – and tried to court – tyrants or men of political power. As Christ associated with the lepers and other outcasts, so Socrates had in his retinue not only Alcibiades but also Critias and Charmides, both of whom were to be implicated in the infamous reign of the Thirty Tyrants after Athens' defeat in the Peloponnesian War. If the image of Socratic education is one of self-knowledge attained through seeking out some mirror in the soul of others, what was it that drew Socrates to these morally questionable men?

The answer that immediately presents itself is that the tyrannical man's desire has something of a universal, and hence transpolitical, character about it that also governs the philosopher's desire for universal truth. The philosopher, as philosopher, cannot remain content to accept without questioning the opinions and conventions that are binding in his city. Using evidence available to all, and his reason, it is the philosopher's business to seek out what is true. This includes when what he discovers not only transcends, but opposes what is conventionally held to be true. In this native *metanomia*, as we might call it, lies the basis for most people's continuing bewilderment concerning the value of philosophy.

But similarly, Alcibiades' political career – with his proven willingness to betray his homeland to Sparta, then Sparta to the Persians, before returning to Athens – is a living illustration of how the tyrannical desire for universal political recognition transcends the usual attachments to place, nation, or regime that bind most human beings. Thucydides (6.15) refers to Alcibiades' great and habitual 'transgressions of law and custom (*paranomia*)'. Aristophanes in the *Frogs* (1431-2) has his Aeschylus describe Alcibiades as a lion cub whose nature may well prove to be at odds with his native city. Plutarch and other ancient sources confirm that Alcibiades' personal life was largely a continual debauch, including rumours concerning incest. Perhaps the most infamous alleged instance of

## 9. *Revaluing* Megalopsuchia

Alcibiades' *paranomia*, however, was some involvement in the destruction of the Hermae in 415, on the eve of the Sicilian expedition. Although his guilt was never established – for Alcibiades chose exile and high treason over returning to Athens for trial – the very accusation is potent testimony to Alcibiades' scant concern for the religious sensitivities of his homeland.

The *Alcibiades* II attests, every bit as strongly as the *Euthyphro* and the early books of the *Republic*, that the practice of philosophising brought into political life by Socrates stood in real tension with the ancestral beliefs of the Greeks, and the Olympian pantheon (cf. *Euthyphro* 7a-9b). Socrates' final, surely highly risky, caution against Alcibiades' praying to the ancestral gods at all is for instance preceded by a first recommendation. This recommendation, taken from an unnamed, probably Pythagorean poet, already represents a 'wise' philosophical tempering of the folk belief that one can pray to the gods for one's particular goods. Socrates' prayer, confirming Xenophon's report in the *Memorabilia* (1.1.2), reads:

> King Zeus... grant us good whether prayed for or unsought by us. What is bad for us, give us not, however hard we pray for it (*Zeu basileu ... ta men esthla, phêsi, kai euchomenois kai aneuktois ammi didou, ta de deila kai euchomenois apalexein*, 143a1-2).

Beyond the opening appeal to Zeus, it is in fact perfectly consistent with all (or no) bodies of positive religion: an intuition confirmed by Socrates' second long speech, wherein it is the Egyptian god Ammon to whose oracle Socrates refers Alcibiades (148d-150b). What Socrates' poet in fact proffers is less a prayer than what might humorously be called a 'meta-prayer'. A contemporary reader is reminded of the story told about Niels Bohr's response to a friend's query concerning a horseshoe the great scientist kept over his front door: 'they say it works even if you don't believe in it'.

As in the *Symposium*, Socrates does not protest when Alcibiades offers to award him the crown (*stephanos*) of laurels at the end of the dialogue (151a-b; cf. *Symp.* 213e). Indeed, Socrates answers that he will gladly receive any gift Alcibiades gives him in the period in which he will instruct him concerning the good for which he should pray. Yet in the classical world such crowns were generally reserved as votive offerings for the gods. Where the gods were for Alcibiades, Socrates is offering philosophy and himself; the Athena, as he says, who can clear the fog from the eyes of Alcibiades' Diomedes (150d-e). The author of *Alcibiades* II has skilfully intimated Socrates' philosophic *hubris* to us previously, when he had substituted 'men of wisdom' (*anthrôpois tois noun echousi*) for the gods, in explaining why Ammon scorns ostentatious gifts and sacrifices, preferring reverent silence:

> For the gods are not venal, and scorn all these things, as Ammon and his prophet told us. Gods and men of wisdom are more likely to hold justice and wisdom in especial honour. (*kinduneuei goun kai para theois kai par' anthrôpois tois noun echousi dikaiosunê te kai phronêsis diapherontôs*

*tetimêsthai*), and none are just or wise but those who know how to behave and speak to gods and men (*phronimoi de kai dikaioi ouk alloi tines eisin [ê] tôn eidotôn ha dei prattein kai legein kai pros theous kai pros anthrôpous*). (150a-b)

Socratic philosophy, or at least Socrates himself, hence seems not inconsistent with a kind of *megalopsuchia*: a sense of the near-divine enlargement of soul which comes from a more comprehensive vision of the truth of the whole, or desire for such contemplative vision.[5] Similarly, as we commented in passing, Alcibiades' desire 'to fill with [his] name and [his] power all men, so to speak' (*emplêseis tou sou onomatos kai tês sês dunameôs pantas hôs epos eipein anthrôpous*, *Alc.* I, 105c3-4) is rooted in a sense of his innate worth. When Socrates comments in the *Alcibiades* I that Alcibiades seems to consider himself to be 'more worthy of honour than Pericles or anyone else who ever lived, except perhaps Cyrus and Xerxes' (*kai oimai se plên Kurou kai Xerxou hêgeisthai oudena axion logou gegonenai*, *Alc.* I, 105c4-6), Alcibiades does not bother to correct him. There could hardly be a better example of someone who deemed himself a *megalopsuchos* in the exact sense Aristotle describes in *Nichomachean Ethics*: namely, 'the man who, deeming himself worthy of great things, really is worthy of them' (*NE* 1121b1-2).

## On philosophy, tyranny and self-knowledge

Nevertheless, Plato's *Republic*, alongside the *Gorgias*, denounces tyrannical ambition as the most unhappy of all forms of life, and that most distant (exactly 729 times less happy, says the *Republic*) from that of the philosopher (*Rep.* 587c-588b). In *Republic* X, moreover, the tragedians (with Homer first of all) are denounced primarily for dramatising figures, like Oedipus, Alcmaeon, or Orestes, who pre-eminently embody this unhappiest of lives (*Rep.* X, 605c-606e). In this vein, the *Alcibiades* II from its beginning, and not without some artificiality (see 138b-138c), serves to frame our consideration of both Socrates' and Alcibiades' careers in the light of Oedipus, the tragic figure *par excellence*. Considering why this is so can lead us towards our conclusions.

Critics have noted the comparison between *Oedipus Tyrannus* and the Socrates Plato presents in the *Apology*.[6] In both cases, we have men whose lives have been lived in the light of a pronouncement of the Delphic oracle. Both men are fearless seekers of truths, to the point of courting exile or personal disaster. Oedipus was himself a parricide; Socrates was accused of the indirect parricide of corrupting the youth of Athens. Both men were sacrificed as *pharmakoi* – at once pollutions and a potential salvation to their cities – to restore civic order. And just as Oedipus in exile calls down disaster on Thebes, so Socrates at the end of the *Apology* claims divining powers, to decree that his killing will not save the city, but heighten its internecine strife (*Ap.* 39c3-d3).

## 9. Revaluing Megalopsuchia

In modern times, psychoanalysis' transposition of the story of Oedipus draws our attention to the deep psychological wish for autarchy this story dramatises. The child wishes to replace its own father, as if to father itself – just as Oedipus is both father and brother to his siblings, through his unholy union with Jocasta. In Sophocles' play, in this vein, Oedipus' tyrannical claim – before his own tragic attainment of self-knowledge – is that he is both Thebes' saviour and the source of the life of his 'earth-born brothers' (*OT* 37-39). Oedipus even identifies himself with the pre-Olympian gods – as a 'son of Chance' (*Tuche*) and 'kin to the moon' – who preceded the Olympian gods, fathers to the laws of the *poleis* (*OT* 1082-83). If we take the origin of human political life to lie in common human neediness or self-insufficiency, the point is, we can also say that Oedipus' tyrannical desire, and tyrannical desire as such, is definitively anti-political. The tragic recognition (*anagnorisis*), at least in *Oedipus Tyrannus*, is in its turn at base the recognition of the falsity of any mortal's claim to this self-founding, Uranic status (cf. Howland 1990, 73).

By posing to Alcibiades the possibility that his ambition might well lead him towards killing his adoptive father Pericles (143e-144c), the pre-eminent politician of the day, the Socrates of *Alcibiades* II is also drawing us to reflect that Alcibiades is caught in both the *hubris* and the profound self-ignorance that ensures Oedipus' downfall. On the one hand, it is clear from the *Alcibiades* I that Alcibiades – at least when he is not before Socrates – feels that he has 'need for no other human being for anything' (*Alc.* I, 104a1-2). He has scorned all his other lovers who fled, we are told, since they were 'outstripped by his pride' (*Alc.* I, 103a5). On the other hand, in both dialogues Socrates stresses that his philosophical love for Alcibiades pits him against another, more fearsome rival: namely, the adoration of the many. The final, tragic words of *Alcibiades* II express Socrates' hope that even now he might have the victory over this rival lover, who, as he has again persuaded Alcibiades, is hopelessly mired in untutored opinion, and so is no certain guide concerning even its own good (146c-d).

It is this component of tyrannical desire, above all, that we can say Socrates as the dialogues present him singularly lacks. Indeed, again and again, the many are presented as the greatest sophist, and the single greatest cause for the snatching of potential philosophers, like Alcibiades, away from the philosophical life (e.g. *Rep.* VI, 492a). The philosophical desire for contemplative self-sufficiency, so emphasised by Aristotle, finds its standard in nature or being. In contrast, the tyrannical desire for universal honour, on one side, opens itself towards such a higher standard. This is because people will not freely grant their love and admiration except to that which they spontaneously experience to be independently worthy of that love and honour. As Howland comments:

> Alcibiades' love of honour manifests, albeit incoherently, an underlying desire to regard his own works in the light of standards which are prior to,

more authoritative and more universal than those sanctioned and sustained by indigenous custom (*nomos*). (Howland 1990, 79)

For this reason, Socrates tries to temper Alcibiades' tyrannical *eros* by making him reflect directly on such standards as his honour allows him to envisage: first of all, the alleged moderation and virtue of the Persian Princes, then justice and the good.

On the other hand – and herein lies the difference with a Socratic philosophic motivation – the love of political honour (*philotimia*), as political, involves its 'great-souled' pursuer by its nature in dependence upon others. As Xenophon's *Hiero* attests, the tyrant's tragic unhappiness comes in no small measure from how the tyrant depends on the admiration of others he at the same time despises as beneath him. This is perhaps the deepest reason why, we propose, the author of the *Alcibiades* II so boldly lists *megalopsuchia* as a species of ignorance or mindlessness (140c-d, 150c). It is again exactly Alcibiades' *megalopsuchia*, 'for this is the best of names for mindlessness' (150c), which Socrates tells us will prevent Alcibiades from ever using the wise poet's prayer or meta-prayer – and so which justifies his bold claim that it were best for Alcibiades to keep silence, rather than continuing to pray for unwise and unjust things to the city's gods (150c-d). The tragic self-conflict at the heart of the tyrannical desire for autarchy, we might well speculate, may have underlain Alcibiades' destructive rage against the city that raised him, and the indiscretions which shaped both his own destiny, and thereby that of Athens.

## The philosophic revaluing of *megalopsuchia*

Let us make now some concluding remarks, bringing these thoughts together. In *Nicomachean Ethics* I, Aristotle gives a principal reason for the philosophical devaluation of the political life. Such a life depends for its happiness on external goods whose acquisition and lasting possession depends upon chance. These external goods, like the recognition of others, are beyond our volitional control. It also depends ultimately on our living in a good, or non-tyrannical, regime, which, Aristotle says (*NE* I.5, 12), is a further species of thing about which we can only pray. Book II of the *Ethics* opens by specifying further the limits to voluntary action in the varieties of ignorance which lead to the type of non-voluntary actions pre-eminently on stage in tragedies like *Oedipus Tyrannus*, wherein the hero has acted, but does not know the significance of his action before the laws of gods and men (*NE* II.1-3).

There is perhaps no dialogue in the extended Platonic corpus that deals as directly as the *Alcibiades* II or *On Prayer* with this constellation of issues, crucial to the delineation of the new philosophical ethos or way of life from 'the tragic age of the Greeks'. Yet, characteristically, the Platonic writer emphasises that it is above all ignorance of the true end of action,

## 9. Revaluing Megalopsuchia

and hence the nature of the good, that is decisive in causing the types of tragedies staged in the 'theatrocratic' culture of Periclean Athens. While this is certainly consistent with Aristotle's position in the *Ethics*, it is not the point of greatest emphasis. Socrates sees in the transpolitical, tyrannical *eros* of Alcibiades one component of his own philosophic *eros*, whose religious heterodoxy and heteropraxy the dialogue boldly and amply shows. Yet the cause and hope of Socrates' repeated attempts to educate Alcibiades is to draw him to reflect, via the topics of justice and the Good, on the inconsistent nature of his own honour-loving conception of the best life. This conception, that of the *megalopsuchia* praised above all in the aristocratic Greek heritage, the Platonic author suggests is the deep, necessary condition for tragic *mania* and *atê*. The happiness of the non-philosophical *megalopsuchos* depends on the approval of others whom he nevertheless feels himself, autarchically, to be above.

That Socrates will finally fail in his philosophic education of Alcibiades is indicated by the author in the final poetic borrowing in the *Alcibiades* II. Alcibiades' love of fame, however tragically divided against itself, is much too strong a force in his character when set against the philosophic *eros* Socrates can only occasionally light within him. In the last Platonic rewriting of the tragic corpus in *Alcibiades* II, Socrates thus shows himself willing, invoking Book V of the *Iliad*, to take the place of Athena, the wise patron goddess of the Athenians (cf. *Apol.* 20e-22e), to clear the fog from the Diomedes of Alcibiades' 'downcast eyes', 'so that he may recognise both god and man' (150d-e). The reader is asked in this way to recall what ensues in the *Iliad*. For Diomedes disregards the warning of the goddess. Instead, he becomes 'over-spirited' (*huperthumos*) and 'overweening' (*huperêphanos*), so that – as Alcibiades was soon to do in Athens – he 'rages furiously against immortal gods' and 'would even fight father Zeus' (*Iliad* 5.121ff.).

### Notes

1. Jowett considers this a clumsy, confected attempt to cite the *Symposium* (Jowett II, 4).

2. The structure, found in other dialogues of doubtful authenticity such as *Minos* and *Hipparchus*, has been termed 'pedimental' (see Thesleff 1967, 34 = 2009, 28).

3. I adhere to the chronology that is usually envisaged, and rendered plausible by some 'late' features of the language of the *Alcibiades* II; nothing that is said here should be taken to indicate that we have firm dates for either dialogue.

4. For such anachronisms, however, the reader can compare the *Menexenus*, whose dramatic setting seems to be no earlier than 387 BC, some twelve years after Socrates' death, and also, perhaps more pertinent here, the reference to Archelaus' own usurpation of royal office in 414 BC at *Gorg.* 470d, without which that dialogue would have a moderately consistent dramatic date in the 420s (Tarrant 2008).

5. A further Platonic hint is suggested in the 'supposition' Socrates presents to

Alcibiades at 141a-b. This supposition reads: 'Suppose that the god to whom you are about to pray were to appear to you and to ask you, before you began praying, whether you would be happy to be the sole ruler of the city of Athens – or, if that seemed mean and tiny, were to offer you all the other Greeks as well – or, if he saw that you regarded that too as insignificant unless the whole of Europe were included, were to promise you all that plus simultaneous recognition by the whole human race of the rule of Alcibiades son of Cleinias ....' This however is nearly literally the offer Socrates, not a god, has made to Alcibiades in the *Alcibiades* I at 105b-c. The contradiction can only be resolved if, as per the closing of the *Alcibiades* II, Socrates is putting himself and philosophy in the place of this god.

6. See Howland 1990.

## 10

# Improvement by Love:
# From Aeschines to the Old Academy

*Harold Tarrant*

**Introduction**

The *Alcibiades* purports to offer us the very first conversation between Socrates and Alcibiades. Previously, it seems, Socrates has just lingered at the back of a crowd of lovers looking rather stupid. This is hardly surprising. Socrates *did* look stupid, and both Aristophanes and his rival Ameipsias thought that he was good enough material for a laugh to present him on stage in their comedies at the Dionysia of 423 BC. The only slight surprise here is that Alcibiades, though he is mentioned in other Aristophanic comedies (and already in the *Acharnians* two years before), is never actually named in the *Clouds*. One might suspect that the young man Pheidippides, whom Socrates exposes to the corrupting influence of philosophic argument and the ensuing amoral attitudes, bears some relationship to Alcibiades. He shares with him a partially Alcmaeonid background (46-70), a passion for horse-racing (14-29), and an interesting lisp (870-3, cf. *Wasps* 44-6), but as the play stands Pheidippides is never seen as having been in any way close to Socrates.[1] Their relationship is in fact akin to one between the principal of a college and an individual first-year student, with no sinister overtones whatever. I doubt that the relationship with Alcibiades had by that stage been seen as in any way unusual; either its bizarre nature was a well-kept secret (in spite of the very public lives that both participants led), or it was not seen as very unusual after all. Alcibiades had experienced the attentions of a host of would-be lovers, so what would have made Socrates special?[2]

The focus in this paper will be on the growth of a legend of an educational relationship, one in which the teacher had neither knowledge nor craft to pass on to the pupil. What was needed to begin the relationship was a kind of educational seduction by a master lover; what was needed thereafter remained largely unclear, but may have owed more to luck or divine intervention than to judgement. What is the purpose of the seduction, and where can it lead? And how could one exempt the seducer from the blame that might follow if the relationship proved bad for both the person seduced and his city?

*Harold Tarrant*

**Aeschines and the growth of the love-legend**

Once Socrates had been put to death in such controversial circumstances both his defenders and his detractors gave their own colouring to episodes in his life in ways that contributed to what one might call Socratic mythology. Xenophon is forced to defend Socrates (possibly against the Polycrates who wrote a literary *Accusation of Socrates*) on charges that he had as his pupils two individuals who did great harm to Athens, Critias, leader of the Thirty, and Alcibiades who repeatedly and treacherously changed sides in the war.[3] Aeschines has his 'Socrates' explain his relationship with Alcibiades, and, even more than the author of the *Alcibiades*, he seems rather apologetic for Socrates' having made a mistake, albeit a glorious one.

Our information comes from a few pages of the orator Aelius Aristides.[4] To begin with he thinks that Plato will agree with the following:

> If I hoped I'd be able to benefit him by some craft, I'd be convicting myself of a great deal of folly. But as things were I thought that this [power] for [use on] Alcibiades had been given to me by some divine dispensation (*theia moira*). There's nothing surprising here.

We meet immediately the Socrates who is dubious about any special skill that he might have, but somehow expects to be able to benefit Alcibiades, i.e. to improve him. The idea that a worthy lover can *improve* the beloved is particularly associated with Pausanias' seemingly rather conventional speech in the *Symposium*, but it is seldom made much of by Plato's Socrates. Aeschines resorts to the same second line of defence as Plato in the *Meno* when he decides that political excellence cannot be attributed to knowledge. If not knowledge, then perhaps there is some divine dispensation at work, a *theia moira*, so that one can somehow determine the right course of action even though one does not know why. Perhaps some inspirational force is taking over, leading him in the right direction. The word *theia* in fact suggests that the inspiration is from a god. No doubt many a lover had been led astray by much the same illusion. The fragment continues with a physical analogy for Alcibiades' presumed psychical deficiency:

> Many physically sick people also become healthy, some by human craft, others by divine dispensation – all those who do so by human craft getting healed by doctors, while in the case of those who do so by divine dispensation desire leads them to what will be beneficial. They desired an emetic exactly when it would be of benefit, or to hunt exactly when the exercise would do them good.

Desire here is *epithumia*, the appetitive force of which Plato is so suspicious, yet it can scarcely be questioned that sometimes our bodies do

*10. Improvement by Love*

indeed have an appetite for what is good for them. It sounds sinister here precisely because of the link with *erôs*, as if Socrates is claiming that love has a good effect precisely because our sexual appetite is naturally good. But reflection will reveal that the desiring patient here is analogous not to Socrates but to Alcibiades, so that the appetites concerned should be those of Alcibiades rather than those of Socrates. Perhaps the beneficial effect of Socrates' love is intended to work through Alcibiades' natural desire for improvement. At the end of this narration Socrates is made to say:

> Because of the love that I happened to conceive for Alcibiades I had an experience the same as that of the bacchants. For bacchant women, when they become divinely inspired (*entheoi*) are able to draw milk and honey from sources others cannot get water from. So I, even though I knew no subject by teaching which one could benefit a man, still believed that if I got together (*xyneinai*) with him I could make him better on account of my loving him.

Somehow Socrates' love is supposed to make him *entheos*, suggesting the presence of a god within him, and it is this god perhaps who is meant to be inspiring Alcibiades in turn to follow the course that is good for him.

## The guiding god of the Alcibiades

When we come to the *Alcibiades* itself we find that it agrees with Aeschines in a very significant respect. Aeschines has Socrates inspired not simply by a *daimôn* but by something fully divine: both *theia moira* and *entheos* suggest the involvement of a *theos*: a being of recognised divine status. Although the *Alcibiades* introduces the divine element by speaking of a 'daimonic obstacle' (*daimonion enantiôma*) to all his earlier desires to converse with Alcibiades, it thereafter prefers to speak of a god controlling his actions. Although one may perhaps conceive of a god that controls the sign, there would still be no reason why any sign sent by a god could not be called *theios*, which is not of course Plato's usual practice. The *Alcibiades* stands apart from the rest of the corpus in the unusually direct way that the sign is linked with the divine. The key idea at the climax of the dialogue at 133c seems to be that there is something divine at the very core of Socrates' being, something divine that now denies and then permits his contact with Alcibiades.

In this regard one might suspect that the erotic power is no longer to be associated with deeply felt need as it was in the *Symposium*, for even though Socrates insists upon his own continuing need for education at 124c, he acknowledges in the same context that he is blessed with a superior guardian to that of Alcibiades – none other than this god himself. So whereas the *Symposium* had postulated a clear difference between the divine and the *daimonic*, regarding Eros as a *daimonic* power, and tended to paint Socrates as a *daimonic* man rather than a divinely blessed one, the 'Socrates' of the *Alcibiades* informs us that he is under *divine* control and makes us wonder whether he can really lack anything at all.

Now one might argue that the *Phaedrus* takes a more elevated view of Eros, and does so in the very passage that most invites comparison with the *Alcibiades*, insofar as it too makes important use of (i) the gaze of one eye into another (255c1-d3, cf. *Alc.* 132e4-133a7) and (ii) the notion of love reciprocated (*anterôs*, 255e1, cf. *Alc.* 135d9-e3). The lover is described as *entheos*, 'divinely inspired' or more literally 'with (a) god within' at 255b6, and thus contrasted with ordinary friends. This is in agreement with the view expressed earlier that *erôs* is a kind of madness that stems from a divine gift (244a7-8), making it literally a gift *from the gods* (245b4-c1). What the *Phaedrus* does not do is to make this divine gift a special favour to Socrates himself. We appear to be talking of any lover who loves *correctly*, not of the philosopher alone,[5] though the qualification is of course an important one. The correct lover cannot perhaps be conceived apart from philosophy (cf. 249a2) or from the internal struggles that proceed from the voice of reason as represented by the charioteer (256a-b), and to this extent there are limits to the achievements that the lover can bring about 'if they follow a less elevated and unphilosophical lifestyle, but an honour-loving one' (256b7-c1). So it would not be likely that a lover could bring about substantial improvement in the beloved 'through love alone' without philosophy.

So where exactly does the *Alcibiades* stand on such issues? Socrates as lover is as divinely inspired (*entheos*) as in Aeschines' account of Socrates' disappointed expectations or in the actual theory of the *Phaedrus*, and his love is of a distinctly philosophical kind as evidenced by his attraction to Alcibiades' beautiful soul rather than his body (131c5-132a2). If he is to keep this beloved soul for himself he knows that he must strengthen it against the opposing influences of the people of Athens, and in a word improve it by exercise and the requisite learning (132b1-3). Socrates here is not afraid to offer lessons:

1. revealing Alcibiades' own ignorance;
2. convincing him that he requires self-knowledge;
3. persuading him that his 'self' is in his soul rather than his body;
4. and exhorting him to care for the soul and to fix his gaze on this.
   (132c1-2)

It is the nature of these lessons that determines how far the *Alcibiades* agrees with Aeschines. Socrates acts like a *mentor*, and like the kind of mentor that offers himself as an *example* of the practices that he is advocating. He is baring his own soul in an effort to show Alcibiades the importance of his. Just like the Socrates of Aeschines, this Socrates believes that he can rescue Alcibiades without offering any particular brand of knowledge that the young man will learn from him – for it is

## 10. Improvement by Love

non-technical self-knowledge that he requires. Just as he thinks of himself as Alcibiades' only true lover (131e), so too he claims to be the only one to possess great power over his future career, without offering any adequate explanation of how he might control it (105d-e). He does not see his own role as being that of the teacher (*didaskalos*), nor is it clear that the other's role will be that of the learner (*mathêtês*) in any normal sense. All this is not unexpected, since it is Socrates' normal position that he is not an educator in the strong sense in which the sophists are educators, so that he cannot be blamed for any failures owing to lack of professional expertise or for failing to fulfil contractual obligations. But even without the communication of any technical knowledge, the right kind of love-relationship can still be depicted as an *educational* experience for the beloved as well as a salutary one for the lover, as we regularly hear from the participants in the *Symposium* – and especially from Pausanias at 184b5-d3. So, even if Socrates' hopes of rescuing Alcibiades are full of self-deception, there is at least something traditional about them.

### How did Alcibiades learn?

So how is it that Socrates expects to have this educational power and influence over the young Alcibiades? The reader of the *Apology* would expect him to aim at controlling the youth by elenctic argument, getting him to observe his weaknesses, and prompting him to care more for the well-being of his own soul. However, that is not the kind of control that we should expect a lover to be exercising, since elenchus is ordinarily a confronting if not hostile experience (cf. Tarrant 2001). There is both elenchus and confrontation in the *Alcibiades*, but it is what makes Alcibiades take Socrates seriously and listen further, and therefore *precedes* his formal role as a lover-educator. What Proclus (*in Alc.* 14) and Olympiodorus (*in Alc.* 11) refer to as the 'elenctic' part of the dialogue is over by 119a, but Alcibiades does not ask Socrates about what is required for his education until 124b, nor how they may advance in the self-knowledge advocated by Delphic Apollo until 132b4-5. What is it that will come *after* the elenchus, indeed *after* Alcibiades has declared Socrates' love to be reciprocated at the end of the dialogue?

Here I acknowledge that I am influenced, perhaps too much influenced, by the commentary tradition, and particularly by the reading of Olympiodorus. This latter reads the passage at 132b-133c as promising that Alcibiades will find the clearest available image of his inner self within Socrates' own intellectual being. The notion of the beloved's eye finding its own self-reflection in the gaze of the lover who looks upon him (*Phdr.* 255c-d) is reproduced non-erotically at 132e-133a, and then transformed, with scarcely a nod to the idea of intellect as eye of the soul (*Rep.* 533d), into the notion that the soul may best be acquainted with its own true self if it 'gazes' into the supreme part of a soul where its excellence – exhibited in knowledge and awareness – is particularly to be found (133b-c). To me it makes little sense that Alcibiades should be being asked to gaze into his own soul in order to achieve self-knowledge, since the comparison with the eye, best able to gaze upon itself by gazing into the most life-like of the images beyond it, would then be redundant. Rather he must be asked to look into another soul, a soul in which he may more easily become acquainted with the nature of the divine as it resides within himself too. And that divine nature may most easily be seen operating *within Socrates*, and guiding his approach to Alcibiades. After all, Socrates has been trying to explain to Alcibiades the rationale behind his guiding divinity's ways since 124c8-10:

> The god, Alcibiades, [sc. is my guardian], who would not let me converse with you until this day; trusting in him I declare that the unveiling you seek[6] will come about through nobody else but me.

This god and its rational guidance had earlier been the source of Socrates' confidence that he was the right person to control Alcibiades (105d4-6, 105e5-106a1). The god is essential to Socrates' plans, and makes Socrates *the only* lover able to offer Alcibiades the secret to the fame he desires. The rightness of this god is forcefully if indirectly confirmed at 131c-e.

Olympiodorus expounds his interpretation of the key passage in two places. I omit material that is heavily laden with Neoplatonic theory:

> (a) ... so you too Alcibiades, ... because you are unable to turn around upon your own self, look into me, i.e. into Socrates' soul, and not into any random part of it but into the highest, and you will see in me intellect and (a) god. (Olymp. *in Alc.* 8)

> (b) So you, ...because you are unable to turn around upon your own self, look into my soul, and through it you will recognize your own as well. By looking into my soul you will discover that there are 'images of gods' [*Symp.* 215b3] within it, for intellect is there and (a) god. (Olymp. *in Alc.* 271)

There is a clear reference to Alcibiades speech in the *Symposium*, where Socrates is compared with the ugly statues of Marsyas that open up to reveal divine images within. Alcibiades insists that he has seen *inside Socrates* in a way that none of the rest of the company has done (216c7-d1). He caps his speech with a reference to all the divine images of virtue that are to be found by the acute observer in his conversations (222a). The connection is with *Alc.* 133c4-6:

> Then this [cognitive faculty of the soul] is like its god, and a person who looks into this and realises all its divine quality, its god and its wisdom, would thus be in the best position to know himself too.

As Olympiodorus understands it, the *Alcibiades* and *Symposium* make reference to the same divine element in the soul, but the former speaks of

## 10. Improvement by Love

one god so that the reader will naturally think of the divinity providentially controlling Socrates' *erôs*, while the latter speaks of many so as to enhance the comparison with Marsyas. And it is also his understanding that the soul of Socrates has an especially important status here, not because other souls cannot contain this divine element (for how else could a beholder behold his own self within Socrates?), but because Socrates alone has not buried or corrupted it. Hence Alcibiades' need for self-knowledge has become a quasi-erotic opportunity for Socrates alone, since in him alone can the true inner self be seen by those who most closely observe him. A close relationship with Socrates therefore offers Alcibiades the educational opportunity that he now desperately needs for public success. There is no doubt that this education will involve philosophy *somehow*, for it will be Socrates' mind that is the attraction, but what is important is constant acquaintance with this mind rather than simply learning what it says or surrendering oneself to its *elenchoi*. It will function as a potent paradigm of the voice within rather than as a direct source either of truths or of the exposure of falsehoods.

It may be going too far, then, to claim that the *Alcibiades* looks forward to a relationship in which the young man will be educated by love alone. The relationship must be a meeting of minds. Yet if the relationship should fail to educate Alcibiades, the actual outcome as the ancient readers knew, it would not be a failure of philosophy or a failure of Socrates to live up to his educational obligations. It would be a failure of love. Socrates struggles with the people of Athens for Alcibiades' affections; if he is corrupted by them, Alcibiades will cease to have the same attraction for Socrates, and the relationship will fail (132a1-5, cf. 135e6-8). One might almost say that the relationship *must* fail, assuming that the god still controls it. Here 127e4-7 is important:

> Alc.: So what must the one who realises [his culpable condition] do, Socrates?
> Soc.: Answer the questions, Alcibiades, and if you do this, if the god is willing, and if one ought also to put any trust in my prediction, you and I shall be in a better condition.

The repetition of 'if',[7] even allowing for the slight variation in Greek (*ei ... an ... ean ...*), underscores three conditions affecting the truth of Socrates' promise. The first is the most basic: Alcibiades' willingness to answer. The second, the god's willingness for them to succeed, might on the lips of another have been no more than a pious addition, but the god's willingness has been a factor from the beginning of the dialogue (105e7) to its end (135d6). The third, the reliability of Socrates' predictions, might again have had little significance but for his legendary prophetic sign that had again featured at the beginning of the dialogue (103a5-6), and his uncanny knack of sensing what is to come in the closing words. In these circumstances his prediction (*manteia*) is that of the soothsayer (*mantis*). Alcibiades will answer, Socrates is to be believed, so two out of three conditions are met. The remaining condition, the god's willingness, seems to have been flagged as the eventual problem.[8]

The *Alcibiades*, in its keenness to avoid attributing Socrates' failure with Alcibiades to a failure of philosophy, appears to be denying any precise correlation between his philosophical effort and the degree of excellence ultimately exhibited by his younger friend. As in Aeschines there are no educational techniques available to him that could guarantee the right outcome, and much seems to depend upon Socrates' strange conviction that he and he alone is the lover who can save Alcibiades. If he is deluded it is not so strange, as lovers are often deluded, and if all is subject to the seemingly capricious whims of a divinity, then that too may be explained in terms of the traditional capriciousness of Eros himself. It may be inaccurate to say that Socrates thinks to restrain Alcibiades 'by his love alone' as in Aeschines, but it is utterly unclear what place there will be for philosophy in the education of Alcibiades once he has found his own true self reflected in the mind of Socrates.

## Education in the *Theages* compared

The pseudo-platonic *Theages* is also presumed to have been influenced by Aeschines (cf. Joyal 2000, 40-7, 54-7), and, in a narrative by Socrates designed to show the uncertainties inherent in picking him as a mentor (130e), the young Aristides gives an account of how his *synousia* (literally 'being together') with Socrates facilitated his progress. It is quite explicit that Socrates taught him nothing, which thus far is a commonplace of the Platonic portrait of Socrates. But normally this 'teaching nothing' involves getting the interlocutor to think problems through logically and to realise quite a lot, beginning (but not necessarily ending) with his own mistakes. And, if Socratic education is to have any long-term purpose, the goal must involve more than just the interlocutor's recognition of his state of ignorance – as indeed it does in the case of the *Alcibiades*. The *Theages* is suggesting that the pupil must *stay* with Socrates, and that the effectiveness of the educational relationship corresponds to the degree of closeness of teacher and pupil – a worrying assumption today, but perhaps one that many a disgraced priest has deceived himself into believing. The very word *synousia* that the *Theages* uses systematically for educational relationships doubles as a word for sexual intercourse, and, as I have been at pains to show before (Tarrant 2005), it is generally a word that Plato chose to avoid in the case of Socrates' encounters with young men. Closeness is generally conceived in spatial terms, and begins with simply being in the same house, but there are suggestions (necessarily weak as the potential pupil's father is present) of a different kind of closeness:

## 10. Improvement by Love

> 'I have never ever learned anything from you, as you yourself know; but I made progress whenever I was with you – even if I was in the same house, but not in the same room, but more when I was in the same room; and I used to think I made much more progress whenever I was in the same room and was gazing at you while you spoke than when I was looking elsewhere; and I made progress most reliably and to the greatest degree of all whenever I was sitting next to you, holding you or touching you. But now', he said, 'that whole feeling (*hexis*) has vanished.' (*Theag.* 130d4-e4)

Aristides' feeling that he was undergoing some improvement at Socrates' side is linked not to the quality of Socrates' words but to the kind of closeness that is more usually missed by a partner in love. This agrees well with the fact that Socrates has already given a warning about his lack of expertise in all fields except matters of love, in which he thinks he stands comparison with anybody, past or present (128b). Aristides had been away on expedition after an initial period of promising progress with Socrates, and had returned with none of the facility for holding his own in a serious conversation that he had had previously (130a-c). Note what Aristides' idea of progress had been: a kind of *dialectical* ability (130c2: *dialegesthai*), enabling him to engage successfully with others who could argue (c3: *en tois logois*). It seems to have nothing to do with *moral* progress, and to bear a curious resemblance to eristic debate with its *competitive* element. In other words Aristides' idea of progress is one that values skills that Plato came to reject, at least for their own sake. Correspondingly, the term *epididômi* (in the sense 'I make progress') is something that we mainly hear of in sophistic contexts, and is worth examining briefly.

That *epididômi* is employed seven times in this same sense at *Theages* 129e-130e is in itself remarkable. The verb is found a maximum of five times in any other work, for there are five scattered cases in various senses in the rambling *Laws*.[9] There are four related cases at *Prot.* 318a-d, arising from Protagoras' sophistic claim that the pupil will 'make progress' every day that he studies with him. There are four cases too at *Hippias Major* 281d-283e, all but the last applying to the progress of the sophistic craft or comparable crafts. The final case is the most revealing:

> Then were you unable to persuade the young men in Lacedaimon that by being together with you (*soi synontes*) they would *make more progress* in excellence than with their own people? (283e2-4)

Compare Protagoras:

> Young man, the result for you, if you are together with me (*emoi synêis*), on whatever day you get together with me (*emoi syngenêi*), that you return home improved, and the same on the next day; and that you always *make progress* for the better in the course of every day. (*Prot.* 318a6-9)

My main concern about the *Theages* in my 2005 article had been its repetitive use of the terminology of 'being together with' or 'getting together with', which is applied freely to educational relationships with Socrates, when Plato ordinarily discourages us from thinking that this is the correct description for Socratic education. The only other place where I found this concern overridden was *Theaetetus* 150d2-151a6, another description of the vagaries of trying to study with Socrates that uses the same Aristides as the *Theages* as principal example, and fails to advance the comparison between Socrates and the midwife as 150b6-d2 and 151a6-d3 have done.[10] There are here three cases of the noun *synousia* ('being together with'), one case of the verb *syneinai* ('be together with'), and two cases of *syngignesthai* ('get together with'), at least one case of each term clearly applied to study *with Socrates*. There are likewise two cases of the verb *epididonai* in the sense of 'make progress'. All this terminology has a similar effect – to make Socrates look as if he is offering the kind of educational service that is associated with sophists such as Protagoras or Hippias.[11]

At that time I found this talk strangely misplaced in the midwifery episode, given that the whole point of the midwifery analogy is to make Socratic education (if there is such a thing) seem utterly remote from anything that the sophists and other contemporary educators made available, and yet I do not think that it is foreign to the *Theaetetus*. Rather, I suppose, its original role has been obscured by revision,[12] and we should recognise that it was Theodorus who has first introduced an alien concept of progress (*epidosis*) at 146b, using both the verb and this rather uncommon noun.[13] He has heard Socrates in discussion, and makes certain assumptions about this activity:

1. that it is a *dialektos*, a word never directly employed by Socrates for his kind of discussion,[14] but used by Theodorus later (183b6) for Heraclitean discourse;
2. that it is fitting for the young, an assumption shared above all by the questionable authority Callicles (*Gorg.* 485c-d);
3. that the young are able to make great progress in it, as in everything.

He will later also assume that it is a type of exercise (162b6), comparable with wrestling (169a-b). This is natural for Theodorus, himself a close friend of Protagoras (161b, 162a), so that he assumes a certain affinity between Socratic practices and the short question-and-answer combat in which Protagoras used to engage (*Prot.* 334e-336d). The sensitive reader may still recognise Plato's problems with such a concept of progress at 151d4-6: those whom the god permits make amazing progress 'as it seems both to themselves and to others'. Their progress *seems* so obvious, but the very fact that their discoveries can be lost suggests that it may not be as real as is thought.

Commentators do not doubt that *Theages* and *Theaetetus* 150d-151a are

## 10. Improvement by Love

related in some fashion, with those who regard the *Theages* as spurious generally assuming that the author was influenced by the other passage, but without being able to interpret it properly, particularly insofar as he had wrongly associated the intellectual midwife's *god* (150c8 etc.) with the *daimonic* sign (151a4).[15] The signs of spuriousness seemed to me then to be overwhelming, but more recently I have discovered that this is the most difficult of the suspect dialogues to separate stylometrically from undisputed Plato. Appendix 2b treats this issue briefly for those who want further detail, but the main observation to be made is that when the dialogue is split down the middle, the second part yields results that seem almost too Platonic, while the first part is much more equivocal, and shares some of the features of the *Alcibiades*-dialogues and *Hipparchus*. While all this proves little, it does suggest that *Theages* part 2 is a great deal closer to the expectations for Plato than *Theages* part 1, and that the second part (as distinct from the first) may be a slight reworking of genuine Platonic material, possibly including material discarded from a dialogue in the course of a revision.[16]

Whatever has happened here, it seems to me highly probable that the ultimate author has, in reworking such material and giving it a different context, been chiefly responsible for the overall educational philosophy of the work. That applies to the depiction of a type of philosophic progress dependent more on close physical proximity than on argument or increasing moral awareness. It is clear that Plato would dismiss this as false educational progress, for much the same 'education by proximity' is effectively rejected at *Symposium* 175d-e. At best such progress-through-contact would be a type of quasi-magnetic inspiration, caught by one participant from another as at *Ion* 535e-536d. The problem with such inspiration is that is does not proceed by craft (*technê*) or science (*epistêmê*), but by divine apportionment and possession (535c1-2), and thus will lack the systematic nature and the permanence that genuine progress would have. But all this seems to have by-passed the author, who has taken this shadow of philosophic progress for the real thing. In so doing he has forgotten the midwife's art with its facility for judging true and false (*Tht.* 150c1-3, 151d2-3, 160e6-161a4, 210b8-9), and left Socrates devoid of any art but the erotic (*Theag.* 128b2-6). Admittedly Plato sees *erôs* as something that can be caught by the beloved and so passed on, but like other forms of inspiration it is to be explained in terms of the god within, making one *entheos* (*Phdr.* 255b6), and thereby leaving control in the hands of the divine rather than of a suitably rational human agent.

My reading of the *Theages* is certainly complicated. The basic material of 128d-130e, I suppose, had the intention of questioning the whole concept of philosophic progress that Aristides is seduced by, exposing it as deficient and unreliable, for it is without any firm epistemic foundation. The ultimate author, however, reads quite a different meaning into the story, embracing the notion of educational inspiration that flourishes through long and close familiarity with the inspired teacher. That must, I believe, mean that he is working within a school whose ideology has changed significantly from that of Plato's day, and no doubt operates according to a system where the succession requires a long apprenticeship in the closest possible proximity to the leader from whom one's alleged inspiration will be inherited.

## Polemonian school culture

Such close relationships became the norm under Plato's third successor Polemo, who took over the Academy in around 314 BC and held office for forty years or so. The relationship between Polemo himself and his own successor Crates was extremely strong, as was that between their close colleagues Crantor and Arcesilaus (cf. D.L. 4.29). Polemo and Crates shared a house, shared a tomb, and shared a reputation as a pair of Golden Age individuals, speaking divine words from daimonic lips (D.L. 4.21-2). Their followers were encouraged to make improvised dwellings nearby (D.L. 4.19), as if to share in some of this proximity. Fragments of Polemo's philosophy are mostly rather unrevealing, centring on ethics, and little concerned with pure theory (D.L. 4.18); it is no accident that one of the most significant is his customary definition of love as 'service to the gods for the care and salvation of the young'.[17] The definition harmonises particularly well with the picture of divinely-guided Socratic love operating in the *Alcibiades*, so that it is natural enough to think that there may be some connection here. In fact it is highly likely that Plutarch (*Life of Alcibiades* 4) took such a connection for granted, since he reproduces the Polemonian formula 'divine service for the care and salvation of the young' in a chapter that up to that point had seemed dependent in part upon our *Alcibiades* dialogue.

Previously I have more fully made the case that the *Theages* stems from the period of Polemo's Academy (Tarrant 2005; 2006-7), but the focus of the present volume is the *Alcibiades*. If one dialogue that combines the divinely-inspired and the erotic Socrates could have arisen in the Academy of Polemo, then it might be thought possible that the *Alcibiades* was a product of this era too. John Dillon (1994) postulated a link between the *Alcibiades* (a 'Hellenistic *Ars Amatoria*') and Polemonian Academic culture, and most will prefer to see the dialogue as cause and the erotic culture as effect. However, the reverse is not impossible, and the following should also be considered.

While it might have been possible to derive both Polemo's definition of philosophic love and the seemingly new erotic culture in the Academy from the *Alcibiades*, we do not actually need to look any further than to Polemo's own relationship with Xenocrates to provide the necessary archetype. The fact that Polemo was rescued from a dissolute life by Xenocrates (e.g. D.L. 4.16) was widely known in antiquity. In this respect Xenocrates had acted

## 10. Improvement by Love

for the care and salvation of the young Polemo. The younger Aristippus had apparently written that Polemo had become enamoured of Xenocrates (*erasthênai*, D.L. 4.19), though there is no suggestion in this case of advances on Xenocrates' part or any physical relationship between them. The context in fact emphasises Xenocrates' dignity and understated emotions in all things, and it was only Polemo's feelings for Xenocrates that are described by Aristippus. Strong feelings on the part of the younger man for a mature, relatively unmoved philosopher immediately bring to mind Alcibiades' speech in the *Symposium*, where Alcibiades complains of Socrates' widespread use of a lover's guise only to metamorphose into the hard-to-get object of love himself (222b1-4). According to Diogenes, Polemo subsequently modelled himself upon Xenocrates in everything that he did, adopting the Xenocratean manner himself. It might be said that Polemo *discovered his true self by what he saw in Xenocrates*, and endeavoured to lead others younger than himself to that same discovery. The principal explanation of the culture of philosophic love that flourished under Polemo was therefore Polemo's own understanding of how he was rescued by Xenocrates. Since he was once as dissolute as Alcibiades, came from a wealthy background, and was no stranger to chariot-racing, comparisons with Alcibiades may easily have arisen, with the consequent feeling that he understood the relationship between Socrates and Alcibiades better than others did.

Therefore the dialogue could have been written, by Polemo or a close friend, with a view to bringing Polemo's insights into the understanding of the Platonic Socrates, so that Socrates fell more into line with later school culture. After all, one thing that clearly emerges from a study of the Academy at this time is that not only Polemo (D.L. 4.20) but also Crantor (4.26-27) and Crates (4.23) had strong literary interests that might well have equipped them to write dialogues that could pass for Plato's own. The *Alcibiades* is actually more likely to have arisen in this way than the *Theages*, since this latter sees Socrates less as a divine servant and more as an independent agent whose activities can be curtailed by divine prohibition. Technically the *Alcibiades* is not so different, but the divine will does seem somewhat more positive at 105e, 127e and 135d. Though serving the god of love rather than the god of prophecy, Socrates is as much on a divine mission here as in his elenctic activities described in the *Apology*.

There is perhaps also an argument for postulating that the *Alcibiades* is later than the *Theages*.[18] Like the *Theaetetus* (150e1-151a5), it is greatly concerned with the way in which those who try to learn under the guidance of Socrates may rapidly go backwards if they leave his company too soon. Both *Theages* and *Theaetetus* employ Aristides as the primary example of one who did so, while the *Theages* also mentions Thucydides, son of Melesias. Yet it is rather Alcibiades who became the primary example of one who had received no long-term help from his relationship with Socrates – the case that really needed explaining. The *Alcibiades* highlights the danger that Alcibiades may fail to benefit from his relationship (132a, 135e), and that failure would have been well known by the dramatic dates of the *Theages* and the *Theaetetus*, so that there is no easy explanation why his case should have been omitted if the *Alcibiades* had been already circulating. It would certainly have been natural that Alcibiades should have been mentioned in the *Theaetetus* as an example of somebody who had gone backwards as a result of corrupting associations (*dia ponêran synousian*) if Plato had at that stage seen his relationship with Socrates as an educational one. The case may be less obvious in the *Theages*, where corrupting associations are not the focus, but it would have had other compensating reasons to mention Alcibiades, given its determination to show how the supernatural sign could exercise control over all Socrates' educational relationships (128d3-7). This control may actually be seen operating in the *Alcibiades*, and some allusion to that work would have been natural *if* it were already in circulation.[19]

## Education by love alone?

Unlike Aeschines, the *Theages* and the *Alcibiades* never openly raise the idea that love might be sufficient to improve the beloved. The *Theages* does not openly suggest that the young Theages might be allowing himself to enter an erotic relationship of any kind, but the following circumstances do, however, apply:

1. Socrates represents himself as an expert in nothing but love (128b);
2. Socrates has profoundly influenced Aristides, and seemingly for the better (130a);
3. Socrates has always failed to teach Aristides anything;
4. The relationship with Aristides seems to have been intensely personal, and to have been dependent on a close physical presence (130d-e).

It might perhaps be suggested that Socrates has improved Aristides by *being there together with him* alone, in particular by being there and talking philosophy. Since it is also obvious from the text that Socrates is concerned for Aristides' welfare one might claim the overall requirements for Aristides' progress were:

1. Socrates' care for Aristides;
2. Socrates' being together with Aristides;
3. Socrates' engaging in philosophy;
4. Socrates' willingness to be close to Aristides;
5. The god's willingness that this togetherness should have a favourable outcome.

## 10. Improvement by Love

A better description of the improvement on offer would perhaps be 'education by philosophic togetherness alone, subject to the god's will'.

Let us now compare the *Alcibiades*.

1. Socrates does not really reveal what he is an expert in, though it would not be hard to claim that he shows special skills in the pursuit of philosophic love;
2. Socrates has by the end of the dialogue influenced Alcibiades for the better, particularly insofar as he has recognised his ignorance, recognised the need for self knowledge, and is now committed to practising justice (135e4-5);
3. Socrates has demonstrated to Alcibiades his own ignorance, and showed him the area of concern necessary for further educational advance;
4. The proposed relationship with Alcibiades is represented throughout as a love-relationship, albeit as an unusual type of love relationship, and might therefore be held to depend upon a degree of closeness.

Socrates has so far improved Alcibiades, and this improvement has depended not just on physical presence but also on his willingness to address strong words to him about his lack of preparation for the political tasks ahead. Even so, one might still claim that success is dependent on the following:

1. Socrates' care for Alcibiades;
2. Socrates' being together with Alcibiades;
3. Socrates' engaging in philosophy *with Alcibiades directly*;
4. Socrates' willingness to be close to Alcibiades and *vice versa* – this is particularly true if Olympiodorus is correct in supposing that Alcibiades must look into Socrates' soul as a kind of 'mirror' of his true self;
5. The god's willingness that this togetherness should have a favourable outcome.

One might be tempted to add a further condition, that the people of Athens should not lure Alcibiades away from Socrates in accordance with 132a and 135e, but that seems implicit in conditions 2 and 4. I suggest that the improvement of Alcibiades is intended to come about through 'education by philosophic togetherness *and engagement* alone, subject to the god's will'. Aeschines' Socrates had probably not hoped for anything much different, but he was peculiarly conscious of his lack of skills, as was the Socrates of *Theages*. The Socrates of the *Alcibiades* is not expected to lament his lack of skills in the presence of somebody whom he wants to impress (albeit in unorthodox fashion), but since Schleiermacher (1836) readers of the dialogue have often remarked that the arguments are not especially impressive, and we are not given the same feeling as in many dialogues that Socrates is falsely concealing his philosophic expertise. On the contrary, when he declares at 124c that he stands in the same need of education as Alcibiades does we might just be prepared to believe him. His skills in philosophic seduction (part of which does of course require clever talking) exceed his skills in philosophic argument throughout, and at no point does he ever suggest that he is going to teach Alcibiades philosophy. And I wonder whether the author of the *Alcibiades* thought that Socratic philosophy is, when properly conceived, a joint journey towards *mutual* self-improvement through techniques of question and answer (cf. 128e) – a journey involving a relationship rather than a mere encounter. The ancient biographic tradition suggests many relationships that might have acted as the real model for such a conception of philosophy, and the relationships between Xenocrates and Polemo, and between Polemo and Crates, might be numbered among them. Whether they were indeed providing an archetype or merely following an archetype already represented in the literature of the Academy is, and will no doubt remain, quite unclear.

## Notes

1. It is of course Wrong Argument who personally supervises Pheidippides' education. Socrates is never seen alone with him, only in scenes where his father is present, and it is his father whom he prefers to address. The erotic Socrates is never seen in this play.

2. Plutarch (*Alc.* 4) mentions people's surprise at their dining, exercising, and even sharing a tent with each other, but he may ultimately be dealing with Socratic sources rather than anything independent of the legend.

3. He tackles these questions directly at *Memorabilia* I.2; we know from hostile remarks in Isocrates' *Busiris* 4-5 that Polycrates' *Accusation of Socrates* made Alcibiades a pupil of Socrates; Isocrates for his part denies that anybody ever saw Alcibiades taking lessons from Socrates as his pupil.

4. Speech XLV = *de Rhet.* I pp. 19-20 Dindorf = fr. 12 Dittmar = fr. 53 SSR.

5. Note that there is a close connection between the life of the philosopher and that of the lover, both being first in the chain of nine lives at 248d2-4, while success in either life (provided that the lover heeds philosophy) may qualify one for early release from this chain at 249a1-4.

6. Either the revelation of Alcibiades to the world or the revelation of higher truth to Alcibiades; for the ambiguity see Denyer 2001, 192.

7. Denyer 2001, 208, talks of 'three protases for one conditional'.

8. If it seems far-fetched that the god should wish to destroy Athens by sabotaging this intellectual relationship, one can point to the spurious *De Virtute*, a reworked précis of some political material in the *Meno*, where the penultimate sentence (379d) reads as follows: 'And whenever (a) god wishes to benefit a city, he has put men of excellence into it, while, whenever a city is about to fare poorly, the god has removed the men of excellence from this city'.

9. 694b6, 747b6, 769c7, 913b6, 944a6; at 747b6 the sense is clearly similar, and applied to progress in arithmetic, as in the only case in *Republic* at 526b9. The mathematical sciences seem to be a clear case of cumulative learning in Plato.

## 10. Improvement by Love

10. That is not to say that the terminology of conception, miscarriage, midwifery and nursing disappears (see d9, e4, e5), but none of it has been prepared for (as the rest of the passage has) in the description of physical midwives at 149b-150a.

11. The only use of *epididômi* in Plato's dialogues (in approximately the right sense) to which we have not otherwise referred is *Cratylus* 410e2, a remark by Hermodorus to the effect that Socrates is making good progress (in etymology). Socrates' reply directly links the remark to *Euthyphro* 4b1-3, thereby continuing the ploy of associating this etymological expertise with Euthyphro, with whom Socrates had 'been together' (*sunê*, 396d6) that very morning. Hence the progress teasingly referred to is in quasi-sophistic studies with Euthyphro.

12. The case for the revision of *Theaetetus* has been further developed in Tarrant 2010; the details concerning the terminology of *epidosis* and how it related to the revision of this work will be discussed in Tarrant (forthcoming).

13. For the noun see also *Symp*.175e4 (of Agathon's progress in the tragic art), as well as *Laws* 676a5, 679b3, 700a8, 769b2.

14. The nearest he comes is *Republic* 454a8, where it is contrasted with eristic. At *Symposium* 203a3 it seems to mean something like 'communication'.

15. The view of Joyal 2000, 82-7, 144; Bailly 2004, 272-9, has an appendix on the similarity, but cannot determine which passage is earlier.

16. For material that was, or should have been, discarded in the course of a revision, see Sedley 2003, 6-16. Since I hold the *Theaetetus* to have been revised, and the ending to have been adjusted to look forward to its eventual sequel the *Sophist* rather than the *Euthyphro* (Tarrant, 2010), it is natural for me to see 128d-130e as a reworking of an earlier discarded ending in which Theodorus had sought to have Theaetetus study further with Socrates, on the grounds that he had already been 'making progress' through 'being together' with him. This would account for the vocabulary of *epidosis* and *synousia* as stemming from Theodorus' misconceptions, and could also explain why parallel material has been woven in the final version into the section of midwifery. I decline, however, to commit myself to this explanation.

17. Plut. *Mor.* 780d; see Dillon 2003, 165. That it was a customary definition is indicated by Plutarch's use of the imperfect tense, and in such cases it may well come from the reports of somebody who had studied with Polemo, rather than from Polemo himself. This is made all the more plausible when another passage of Plutarch (*Theseus and Romulus Compared* 1.6) refers to it, in the context of Ariadne's heaven-sent love that preserved Theseus, simply as a definition 'of the philosophers'! Cicero (*de Leg.* 1.18), perhaps following Antiochus of Ascalon, is apparently prepared to represent a *Stoic* definition as virtually a pan-philosophic one, and Zeno's studies with Polemo make him the likeliest source for having preserved a concept of love consistently promoted by Polemo. It ought therefore to be noted that Zeno is known to have seen Eros as a divine and cohesive force, bringing friendship, freedom, and concord, and hence contributing to the preservation (again *sôtêria*) of the city in some way (Athen. 13.561c = *SVF* 1.61.13-17), a deduction that might easily be made on the basis of *either* Polemo's definition *or* the *Alcibiades*.

18. Joyal 2000, 56-7, 219, suspected the priority of the *Alcibiades*, but Bailly 2004, in another appendix (279-84), again decided that there is no compelling evidence either way.

19. Note that this would not imply a very late date for the *Alcibiades* if the ending of the *Theages* were intentionally based primarily upon a discarded draft ending of the *Theaetetus* as speculated above.

# 11

# Ice-Cold in Alex: Philo's Treatment of the Divine Lover in Hellenistic Pedagogy[1]

## Fergus J. King

The Judaism of the Second Temple period was not an isolated culture. Modern research shows that, as a result of the long-standing interplay of Greek, Roman and Judaic cultures, Judaism developed its thinking and practice in dialogue with its neighbours' and conquerors' cultures, though the extent of the interplay remains contentious. That interplay can be seen in the work of the Alexandrian Jewish writer, Philo, whose work is a fusion of Greek philosophy and Judaism. Platonic ideas and literature figure heavily in his writing. However, the relationship which exists between pupil and teacher does not adopt wholeheartedly the patterns which can be seen in the Platonic corpus.

Philo wrote prodigiously (ten volumes and three supplements in the Loeb Classical Library) across a diverse number of subjects. Much of his work engaged in an allegorical interpretation of Scripture in an attempt to show that Judaism was as philosophical as the various schools, usually Greek in origin, which still existed in the late Republican and early Imperial periods of Rome. He lived in Alexandria, where Greek and Jew had co-existed for a long period, not always in peace. Philo's own lifetime saw a period of unrest between the two groups. Philo's work reveals not just an active and full knowledge of the Jewish Scriptures but of the philosophies of the Stoa, Aristotle and Plato. It appears that he aimed to convince Greek-speaking, non-Jewish readers that Judaism possessed the philosophical knowledge or wisdom that their own great thinkers had sought: 'It was Philo's triumphant boast that what the gentiles sought in ignorance the Jews had actually possessed in Moses' (Goodenough 1940, 39).

However, there are a number of different approaches in recent scholarship as to how this might actually work. Even the titles and names by which Philo is identified may shed light on how he is perceived at various points.[2] Great attention is also paid to his exegetical and interpretive methodology. Thus in detailed analyses of Philo's allegorical method, Dawson (1994) presents Philo as a cultural revisionist attempting to show that Greek culture is subordinate to Jewish, while Boyarin (1994) suggests a universal worldview which is not restricted by Jewish particularity. This chapter does not focus so much on the content of those well-researched

## 11. Ice-Cold in Alex

areas (although I will suggest that they have implications for this wider topic) but looks specifically at Philo's pedagogy, notably the 'divine lover' motif.

### The divine lover in the Philonic writings

Given the extent of the Philonic corpus, a word search was undertaken to isolate instances of the vocabulary used elsewhere to describe relationships of this type. It goes without saying that these terms encompass lexical fields which are wider than this one specific instance, so the search is somewhat like a fishing net which is cast and draws in a catch: the catch is then sorted for what is wanted or rejected.[3] For our purposes, only three matches relate directly to the divine lover: *erômen-* in *Contempl.* 61.1 and *paidik-* in *Contempl.* 61.1 and 4.

This passage, as it turns out, is one of three key texts in which Philo discusses, in broader terms, the issue of 'homosexuality': *Abraham* 133-37, *Spec.* 3.37-42 and *Contempl.* 59-62.[4] I purposefully place 'homosexuality' in inverted commas, aware that the term is fraught with difficulties and may well be, at least in our usage, alien to the ancient world, though the question of whether 'homosexual' may be used to describe behaviour from the time before the word itself was coined in the 1860s is hotly contested by 'essentialists' and their critics.[5] I will subsequently use the term 'masculine same-sex activity' to avoid getting dragged into this debate, which is best left for other forums. Similarly, I purposefully use 'masculine'. I do not exclude the possibility of feminine same-sex behaviour in the ancient world, but simply honour the fact that we are dealing with honour and shame societies in which the criteria for men and women were different, that the issue that stands before us is of masculine behaviour, and that we cannot pretend that one code of behaviour fitted both genders.[6] The texts which we will examine in the Philonic corpus do not speak of feminine same-sex behaviour so, with apologies to Wittgenstein, thereof I must keep silent.

Here we must be careful that we do not allow anachronistic thinking to intrude, and need to bear in mind the numerous caveats which have been made in recent scholarship. Many of these come from New Testament theology and Christian ethics where the debate about the ethical dimensions of homosexuality in the modern world has ebbed to and fro over the last forty or so years. Scholars in this field remind us to be vigilant in assuming that ancient texts can be imported directly into the modern debate as though they address the issue in exactly the same way that we do. It must also be said, and I say this as a member of that Christian theological community, that the debate has not been helped by scholars prejudging the issue, either from a liberal or conservative position, and exploring the texts in ways which lead to the very conclusions which they held as their research began. Some have been, I would venture, wilfully misleading in their methodology. Consider, for example, Horner's small volume, *David Loved Jonathan: Homosexuality in Biblical Times*, which argues that there was at least a 'strong possibility' of homosexual activity in cultic situations where there were eunuchs even though there are no official records: the footnote supporting the argument turns out to be the *Kama Sutra*.[7] Both parties are equally guilty of bending texts to suit their own modern purpose in ways which effectively dehistoricise them. Part of the problem here arises from the influence of reader-response criticism which, while it admirably reminds us of the potential number of readings which are valid for any text, fails, on occasion, to recognise the historical dimensions of text and meaning.[8]

That said, we are still free to explore what it is that Philo says in his own terms, aware that the premises from which he argues are potentially very different from those of our own day and age. I have no intention of addressing the contemporary debate in this paper; my interest is to shed some light on why Philo thought as he did, and venture to understand this as a specific reaction to the context in which he lived. It may be, however, that this may inform the modern debate.

Returning to the three Philonic texts, it can be seen that the last two of these in particular are germane to the 'divine-lover' motif. Let us start by considering their substance. I summarise the key points here for brevity, focusing on two: *On the Special Laws* and *On the Contemplative Life*.

## On the Special Laws *3.37-42*

This passage is part of a longer exposition of the sixth commandment of the Decalogue, which makes 'thou shalt not commit adultery' an extended reflection on appropriate and inappropriate sexual behaviour. Thus Philo speaks out against adultery (7-11), incest and relationships prohibited by kindred or affinity (12-31), intercourse during times of menstruation (32-3), intercourse when barren or sterile (which he appears to consider purely a feminine health issue) (34-6), pederasty (37-42), bestiality (48-50), prostitution (51), adultery per se (52-63), rape and seduction (64-71), intercourse with the betrothed (72-8) and slanders about virginity (79-82).

On pederasty, Philo describes it as a graver evil (*meizon kakon*, 37) which has become even 'a matter of boasting not only to the active but to the passive partners' (*nuni d' estin aukhêma ou tois drôsimonois, alla kai tois paskhousin*, 37).[9] On what is his condemnation based? Two things:

1. that taking part in such activities makes men effeminate and is damaging to both their physical and psychological male health (*hoi noson thêleian nosein êthizomenoi tas te psukhas kai ta sômata diarreousi mêden empureuma tês arrhenos geneas eôntes hupotuphesthai*, 37).
2. that such activities destroy the means of procreation (*diaphtheirôn tas gonas*, 39), promote sterility and render effeminate young men at the

flower of their development (*tous neous hôraizôn kai to tês akmês anthos ekthêlunôn*, 39).

His critique takes on a specifically religious dimension as he singles out for particular attention those who take part in religious feasts and mystery cults.

## On the Contemplative Life 57-63

This passage speaks directly to the symposium tradition found in Greek philosophy. Given that the symposium is in some ways a microcosm of the school, we may read this passage as an attack on the nature and character of the philosophical schools, and even, perhaps, of wider Hellenistic practice.[10] Thus this passage is a foil to diminish the worth of such traditions in comparison with the practice of the Therapeutai, a Jewish contemplative movement best described as an Egyptian Jewish order, who apparently were based at Lake Mareotis.[11]

In common with other Judaic groups of the Second Temple period, their meals are characterised by table-fellowship, salvation expressed in right eating and purity (cf. King 2007, 88). The meal of the Therapeutai takes the shape of a classic Hellenistic banquet with sections which correspond to a *deipnon* (64-85) and a *sumposion*. To summarise very briefly, these are characterised by order, decorum, lack of excess, and praise of God. Before this account is given, the banquets of the Greeks are unfavourably, or even inadequately (thus Szesnat 1998, 91), described: they, in Philo's opinion, are marked by drunkenness and fighting (40-7), luxury and ostentation, including beautiful slaves (with the implication of voyeurism or immorality) and rich foods (48-50): all indications of a lack of self-control and, thus, weakness.[12] The two symposia at which Socrates was a guest are held up as noble counterpoints to these practices, but there is a sting in the tail: compared to the meals of Philo's contemplatives even these appear somewhat contemptible (58). First, there is an element of pleasure, of which Philo disapproves (58; cf. Szesnat 1998, 93). The discussion is also disappointing: a discussion of love which, whilst initially promising soon becomes an excursus on 'common vulgar love' which Philo interprets as masculine same-sex love. He interprets this literally, with no consideration of the possibility that this language might be symbolic or metaphorical for the philosophical quest.[13] Why is this love so criticised? Because it induces an effeminate sickness (*thêleian de noson*, 60)[14] or renders the participants androgynous (*androgunous kataskeuazôn*, 60).[15] Love corrupts both the lover and the beloved: the boys are reduced to the condition of being girls (*erômenês*, 61, a feminised form of the masculine *erômenos*) and the lovers (*tous erastas*, 61) are damaged physically, mentally and in terms of their possessions (*sôma kai psukhên kai ousian*, 61). Further, 'sterility and childlessness' ensue (*anthrôpôn kai steirôsin kai agonian tekhnazontai*, 62). For Philo, male same-sex behaviour is, literally, the end of civilization as we know it (Szeznat 1998, 95-7).

*Summary*

Both passages really cite the same arguments against masculine same-sex activity: effeminacy and the destruction of procreative ability. It is now our task to see why Philo has singled out these reasons for his moral stance. It would be easy to take an ahistorical approach to this question. Yet, it is worthwhile to look at the context in which Philo lived and wrote, and how that may have shaped or driven some of his reflections.

## Philo: an Alexandrian Jew

Let us start with two obvious statements: the first, that Philo was Jewish, and the second that he lived in Alexandria. These two points show us that Philo lived in a time and place where issues of culture and identity were of crucial importance. Tracing its origins to Alexander in 333 BC, the city was predominantly Greek, with few native Egyptians living there (cf. Schwartz 2000). Jewish immigration meant that they came to predominate in 'two of its five quarters' (*sic*) (Schwartz 2000). The first anti-Semitic writings appeared in the third century BC and Apion's writings (contemporary with Philo) were refuted by Josephus, *Contra Apion*. Philo has a particular view of the problem: Philo was aware of the anti-Semitism in his native city and referred to it a number of times in his essays. His tone mixes apology with self-righteous innocence. Racial and religious harmony is a fond hope. The Jews, he declares, are ready for friendship with any whose intentions are peaceful, but let our good will not be mistaken for cowardice ready to surrender to aggressors. Philo is disturbed by charges of Jewish misanthropy. It is astonishing, he laments, that some people accuse the Jews of inhumanity, that nation which shows such profound fellowship and good will to all mankind and which offers prayers and sacrifices for them (Schwartz 2000).

Thus Philo's Alexandria was not a happy multicultural city, but rather one split by issues of culture and identity. Matters came to a head, so Philo reports, with the visit of King Agrippa I to the city.[16] An unruly mob insulted and parodied the king, and called for his images to be placed in the synagogues. Synagogues and Jewish business were attacked and burned. Later there were indignities for Jewish senators and women. The quarrel was not distinct from Roman politics, whether of the regime or individual interests.[17] Anti-Semitism was fomented by Flaccus, the Roman governor, increasingly under threat since the death of Tiberius and the accession of Gaius Caligula earlier in 37 AD, who was offered support by anti-Semitic factions. Issues of citizenship for Jews may also be intertwined in the problem (cf. Colson 1967, 296). These

## 11. Ice-Cold in Alex

political actions raised other issues: they asked who might be considered 'authentically Greek'.[18]

### Philo's multi-cultural context

What is of interest here is not the precise details of the conflict but some of the longer standing mythologies which informed the positions which the protagonists took. Thus Philo's work not only describes Jewish aspirations, but becomes an apologia for Judaism, in which Philo argues that it is a viable and credible alternative to Hellenism. He wishes to show not only the commonalities between Judaism and Greek philosophy (a defensive strategy), but even, if Dawson is right, its superiority (an offensive strategy). His comments on masculine same-sex activities exemplify this broader agenda. Why? Because sex is one of the important boundary markers for the Jewish way of life.

### Philo's Judaic context

Let us defend this statement with an observation on the nature of Judaism by Jonathan Klawans. Klawans notes that sacrifice and cult were significant factors in Jewish life and identity. In turn, sacrifice is important because it deals with issues which are paramount and closely connected with the social identity of the Jewish people. Sacrifice ensures purity, and purity is purity from what? Pollution caused by sex and death (Klawans 2001, 145). We may dispute the importance placed on these two matters by Jewish thought and praxis of the period, but let us acknowledge the reality of their significance in what Girard calls the 'mythic realisations' of the Judean people.[19]

The long-standing significance of sexual matters as part of Jewish identity surfaces in the Maccabean literature which describes conflict between Judaic nationalists and the Seleucid regime.[20] 1 Macc 1:14 mentions the building of a gymnasium in Jerusalem as a source of outrage, because such places encouraged nudity and were considered to be places where masculine same-sex relationships were cultivated.[21] Alexandrian Jews apparently availed themselves of the gymnasium culture, and Philo himself was most likely a product of it. It was a means for Jews to assimilate with Hellenism and Romanism to the extent that they might obtain citizenship.[22] However, it must have raised questions of identity. Gymnasia bore the hallmarks of Greek polytheistic religion both in their design and the literature which was studied in the educational syllabi offered. Jews who studied in such places must have been aware of a major theological difference, if not a difference of identity. Other Jews definitely were. Groups like the Maccabees had no doubts that those who assimilated Greek culture betrayed their faith (1 Macc 1:15). Yet it is equally likely that those who attended the gymnasia for purposes of social advancement might well have felt that they could undergo instruction there without 'selling out'. As Hengel sums up, participating in activities held in a polytheistic environment 'was not to be taken as an evasion of Jewish belief: partly, it is also a sign that the Judaism of the Diaspora had won an inner self-assurance over against its polytheistic environment' (Hengel 1991, 68). Philo would appear to fit here: confident in his claim of showing that Judaism is not just the equal of the Greek schools, and keen to show how it both conforms to and diverges from their standards – for the better. And for Philo, rejection of the erotic element was part of this superiority.

Sociological analysis suggests that questions of identity involve a number of different boundary markers. In her *Purity and Danger*, Mary Douglas (2002, 142) notes the symbolism of boundaries, and how they are part of social identity. The human body is often used to describe societies or groups:

> The body is a model which can stand for any bounded system. Its boundaries can represent any boundaries which are threatened or precarious. The body is a complex structure. The functions of its different parts and their relation afford a source of symbols for other complex structures.

Particular attention must be paid to the weak boundary points of the body:

> All margins are dangerous. If they are pulled this way or that the shape of fundamental experience is altered. Any structure of ideas is vulnerable at its margins. We should expect the orifices of the body to symbolise its especially vulnerable points. (Douglas 2002, 1)

Sexual activity becomes part of the business of boundary and identity:

> Sexual collaboration is by nature fertile, constructive, the common basis of social life. But sometimes we find that instead of dependence and harmony, sexual institutions express rigid separation and violent antagonism. So far we have noted a kind of sex pollution which expresses a desire to keep the body (physical and social) intact. Its rules are phrased to control entrances and exits. Another kind of sex pollution arises from the desire to keep straight the internal lines of the social system. (Douglas 2002, 173-4)

We see these patterns in the Levitical material which forms a major plank of Philo's sexual morality. This material covers a wide range of ground. Eating, sex, and death are three key areas, but they are united by a common premise that keeping these instructions is necessary for holiness and the receipt of God's blessing:

> Holiness is the attribute of Godhead. Its root means 'set apart'. What else does it mean? We should start any cosmological enquiry by seeking the principles of power and danger. In the Old Testament we find blessing as the source of all good things, and the withdrawal of blessing as the source of all

## 11. Ice-Cold in Alex

dangers. The blessing of God makes the land possible for men to live in. (Douglas 2002, 62)

Keeping the commandments of God has the effect of guaranteeing prosperity, and offers wholeness and completeness. Completeness is signified by the stress that sacrificial victims must be perfect or unblemished, and that the body must not be defiled (Douglas 2002, 63-4). When we see Philo's views of masculine same-sex behaviour, it is apparent that he views such behaviour as defiling: it literally ruins the prosperity of society by the denial of the procreative purpose:

> Holiness means keeping distinct the categories of creation. It therefore involves correct definition, discrimination and order. Under this head all the rules of sexual morality exemplify the holy. Incest and adultery (Lev. XVIII, 6-20) are against holiness, in the simple sense of right order. Morality does not conflict with holiness, but holiness is more a matter of separating that which should be separated than of protecting the rights of husbands and brothers.[23] (Douglas 2002, 67)

Leviticus 18:20 includes masculine same-sex behaviour in the list of prohibitions.[24] So it appears that Philo is arguing his point in a way that is consistent with a Jewish pattern of perfection, which we can identify as holiness. However, his argument may well be informed by other non-Judaic thinking.

### Philo's philosophical context

The Platonic corpus is not univocal in an affirmation of the 'divine lover' motif and approval of masculine same-sex behaviour. In the *Laws* (8.836b-c), Plato is critical of non-procreative sexual behaviour in the constitution he draws up for his putative state. Three arguments are advanced: first that it is 'unnatural', second that such unions do not occur in the animal world, and third that these relationships do not promote military courage. Space does not permit us to do more than note these points, which would be unlikely to stand up to modern scientific scrutiny. For our purposes, we note a commonality between Judaic and Platonic writing; a convergence which is particularly useful to Philo who is thus able to advance his case using arguments and citations which some of his interlocutors might hold themselves. A simplistic 'Judaism says "yes" and Hellenism says "no"' dichotomy will neither stand up, nor will it do justice to the complexity of the materials still available to us.

However, this is not the only point where the different cultures of the first century BC overlap: ideas of masculinity also impinge on the arguments and again suggest some convergence, or, at least, that Philo is using arguments congenial to his interlocutors to make his point. To get into these arguments we need to look at constructions of masculinity in the

*Fergus J. King*

period, and be precise in our use of texts. The criticism levelled by Camille Paglia (1992, 170-248, especially 189) at David Halperin's work (of mixing documents from different locations and epochs like gravel off the back of a truck) still holds good, and is a remedy against excessive generalisation which fails to respect the individual niceties of different periods of Greek, Roman and Jewish history.

## Masculinity in the first century BC

When we look at definitions of masculinity in the Greek and Roman cultures of Philo's times, two protocols become apparent: dominance and self-restraint (Ivarsson 2008, especially 185). These protocols are constructed along very different lines from ours. Modern society is highly critical of those who use their authority as teachers as a means of developing sexual relations.[25] In the Greek and Roman world of Philo's time this was less of a concern, though there are reports of pedagogues whose duty was to chaperon their charges, and this involved protecting them from sexual harassment (Bradley 1991, 53). The poet, Ovid, has different objections: he is critical of pederasty because the boy will get no pleasure, and mocking of homosexual males (cf. Makowski 1996, especially 30). Thus we may note that certainly within popular thinking there was not a whole-hearted adoption of the idea that same-sex male behaviour was beneficial or positive for the youths involved.

In the ancient societies of Philo's time, all 'real men' are expected to hold these protocols of dominance and self-restraint or risk being branded as effeminate or soft (Lat. *mollis*, Gk. *malakos*; cf. Edwards 1993, 63-97). Further, failure to be 'masculine' is a sign of moral weakness: masculinity is equated with virtue, its lack with vice (cf. Stenström 2008, especially 206-7). Furthermore, masculinity is not unchanging, nor a biological fact:

> Rather, a person's masculinity is always under threat and must be guarded. Masculinity is continuously constructed by defending one's honour, shunning everything weak and feminine, behaving in a way that befits a man, and by being in competition with other men. (Stenström 2008, 204)

This last point needs some clarification. The competitive element arises from the fact that the ancient cultures which we examine were essentially honour/shame cultures in which honour was to be sought and was considered to be in limited supply: George Foster (1965, 296) calls this the 'image of limited good'. It means that in such societies there is not enough honour to go around, that one man's gain of honour is another's loss, and therefore competition, aggression and envy become driving forces for behaviour.[26] Given Philo's immediate context, we might argue that not only are individuals in competition for the limited good of honour, but this competition has extended to the rivalry between Jew and Greek in Alexandria, and is

## 11. Ice-Cold in Alex

part and parcel of Philo's wider apologetic and philosophical agenda: to show the value of Judaism and the Mosaic tradition to its Hellenistic counterparts.

### Masculinity and sexual behaviour

In this competitive arena, dominance becomes a protocol, and masculine sexual behaviour is graded on hierarchy. At the risk of being graphic, penetration is power:

> Masculine sexual behaviour means penetrating a socially inferior person, whether a woman or a boy. A man must not be penetrated himself. Nor must he seem to be submissive in any other way. The most flagrant deviance from this protocol is a man who desires and finds pleasure in being penetrated by other men. (Ivarsson 2008, 185-6)

For some this meant that actions were inappropriate for older men (with, presumably a tacit acceptance of the suitability for younger men to be penetrated), but for others, the whole business meant that masculine same-sex behaviour could not be legitimate at all. Thus, in describing Paul's critique of such behaviour, Balch notes:

> It seems likely that with this term (*arsenokoitia*) Paul is picking up a thread of Greek and Jewish tradition which regarded pederasty as an illegitimate form of erotic love not only because of the lover's loss of self-control but also because of the younger male's disgrace in being penetrated. Stock arguments against the practice of pederasty turned inevitably to the *hubris* inflicted on the boy.[27]

What is of interest is that Philo does not refer to this *hubris* in his critique. Nor does he appear to differentiate between hubristic and non-hubristic love.[28] Nor does he make any argument to the effect that such damaging behaviour might be inappropriate to the formation of an educated person (i.e. that the means frustrates the ends). His concerns appear solely with effeminacy and sterility.

The second protocol is that of self-restraint (*enkrateia*). This signifies weakness to the extent that a man is driven by, and does not control, his own passions and desires (Ivarsson 2008, 186-8). 'Mastery' is a common trait in masculinity beyond and including sexual behaviour'(Stenström 2008, 204-5). Note, too, that there is no distinction between private and public morality. What might be described as a lack of mastery manifested as improper masculine behaviour becomes a signal that an individual is not fit for public office, a connection which is explicitly drawn in the use of sexual slander in Cicero and Suetonius.[29] Philo includes this element in his *Contemplative Life* by placing this kind of behaviour alongside luxury and voluptuousness as compared to the practices of the Therapeutai.

*Fergus J. King*

In this respect, it is possible to say that he echoes popular contemporary opinion which not only manifests itself in a number of different cultural critiques, but also exemplifies a standard theme in Jewish polemic:

> Just as the Greeks considered barbarians effeminate, and the Romans questioned the masculinity of the Greeks, so the Jews often stereotyped gentiles as effeminate. For example, the books of Judith and 4 Maccabees both demonstrate the inferiority of elite, gentile men (Holofernes, Antiochus Epiphanes) compared to Jewish women and youths (Judith, the seven martyrs and their mother) with respect to courage, self-restraint and masculinity. Gentile effeminacy is often connected with sexual licentiousness, as e.g. in the Wisdom of Solomon (14:22-28), where idolatry is the specific origin of *porneia*. Gentile idolatry leads to all kinds of evil and excessive behaviour, and different kinds of sexual excess and deviance are prominent among these vices.[30] (Ivarsson 2008, 190-1)

Philo takes up this theme but specifically directs it towards masculine same-sex behaviour. We must also point out that Philo here takes a very literal view of 'common vulgar love' which is neither used as an allegory or metaphor as it may have been within some of the philosophical traditions. This is a conscious choice of Philo's. Elsewhere he is capable of describing the erotic or bodily (albeit in different sex unions) in a positive manner (cf. Winston 1998, 41-62, especially 48-50). The connection made explicitly to Greek religion in his writing strongly suggests that he is not influenced purely by the debate within Graeco-Roman society but is drawing upon the history of Jewish polemic (Gaca 1999, especially 167-71).

It is also possible that this treatment of same-sex masculine behaviour may shed light on Philo's aims and intentions. We have already asked whether he aimed to subvert Greek culture or to reveal universality. The passages analysed here appear to contain elements of both: a Jewish way of life (the Therapeutai) is viewed as superior to its Greek counterparts. However, the arguments which buttress this are not purely Jewish; they contain elements common to both Jewish and Greek philosophical and popular thought. Thus, in addition to the variety in popular beliefs noted above we may also note the philosophical dimension to issues of masculinity and effeminacy.[31] If Judaism is being hyped up here, it is on the grounds that it is a better way of fulfilling values which are already found in Greek thought: we might put it crudely, 'if you want to be really Greek, act Jewish', at least in regard to sexual behaviour. This conclusion resonates with Dyck's conclusions (2002, 174) about Philo's allegorical method:

> It is my view that, far from revising (let alone subverting) Greek culture and imperial rule, Philo was endorsing it. Not necessarily in a conscious way but rather by participating in a discursive tradition that sought to recast Judaism in a form appropriate to its imperial and cosmopolitan environment. Philo represents a form of Judaism which had come to terms with a high

## 11. Ice-Cold in Alex

degree of socio-cultural and political assimilation and acculturation. Furthermore it accommodated Judaism to the dominant culture via practices such as allegorical interpretation without abandoning its distinctive traditions and practices.

We might add that, in this case, accommodation involved the use of philosophical reflection (exemplified by the *Laws*) and popular values.

### Conclusions

Philo's approach to the 'divine-lover' material is highly critical, and his rejection of any such value draws from a mixture of popular and philosophical traditions. Attitudes to male same-sex behaviour were not uniform, and Philo draws on the critical elements within popular thinking, Greek philosophy and Judaism to criticise male same-sex behaviour as 'un-masculine' inasmuch as it encourages effeminacy and indicates a lack of self control. He is, however, running a particularly Jewish line when he draws links between this behaviour and idolatry. The shrewdness of his approach is to link this particularly Jewish dimension to sentiments which might well have been held by some of his interlocutors (e.g. the disapproval of effeminacy). Thus his argument about male same-sex behaviour, whilst strongly Judaic, is not without its echoes in the *Laws*, or contemporary understandings of law manifested in the legislation passed by Augustus (e.g., pertaining to procreation and sterility; cf. Stenström 2008, 206-7).

Philo's writing is not meant for the 'ivory tower': he is engaged in a critical polemic in a competitive society for honour – in this case the honour of Jewish culture and practice in a highly divided Alexandria. This is no abstract philosophical speculation but one rooted in a highly contentious social and political context. It is as much a work of rhetoric, for persuasion, as philosophy, for the honour and status of Philo and his people are at stake, and the competitive or aggressive element of discourse in an agonistic 'limited good' culture is well to the fore.

### Postscript: the Philonic legacy

The evidence presented above suggests that Philo stands within a broader sweep of Judaic thought which condemned masculine same-sex behaviour, often associating it with idolatry and effeminacy. However, he certainly cannot stand as a representative of Christian tradition. Space does not permit a full examination of Philo's impact on Christian tradition, but let us start by noting his location in Alexandria, an African city, and the crucial role that Alexandrian and African Christians took in the shaping of Christianity in its earliest centuries.[32] Theirs was a legacy which was to have an impact on subsequent theologians of the patristic periods and beyond, of both the theological East and West. Philo's contribution to this was not inconsiderable. His influence may also have led to the side-lining of the 'divine lover' motif in traditions which evolved within that Christian context, notably by treating it literally rather than symbolically.

If we turn our attention to issues of male same-sex behaviour we find that Philo's influence on emerging Christianity was immense. His interpretation of Scripture dominated Christian biblical interpretation (Crompton 2003, 136-8; Dockery 1992, 77-9), and his exegesis of the Sodom and Gomorrah story,[33] which firmly linked the condemnation of the people of Sodom with masculine same-sex activity, was adopted wholesale within the earliest Christian traditions, but not in rabbinic interpretation (cf. Bailey 1975, 26-7). It is only in the modern period that the stress on the abuse of guests and hospitality has been strongly pushed as an alternative reading, even if this cannot be fully divorced, philologically, from sexual behaviour.[34] However, an analysis of Philo's interpretation within the context which shaped it shows how different the dynamics of same-sex unions were, and must caution against an overly simplistic relocation of his argument, and indeed subsequent reflections based on these, to ethical debates in other times and places, including contemporary Christian controversy. There is a further consideration. When an interpretive tradition has become as influential as Philo's, care must be taken to ensure that the original texts are allowed to speak for themselves and are not obscured by later interpretations.

Further, the traditions of Christian monasticism came out of this African context (cf. Oden 2008, 52-5). It does not require a great leap to see a link between those early Christian traditions and their antecedents in groups like the Therapeutai described in the *Contemplative Life* (cf. Oden 2008, 158). Christian monastics were to spiritualise same-sex relationships and exclude the physical and erotic, though modern revisions of these traditions contest whether the physical was truly absent. Even married Christians were to choose the way of abstinence in what were called 'spiritual marriages' (Boswell 1996, 119-21). In *Confessions* 3.1, Augustine describes a relationship with a strong physical component which may or may not have been homosexual, yet his Christian persona will not see any value either to masculine same-sex behaviour, or, indeed, to the physical aspects of that friendship.[35] Thus, whatever positive aspects might have been drawn about masculine same-sex behaviour in the divine lover of Greek philosophy were not adopted in either Jewish or Christian tradition, which rather classed such activity as sinful, idolatrous and/or detrimental to the fabric of society.

It is, however, important to remember the context of Philo's argument. His scathing critique of masculine same-sex behaviour is forged in a battle for identity and value. In the modern period, the issue of human sexuality in the church may equally be such a crucible, particularly when the church goes global in a post-colonial world. The modern debate may not be so

## 11. Ice-Cold in Alex

much about sex, as about being Western, African, Asian, and/or powerful. Even if the arguments advanced by Philo appear outdated, it would seem that the struggles for power and identity which make debates on such topics so controversial remain.

### Notes

1. This chapter is dedicated to the memories of Prof. Ian Mueller, late of Chicago, and Prof. Ian G. Kidd, late of St Andrews. It is a reworking of a paper read at the Australasian Society for Ancient Philosophy Conference, 4-6 December 2008, on *Socrates, Alcibiades, and the Divine Lover/Educator: A Research Conference revolving round the Platonic Alcibiades I* at the University of Newcastle, NSW. I am most grateful to Professors David Runia and Harold Tarrant for their corrections and suggestions to improve the paper.

2. Runia 1994, 1-27. Whilst Runia notes the modern tendency to designate Philo 'the Alexandrian', this paper suggests that both his Judaic and Alexandrian roots are fundamental to understanding his treatment of the erotic element in Greek pedagogy.

3. At this point I must gratefully acknowledge the assistance of Professor Tarrant who ran, on my behalf, searches conducted with *Thesaurus Linguae Graecae* (Disk E), using *Silver Mountain* software, for the following terms: *erwn, erwth-* and *paidik-*. These yielded, respectively, 9, 9, 5 and 17 matches. Of these, a number related to vocabulary other than that relevant to the 'divine lover' motif. To maintain the fishing metaphor, they have been returned to the water for others to catch and utilise later.

4. See also the summary of Ward 1997, 263-84 esp. 269-75.

5. Chauncey Jr., Duberman and Vicinus 1991, 1-13, esp. 5-7. Further, in the same volume, Boswell (37-53) and Padgug (54-64).

6. For female same-sex behaviour, see Crompton 2003, 15-20; 97-9. On the different roles for men and women in honour/shame societies see Neyrey 1998, 29-30. For a further treatment of feminine same-sex behaviour, see Brooten 1996; Hallett 1989; Smith 1996. Szesnat 1999 examines three Philonic texts dealing with female same-sex behaviour.

7. Horner 1978, 101, 140 n. 2. I cannot but feel that the cross-reference suggests a weakness in the claim: surely a strong argument would be able to cite evidence which was closer geographically and chronologically. Nor am I sure what the footnote actually contributes to Horner's argument, which proposes that male prostitution was secular rather than cultic in Ephesus.

8. Thus Levine 2007 for a critique of the impact of ideology, often unconscious or unexamined, on the reading of Biblical texts. Her n. 2 (57-8) quotes extensively from Horsley 1994, especially 1133, for criticism of reader-response methodologies as rendering knowledge of the ancient world superfluous for the reader/critic, holding affinities with modern American middle-class culture and following through a 'secularized Protestantism'.

9. Smith 1996, 227-38 is critical of Scroggs' theory that ancient same-sex behaviour was essentially pederastic, noting that there is an increase in non-pederastic (i.e., of more similar ages) same-sex behaviour by the first century AD. It is worth noting, however, that Philo's inclusion of pederasty implies that same-sex behaviour between different age groups was still a social practice open to criticism: why criticise what is no longer taking place? In turn, Millar 1997 offers a corrective

to Smith's perceived over-reliance on earlier Greek sources and readings of contemporary material such as Martial.

10. As presented by Philo, the meal practice of the Therapeutai is a manifesto of their beliefs: this is essentially a Judaic variation of a pattern identified by Lukinovich 1990. The literary symposium sets up a mimetic similarity between the account of the meal, its actions and dialogue, and the aspirations of the group (269-70).

11. Szesnat 1998. On the Therapeutai/Therapeutides, see 89-90. Szeznat notes that Philo's account is shaped by his own interests and may differ considerably from the sectarians' self-perceptions. There is considerable division over the validity of Philo's account. Engberg-Pedersen 1999 considers it essentially fictional, whereas Beavis 2004 thinks it is an idealised account which contains some factual details. For the implications of the work as rhetoric, see Braun 2004.

12. Szesnat 1998, 91, notes a common linking of gluttony and outrage in Graeco-Roman antiquity.

13. For a minimalist interpretation of the 'divine lover' material, not considered by Philo, see Blyth in Chapter 2 above.

14. For a minimalist discussion of the term, see Szesnat 1998, 104-6, who sees this springing from a rigid gender stereotyping and hierarchy in Philo's anthropology.

15. Szesnat 1998, 98 notes that *androgunous* may not demand a literal physical hermaphroditism, but rather the transgression of customary sexual boundaries.

16. See the account in Philo, *Flaccus* 1-103 in Colson 1967.

17. Elliot 2008, 191 n. 143 for Philo's reading of the revolts as miscalculated defiance of the ruling powers. It is possible that the Roman authorities exploited ethnic rivalries to consolidate their own power.

18. Dyck 2002 notes that the Roman introduction of a poll tax raised issues of who was 'authentically Greek' (164), cross-referring his remarks to Dawson 1994, 116.

19. Burkert 1983, 141; Mack 1987, esp. 11.

20. See De Young 2000 for a detailed analysis of the treatment of homosexuality in the Apocrypha and Pseudepigrapha. At times the Maccabean literature has more than a tinge of Asterix about it ('All Gaul was conquered? No, one small village of indomitable Gauls held out against the invaders …'), and it certainly should not be read as a pure and simple historical account of reaction against a powerful foreign regime. In many ways, it is a reflection on what it means to be Jewish, with the added irony that it is written in Greek, suggesting that those who saw themselves as proper Jews had been more tainted by Hellenistic culture than they may have wished to admit.

21. Thus in classical Athens, see Dover 1989, 54-7. Note that the Romans did not adopt the gymnasium culture (Crompton 2003, 79, 84). However the gymnasium persisted as a Hellenistic social institution, notably in Alexandria where it was an 'important point of transition' between Hellenistic and Jewish culture (Hengel 1991, 66; see also 65-70).

22. Hengel 1991, 68. Thus Claudius' edict of 41 AD which banned Jews from the gymnasium in Alexandria effectively barred them from citizenship.

23. See also Crompton 2003, 34-6.

24. For a detailed analysis of the Levitical texts, see Olyan 1994, in which Olyan notes that Judaic culture was unique in the wholesale proscription of male-male intercourse without qualification.

25. Garner, R., 'It Started with a Classroom Kiss', *The Independent,* 6 October

## 11. Ice-Cold in Alex

2008 [On-line]. http://www.independent.co.uk/news/education/education-news/it-started-with-a-classroom-kiss-952473.html. Things get even more complicated when these are same-sex relationships, e.g., J. Dart, 'Ex-teacher faces More Child-Sex Charges', *Sydney Morning Herald,* 10 November 2008 [On-line]. http://www.smh.com.au/news/national/exteacher-faces-more-child-sex-charges/2008/11/10/1226165431819.html. I cite these two examples purely to note the very different climate of the ancient world.

26. See Neyrey 1998, 16-20 for a description of the consequences of 'limited good' in ancient Mediterranean cultures.

27. Balch 2000, 221. I note in passing that the terms used by Paul are still highly contentious and hotly debated. See the summaries and discussion in De Young 2001, 175-203, and the influential conservative treatment of Wright 1984. Scholars variously interpret *arsenokoitia* and its cognates as referring to male cult prostitution, pederasty, ritual impurity or homosexual behaviour in general. The main implication which the modern writers, both liberal and conservative theologians alike, seek to draw is whether these terms refer to situations which are still 'live' or redundant, and thus whether or not their proscriptions have any value in the contemporary debate about homosexuality. For primary references, albeit of a slightly later period, see Plutarch, *Amatorius* 768E; Dio Chrysostom, *Discourse* 7.149-52; Ps.-Lucian, *Affairs of the Heart* 27; Achilles Tatius, *Leucippe and Clitophon* 2.37.3; Clement of Alexandria, *Paedagogus* 2.10.89.2.

28. For the distinction of hubris, see Dover 1989, 20, 27-9, 34-9, 45-6.

29. Ivarsson 2008, 187. See further, Crompton 2003, 82-4 (Cicero), 101-3 (Suetonius).

30. See further Ivarsson 2008, 187-8 and 187 with n. 20. See also Satlow 1994 for a wider reading of later rabbinic reactions to same-sex activity, identifying Philo as one of the precursors to their views. For a detailed example of Jewish constructions of masculinity, see Moore and Anderson 1998.

31. Ward 1997, 264-9, for the Platonic traditions recorded in the *Timaeus* and the *Laws*. The *Timaeus* passages resonate strongly with polar thought in that they associate masculinity and femininity with an active/ passive dichotomy.

32. For the legitimacy of using 'African' in this period see Oden 2008. This designation differs from the predominant tradition which would distinguish North Africa from the rest of the continent. It is Oden's contention that this is a racial rather than a cultural distinction and thus is no longer sustainable.

33. E.g. *On the Life of Abraham*, 133-7 in Colson 1966, 68-73; Marcus 1979.

34. Thus while Bailey would deny any possible sexual component in the criticism of Sodom (1975, 28), the vocabulary used in Genesis 19:5, and often translated in English as 'know' has a strong sexual component, and is often brought forward to criticise his sweeping conclusions as it suggests that sexual activity may indeed form part of the condemnation of Sodom (De Young 2000, 114-21).

35. Those who interpret this as a same-sex relationship cross-refer to *Confessions* 4.4, which describes the death of his friend. Both passages describe the relationships as 'friendships', but the relationships seem to be located in different towns; Carthage (3.1) and Augustine's native town, Thagaste (4.4). See Farmer 1987, 28-9. For a same-sex interpretation, see Crompton 2003, 137-9.

## 12

# Proclus' Reading of Plato's *Sôkratikoi Logoi*: Proclus' Observations on Dialectic at *Alcibiades* 112d-114e and Elsewhere[1]

*Akitsugu Taki*

### 1. Introduction

In the early nineteenth century, Stallbaum in his commentary on the *Alcibiades* I (hereafter cited simply as the *Alcibiades*) already had to use strenuous philological argument to vindicate its authenticity against Schleiermacher and Ast.[2] Even Denyer's ingenious proposal of dismissing the modern developmental view of Plato's thought in defence of its authenticity[3] could not completely hide the dialogue's deviation from other Platonic dialogues.[4] However, despite its chequered recent history, many an ancient reader of Plato respected the dialogue as authentic. Some Platonists even thought that it should be the first to be read in their educational curriculum based on Plato's works.[5] Among these the later Neoplatonic school after Iamblichus first left us the literature with which we can properly discuss their interpretative assumptions concerning the curriculum. Why did they pursue such a reading practice beginning with the *Alcibiades*, and why did they choose twelve dialogues as canonical for their curriculum?[6] How could they choose some and remove others? Specifically, how did they dispose of what modern interpreters often call 'Socratic' dialogues?

In what follows, I will inquire into the criteria by which they could have chosen their canonical works. Our task, since we have few other resources, is to analyse their extant commentaries on these works. However, I do not here focus on the ideas they deduced from the reading of the canonical works but rather on the interpretative assumptions behind their methods. Although their reading of the non-canonical dialogues may not be a major concern in their commentaries, I will discuss what is methodologically implied in their exegeses of the canonical works and thus how they read 'Socratic' dialogues.

In what follows I shall argue that Proclus, in his commentary on the *Alcibiades*, is exploring a mainly respondent-centred interpretation of Plato's dialogues, and that one can read Socratic discussions with each separate interlocutor by proceeding from that interlocutor's response in Plato's text; or, more specifically, that Proclus points to the possibility that

*12. Proclus' Reading of Plato's* Sôkratikoi Logoi

in every spontaneous response in Plato's dialogues the respondent is ultimately being subjected to a question-and-answer examination, not simply by Socrates but also by himself, that is, in Iamblichus' terms, that the soul is 'projecting *logos* (*logon proballein*) from itself'.

## 2. Resources for 'Socratic' dialogues in the Proclan corpus

Proclus in extant works refers to all the 'Socratic' dialogues except the *Hippias minor*, but in these references he does not propound how he reads either the parts or the whole of them.[7] In most cases he just gives an outline, or the subject-matter, of either a dialogue or Socrates' argument.[8] Apropos of Proclus' commentaries on 'Socratic' dialogues, the essay on the argument with Polemarchus in *Republic* I is mutilated in the manuscript of his *Commentary on the Republic*. Even the remaining part of the next essay on Thrasymachus' session does not concern Socrates' dialectic. To make matters worse, Proclus' lost commentary on the *Gorgias* is at present hard to reconstruct. First, Mettauer conjectures (1880, 23) from Arethas' use of Proclus' and Olympiodorus' commentaries on the *Alcibiades*, that Arethas' scholia on the *Gorgias* in cod. Bodleianus MS E. D. Clarke 39 (Codex B), if they do not accord with Olympiodorus' commentary, come from Proclus; but he admits that he has no convincing argument for the conjecture, which Greene (1938) follows with reservations. Secondly, there has been found no trace of Proclus' commentary on the *Gorgias* in the extant manuscripts now scattered over Europe but supposed to have been copied in Arethas' *scriptorium* (cf. Allen 1893, 48-55). Thirdly, considering the relatively low correspondence in technical terms between Proclus' and Olympiodorus' commentaries on the *Alcibiades*,[9] it is less likely that Proclus' lost commentary on the *Gorgias* could be excavated from Olympiodorus' extant one. In fact, Olympiodorus, although he refers to Proclus' commentary in his own commentary on the *Alcibiades*, does not mention Proclus even once in his commentary on the *Gorgias*. Fourthly, the extant scholia on Codex B, when compared with Proclus' extant commentaries, lack Proclus' usual devoted attention to the philosophical issues relevant to the passage concerned.

Therefore, if modern readers go to Proclus for his line-by-line interpretation of a particular passage from so-called 'Socratic' dialogues, they will usually be disappointed. However, in his commentaries on the discussions between Socrates and Alcibiades in the *Alcibiades* and between Zeno, Socrates and Parmenides in the *Parmenides*, which he sees as parallel to certain other discussions in 'Socratic' dialogues, Proclus offers a number of remarks on the way he interprets either Plato's works in general or a specific work, and also on the classification of Socratic modes of conversation. Accordingly, if one is attentive to these remarks, one can reasonably inquire about Proclus' reading practice.

*Akitsugu Taki*

Michael Erler (1987, 153-63) has already made such an attempt. On the basis of Carlos Steel's work on Proclus' interpretation of *aporia* in his commentary on the *Parmenides* (1987, 101-28), Erler applied its results to the aporetic dialogues. He argued that, as in the *Parmenides*, Proclus would interpret *aporia* in the aporetic dialogues to be apparent, not genuine, and, therefore, designed to be solved by finding a hidden key. I agree that Proclus' intention was to read all Plato's dialogical exchanges according to one and the same principle, but I will here bring to light a further assumption underlying his implementation of this intention.

### 3. Proclus' reading assumption: every dialogical discussion in Plato's dialogues is Socratic

Statistically, Proclus mentions Socrates more often than anybody except for Plato. From the viewpoint of modern criticism, his exact reference to Socrates, not Plato, as speaker in the drama seems a sign of a mind that is highly sensitive to Plato's literary form. However, this may rather be an anachronistic mistake on our part. Certainly, Proclus, unlike some other ancient readers, does not make a habit of carelessly confusing Socrates with Plato; however, the care that he takes is not motivated by the concerns of modern criticism. At least in the *Parmenides* commentary he is trying to find the *historical* Socrates' mind in Plato's representation of him.[10] General remarks on the literature of Socrates' trial in his *Timaeus*-commentary may be taken to indicate his historical concerns in his reading of Plato's dialogues (e.g. *in Tim.* 1.65-6).

We have further indications of a *Socraticising* reading practice also in the classification of Socrates' dialectic that Proclus puts forward[11] in the course of defending his (and probably his Athenian predecessors') interpretation of the *Parmenides*.[12] Three subordinate classes, refutation (*elenchos*), practice (*gymnasia*), and a discourse by division or hypothesis, are collected under a single category, regarded simply as Socrates' dialectic. Modern readers of Plato who see a philosophical development in Plato can readily blame Proclus for oversimplifying the differences in style and topic pertaining to Plato's compositional techniques, claiming that Proclus is unjustifiably superimposing upon Socrates' use of refutation in the aporetic dialogues a more constructive purpose, and amalgamating different ideas of Socrates' interrogation that appear in quite different contexts, ideas originating primarily in the *Meno*, *Theaetetus* and *Sophist*.[13] However, Proclus does not hesitate to include different types of discourse under a single genus, i.e. Socrates' dialectic. As a result, in every dialogical exchange in Plato's works he can observe the Socratic mind revealing itself and the respondent progressing in the educational curriculum by means of dialectic. In the Proclan picture of these dialogical episodes, a single story is going on, as if one and the same person, in the course of responding to Socrates, were for the goal of human perfection being purified of 'double

## 12. Proclus' Reading of Plato's Sôkratikoi Logoi

ignorance' or pretended knowledge, then being trained in examining the logical implications of each of a pair of contradictory hypotheses, and finally being led up to the principle that lies beyond the need for hypothesis.

In parallel, Proclus also goes to the length of warranting the respondents more than consistency in their beliefs. Against what he regards as the Peripatetic criticism of dialectic, Proclus identifies a truth-finding capacity, at least within Socrates' version of dialectic.[14] Even in Socrates' disavowal of knowledge in the *Apology* he assumes that, if the disavowal is justified, Socrates knows by what criteria he must judge.[15] Specifically, he attributes to Socrates three kinds of knowledge: dialectic, truth-eliciting midwifery, and the art of love.[16] Hence, dialectic is for Proclus a truth-finding process in a question-and-answer discussion. Even *elenchos*, as subclass of dialectic, is not the mere exposition of a contradiction in an interlocutor's beliefs but a *proof* of the falsehood of a particular belief. Gymnastic discourse is not a mere practice of finding logical implications but a way of finding truth in some of those implications.

Furthermore, for his unifying interpretation of the dialogical episodes he simply sets aside the Peripatetics' criticism of sophisms, which are not inapplicable to Socrates himself, and also skates over the distinction between *agonistic* and *elenchos*.[17] For all possible criticisms, however, Proclus collects Socrates' various respondents such as Callicles and Thrasymachus under one heading as participants in Socrates' dialectical pursuit of the truth. Hence, one can conclude that Proclus, if he is to justify such simplification, must assume something potentially common to all dialogical exchanges.

### 4. Proclus' interpretative key: the soul's intrinsic projection (*probolê*) of *logos*

Proclus does not discuss why his unifying reading can be justified; however, his interpretation of the *Alcibiades* suggests a key to his reading practice.[18] Some Middle Platonists previously divided the *Alcibiades* into ten parts represented each by the conclusion of an argument (*sullogismos*), but in the introduction of his commentary Proclus modifies their division by relating each of the arguments' conclusions to a single topic (*skopos*), knowing oneself, including additional comments of his own. Apart from a long commentary on the preamble (*prooimion*) of the *Alcibiades*, Proclus' extant work takes the form of a running commentary, while sometimes referring to this division.

However, this method of relating the conclusions of the various arguments to the single topic of a dialogue seems to be limited to the interpretation of the *Alcibiades*. In his other extant commentaries on Plato's dialogues Proclus repeatedly argues for a single topic for each dialogue by criticising the previous interpretations and their methods,[19] but he is not arguing from the arguments' conclusions in the dialogue. Nor is he applying the method systematically even in the extant main body of the *Alcibiades* commentary which contains the first six arguments. However, the method as he states it (*in Alc.* 10.4-17) should in theory be applied to all the dialogues in the sense that in every dialogical exchange throughout Plato's dialogues the respondent is supposedly *projecting* the arguments so as to focus on a single topic. In the analogy between the ontological structure of the universe and that of a Platonic dialogue, which Iamblichus first propounded, *what the arguments are to the skopos, the soul is to the intellect*. However, as Proclus shows in the immediate context, '*skopos*' is interchangeable with '*problema*' (*in Alc.* 10.1), that is, the product of the respondent's *probolê* of *logoi*, as he had just suggested (*in Alc.* 7.20), and as the sixth-century author of the *Prolegomena* suggests in expounding Iamblichus' theory of the analogy (*Prolegomena* 17).

We can see the key also in Proclus' commentary on the third argument of the *Alcibiades* (112d-114e), that in the question-and-answer exchange it is the one who answers a question who *legei* (speaks or affirms), not the one who asks (*in Alc.* intr. 12.24-13.2). A theoretical generalisation that he attempts to read in the argument's conclusion is that the respondent, in answering questions, is not simply being examined by the questioner but ultimately examining himself or herself by dint of divinity. Also, on the assumption that the soul in essence knows all things prenatally, he reinterprets the respondent's supernaturally assisted initiative as the learning of the truth, and, furthermore, in psychological terms, as the soul's projecting of *logoi* from itself (*in Alc.* 15.12-16, 280-2).

The theory of the soul's intrinsic projection of *logoi*, or interchangeably, of Forms,[20] which also derives from Iamblichus,[21] is related to the universal soul's creation,[22] and to the individual soul's reminiscence,[23] discursive reasoning in mathematics,[24] and perception.[25] Therefore, in the comments on the third argument, Proclus is trying to subsume the respondent's initiative under a more comprehensive theory of the soul. Hence, he is implying that the soul's universal activity can be viewed in the respondent's conduct in the course of a question-and-answer exchange.

As a result, such an underlying universal capacity of the human soul can be Proclus' key justification for adopting a unified approach to Socratic conversations in Plato's dialogues. This is not only a theory; Proclus applies it. First, he connects the activity of the individual soul with that of the universal soul, especially when it undergoes *elenchos*.[26] Secondly, he assumes that the souls of Socrates' adversaries undergoing *elenchos* are aiming for the truth.[27] Even if they are not convinced, Proclus emphasises, they will progress in another life: at present they are simply unaware of their own souls' activity.

## 12. Proclus' Reading of Plato's Sôkratikoi Logoi

### 5. An assessment of Proclus' interpretative method

That Proclus detects the presence of self-examination in the spontaneous responses of interlocutors also opens the possibility of a universal reading of their responses, not only to questions but also to suggestions or even statements. This respondent-centred reading method goes hand in hand with Proclus' universalisation of the propositions embodied in an individual interlocutor's responses and with his examination of their truth and validity for the joint intellectual benefit of himself and his audience.

To what extent Proclus applied this *Socraticising* reading remains hard to determine. He has left us no line-by-line commentary on the answers of Socrates' respondents in the aporetic dialogues. However, his respondent-centred reading practice points towards the conclusion that, for him, Plato's readers in general can, by joining the inquiry into the truth, proceed towards perfection step by step with a single idealised interlocutor. All dialogical conversations thus become part of an inquiry into the same universally applicable truths, necessitating an inter-dialogical reading of Plato's dialogues.

Proclus' strategy is worthy of consideration as a general methodology for reading Plato. It shows how even a doctrinal reader of Plato, who assumes that Plato's own argument can be deduced from a dialogue and that Plato reveals his views directly to us, can admit the respondent-centred reading, which some sceptical readers of Plato also favour. It shows that the doctrinal reading is not necessarily based on 'mouthpiece theory', which holds that leaders of the discussion in any given dialogue argue on behalf of Plato, nor on constructive interpretations of Socrates' role as questioner.

However, Proclus has neither identified nor solved all the problems in his method of reading the arguments. In the introduction to the commentary on the *Alcibiades* Proclus fails to distinguish between mere inference and proof.[28] Later, in his exegesis of Socrates' proposal at *Alc.* 114b that Alcibiades should *prove* his claims while himself asking questions, taking it to apply also to Socrates' contribution to arguments before and after, Proclus shifts the responsibility for *proving* the argument from Alcibiades the respondent to Socrates the questioner.[29] Furthermore, in many places he includes some remark implying Socrates' own knowledge of what he is asking about.[30] Therefore, in the extant parts of the commentary, Proclus is shifting, without adequate discussion, the responsibility for the argument, from the respondent's mere discoveries in the course of an argument to Socrates' sound grasp of the proof. Unfortunately, the extant commentary ends short of Socrates' reconfirmation, at *Alc.* 116d, that Alcibiades the answerer affirms the conclusion of the argument, which would perhaps have given Proclus the opportunity to explain his theory better.

Furthermore, Proclus has not described how the soul is projecting *Logoi* even when the respondent makes no advance. For Proclus, Socrates might have been fully trained by Parmenides when young.[31] However, as Proclus is well aware, even those as young or good-natured as Socrates in the *Parmenides*[32] will lose their acquired self-knowledge, as shown in history by Alcibiades[33] and by Parmenides' ultimate respondent, Aristoteles,[34] the youngest among the interlocutors, who later will become one of the infamous Thirty Tyrants. This will apply even more to the mature and ill-natured, such as Thrasymachus and Callicles.[35] Then how could Proclus explain their descent or deviation? How might the mature and ill-natured, in *honestly* answering Socrates' questions, be slipping backwards even while their own souls, unbeknown to them, are projecting *logos*? His extant corpus remains silent.

If retrieving prenatally acquired knowledge is explained as the soul's projection of *logos*, and if a false opinion is some failure of this retrieval, it seems that a false opinion should be explained as the denial of the soul's projection of *logos*. Yet this projection is for Proclus an undeniable universal law. Furthermore, even if a false opinion is instead explained as a lack of awareness of the soul's projecting *logos*, how could simple ignorance be explained? If the theory explained that simple ignorance is simple unawareness whereas a false opinion is double unawareness, the false-opinion holders, if purified, must become aware of their doubly unaware selves in getting to know their souls. This might result in us having a multiplex single self or multiplied selves along with our soul; or rather, our most immediate self might have to observe other mediated multipliable selves as we look to our soul. If so, according to how much the most immediate self has deviated from the soul's *probolê*, the truth might also be multiplied and graded.

## 6. Conclusion: Socratic argument in the *Alcibiades*

As our discussion of Proclus' interpretation has shown, the *Alcibiades*, whether authentic or not, is problematic for an understanding of Plato's 'Socratic' dialogues. Whereas the problem of how one could make an affirmation while asking a question is raised, Alcibiades in the immediate context (and often elsewhere) answers unproblematically: 'You say truly' (*alethê legeis*), etc. This is a reply form characteristic of Plato, used mostly in reply to statements, but sometimes to questions, and sometimes even with ambiguity as to the first speaker's intention (cf. Taki 2008). Further, the problem of proving a statement by asking questions is raised at *Alcibiades* 114b, where the crucial verb *apodeiknumi*, 'point out', implies, like the English 'prove', the truth of the embodied proposition. This is suggested by Socrates later at 130c and earlier, at 112e, in his promise concerning the ensuing question-and-answer argument, 'You will know in the following fashion'. This problem is one that Plato, with his linguistic subtleties, will raise often for readers of his dialogues. It is the kind of problem that may easily be explained in terms of the author's desire to set snares for challenging the reader. If Proclus, with

## 12. Proclus' Reading of Plato's Sôkratikoi Logoi

his respondent-centred reading method, also stumbles over such difficulties, he may be forgiven.

### Notes

1. Earlier versions of this work were read in Japanese at the seventh conference of Philologika (Japan) held at the Japan Academy on 25 October 2008 and pre-circulated in English at the Research Conference *Socrates, Alcibiades, and the Divine Lover/Educator* at University of Newcastle, NSW, Australia, 4-6 December 2008. The second and third paragraphs of Section 4 and the fifth paragraph of Section 5 are based on my research for a paper in Japanese, entitled in translation, 'Proclus' interpretative method of Plato: a problem in his identification of inferences in a dialogue in his commentary on the *Alcibiades* I' in Oshiba and Koike (eds) 2010. For Proclus' commentary on the *Alcibiades*, I use A.-Ph. Segonds 1985 (= *in Alc.*). For his commentary on the *Parmenides*, up to 137c I use Steel 2007, 2008 and thereafter, Stallbaum 1839 (= *in Parm.*). Other reference to ancient works is made according to the abbreviations listed in LSJ 1996.

2. Stallbaum 1857, 193-217; Schleiermacher 1996, 319-26; Dobson 1836, 328-36; Ast 1816, 435-41.

3. N. Denyer 2001, 14-26.

4. Pace Stallbaum 1857 and Grote 1865: neither Herodotus nor Xenophon refers to Zoroaster (*Alc.* 122a). The reply form *alêthê legeis*, although used Platonically in reply to a question (*Alc.* 120a4, a8, e3, 135a3) is slightly too frequent, as in the so-called later dialogues of Plato; see Taki 2008, 83-93, n. 13. The Hellenistic, not classical, currency of the hapax legomena in the *Alcibiades*, e.g. *akrocheirizesthai* (*Alc.* 107e6) and *anaplattontas* (*Alc.* 121d6), comparatively diminish its authenticability.

5. Albinus, *Eisagoge* 6. Cf. Hermann 1853, 147-51; Diogenes Laertius 3.62.

6. Westerink, Trouillard and Segonds 2003, 26 [= Prolegomena]; Procl. *in Alc.* 11.1-21.

7. E.g. *Euthph.*: *Theol. Plat.* 5.131-2, *in Parm.* 986.1-6, *in Crat.* 116.1-15; *Cr.*: *in Tim.* 1.80.11-15; *Charm.*: *in Alc.* 166.18-167.4, 185.13-17; *La.*: *in Alc.* 235.7-9; *Ion*: *in Rep.* 1.182.24-183.9; *H. Ma.*: *in Parm.* 987.15-22; *Prot.*: *Theol. Plat.* 1.28-9, *in Alc.* 252.19-253.7, *in Tim.* 1.344, *in Parm.* 655.6; *Gorg.*: *in Rep.* 1.156-7, 2.103, *in Crat.* 51, *in Parm.* 655.6; *Lys.*: *in Parm.* 654.18-21, 989.17-19; *Men.*: *in Rep.* 1.33.3; *Rep.* I: *in Parm.* 655.6-7.

8. E.g., for an outline of the *Lysis* see *in Parm.* 654.18-21; for the main topic of the *H. Ma.*, *in Parm.* 987.15-16; for Socrates' unilateral argument, *in Alc.* 323.11-324.22 (*Rep.* I 348b-350c) and *in Alc.* 329.4-6 (*Men.* 77b-78b).

9. See Indices in Westerink 1954.

10. *In Parm.* 729.20-730.3, 784.3-10, 987.5-12, 988.23-30.

11. *In Parm.* 652.21-656.11, 987.31-989.23.

12. The aim of *Parm.*, as Proclus and his predecessors interpret it, is not mere logical practice, but on the theory of Forms (*in Parm.* 619.21-624.15, 630.26ff.). Specifically, unlike their previous and contemporary interpreters, they see a maieutic discourse in an apparently refutative discourse in the first part of the dialogue (*in Parm.* 781.14-15, 838.15-25 *et passim*) and also a dialectic discourse in an apparent logical practice in the second part. For Proclus, both discourses are an inquiry for the truth: the former signals how to overcome the apparent puzzles arising from a physical understanding of participation; the latter concerns not only logical implications from contradictory hypotheses but also their truth.

13. *Men.* 81a-86c, *Tht.* 148e-151d, *Soph.* 226a-231c; cf. *in Alc.* 28.16-29.7.
14. *In Parm.* 653.2-3, 984.7-985.9, 989.1-23, 994.5-9, 995.13-20, In *Crat.* 2. Aristotle distinguishes between a proof from a principle and dialectical reasoning. Thus his dialecticians converse with their respondent without knowledge about what they discuss; they have recourse at most to common opinion. However, he leaves room for dialectical reasoning in his discussions on the first principle (*Metaph.* 1004b17-26, *Apr.* 24a22-24b12, *Top.* 100a25-101a4, 105a3-9, 159a25-37, 161a16-b18, 163a29-b4, 164b8-15; *SE* 165a38-166b11, 169b18-170a11, 171b3-6, 172a11-b4, 183a37-b8).
15. *De providentia et fato* 48, 51; cf. the fifth objection to New Academics, *Prolegomena* 10.
16. *In Alc.* 27.16-30.4; cf. *Prolegomena* 11.
17. *In Alc.* 283.24-285.14; *in Parm.* 987.15-22.
18. *In Alc.* 11.22-18.12.
19. *In Alc.* 5.15-7.11, *in Parm.* 630.11-17, *in Crat.* 1, *in Rep.* 1.5.1ff., *in Tim.* 1.1-4; for Iamblichus' inquiry about the *skopos* of a dialogue, see Dillon 1973; *in Phd.* fr. 1, *in Phdr.* fr. 1, *in Phlb.* fr. 1, *in Tim.* fr. 1; for Olympiodorus' inquiry, see Olymp. *in Alc.* 3-6; *in Grg.* 4; *in Phd.* 4.11; cf. Thrasyllus' *epigraphê* or sub-title at DL 3.49, 58-9; Procl. *in Rep.* 1.8.11; *Prolegomena* 21-5 and for its historical and philosophical significance, Tarrant 1993.
20. *In Alc.* 191.12-192.14, *in Parm.* 789.17-21, 896.24-6, 987.5-12, *in Tim.* 1.102.29-103.3, *in Euc.* 13.6-13, 56.15-16; cf. Simplicius, *in de An.* 11.166.5-9, 11.192.12-20; Porphyrius, *in Ptolemaii Harmonica* 12; cf. for *logos* as the formular of the causal form (*eidos*), Arist. *Phys.* 194b26-7, *Metaph.* 996b8, 1039b20-3, 1044a32-b15.
21. The noun phrase *probolê* of *logos*, or Forms, is used along with the verbal form *proballein* in Simplicius, Proclus, Iamblichus and Valentinus cited by Irenaeus but not in Plato (for the colloquial phrase *logon proballein*, *Symp.* 180c), Aristotle or Plotinus and not even in *Procl. Inst. Th.*, where mainly *prohodos* is used. Proclus' usage is related in the wider context to some associated phrases: (1) *logon proballein* (i) a kind of colloquial periphrastic verbal phrase, (ii) a Gnostic analogy of God's creation with male ejaculation or female delivery: Valentinus on John 1:1-8 (Irenaeus, *Adversus haereses* 1.1.1.22, 1.1.18.3-1.1.18.9; cf. E. Osborn 2001, 267ff. (*probolê* = 'emanatio'), (iii) a sensation in analogy with female delivery: Ps.-Gal. *Ad Gaurum* 14.1-2; (2) *sperma ... ballein* (i) [agr.] seed-sowing: Xen. *Oec.* 17.11.2-3, (ii) [med.] insemination: Gal. *de sem.* 4.516; (3) *logon ... speirein* (i) a colloquial phrase for the dissemination of a rumour or story: Ar. *Ran.* 1206, (ii) the dissemination of teaching: New Testament: Mk 4:14, Mt 13:19, Lk 8:11; cf. Mk 4:26-9; OT: Is. 55:10-11. However, the origin of the *logos* theory assumed in Proclus' and Iamblichus' phrase can be traced to many sources but is hard to identify with any specific one (s.v. *logos*, Pauly-Wissowa; Kittel 1932).
22. For Iamblichus, Simplicius, *in Ph.* 9.786.11-22; Iamblichus, *in Tim.* fr. 58, 59 (Dillon, op.cit.) (fr. 58 = Procl. *in Ti.* 2.306.1-5, fr. 59 = Procl. *in Ti.* 2.309.23-9; for Proclus, Procl. *in Parm.* 894.26-895.1; cf. Syrianus, *in Metaph.* 26.33-7).
23. *In Alc.* 171.2-3 (projection of the truth), *in Rep.* 2.95.2-4, 2.350.17-21, *in Tim.* 1.446.23-29; cf. Porphyrius, *Sententiae ad intelligibilia ducentes*, 29.1-15; cf. *in Alc.* 8.15-19.7, 27.16-30.4, *in Parm.* 653.6-14, 864.11-865.1, 873.31-874.6, 932.13-17; cf. Iamblichus, *Comm. Math.* 11.20-2.
24. Iamblichus, *Comm. Math.* 11.20-2. (cf. Merlan 1975, 11-33); Proclus, *in Euc.* 44.25-47.8, 78.8-79.2.
25. Iamblichus, *de An.* (Stobaeus 1.48.8.6-9); Proclus, *in Tim.* 1.248.29-250.11;

## 12. Proclus' Reading of Plato's Sôkratikoi Logoi

cf. Simplicius, *in de An.* 11.128.28-9, 11.138.13-15, 11.189.33-11.190.1, 11.192.35-11.193.13, 11.225.28-9.
    26. *In Parm.* 894.26-895.1; *in Tim.* 3.340-1.
    27. *In Alc.* 90.3-12, 277.5-278.7, 279.21-280.23.
    28. *In Alc.* 10.10-13, 14.22-3 (14.12-13), 16.9 (15.1, 15.13, 17.7, 17.17, 18.5, 18.9-10); cf. 15.13 (276.20-277.1; 313.19-314.3), 16.14 (337.23, 338.9), 17.4 (*Alc.* I, 117b), 18.5 (*Alc.* I, 130c); *Eisagoge*, 6.
    29. *In Alc.* 303.1-19; cf. 302.9-12, 314.10-11, 18-19, 323.11-19, 329.4-6, 338.8-10, 339.8-11.
    30. *In Alc.* 229.10-13, 230.18-231.2; 312.20-2, 313.19-314.7; cf. 336.15-337.26.
    31. *In Parm.* 691.17-22.
    32. *In Alc.* 166.20-167.4, 299.22-6; *in Parm.* 687.21-2, 722.8-9, 10-11.
    33. *In Alc.* 85.19-92.3.
    34. *In Parm.* 690.26-691.4, 691.22-14.
    35. *In Alc.* 322.23-323.11.

13

# Socrates' Divine Sign: From the *Alcibiades* to Olympiodorus[1]

*François Renaud*

## 1. An ancient approach to an elusive issue

What is the nature and function of the divine sign of Socrates as both lover and educator, in the *Alcibiades* in particular? The importance of the divine sign is as undeniable as its elusive character. According to both Plato and Xenophon,[2] the divine sign led to the charge of impiety (*asebeia*): Socrates was accused of not acknowledging the ancient gods of the city and of introducing new, private ones (*daimonia kaina*).[3] The accusation presupposes the opposition between the gods that the city officially recognised and the vague, apparently private daemonic forces that Socrates introduced. In the dialogue bearing his name, Euthyphro simply assumes that Socrates' divine sign provides the ground for Meletus' accusation of introducing new divinities (*Euthph.* 3b5). Moreover, Socrates seemed to have complete trust in the sign and its counsel (*Ap.* 40a8-c3; *Euthd.* 272e1-4). In Plato's *Apology* (31c-d), the divine sign is presented as the reason why (*aitia*) Socrates turned away from political life, and therefore as the indirect reason why he opted instead for the philosophical life. Socrates presents his philosophical engagement as the mission he received from the god of Delphi (*ho theos*).[4]

The difficulties involved in understanding the exact nature of the sign are many. First, there are few references to the sign in Plato (and Xenophon), and those few references are vague, most often associated with phrases such as 'the daemonic (sign)' (*to daimonion* [*sêmeion*]), or 'the voice' (*hê phonê*).[5] Secondly, Socrates readily speaks of the sign as something influencing his daily life and his relation to his fellow human beings (usually by hindering him from doing something), but he hardly ever speculates – at least aloud – about its underlying philosophical or conceptual implications. Thirdly, when discussing the theme of 'daemonic beings' (*daimones*), Plato hardly ever makes any explicit connections with Socrates' daemonic voice (cf. Hoffmann 1985, 421). Given these difficulties, it is not surprising that scholars have had little success in illuminating the meaning and wider implications of the divine sign.

Given the meagre textual evidence at our disposal, what kind of interpretative strategies is the reader to adopt? Are Plato's readers expected to

## 13. Socrates' Divine Sign

establish indirect, implicit connections between Socrates' divine sign and discussions about *daimones* and other fundamental questions about love and education? Most modern scholars refuse for methodological reasons to go beyond the explicit statements of the text, and consequently many argue that our knowledge of the divine sign must be limited to the fact that it is a phenomenon unique to Socrates, the irrational side of this otherwise eminently rational figure. The ancient interpreters, by contrast, supposed that Plato systematically taught by hints and riddles, and therefore fully took up the challenge of establishing implicit connections between statements about the sign and other general remarks made about *daimones* and other overlapping themes found in the Platonic corpus. The corpus known to them is similar to ours, apart from the inclusion of dialogues considered today to be *dubia* or *spuria*, among which, the *Alcibiades*. Most scholars today generally ignore the ancient Platonist interpretations. This is especially true of ancient interpretations of Socrates' mysterious divine sign, which interpretations most scholars deem to be fanciful. Indeed two recent books on Socrates' religious beliefs scarcely consider the ancient interpretations.[6]

The significance of the Neoplatonist approach to the dialogue generally lies in the central importance granted to the *Alcibiades* as the first dialogue to be read in the curriculum as prerequisite to self-knowledge. Olympiodorus of Alexandria (c. AD 500-565) is the author of the only fully extant ancient commentary on the *Alcibiades* (Proclus' is incomplete), offering an interpretation that is still worth considering.[7] The merit of his commentary specifically lies in its ability to unite the daemonic and erotic aspects of Socrates' relation to Alcibiades.

### 2. The related context: Prologue (103a-106a) and climax passage (132d-133c)

In the *Alcibiades*, the divine sign (*daimonion ti*) is explicitly linked, perhaps even identified with (the) god (*theos*).[8] At the outset Socrates declares to Alcibiades that the sign or the god – nothing human (*ouk anthrôpeion*) – is responsible (*aition*) for his approaching Alcibiades at last, after following and observing him in silence for many years (103a). The patient waiting demanded of Socrates by the god proved necessary in order for the young man to mature and become receptive to Socrates' pedagogical zeal, so that their discussion could be fruitful. The waiting over, the sign at last allows, indeed apparently incites, Socrates (*nun d'ephêke*, 'has now let me loose', or, 'has set me on') to speak to and court the young man. In the lengthy introductory speech, Socrates presents himself to Alcibiades as his only true lover, the first and most faithful, who remains attached to him while all the others have deserted him. This is because, as Socrates reveals later in the climax of the dialogue (132d-133c), he loves Alcibiades truly, meaning that he loves what Alcibiades truly is, namely his soul, the higher, divine (*theion*) part of his soul (also characterised as god: *theon*, 133c5), as opposed to Alcibiades' other lovers who are only attracted to his body. Socrates is also his most indispensable lover, the one without whom it will be impossible for Alcibiades to realise his vast, indeed tyrannical ambitions. But Socrates can achieve this only with the help of the god (*meta tou theou*, 105e5), or 'god willing' (*ean theos ethelêi*, 135d).

## 3. Indirect exhortative function and identification of the *daimôn* with god

This brief summary of the prologue and the climax of the dialogue tells us that the divine sign is inseparable from the god, stemming from or even being identified with him. The sign no longer holds Socrates back, but apparently encourages him to speak to the young man as someone ready to accept his aid. As Socrates points out at the very end of the dialogue, with the help of god their relationship will be long-lasting. But despite what Alcibiades might wish, god's help ironically consists in philosophical, intellectual education of his true self, not in political training.

Two objections are at this point routinely raised by modern scholars against the *Alcibiades*' authenticity. First, in Plato the divine sign is exclusively apotreptic, that is, always dissuading Socrates from doing something he is about to undertake and never pushing him to take any action, while in Xenophon the sign has both prohibitive and exhortative functions.[9] Secondly, in Plato the divine sign is never explicitly identified with a *daimôn* or with a (the) god (*theos*). The expressions used to refer to the divine sign usually involve the adjectival sense of *to daimonion* as a shorthand implying *sêmeion* ('the daimonic *sign*'), and does not signify a god or even a *daimôn* (as substantive). I shall discuss these two objections briefly, not because I am particularly concerned with the question of authenticity *per se*, but because I wish to examine the implications of the *Alcibiades* in connection with dialogues that are unanimously agreed to have been written by Plato, as well as to explore the conceptual coherence that Olympiodorus attributes to the *Alcibiades* in conjunction with other dialogues taken together (such as the *Phaedrus* and the *Symposium*), especially concerning the divine sign.

Despite what some scholars have argued, there is textual evidence that suggests a link between the divine sign and positive exhortation. In Plato the divine sign sometimes does seem indirectly to encourage Socrates to act. In a passage in the *Theaetetus* (151a2-5) on his maieutic art Socrates claims that the sign sometimes forbids him to associate with certain people, while at other times it permits him (*eân*, the same verb as is used in the *Alcibiades*) to do so. In the *Phaedrus* (242b8-9) Socrates' sign also seems to spur him to action. There Socrates says: 'my *daimonion* forbids me to leave until I make atonement for some offence against the gods' (*ouk*

## 13. Socrates' Divine Sign

*eâ apienai prin*), that is, before he gives a second speech concerning the god Eros after giving a first inadequate description of him.[10] Such passages suggest that the divine sign in Plato occasionally fulfils – indirectly – an exhortative function, presumably through the act of the god sending the sign.[11] Moreover, Plato does regularly link the divine sign (*to daimonion* [*sêmeion*]) and the *daimôn*, as the later Platonists assume. Socrates himself links the two in the *Apology* when cross-examining Meletus (26b-28a). There Socrates accepts the old popular belief that *daimonic* voices stem from a *daimôn*, that is, a god or half god: 'But if I believe in spiritual things (*daimonia*), it is quite inevitable (*pollê anankê*) that I believe also in spirits (*daimonas*)' (tr. Fowler).[12] Later in the *Apology* Socrates calls his sign 'the sign of the god' (*to tou theou sêmeion*, 40b1).[13] Consequently it appears worthwhile to reconsider the late Platonist interpretation, which links the sign with both *erôs* and god. Let us recall very briefly the larger, pre-Platonic and Platonic context surrounding the notions of *daimôn* first, before examining Olympiodorus' interpretation of the divine sign in the *Alcibiades*.

### 4. Pre-Platonic and Platonic notions of *daimôn*

The Greek word *daimôn* could be translated alternatively as something divine or semi-divine, a divine power, or protective spirit, a god or even fate (lit. probably 'the one allotting fate'). Plato's conception of *daimôn* is far from monolithic, borrowing from old popular traditions while also inventing images and tales of his own. In Homer, the Greek word *daimôn* can be synonymous with *theos*. More commonly however it does not designate an individual god but rather the (vague) power of the divine.[14] While *theos* most often signifies a particular god associated with a myth or cult, *daimôn* is typically used to designate a divine force that manifests itself in a particular situation and is not (yet) the object of a cult. A *daimôn* can be a personal protective spirit, such as in the case of Socrates' sign or 'genius.' It can also be a deceased hero such as those of Hesiod's Golden Age.[15] The latter meaning prepares the way for the wide-spread conception of *daimôn* as an intermediary being, whether good or evil, between gods and human beings. In some Platonic dialogues, the word *daimôn* referred to the gods (*theous*) and heroes (*herôas*),[16] in others to a divinised human being,[17] in yet others to an accompanying *daimôn* leading the deceased souls to the Last Judgment in Hades.[18] Moreover, in an important passage in the *Timaeus* (90 a-d), the word is used to refer to the sovereign, rational part of the soul, the 'divinity' (*daimona*) inhabiting us all, which god (*theos*) gave to each of us, and the cultivation of which constitutes the aim of human life. In a passage in the *Symposium* (202e1), a *daimôn* is an intermediary being between gods and humans (*metaxu esti theou te kai thnêtou*). This last meaning needs to be treated separately.

*François Renaud*

### 5. *Daimôn-erôs* in the *Symposium* and Olympiodorus

In the *Symposium* (202d-203a) Socrates has recourse to the notion of *daimôn* as an intermediary being (*metaxu*) in order to explain the nature of Eros. In this passage *daimones* are said to communicate human beings' prayers and sacrifices to the gods and to convey the gods' orders to humans. This notion of *daimones* as intermediary and benevolent beings is then applied to *erôs*, the desire for wisdom (*philo-sophia*) in the human soul (*psychê*), the force mid-way between utter ignorance and divine wisdom. Born of poverty and resourcefulness (*penia* and *poros*), Eros is said to be a great *daimôn* (*megas daimôn*), half mortal, half immortal, the striving that leads humans to the good.

The influence of the *Symposium* passage on later Platonism proved to be immense. It became the *locus classicus* on *daimones* and the starting point of an increasingly systematised demonology in Middle Platonism and Neoplatonism.[19] Like his predecessors, Olympiodorus draws explicitly upon the *Symposium* passage, conceiving Eros and everything daemonic as an intermediary lying in the Middle (*to meson*). Since the soul itself is partially mortal and partially immortal, situated between god and mortal, Eros is the force uniting the contradictory impulses within the soul, analogous to the two horses in the *Phaedrus* (*In Alc.* 226.18-26). Thus, according to Olympiodorus, Socrates' *daimôn* is at once unique and universal, as it represents the highest rational activities of every soul. Socrates' *daimôn* is unique insofar as Socrates as an individual is exceptionally free from the contingencies of bodily life,[20] but this is also the reason why his *daimôn* is an *exemplum*, a universal model for all to follow. This is also why Socrates is in need of self-protection and self-restraint with regard to political life. Olympiodorus contends that there can only be one *daimôn* allotted to each soul, on account of the unitary character of life. Soul and *daimôn* thus more or less coincide.

### 6. A moderate defence of the universalisation of *daimôn-erôs*

What are we to think of this conceptual extension that links Socrates' private *daimôn* with a universal *daimôn-erôs*? Most scholars refuse to link Socrates' sign with the doctrine of *daimôn* in the *Symposium*. To be sure, for Plato the divine sign stands for the uniqueness of Socrates as someone out of place in the city (*atopos*) and banned by it. In a passage in the *Republic* (496c2-4) Socrates claims that the divine sign is something that has been granted so far to few or none before him. It can, however, be argued from this *Republic* passage that Socrates' divine mission, as expounded in the *Apology*, is to transform other human beings into philosophers, so as to make them similar to him by having them share his *daimôn* or one of the same kind. Can the late antique interpretation about a common *daimôn-erôs* be shown to be defensible? Here are a few preliminary arguments in its favour.

In the *Symposium* Alcibiades praises Socrates as a daemonic man (*daimonios anêr*, 219c). His depiction of Socrates also contains striking similarities with that of Eros. As the incarnation of the lover of wisdom (*philo-sophos*), situated as he is between utter ignorance and divine wisdom, Socrates seems to appear as the 'great *daimôn*' Eros himself. Moreover, the *Phaedrus* more explicitly describes the philosopher as the true erotic human being (*erôtikos*), spurred by the power of Eros with his mind resolutely turned towards the good and the beautiful. In the *Symposium*, as elsewhere, Socrates himself claims to know nothing but matters erotic (*erôtika*).[21] Further possible connections between Socrates' *daimonion* and philosophic *erôs* are to be found in the *Apology*. A passage referred to at the beginning of this paper (31c-d) links the divine sign with Socrates' choice of the philosophical life. There the sign is said to be the cause (*aition*) turning him away from political life. The *Republic* passage just referred to (496a-e) also presents the sign as indirectly responsible for his choice of the philosophical life (cf. Hoffmann 1985, 423-4). Finally, according to the *Apology* (similarly to the *Symposium*) the god's (or gods') care for humanity is made manifest in the person of Socrates: his life is guided by the Delphic god's commands through oracles, dreams and other means of communication (33c5-6; cf. 41c8-d2). Such passages testify to the affinities of Socrates' *daimonion* with philosophic *erôs*.[22] In that sense his *daimôn* would be an analogical term for the Intellect.[23]

## 7. The Socratic art of love

*Benevolent love*
Olympiodorus considers the *Alcibiades* to be an emphatically erotic dialogue (*erôtikos dialogos*) and Socrates to be an eminently erotic figure (*erôtikos*). As a divinely inspired lover, Socrates is beneficent (*euergetikos*) toward his favourites (*in Alc.* 21.5). His help consists in turning and leading his younger lovers, by means of dialectic, towards the good and the beautiful in their own souls.[24] To do this, Socrates must turn them away from the political life (*bios politikos*) and towards the philosophical life (*bios philosophikos*). The contrast between 'the two lives' in the *Alcibiades* is underscored by Olympiodorus: the great obstacle to Alcibiades' education is precisely 'the many' (*hoi polloi*), who have been his first corrupting teacher (*in Alc.* 221.9-16). As Socrates prophesies at the very end of the dialogue (135e), the greatest threat to Alcibiades is the attraction of the city (*dêmos*) and conversely Alcibiades' love for it. Socrates, by contrast, is radically self-sufficient, and indeed an image of divine self-sufficiency (*autarkeia*).[25]

*François Renaud*

*Erotic expertise*
As an inspired lover (*entheos erastês*), Socrates couples knowledge and sympathy.[26] In the *Alcibiades* he is an 'erotic' teacher but also a dialogical one, leading his interlocutor to maieutic discoveries. This is why, according to Olympiodorus, the *Alcibiades* is divided into three successive parts: elenctic, protreptic and maieutic. Socratic expertise in the *Alcibiades* necessarily involves dialogue consisting in questions and answers between student and teacher, the only form of philosophical instruction.[27] This presupposes the active participation of the student, giving explicit approval at every stage of the dialogue. The Socrates of the Platonic *Alcibiades* contrasts with that of Aeschines,[28] in which the key factor in Socratic education is not expertise (*technê*), but divine dispensation (*theia moira*) alone.[29] Moreover, self-knowledge is inseparable from one's *daimôn*, for to know oneself means to see what one has in common with all other human beings through nature. The return (*epistrophê*), as the ultimate goal in education, is a reversion within oneself. Indeed to hold a discussion with Socrates means to discover the divinity of the intellect in oneself – the rational, highest part of one's soul – and thereby to become like the divinity itself.[30] The personal *daimôn* of Socrates, pure and authentic, is somehow the divine intellect made visible (cf. Pradeau 1999, 78, n. 2). The erotic expertise which Socrates possesses shows deep affinities with the doctrine of rational desire or philosophic *erôs*, presented by Diotima in the *Symposium*, although it may not be quite simply an illustration of it, as the ancient Platonists thought (cf. Joyal 2000, 52-5).

*Illustration of the art of love*
For Olympiodorus and the other later Platonists, the *Alcibiades* represents *the* introduction to self-knowledge, but it is also the dialogue *par excellence* on the 'art of love'.[31] The late Platonists read the dialogue as an illustration of the Platonic art of love as elaborated in the *Symposium* as well as the *Phaedrus*.[32] The favouring of the *Alcibiades* over the *Symposium* and *Phaedrus* as the guide on the art of love, might be due to the fact that the *Symposium* and the *Phaedrus* emphasise the advantages to the lover, while the *Alcibiades* portrays the 'altruistic' concerns of the lover, that is, the educational benefits to be derived by the beloved. The *Alcibiades* presents Socrates as a wise man intent on establishing a long-lasting relationship based on love, by bestowing on the young man who is in need of help and capable of receiving his love all the benefits that his wisdom can provide him (Dillon 1994, 392).

In his *Alcibiades* commentary Olympiodorus sharply distinguishes an inspired lover (*entheos erastês*) like Socrates from the common, vulgar lover (*phortikos*), like those who have deserted Alcibiades. Olympiodorus identifies three important differences between Socrates and these other lovers (*in Alc.* 14.5). First, the common lover admires his favourites, while the inspired lover is admired by them. Secondly, the common lover quickly

## 13. Socrates' Divine Sign

leaves his love; the inspired one chooses a worthy object of love (*axieraston*) and remains faithful to him, accompanying him throughout. Thirdly, the inspired lover is divine-like (*theoeidôs*) and therefore an object of imitation, while the common lover only seeks sensation and bodily touch (*haphên*). On the last aspect, the *Alcibiades* displaying restraint in sexual matters contrasts with the *Theages*, in which bodily contact (*haphê*) seems surprisingly to take the place of argumentation.[33] Socrates' 'art of love,' as portrayed in the *Alcibiades*, consists in selecting the proper soul, that is, the object worthy of love (*axierastos*), namely a large-minded or exceptionally ambitious soul who despises bodily things. He awaits the moment when the young man is ready to listen to him and to participate with him in dialogue. He then teaches him the principle of philosophic *erôs* and self-knowledge. This encounter is meant to result in reciprocal love (*anterôs*), which indeed occurs at the end of the dialogue.[34]

*The service of the gods to the youth*
There is a dictum by Polemo (c. 314-c. 270), the last head of the Old Academy, which we find in Plutarch's *Moralia* (*To an uneducated ruler*, 780d): 'Polemo used to say that love is the service of the gods in the care and salvation of the youth'.[35] This description of love as a close relationship between an older and a younger man explicitly links the erotic dimension of Socratic and Platonic education to its professed divine mission. John Dillon (1994, 390 n. 7) and Harold Tarrant (2006, 4) have drawn our attention to this dictum as a possible description of both the doctrine of the *Alcibiades* and the practice of education at the Academy under Polemo. Interestingly, the link between this dictum and the *Alcibiades* is confirmed by Plutarch's own interpretation of Alcibiades' relationship with Socrates and presumably of the *Alcibiades* too in a passage at the beginning of his *Life of Alcibiades* (4.4). There Plutarch optimistically remarks that Alcibiades had come to understand the real nature of Socrates' love for him: 'And he [sc. Alcibiades] came to think that the work of Socrates was really (*tôi onti*) a kind of service of the gods for the care and salvation of the youth.'[36] The last words are an exact quotation of Polemo's dictum (except for the position of the verb *einai*), although Plutarch does not mention him by name this time. The phrase *tôi onti* ('really') testifies to the truthfulness of Polemo's saying and of the conception of love underlying it, in Plutarch's eyes. According to this interpretation, the doctrine of the *daimôn-erôs* is inseparable from the care of the gods for humanity. In the *Apology* Socrates claims that his life has been guided by the god's commands (33c), and that, more generally, the gods do not neglect the good man, and this is why he interprets his divine sign's silence as meaning that his death must be a good thing (41d).[37] Thus, according to the *Apology*, the life of Socrates does seem somehow to fulfil a specific purpose in a divine plan (cf. Rist 1963, 16).

The rest of the passage from Plutarch's *Life of Alcibiades* also refers to

*François Renaud*

the *Phaedrus* and the *Symposium*, and is worth quoting also because of its emphasis on the concrete, practical dimension of that education: 'Thus, by despising himself, admiring his friend, loving that friend's kindly solicitude and revering his excellence, he [sc. Alcibiades] insensibly acquired an "image of love", as Plato says [*Phaedrus* 255d], "to match love," and all were amazed [*thaumazein*] to see him eating, exercising, and tenting with Socrates [*Symposium* 219e], while he was harsh and stubborn with the rest of his lovers' (tr. Perrin).[38] These remarks by an ancient reader of Plato, and no doubt of the *Alcibiades*, recall what was then most admired – and might indeed be most admirable – in the figure of Socrates, namely the harmony between what he thought (*logos*) and what he did (*ergon*), between thinking and life (Tarrant 2006, 8). The imitation of Socrates as *exemplum* will thereafter mean the call on everyone to strive to embody that elusive unity,[39] and the divine forces at work in him as an educator (cf. *Tht.* 176a5-b3).

**Notes**

1. I would like to thank Jeremy Hayhoe for his kind proof-reading of the text.

2. *Ap.* 26d-28a (for Plato's text I follow Burnet's text throughout unless indicated); Xenophon, *Mem.* I, 1.1-5 (ed. Marchant).

3. *Ap.* 24b8-c1: ἔχει δέ τι πως ὧδε· Σωκράτη φησὶν ἀδικεῖν τούς τε νέους διαφθείροντα καὶ θεοὺς οὓς ἡ πόλις νομίζει οὐ νομίζοντα, ἕτερα δὲ δαιμόνια καινά.

4. *Ap.* 30a5; 31a7-8; 33c4-7; cf. the Delphic oracle: *Ap.* 20d4-22e5; cf. Xen. *Apol.* 14.

5. E.g. *Ap.* 31c7-d1; *Alc.* I, 103a5-6; *Euthd.* 272e3-4; *Rep.* 496c3-4; *Phdr.* 242b8-c2.

6. Smith and Woodruff 2000; Destrée and Smith 2005.

7. *In Alcibiadem* (hereafter: *in Alc.*) (ed. Westerink). See Renaud (2008) for an account of Olympiodorus' general exegetical approach to Plato and Aristotle.

8. *Alc.* 103a5; 105b8, 105d5, 105e5, e7, 124c8, 127e6, 133c5, 135c5, 135d6.

9. The best-known passage in Plato on the strictly apotreptic quality of Socrates' sign is in the *Apology* (31d3-4): ἀεὶ ἀποτρέπει με τοῦτο ὃ ἂν μέλλω πράττειν, προτρέπει δὲ οὔποτε. Cf. Xenophon, *Mem.* 1.4.14-15; 4.3.12; 4.8.5-6.

10. See Opsomer 1997, esp. 115-21, as well as Joyal's response (2001, 352-6).

11. The twofold aspect of the sign led some Ancients, such as Euclides the Socratic, to suppose that two different *daimones* were involved here; on this see Brancacci 2000), esp. 152-4.

12. *Ap.* 27c8-9: εἰ δὲ δαιμόνια νομίζω, καὶ δαίμονας δήπου πολλὴ ἀνάγκη νομίζειν μέ ἐστιν. οὐχ οὕτως ἔχει; ἔχει δή.

13. See Bailly 2003, 106, n. 1.

14. See Liddell and Scott 1940, 365-6.

15. *Works and Days* 122ff. (ed. Solmsen et al.).

16. E.g. *Ap.* 27c10-28a1; *Phdr.* 246e6; *Rep.* 392a4-6; *Laws* 801e2-4, 818c1-3, 828b1-3, 906a7.

17. *Crat.* 398b5-c4; *Rep.* 540b7-c2.

18. *Phd.* 107d6; *Rep.* 620d8-9; *Laws* 877a6-b2.

19. E.g. Proclus on *Symp.* 202d13-e1: *in Alc.* 46.5-6 (ed. Segonds); Hermeias, *in Phdr.* 66.1-3 (ed. Couvreur).

## 13. Socrates' Divine Sign

20. According to Plutarch (*De gen. Soc.* 591e, ed. de Lacy and Einarsen), Socrates' divine sign corresponds to his *nous-daimôn*: his soul is less submersed in the body than those of other human beings.

21. *Symp.* 177d7-8: οὐδέν φημι ἄλλο ἐπίστασθαι ἢ τὰ ἐρωτικά. Cf. 193e5-6; *Theages* 128 b2-4. Cf. Joyal 1995, 51.

22. See Mühl 1966, 249-51; Motte 1989, 217.

23. *in Alc.* 15.5-17.9. See Rist 1963, 16. Similarly in Plotinus the concept of *daimôn* is transposed to *erôs* as the activity of the human soul: *Enn.* 3 [50] 5, 3-7.

24. *in Alc.* 215.19: καὶ ὅτι ὁ ἔρως τοῦ καλοῦ ἐστίν, ὄντως δὲ καλὸν τὸ ἐν ψυχῇ.

25. *in Alc.* 55.20-3: ὅτι σπουδαῖος ὢν ὁ Σωκράτης αὐτάρκης ἐστὶν καὶ τῇ τοῦ θεοῦ αὐταρκείᾳ συγγενής· ἐντεῦθεν ὡς ἐρωτικὸς οὖν σπουδάζει τῆς τοιαύτης αὐταρκείας μεταδοῦναι τοῖς παιδικοῖς καὶ πρὸς τὴν τοῦ θεοῦ αὐταρκείαν τελειώσας ἀναγαγεῖν. Cf. *in Alc.* 42.14-15.

26. *in Alc.* 41.10-12: στοιχεῖα δὲ καὶ τεκμήρια ἐνθέου ἐραστοῦ λέγει δύο ταῦτα, ὅτι δεῖ τὸν ἔνθεον ἐραστὴν καὶ κρίσιν ἔχειν καὶ συμπάθειαν.

27. *Symp.* 209b-d; *Phdr.* 276a-277a; *in Alc.* 213.5-7: πρέπει γὰρ τῷ ἔρωτι καὶ ἡ ἀποκατάστασις, ἐπιστροφῇ ὄντι, καὶ τὸ διαλέγεσθαι τὸν ἐραστὴν τῷ ἐρωμένῳ· ὄργανον γὰρ κοινωνίας ὁ λόγος. τοῦτο δὲ τὸ διαλέγεσθαι πάλαι μὲν ἑνόει.

28. Aeschines Socraticus, fr. 52 (ed. Giannantoni).

29. Hoffmann 1985, 427; Joyal 2000, 82.

30. *Alc.* 127e-133c, esp. 132c-133c; cf. *Theaet.* 176a-b; See e.g. Renaud 2007, 238-41; Tarrant 2007, 10-12.

31. Dillon 1994, 388; cf. Alcinous, *Didaskalos*, 33 (ed. Whittaker).

32. Hermeias' and Proclus' exegetical procedure, like Olympiodorus', consists in explaining the *Phaedrus* in the light of the *Alcibiades* and inversely: Hermeias, *in Phaedr.* 207 (ed. Couvreur); Proclus, *in Alc.* 133.1-134.15 (ed. Segonds); cf. Dillon 1994, 388-90.

33. *Theag.* 130e2-3: pol) δὲ μάλιστα καὶ πλεῖστον ἐπεδίδουν ὁπότε παρ᾽ αὐτόν σε καθοίμην ἐχόμενός σου καὶ ἁπτόμενος. By contrast see Agathon's remark in the *Symposium* (175c8: παρ᾽ ἐμὲ κατάκεισο, ἵνα καὶ τοῦ σοφοῦ ἁπτόμενός σου) and Socrates' amused rebuff (175d3-e1). For the connection between the *Theages*' use of *synousia* and related vocabulary and the Academy under Polemo, see Tarrant 2006, 6.

34. *Alc.* 135e1-3; *in Alc.* 220.4: τοῦτο γὰρ τέλος τοῦ ἐρωτικοῦ, τὸ ἀντερᾶσθαι.

35. Πολέμων γὰρ ἔλεγε τὸν ἔρωτα εἶναι θεῶν ὑπηρεσίαν εἰς νέων ἐπιμέλειαν καὶ σωτηρίαν.

36. Plutarch, *Alc.* 4.4: καὶ τὸ μὲν Σωκράτους ἡγήσατο πρᾶγμα τῷ ὄντι θεῶν ὑπηρεσίαν εἰς νέων ἐπιμέλειαν εἶναι καὶ σωτηρίαν.

37. See Plutarch, *De Soc. gen.*, 593a-594a (ed. de Lacy and Einarsen).

38. *Alcibiades* 4.4: καὶ τὸ μὲν Σωκράτους ἡγήσατο πρᾶγμα τῷ ὄντι θεῶν ὑπηρεσίαν εἰς νέων ἐπιμέλειαν εἶναι καὶ σωτηρίαν, καταφρονῶν δ᾽ αὐτὸς ἑαυτοῦ, θαυμάζων δ᾽ ἐκεῖνον, ἀγαπῶν δὲ τὴν φιλοφροσύνην, αἰσχυνόμενος δὲ τὴν ἀρετήν, ἐλάνθανεν εἴδωλον ἔρωτος, ὥς φησιν ὁ Πλάτων, ἀντέρωτα κτώμενος, ὥστε θαυμάζειν ἅπαντας ὁρῶντας αὐτὸν Σωκράτει μὲν συνδειπνοῦντα καὶ συμπαλαίοντα καὶ συσκηνοῦντα, τοῖς δὲ ἄλλοις ἐρασταῖς χαλεπὸν ὄντα καὶ δυσχείρωτον, ἐνίοις δὲ καὶ παντάπασι σοβαρῶς προσφερόμενον, ὥσπερ Ἀνύτῳ τῷ Ἀνθεμίωνος.

39. 215.15: τέλος τοῦ ἔρωτος ἡ ἕνωσις.

# 14

# 'The Individual' in History and History 'in General': Alcibiades, Philosophical History and Ideas in Contest

*Neil Morpeth*

## I. Historical, transhistorical and archetype

Alcibiades is, at once, an historical figure and an archetypal individual. Also, in an anthropological sense and in terms of traditions of thought, Alcibiades is a truly remarkable, individuated moment in history. Alcibiades the historical personage and philosophical character-as-actor has become a source for historical and philosophical memories, that is, a human gathering place, a focus, reference and a trans-historical persona for the passages of history and intellect – a place where singular and collective human actions and behaviours matter and where particular and general social forces remain contentiously in play.[1] With the classical world of the Athenian empire immediately behind the philosophical stage and dramatically present in the foreground of the *Alcibiades* I, and with the Spartan world still presenting intellectual and social puzzles, who better than the exiled, prodigal Athenian son, Alcibiades and Socrates to discuss the deep waters – the social anthropology of a once-real world and its strikingly individuated conduct.[2] Significantly, these modes of human conduct must be clearly seen as situated within the broad agonistic context of Hellenic and Mediterranean civilisations. These 'particular' and 'general' ideas and arguments are swept by Mediterranean scenes and characters.[3]

In a text such as the *Alcibiades*, philosopher-historians are simultaneously encountering intellectual plays within a temporal world held inside a venturous philosophical bubble – a thought experiment on papyrus. Here, readers encounter the *Alcibiades*' uncanny but hypothetical polis of ideas, dialogic argument and contest where a particular if singularly complex late fifth-century history finds literary and general exploratory form in, perhaps, the early years of the fourth century BC.

The challenge for historians of thought and philosophers with an historical figure such as Alcibiades is that he has become an archetypal, political, composite model-type in Classical history and times beyond. Indeed, arguably, Alcibiades remains an atavistic, albeit troubling, his-

## 14. 'The Individual' in History and History 'in General'

torical figure and a classical intellectual caricature of general political ambition and, as events turned out, of overreach. Without Alcibiades' historical and reputational presence, our impression of imperial and imperious Athenian chauvinism would lack much of its verve. Alcibiades is drama and he is dramatically engaged, and moreover, this is not solely a result of the narratives and the intellectual creations of the pens of his voices in history.[4]

And yet there is far more again to this Alcibiades of writers of history and philosophy. There resides in the *Alcibiades* a series of intellectual and historical echoes or foreshadowings of a most interesting kind which deserve further exploration. A deep, abiding friendship (*philia*) between Socrates and Alcibiades is in action here. Whether or not its force is singularly erotic, its practice, politically and personally, is intense – like citizens in arms during the Delium campaign or at Potidaea (Plato, *Symposium* 218c-221b). Moreover, this relationship is teasingly and intensely agonistic.

When a person of remarkable personal and political significance enters the body politic as Alcibiades did – his sense(s) of *realpolitik* and grandiose self-ambition (note *Alc.* 105a-106d and 113d) outweigh his philosophical sense of just and unjust conduct in times of preparing for war and of waging war (*Alc.* 109b-c etc.). Yet, as Socrates pointed out – firmly and persuasively – Alcibiades' original sense of purpose or purposiveness, worth and self-knowing, and of generalised justice-in-conduct in the world, reached back to his complex, youthful years, as seen at *Alc.* 108d-110b, or in the early reference to his guardianship by Pericles (104b) and Socrates' longing and intense overview of Alcibiades' life-in-progress (105d-e). Here we encounter a sense of an almost innate, or perhaps learnt, good conduct in-the-world. However, intellectually and pedagogically speaking, that is, conceptualising and reasoning in the realm of 'true' intelligent discourse, Socrates perceived that Alcibiades had only come into contact with everyday teachers as it were. Moreover, such teachers were lacking in purposiveness and seriousness (*ouk ... spoudaious ge didaskalous*, 110e). In a sure sense, Alcibiades had sought refuge (*katapheugeis*, 110e) in a body of 'teaching persons' who possessed only slight qualifications: that is, in Socrates' eyes *such slight teachers lacked real expertise of a true dialectical kind suited to a polis characterised by seriousness of purpose in conduct in-the-world.*

### II. An intellectual crucible: the formation and shaping of educative ideas

Readers of the *Alcibiades* encounter several orders and layers of intellectual conduct and behaviour in polis society and in-the-world. Questions of 'the just' and what is just are philosophically present (specifically, the ideals and realities of 'just' behaviour, 109b-c), but the extent of expedient political conduct or behaviour at the level of the polis (113d-114b) and its politicians and partisans is, to at least the same extent, a pressing reality and concern. Right governance, let alone just governance, cannot occur in the political arena and assembly (*ekklêsia*, 114b etc.) of the ignorant (note the telling usage of *amathia*, 118b). The questions undergoing forensic interrogation and contest here crossed political and anthropological boundaries of conduct. These questions were and remain bound up with matters of 'political' development and education, namely, the signal, ill-development of one notable citizen and *stratêgos*, Alcibiades, and with cultural/socio-political conduct in the polis – that is, upright governance in times of war and peace (109a-b).

Equally, in this remarkable dialogic encounter, a reader should be struck by the lofty angularity of the discursive questioning: Alcibiades was ('is', if one enters into the immediacy of the drama) acting-in-the-world whilst Socrates was acting upon it (cf. 113d; e). Of course, neither then nor now could any reader easily ignore the dramatic presences or the historical *personae* of these two singular Athenians. Whilst they were equally striking and singularly stubborn Athenians – their society, like later societies, turned upon complex influences, ambitions and always human interactions – friendships and enmities within and outside of their particular world's immediate societal gaze. Socrates and Alcibiades were, at once, key features of this polis world and yet were propelled by their actions and reputations, and by later historical and narrative voices, to another order of formative kinship with what it is (and was then) to be human – human-in-society.

Alcibiades is clearly on the back foot in this dialogic encounter with Socrates. Yet, Alcibiades has his salient moments in the '*true*' or real world of Hellenic political behaviours: the social and anthropological arena of Athenian or Hellenic conduct and action in the world of poleis constitutes that 'true' historical drama and philosophical ground-for-contest. *Alcibiades* 113d is such a moment. In the realm of everyday and 'real' political/ideological behaviour, the questions of comparative scales or degrees of more or less just behaviours being in juxtaposition to their opposites (*dikaiotera ê adikôtera*, 113d2-3) rapidly pass or, rather perhaps descend from, a world of notional justice (*dikaia*) into a realm of 'expediencies' – expedient behaviours-in-practice (*ta sumpheronta*, d5-6). In the realm of practice, namely, the worlds of politics and generalship, of making and doing, action rarely pauses.

## III. An intellectual crucible: social anthropology – questions of power and ideas in action and formation

Significantly, this dialogic encounter is premised upon a cultural and intellectual *milieu* that is similarly predicated on both the particular and the general. Once again, one should flag the social anthropology, the

## 14. 'The Individual' in History and History 'in General'

'*bound sensibilities*', in a true sense of the ideas and terms, '*friendship*' and '*association*', that shape the span of associative relations-in-society, which specially and tightly bind and possess Athenian and Hellenic group behaviours. Socrates quite literally invoked the god 'Friendship', *Philios*, as a bond-in-action between himself and Alcibiades (*Alc.* 109d). Further, Socrates then went on to assert that even Pericles was not one who possessed a 'self-moving wisdom' (*ouk apo tou automatou sophos*, *Alc.* 118c), that is, a singular and solitary independence of thought and wisdom. Even the towering, independently spirited figure of Pericles, whom Socrates has spoken of several times with regard to Alcibiades' parents, his guardianship by Pericles and his ambitions (recall *Alc.* 118b-c and earlier 104b, 105b), was far from alone or 'independently moving' in his leadership of Athens and in his own intellectual formation: again note Pericles' contemporary intellectual and social engagement with currents of thought and currencies of ideas, literally personified by his association with Pythocleides, Anaxagoras and Damon (118c). However, it should be considered, in terms of didacticism and the *Alcibiades* as argumentative dialogue-in-play, that the use of Pericles' reputation was a deadly arrow aimed at Alcibiades. After all, in the dramatic bubble of this dialogue, and in the contest of arguments within it, Pericles' reputation was known and already one of renown while Alcibiades' career was in process, incomplete and under question.

The intellectual contexts and the dramatic and historical settings of the *Alcibiades* are fascinating in their own right. Moreover, the *Alcibiades* has an intellectual relevance and legacy which extends far beyond its Athens-centred, polis-centred, Mediterranean context. It is almost as if, when one considers both the *Alcibiades* and Alcibiades as he is portrayed in the *Symposium*, what matters is not only reasoned insight and the avoidance of the 'expedient' and expedient-driven personal powers and the dangerously naïve seductions which could lead to overreaching political or personal ambition (cf. *Alc.* 113c-116d), but also an equal recognition of the need for painstaking, individualist political and moral development (*epimeleia*) and its attendant socio-cultural skill-set (*technê*, 124b) for action in and on society. Significantly, Alcibiades' singular lack of *epimeleia* and *sophia* – a deadly absence of painstaking care, diligence, and wisdom (123c-d) opened his flawed, self-driven confidence and hubristic political overreach to a potential negation of his social ranking and standing: effectively, to be found wanting (*apoleiphthêsêi*, 124b4).[5]

Moreover, given my foregoing remarks, the reference to Damon, intellectual and musician, if the two fields can be separated, deserves closer scrutiny. The literary and dramatic setting of this Platonic-dialogic engagement, at least at this point of the Socrates-Alcibiades encounter, must have been very near to or in the early years of the Peloponnesian War. The use of the term, *têlikoutos* (118c) with its pointed reference to a venerable old age, is both dramatically and chronologically instructive. Of course, neither Pericles nor Damon were young, yet they both interacted and consulted with one another, unlike Alcibiades who was neither old nor keenly consultative, let alone complete in terms of his own education or his skills in educative leadership (cf. *Alc.* 118b-c). Yet, at this time, when Athens was at or on the cusp of a great war, Alcibiades was entering the political fray (*ta politika*, 118b), and moreover, he was in a state prior to any *educative completion*.[6]

In summary, his education for life was incomplete and he was not ready for any true life in public affairs, let alone participation in the effective governance of a polis-society. This is reinforced in the passage that commences at 124c. The calibre of leadership, the capacity and readiness for leading citizens is central here. Socrates appears to be somewhat wooden in his approach to Alcibiades, but he is undoubtedly singular in his insistence upon a certain real, hard-edged political and educational readiness for polis-life. This is the transformative and transhistorical character of the *Alcibiades* and this is where a writer might make legitimate, common cause with another world, a late modern world and a time with uncommon, yet continuing, links to Western Mediterranean and Classical traditions of thought.

## IVa. Bridges and traditions of ideas: living legacies and transformations

Remarkably and significantly, when Marc Bloch in *Strange Defeat* invoked the Delphic maxim, *know thyself, connais-toi toi-même*, literally, 'know you, you yourself', recalling, famously and originally, Socrates' words in a key, lengthy disquisition addressed to Alcibiades in the *Alcibiades* I, much more than aphoristic Classical intellectual tradition was in direct view and in political play in both Bloch's world[7] and the dramatic polis worldview presented in the *Alcibiades* (especially at 123c-124b). This was and remains an emphatically literal call to personal self-knowing or knowledge at the level of the particular – the immediate, singular self – in society. It is, or could be described as, an ethics of reasoning and conscience, that is, a conscious seizure of why a thinking being should openly and capably stand in the world of the affairs of human beings in society, in action, and in political heat. True acts of intellect and intelligence must possess a moral core of knowledge and a willingness to put intelligence to service in society: here one may again note *Alc.* 123c-124b, with its weight of argument buttressed by its concentration upon the critical importance of what is *phronimos*, 'thoughtful', in the rule of the citizenry in the polis by Athens' hypothetical and idealised intelligent social élite, the *kaloi k'agathoi* (124d-125a). While in an essential, if general and traditional way the Delphic motto *know thyself* has long entered popular, intelligent discourse and education, as signalled later again in Victor Ehrenberg's venturous 1968 work, with its proud, concluding chapter banner head:

## 14. 'The Individual' in History and History 'in General'

'Know Thyself', Marc Bloch's passionate appeal to this worldly maxim and tradition is possessed by an urgent spirit and intellect, namely, an intelligent engagement with a less than rational world.[8] Marc Bloch was a 1940s 'gadfly' – a fierce and stinging critic.

The continuing manifestations of 'The Classical Tradition', embracing many Mediterranean and wider European traditions, whether located near the continental span or afar, presume both passion and intellect. 'Insight' is a key idea and concern in the traditions of thought associated with both the *Alcibiades* and Bloch's *Strange Defeat*. In these works we come face-to-face with ancient and modern forms of contemporaneous questioning and quarrelsome exploration, which were (and remain) concerned with elemental processes of knowledge, knowing and understanding. These traditions of thought remarkably span historical times. What matters here is the following: the capacity for insight, 'vision', understanding, and especially that fleeting intellectual capacity of coming-to-be, of looking meaningfully, and intentionally, a little further into the human condition in time and place, both on the literary page and in dramatic life, both literally and figuratively speaking.[9] This intellectual stage was and remains saliently life itself – historical, dramatic, and always philosophical – of things lost and found, fought for and loved, and simply not forgotten.

It might well be a truism, yet it is a necessary truism, to state that the intellectual, historical and philosophical activities under discussion here (in the attempt to understand a little better the intellectual climates in which traditions of thought – formative, made and remade – played out their passages in historical time and the philosophical arena, whether they are centred on historical personages or on *dramatis personae*) were elementally subject to the art of debate and dialogic encounter and formulation. In a worldly sense, this is a debate which remains very much alive.

Let us now consider and 'recall' Marc Bloch's opening to *The Historian's Craft – apologie pour l'histoire ou métier d'historien*, formulated as a question, a grand question, from his son, Etienne Bloch, to his father, professor in many senses of this venerable word and title, and a man of ideas:

*Papa, explique-moi donc à quoi sert l'histoire.*
Papa, explain to me then of what use or service is history?[10]

Ah, the archer's target. The central question charmingly and essentially posed here is focussed upon the utility and purposive activity and the nature of intellectual accountings, recountings and record. Here, the reader is introduced to reasoning argument and 'the subject' under discussion by a true, doubting enquirer, to borrow from Boyle's seventeenth-century title and treatise, *The Skeptical Chemist*. History is at once *subject* and to be *subject to discussion*. This work, *The Historian's Craft*, with its introductory dialogic encounter-question posed by son to father and recast, or turned back by the father upon readers then yet to come, in an uncertain future, constituted a doubting chemical or elemental enquiry into the human condition through time, in argument, and always in life. This was an inescapably philosophical and historical task-as-calling and an act of learned life, learning and love in the face of exile and death. *Explanation* and the craft of history were inextricably bound to acts of accounting and recounting, argument, tradition and innovation. In terms of traditions of argument and of questioning 'the ways of the human world', Bloch's journeys are across the bridge of Classical traditions of thought and of human presences, traces and passages through past and present worlds.

### IVb. Living legacies: Memory and the passage of historical time

Further, let us turn to Alcibiades' conceptual, historical and philosophical thought-driven place by way of the following two devices: the first will be a general observation, and the second will be concerned with Plutarch's reportage. First, Alcibiades, as historical figure and philosophical actor/interlocutor, could be characterised by the following observation:

> *Many things can be said about Alcibiades and, possibly, many of them are true.*

Such an ironic statement could usefully provide historians and philosophers with the space to pause and wonder at the remarkable transhistorical reputations-as-character of an Alcibiades.

Secondly, Plutarch's story of Alcibiades' prized hound is illustrative of the grandiose, public and edgy personality – political and individual – which characterised Alcibiades' complexity as political player in Athens and abroad:

> Possessing a dog of wonderful size and beauty, which had cost him seventy minas, he had its tail cut off, and a beautiful tail it was, too. His 'comrades' (intimates) chid him for this, and declared that everybody was furious about the dog and abusive of its owner. But Alcibiades burst out laughing and said: 'That's just what I want; I want Athens to talk about this, that it may say nothing worse about me'. (Plutarch, *Alc.* 9)[11]

Of course, the Athenians, among others, did say worse things about Alcibiades.

The striking, elemental human quality of Alcibiades' life in political society and literary imaginings (which could be suggestively characterised as forms of charismatic re-creation) remains the particularist spark of creativity brought to life and human reflection by Greek traditions of thought, historical and philosophical. With particular reference to Alci-

## 14. 'The Individual' in History and History 'in General'

biades (yet, keeping in historical view his intellectual place and presence in the philosophical arena of exploratory Hellenic thoughtfulness, contentious debate, and engagement in-the-world), this flawed, remarkable embodiment of creativity and aristocratic self-ambition might be better understood as a signal or indicator of an elemental emergence of 'individuality' in the complex guise of a 'public personality'.

Alcibiades and the intellectual and societal dynamics which brought him into public life remain simultaneously elemental and paradoxical – 'knowable', capable of empathetic reasoning, yet rather distant and elusive. Intellectual and historical roots, *shared or claimed origins*, if you will, are one thing but proximity, intellectual proximity, remains a challenge. At the heart of such an historical figure, and philosophical actor-in-the world as Alcibiades clearly is, rests, albeit uneasily, an intellectual legacy which could be termed a twinned human drama, namely, a study of intended and unintended consequences. Ultimately, Alcibiades' historical reputation is formed during, around and in times of war suffused in politics, Mediterranean-wide dreaming and dealing, passion and horse-racing.[12] To a distant eye his life could well appear like a contest (*agôn*) with life itself.[13]

In this remarkable classical and perilous Western terrain, one can rediscover and reconsider shared ideas and legacies, actions and inactions, which extend from the worlds of Herodotus and Thucydides, through Plato and indeed Aristotle, and on into European writers and intellectuals such as Marc Bloch. Further, in a general but apposite intellectual context, that is, in terms of legacies and traditions of thought, an historian of thought should consider advancing a claim that a not dissimilar *agonising* presence can be found in the life-works and reputational memories contained in Thucydides' contemporaneous account of *The Peloponnesian War* and Marc Bloch's wartime writings as history, memory, recollection and record.

### V. Climates for the growth of intellectual exploration

When intellectual society or human self-reflectivity rises or awakens, appreciations of the complexity of human society seemingly increase exponentially. These events occur in and out of immediate historical causation, whether or not such intellectual appreciations and activities attract forms of social, political or cultural opposition or, for want of a better term, authoritarian assault. Historians and philosophers should never underestimate the surprising growth and power of human personality and its peculiar waves (thought- and psychology-based waves) of self-confidence, reflectivity or despair – personal and/or social.

How might an historian of thought characterise such challenges? Two observations follow:

(i) The human challenge for the writer, namely, coming to grips with the depth of the cultural and anthropological antiquity and 'ways of seeing' which accompany historians and philosophers when they seek to explore the plurality of the classical traditions of thought, their intimate social, cultural and historical locales, and subsequent transmission (in part, partial or otherwise transformed) to a much later modern and contemporary European and Western world, is always and, at once, great, small and complex. This is a truism but a necessary truism which weighs upon historians of ideas – the past is always, even when it uncannily seems familiar, a foreign land.[14]

(ii) Yet, almost paradoxically, it ('the past') drives historians and philosophers along the road of encounter or even embrace. If you will allow both a light and dark ironic aside: when it comes to questions of matters intellectual – writers, historians and philosophers can and do enter upon strange quests and sometimes even stranger loves.

In the end, the elemental yet complex challenge remains: historians of ideas actively reconsider the intellectual milieu or climate for the growth of independently spirited ideas of history, and social and human conduct (a philosophical realm), within peculiarly cultural, historical and general civilisational contexts – past and present. This challenge additionally remains a pivotal, perhaps the pivotal, exploratory notion whenever one seeks after insight (*dianoia*: conscious and intentional thought/reasoning and awareness as 'understanding') or into the sceptical, robust and yet fragile terrain of classical and Mediterranean traditions of thought.

## VI. Alcibiades and the complexity of history's stage

Allow me to extend my remarks with the following word picture. When accounting for human behaviour, in the singular and in general, through time and/or culture, one should not be surprised if matters of renown (or its opposite) and matters historical, philosophical, and above all, thoughtful, remain messily to the fore in the study of human affairs and their motivating forces and ideas.

Whatever might be made of Aristotle's remarkable comments in the *Poetics* (9.1-5: 1451a36-1451b11), when Aristotle observed, on the difference between poetry and history, that the 'particular fact', or rather, '*history*', moves according to each 'thing that Alcibiades did or experienced' (1451b10-11), it is clear that Alcibiades, as historical figure and individuated personality, had reached an archetypal standing in Aristotle's thought, as elsewhere. One cannot doubt that Alcibiades stood as a 'model-like' testament to the singular, and yet generally complex, stamp of human character in any given chapter of human history – of the particular (that is, of the implacable human character) and the general (the force and play of history's actions and accountings in and through time). Alcibiades is at once recognisable and historical and yet possessed of human character, drama if you will, capable of travel – archetypal travel – in and through

## 14. 'The Individual' in History and History 'in General'

time. In very real senses, states of reality are subject to not only 'general' and 'particular' forces and circumstances but, in some existential sense, divergent and broad plays of likelihood or probability (*to eikos*, 'the probable') whilst also being, in the end, subject to more singular and circumstantial historical matters (*to anangkaion*, 'the necessary'). As Halliwell observed in his translation and commentary, *The Poetics of Aristotle*:

> What Aristotle requires, by probability and necessity, is not the direct reproduction of any one type of reality, but something more like an underlying correspondence to the general concepts and truths which we derive from experience of the world (1987, 109).[15]

Put another way, with regard to things or matters 'tragic' and 'comic', when it comes to human affairs and intellectual or philosophical understandings of the ranging human condition, we, that is scholars, are appreciative prisoners of what is at once a theoretical and an experiential apprehension. That is, if we seek to know a little more about history and philosophy and their interrelationships, we should appreciate that our understandings, or the archetypes that scholars might use to evaluate potentially evidentiary details or positions about human beings and their affairs in history, culture and society, have both theoretical and experiential notions tugging away at any quest toward a more orderly human understanding.

### VII. Lovers of words and accountings: on the 'individualist' character of events and human mutuality – 'mutualities of experience'

'Evocative' is a wonderful word. Historians of ideas and their philosopher colleagues need only declaim 'Thucydides, Plato, Socrates, Alcibiades and Marc Bloch', and classicists and scholars in the warring literal and literary fields of ideas recognise at once the signal individualist character and exilic experiences of those mentioned. Moreover, they each share in the literal, literary and imaginative beginnings, continuities and extensions of the intellectual reach of Mediterranean and Western Classical traditions of thought. A further note on the *idea of exile* is useful here. All of our figures in time and philosophical exposition had remarkable experiences of exile, namely, internal and external exilic experiences and alienations.[16] Wars between states washed over them as did internal wars (often referred to as *stasis* or civil war – a deadly epithet and euphemism), and extremes of discord and violence presented themselves in their lives.[17] The intellectual and/or passionate life is not a quietist zone. Such intellectual reckonings, in real and artistic time are, at once, intimately and inseparably historical and philosophical with also a poetic, Aristotle-inspired dimension. The spirit of *dianoia* and the quest for understanding (and its classical expression in *Symposium*, 219a) remain at the heart of intellectual life.[18]

Significantly and by way of qualification, I am not arguing for simple or linear historical connections here, but rather for agonised, intellectual presences and reckonings with, and upon, our own lives and times. Additionally, predictability is also an absent element here. All the intellectuals under discussion, with little historical or dramatic liberty, were simultaneously courageous, fearless and preoccupied. Moreover, all these historical figures and their philosophical dramaturgy-in-action (that is, their lives on the literal worldly stage and on the page) were characterised remarkably by a certain reflectivity and, to be fair, surging senses of challenging, problematic, remarkable and engagingly singular self-reflectivity.

These intellectual and societal engagements could be called forms of acute, conscious awareness of life, times and intellect-in-action. An intellectual climate is not only made in words and ideas; it is forged in cultural anthropology (really, many social anthropologies – ancient and modern), and external challenge and exchange. All of the preceding intellectual actions, activities and engagements with and in the world were premised upon very real forms of intellectual courage and equally wide-ranging senses of risk and risk-taking.

### VIII. Locating and locations of argument in perilous times: 'initiation' or plunging into war

Times of war and strife – civil and political or in deadly combinations – would appear to be unlikely venues for lovers, intellectual or carnal. Yet, unpredictability, and a certain incongruity when it comes to any true appreciation of the seductively termed 'human condition', is itself a place, a locale where ideas and, alas, war meet. Whatever might be said about war *per se*, once commenced it is fluid (potentially in concept and operation), rarely discreet, and often unscrupulous in its public faces and actions. Ideal terrain, one might almost say, for the likes of an Alcibiades character – and his historical and philosophical interlocutors. When it comes to finding a descriptor for the historical beginnings of a war (individual and conceptual, the events and the soldiery), expansive human-manpower fighting imagery is better characterised by the direct and broad term 'plunging' rather than 'initiation'. That is, any idea of 'initiation' needs to be perceived in the harsh and surprising circumstances of a particular war, or of warring in general, in those particular times and societies. Anthropology and psychology are closer to philosophy and philosophical history than some might imagine.

Of equal significance, in such fraught and intense, yet very much alive climates, we are considering contemporary ideas and traditions of thought

## 14. 'The Individual' in History and History 'in General'

which continue to swirl as flows of human thought in contention in societies beyond the authors' original conceptions. Traditions of thought and contemporary thought and writings are, almost paradoxically, historical and existential states-of-being. These kinds of philosophical and/or historical writings are, to borrow an awkward and provocative notion, 'of their nature' contemporaneous phenomena. They resonate because they make a place for 'sense' and 'argument' in and about contemporary human worlds – intellectual, social and moral. Equally, though truistic, these writings are a form of the recording of human existence. Such writings and their ideas are peculiarly and intensely present yet remarkably possessed of senses of their own past.

At the heart of these traditions of thought and ideas there reside the declamatory voices of writers and 'actors' in their forensic and combative worlds of ideas, their histories, and elementally, their stories from their own worlds. To take but one controversial historical and dramatic figure – a player in events – as example, Alcibiades stands as a larger-than-life historical figure and equally as a Thespian, a dramatic character, on an Athenian/Hellenic philosophical stage. Alcibiades was, at once, historical, individuated, philosophically sprung, and mythic in stature. In these four senses, Alcibiades represented something much greater than himself, and simultaneously, was a signal exemplar of flawed ambition and power in-the-world.

... And this Protean intellectual ferment arose in the Mediterranean generally speaking, and in particular, the Eastern Mediterranean. This not-so-antique world remains a remarkable intellectual and historical geography, and a seedbed of ideas.

### Notes

1. In the leading popular English language journal, *The Economist*, the abiding presence of Socratic argument and the Classical tradition is seen to be robust and in intellectual ferment: 'Socrates in America: Arguing to death – From Socrates, History's quintessential non-conformist, lessons for America today', *The Economist*, 19 December 2009, 63-5. This is a substantial article for this leading journal and a useful insight into popular, contemporary debate and the roles or utility of a public intellectual.

2. Alcibiades' personal and political situation is complex: Pericles was his guardian and, in effect, 'familial' protector and maker (note *Alc.* 104a-b, and yet ...). Moreover, Alcibiades stood in good stead through his own family's long history and social position (cf. Thucydides, 5.43.2ff; 8.6.3). Alcibiades' personal quest for power was, according to Socrates, driven – even all-possessing (*Alc.* 105). For succinct and valuable commentary on Alcibiades and his family, see Davies 1971, 17-21, and generally. Note further, Plutarch, *Alcibiades* 22-7, who pens a vivid and insightful account of Alcibiades' dangerous, oscillating career.

3. The elusive yet central quest of examining this many-faceted world remains common ground for historians, ancient and modern, and scholars of ideas, arts and sciences. Influences, real and imaginary, and renowned scholarly, artistic and

## Neil Morpeth

literary studies abound. Note as a beginning: J.J. Winckelmann, in Irwin (ed.) 1972; Von Wilamowitz-Moellendorff 1908; C.R. Whittaker 1997, 459-72; Purcell and Horden 2000; Harris (ed.) 2006.

4. A general observation: history and literary studies, philosophical and biographical studies – Thucydides, Plato, Xenophon and Aristotle – all embrace or engage with the elemental character, the political manoeuvres and 'lives' of Alcibiades as literary figure and historical personage. Alcibiades is an elemental part of Athenian time and culture. Alcibiades is 'morphic', changing shape or form through historical time and in literary and philosophical space. Note further, on the topic of dealing in things and in ideas, in people-in-exchanges both monetary and 'imaginative', Xenophon, *Ways and Means* (*Poroi*, 5.1-4 and generally). The polis ideally needs peace for the pursuit of these kinds of prosperity and happiness.

5. However, Alcibiades felt no qualms: note Connor 1971, 21. Significantly, the *Alcibiades* is, at once, in dramatic 'historical time' and 'out of time' in the sense of an idealised philosophical discourse: note P. Ricoeur's explorations of this theme (2004; 2006, 168-71). The *Alcibiades* is a dramatic testimony of, and to, an Athenian philosophical past.

6. Note the telling, adverbial weight and deployment of the word *'prin'* at 118b, *prin paideuthênai*.

7. Marc Bloch's father, Gustave Bloch, was a classicist and an eminent ancient historian and 1940 was the hard and salient year for Bloch's deployment of Klio and the Delphic maxim: M. Bloch 1946, 179; 1949, 146. See re. Gustave Bloch, Fink 1989, 1-14.

8. See *Strange Defeat*, 143-9 (= *L'étrange défaite*, 176-82) for the depth of the character of the intellectual challenge and struggle which the events of 10 May, 1940, and earlier, pressed upon Marc Bloch, France, Europe and, beyond, the world at war. The 'nature' of intellectual engagement and the absence of agreement-in-controversy is elemental here: note Gocer 1999, 703-4.

9. For *dianoia* and more, see further Tarrant 2000, 154-5, always keeping in view Plato's *Symposium* 219a and its dialogic encounter – before and after. See also the insightful, broad discussion in Gould 1963, 18-57.

10. Carol Fink 1989, 286-7 grasped not only the essential liveliness and passionate argument in Bloch's work but also his Classical-Socratic intellectual edge. Regarding Marc Bloch's ideas of the historian's intellectual activity and, in many senses of the term, intellectual combat, much remains to be considered.

11. The translation is that of Perrin 1916 with changes. For a very useful and insightful treatment, cf. Pelling 2002.

12. *Thuc.* 6.15 (along with 6.16.1-2ff.) is instructive. These lines in Thucydides are more than partisanship – they deal in dreams and ambitions and signal that cultural and social behavioural traditions set limits to 'individualised' conduct in-the-polis. Not that one should, for a moment, understate the animus in existence between Nicias and Alcibiades (note 6.12.1 and 16.1). For a discussion of the 'contradictions', or social strains existent within the very cultural structures of a polis or Hellenic society generally – and well deserving further reconsideration – note A.W. Gouldner 1965, 1-40.

13. Plutarch is insightful: *Alcibiades* 7-14 and 23. Cf. R.J. Littman 1970, 263-76. In historical and philosophical senses, war, Eros and conquest were ancient relatives – fraught with potential and/or contradiction. Paradox is also nearby. Certainly, for good or ill, Alcibiades' reputation grew rapidly through time. See further, N.F. Minnich 1996, 9-26. Controversy continues: M. Nussbaum 1986, 165-99.

## 14. 'The Individual' in History and History 'in General'

14. For inspiration and reflection see D. Lowenthal 1985.

15. See further, G.E.M. de Ste. Croix in Barbara Levick (ed.) 1975, 45-58. See also Raymond Weil 1977, 202-17. Speaking generally, complexity, interpretation and the transformation of ideas in-and-about society, real and conceptualised, are, at once, the subjects and central preoccupations of Aristotle's forensic explorations. R. Sorabji captures these living traditions and arenas of ideas in theory and practice or action and debate (Tarrant and Baltzly [eds] 2006, 185-93). 'Reading' *Alcibiades*, like reading Plato and Aristotle, is just that – a revelation in ideas. By way of recapitulation, note Aristotle's singular use of Alcibiades in history: *to de kath' hekaston, ti Alkibiadês epraxen ê ti epathen*, 1451b 10-11: see generally, Halliwell 1987, 40-2.

16. To give but one example here, witness Plato as literary and historical voice in his renowned Epistle VII, and see Epistle VIII for broader cultural/Hellenic and Mediterranean perspectives. Still worth exploring is Edelstein 1966.

17. All 'the protagonists' in this essay had direct experience of violence – violence in a range of warring conflicts. This in itself provides key dramatic background to feelings powerfully held – Eros-driven or otherwise. Again, Socrates' and Alcibiades' personal experiences of battle, the natural geographic climates of these conflicts, the singularity of experiences of war and the intensity of human contact (note again, Plato, *Symposium*, truly remarkable encounters at 218c-221b) were unlikely to be in negation of passion and of passions held intensely. Complexity, *mania* (*tês philosophou manias*, Plato, *Symposium* 218b), courage, and the sheer range of the emotional but reasoning *anthrôpos* is on display. Socrates, of course, was unlike other *anthrôpoi* (221c). For a perspective on generational/early twentieth-century changes in ideas and historical reflection on the Classical Tradition as a modern study in its own right, see R.G. Bury 1909; 1932, lx-lxiv; li-lii, and generally. Many more were to follow, among whom: E.M. Butler, Werner Jaeger, W.K.C. Guthrie, J-P. Vernant, G.E.R. Lloyd and K.J. Dover.

18. A general influence but one of many – the emotional range of human beings is at once anthropological, cultural, historical and philosophical, and more, and remains in contest: see Nussbaum 2001. Questions of insight and perceptions of the past, and its imagined shaping, remain powerfully, argumentatively in view in Dover (ed.) 1992.

Appendix I

# Fourth-Century Politics and the Date of the *Alcibiades I*

## E.J. Baynham and Harold Tarrant

As this volume demonstrates, both the authorship and the date of the *Alcibiades* I are highly contentious issues.[1] In theory no fourth-century BC date seems to be excluded, with Tarrant's article in the present volume perhaps even allowing for an early third-century one. The present brief will be to reflect rather narrowly, from a historian's perspective, on such indications there are of an historical context, without dwelling on any of the issues that habitually concern readers of the dialogue as literature or as philosophy.

The question of any Platonic dialogue's date is a double one: first the dramatic date – when the conversation represented is supposedly taking place, and second, the dialogue's actual date of composition. The former date will in most circumstances involve a single day, while the latter could in principle involve several years. In theory, examining Plato's choice of the dramatic date may illuminate the date of composition. We are given evidence for the supposed dramatic date by Socrates himself; he tells us at 123d that Alcibiades is nearly twenty, and later (131c) that his body is 'losing its bloom' (*lêgei anthoun*). This might seem a depressing thought, though all that Socrates is likely to mean is that Alcibiades is now on the threshold of full manhood, so that this is the time when influencing his way of thinking has become particularly urgent. Alcibiades' stunning appearance is something of a literary *topos* – not only in this dialogue, but also in his biographical tradition as a whole. Plutarch says right at the start of the *Life*, that Alcibiades' physical beauty flowered at each time of his growth, as child, as youth and as man; in other words, he never went through an unattractive phase. Even his lisp seems to have contributed. One might well wonder whether there is something Homeric about this magnetic attractiveness: Alcibiades is the Homeric *agathos* in every sense of the word, and as such he will insist on receiving his *timê*.

If Alcibiades is aged around twenty at the time of the purported conversation then one should expect the setting to be around 430/429 at the latest,[2] some two years after the first attested reference to Alcibiades' activity, as an ephebe at the siege of Potidaea (where Socrates famously saved his life, *Symp.* 219e-220e) just before the outbreak of the Pelopon-

*Appendix I*

nesian War. The great statesman Pericles is still alive (104b) and is named as Alcibiades' guardian. Whoever wrote the *Alcibiades* has taken great care to create historical verisimilitude, as Plato did himself in dramas like the *Theaetetus* and the *Symposium* (see Hornblower 2000, 366, with n. 8). For instance, Artaxerxes I is correctly named as the current Great King of Persia (123d) and the identification of the Spartan queen Lampito (probably not the same one as Aristophanes' big breasted 'rump-jumper' in *Lysistrata*) as the daughter of Leotychidas, wife of Archidamus and mother of Agis (124a) is also accurate.

At the same time there are some odd anachronisms for a supposedly fifth century context. David Gribble (above n. 1), in his summary of the main arguments against Plato's authorship, has drawn attention to a range of anecdotal information that appears to have been assembled at a later stage in the Alcibiades tradition, such as his refusal as a boy to learn the aulos (106e; cf. Plut. *Alc.* 2), his tutor's name (112b) and his mythical genealogy. Even so, it is hard to know when these stories developed, and one is not entitled to affirm that they necessarily have to be late. The story about Alcibiades' rejection of the flute perhaps has special significance for us, and we shall come back to it. Also curious is the reference to the recent increase in Spartan wealth (122e), which Socrates claims has been pouring into Sparta 'from all of Greece and often from foreign cities too'. This might be mere careless generalisation, but nevertheless such a statement suggests a Sparta of the first quarter of the fourth century BC at the height of its hegemony, after the defeat of Athens and before the devastating loss at Leuctra in 371.[3] Comparing Spartan wealth favourably with Athenian wealth at the beginning of the Peloponnesian War would be in total contradiction of the evidence of Pericles' address in indirect speech in Thucydides (2.13.2-5). One might have expected Plato to be well aware of this.

Even more intriguing is the reference to Peparethos (116d-e) – a small island-city that was seldom in the news. Denyer (2001: 152) makes much of this, mentioning that it was 'too insignificant even to be the byword for insignificance'. Peparethos was an island in the same group as Halonnesos, off the coast of Magnesia, and an ally of Athens since 377 BC, following Athenian success in capitalising on the unpopularity of Spartan domination (Diodorus 15.30.5). The small island was in the political headlines at least twice, but known examples are in the fourth century, rather than the fifth.[4] The reference to Peparethos has received its share of scholarly attention, but it is worth reminding ourselves of the two occasions when it turns up in our sources; Diodorus (15.93) records that Alexander, the tyrant of Pherae, captured a squadron of five Athenian triremes and one from its ally Peparethos in 361 BC. This was an embarrassing episode for Athens, which not only highlighted its own incompetence but its failure to protect its allies from a thug like Alexander. Polyaenus (fr. 6.2) also discusses a punitive raid on the Piraeus that Alexander conducted in response to Athens' perceived interference in

## Fourth-Century Politics and the Date of the Alcibiades I

Peparethan affairs at that time. This would have added to Athens' embarrassment. The second episode occurs about 20 years later, in 340, as documented by the so-called *Letter of Philip* (part of the Demosthenic corpus) in which the Macedonian king answers Athenian complaints about his treatment of the islanders.

Although Denyer has used Peparethos to argue that the *Alcibiades* I is late Plato, written shortly after 361, it is not clear that it can help his case. At first sight Socrates' reference to somebody claiming to know about justice and injustice when offering advice either to the Athenians or to the Peparethans (whether in Peparethos itself or perhaps in Athens) is rather vague, and could fit either context – in other words it might support a date either when Plato was around seventy years old or after his death, depending on the lost details of either episode. Some attention to detail is therefore required if we are to progress further. The passage may be translated as follows:

> So if somebody gets up to advise either the Athenians or the Peparethans on what's just and what's unjust, and he says that just [actions] are sometimes detrimental, you would surely ridicule him, since you too turn out to be claiming that just [actions] and advantageous ones are identical. (*Alc.* I, 116d-e)

As Denyer shows, the reference to Peparethans is not simply using the proverbially insignificant city to contrast with the most significant one, since that dubious honour went to the island of Seriphos. Nor is it obvious that the city is being mentioned for its insignificance, which might have warranted the addition of an 'even' (*eite <kai> Peparêthiois*). There must be something that caused the Peparethans to come into the author's mind at that moment, and there was presumably some nuance to be picked up. It is plausible that their passing mention is intended to allude, so far as was possible without upsetting the dramatic context, to an actual case when the Peparethans had been induced to act in defiance of the dictates of justice because they had considered it against their interests.

Now in the case of the Athenians it is very easy to think of a case when they were conscious of acting unjustly (as the word was traditionally understood) because they thought that the proposed course of action coincided with their interests. Though Thucydides appears more generally to underline the extent to which all parties in war abandon the unclear dictates of traditional justice in favour of the apparent clarity of self-interest, the Athenians as he represents them are most openly hawkish in relation to Melos, another seemingly insignificant island. The Melians' appeals to fairness in the famous 'Melian Dialogue' fall on deaf ears, since the Athenians consider it inevitable that those who can dominate will act in their own interests and dominate regardless (5.86-93, 105). For the Athenians it was against their interest to be seen to be weak by allowing

*Appendix I*

Melos, a Spartan colony, with the traditional ties of friendship, to remain neutral (5.95). The eventual Melian surrender was followed by the slaughter of all men of military age (5.116). Now Plutarch (*Alc.* 16.6) holds Alcibiades primarily responsible for this perceived act of injustice, since he apparently spoke to the motion – presumably one that condemned the male captives to death, though possibly one that initiated the expedition. Given his influence at this period, and his tendency to advocate the most aggressive policies, it would not have been surprising if this tradition that Plutarch had been following went back to the fourth century. If so, Alcibiades had much earlier come to be associated with the Athenians' naked pursuit of self-interest in its dealings with Melos in disregard of the conventional values that had once held the Greeks together. Socrates is pre-emptively but unsuccessfully warning Alcibiades not to be lured into thinking that injustice can pay, just as he is unsuccessfully warned against other popular influences in the dialogue.

Now the importance of Melos here may lie in its relative insignificance. The reference to another insignificant island whose future had been in the balance because of its allegiances in the fourth century might have brought Melos to mind. It may perhaps be that certain fourth-century events involving Peparethos were similar, insofar as a bullying neighbour was coercing an insignificant island into deserting its previous loyalties, but again, that might apply to the situation in 340 as well as that in 361. A better parallel might involve the following:

1. A situation in which morality and expediency became a topic of conversation;
2. Advice given to the Peparethans based upon a distinction between what was just and what was expedient – and since neither Philip nor the Athenians were likely to have been aware of what was said in Peparethos' local place of assembly, the advice probably needed to have come from the Athenian Assembly.

So far as we can judge nothing like this had occurred in 361. The Peparethans were being harassed by a tyrant who did not need justice on his side, and Diodorus' account at 15.95.1-2 uses language that is as morally neutral as is possible when talking of Alexander's pirates and mercenaries. Athens responded to the duty to assist the Peparethans, without giving their preference to self-interest rather than justice, and it is not clear that any advice was given. Yet in 340 Philip's [alleged] response to Athenian complaints about his conduct towards Peparethos, which he had sacked, is everywhere framed in terms of justice (Dem. *Or.* 12.12-15). 'Philip' complains that he has not fully repaid the Peparethans for their injustices against him. The situation in fact concerns an island of *even less significance*, Halonnesos, from which Philip had recently expelled pirates, leaving a garrison of his own. The Peparethans seized Philip's garrison and annexed the island, seemingly with little excuse, since 'Philip' complains of broken oaths and heavy-handed violence (12.15). But the interesting thing is that the Peparethans apparently asked *Athens* for permission to take the island, so that some kind of advice must have been given to them from Athens at that time. The Athenian response may well have been given in terms of expediency rather than justice. Certainly one Demosthenean address concerning Philip's representations to Athens concerning events at Halonnesos begins with the denial that the speaker will be prevented from telling the Athenians what was expedient for them:

> Gentlemen of Athens, there is no way that the charges that Philip brings against those who speak to you in favour of *what's just* will stop us becoming your *advisers* in favour of what's to your *advantage*. (Dem. *Or.* 7.1)

The terms in italics, which might be expected to reflect the language used generally in Athens concerning this episode, recall the language of *Alc.* 116d7-e1. Even though there is no evidence for such Athenian advice to the Peparethans in particular, the 340 episode is clearly one that did raise issues of justice and expediency in people's minds. It was also a case in which the alleged Peparethan disregard of justice, presumably in favour of expediency, ultimately proved quite as inexpedient as it was unjust, and therefore underlined the Socratic thesis that justice and expediency are inseparable. Thus, those who wish to appeal to Peparethan history as evidence for the date of this dialogue should be prepared to give up claims of Platonic authorship (at least as traditionally understood), for it is the 340 episode that provides the more convincing *terminus post quem*.

However, so far none of the passages discussed completely rule out the possibility that Plato himself was the author of the dialogue, even though they tend to point to a date rather late in Plato's life or later still. But there is one more passage that has drawn our attention, which is also intriguing. In an extended speech from 121b to 124b in which Socrates talks about Spartan and Persian customs, as well as their respective resources, he imagines the rather improbable scenario of Alcibiades challenging Artaxerxes, no doubt appealing to Alcibiades' far-reaching ambition and vanity, which have already been treated at 105b-c. In itself the concept of Greece challenging the Persian Empire is nothing new; the ideology of panhellenism had its origins in the fifth century, although it reached the zenith of its popularity in the fourth – and it had plenty of exponents, from King Agesilaus aspiring to be a second Agamemnon, to Isocrates' *Panegyricus* (cf. Flower 2000). But again a mere allusion to panhellenism does not rule out Plato.

However it is within the context of Alcibiades' challenge to Artaxerxes that Socrates refers to Alcibiades' age – in his twentieth year, as well as his limited resources in comparison with the massive wealth of Persia.[5] The age reference given in that particular context could be significant.

*Appendix I*

What other twenty-year-old took on the Great King of Persia with only limited resources, and yet won?[6] The veiled parallel to Alexander the Great is almost irresistible; both Alcibiades (as represented here) and Alexander have designs on world-wide empire, for want of a better word. Alexander's vision for conquest lay East, whereas Alcibiades' imperialist dreams seem rather to have been centred on the West, in Sicily and Carthage (cf. Thuc. 6.15), as Brian Bosworth points out to us. Moreover, both Alexander and Alcibiades are young men, both have striking physical looks, both have mythical genealogies (as befitting their status), both have the benefit of philosophical instruction – and both are deeply flawed. It might even be added, perhaps on a rather facetious note, that both are associated with qualms about the playing of a musical instrument, although a different instrument and for different reasons.[7] In Alcibiades' case his qualms are actually noted early in the dialogue (106e). The parallel with Alexander is intriguing, and would have added a new dimension to the way in which readers in the late fourth century responded to the *Alcibiades*. No more can confidently be said.

There is one final idea that may be worth recording. If the *Alcibiades* was not written by Plato, then in what social and historical context did it appear? One oddity that suggests an unusual social context is the strange use of the conjunction of father's and mother's name first when Socrates addresses Alcibiades at 105d2 and then when he refers to himself at 131e3-4: very far from Plato's usual practice. And it is Alcibiades' mother's name alone that is used at 123c6, in a context that imagines the difficulty that royal women like Amestris or Lampito would have in imagining Alcibiades as a serious opponent for their own sons. Even the device of having Socrates tell how *females* would be thinking is unusual, best paralleled in the Diotima story from the *Symposium* at 201d-212a, in which the Mantinean visionary does in fact refer to Poros as the son of Metis – though the mother's name is less of a surprise when dealing with the world of divinities. One explanation of the use of the female voice and the recognition of female progenitors might be the intimacy of the conversation, but another might be the intimacy of social context for the reading of the work: perhaps intimate in a different sort of way, perhaps even voyeuristic.

In this context, therefore, we should like to place on record the idea that the work may fit into the genre (if that is the word) of fourth-century sympotic literature. Simon Hornblower has recently argued for a similar origin of the political pamphlet on the fifth-century Athenian empire, whose author, Pseudo-Xenophon, is more popularly termed the Old Oligarch (cf. Hornblower 2000b). One intriguing fact is that the *Symposia* of both Plato (176e) and Xenophon (3.1-2) both temporarily banish the entertainment to which the aulos contributes.[8] According to Hornblower's theory, rather than being a contemporary rant against the Athenian democracy of the late fifth century, the Old Oligarch's pamphlet becomes

*Fourth-Century Politics and the Date of the* Alcibiades I

a hypothetical and imaginary work, deeply influenced by Thucydides (so that it responds intertexually to Thucydides, not the other way around), and its primary purpose is to entertain – albeit in an extremely elaborate, if not laboured way. So, by analogy, one may ask whether the *Alcibiades* might be a parody, written by someone who was deeply steeped in Plato, but who could not resist leaving some clues about the true nature of his piece? One ought surely to remain sceptical – the *Alcibiades* seems to take itself rather too seriously, perhaps, and Platonists in a later age also took it rather seriously. But then again, the Old Oligarch is not obviously funny either.

This contribution has offered some considerations that need to be taken into account when tackling matters of date and authorship. None of the issues discussed lead to clear-cut conclusions. Indeed if we are right in suggesting that the *Alcibiades* may be an example of sympotic literature there might be one final twist: Plato's *Symposium* hints that its own antecedents may have been *oral* antecedents, and that the contributions to intellectual discourse at a symposium were likely to be spontaneous oral contributions. As long as it remains unrecorded, oral literature may mutate, and develop. It is not out of the question that a dialogue should have such an origin, relying on some admirer of its creator to fix it in its final form. In any such case alien vocabulary and oddities that allude to later events may come to be incorporated. The possibilities remain as fluid as oral literature itself.

## Notes

1. A select bibliography of the 'huge literature' on this issue is offered by Gribble 1999, 260, n. 146; to that must now be added Denyer 2001, whose late dating is received favourably in this volume by Benitez and Hooper; also Smith 2004 and Tarrant 2006/7.

2. Denyer 2001, 189 takes it to imply a dramatic date of 433 BC; this would conveniently be before the Potidaean incident, so that we should not be asked to imagine that Socrates had saved Alcibiades without actually speaking to him. Nails 2002 argues that Alcibiades' claim that he was with Socrates on campaign at Potidaea (*Symp.* 219e) implies that he was twenty by the time Callias left Attica in the fall of 432. If Alcibiades were unable to circumvent the usual ban on ephebes serving beyond Attica, then, if he is not yet twenty here, the dialogue is set before the expedition.

3. Cf. Hodkinson 2000, 432-41, where he discusses the domination of Spartan society by a wealthy and extravagant elite in the early part of the fourth century.

4. In Thucydides the island is mentioned only in relation to the perception of seismic effects on the sea in that area (3.89.4).

5. Concerning Alexander's limited resources, Onesicritus said he was already 200 talents in debt at the outset of the expedition; see *FGrH* F 2 = Plut. *Alex.* 15.2; cf. *De Alex. fort.* I 3 p.327 D: 'To provision these forces [for the campaign in Asia], Aristobulus [= *FGrH* 139 F 4] says he had not more than seventy talents; Duris speaks of maintenance for only thirty days.'

6. On Alexander's age at his accession see Arrian 1.1: 'about twenty years'

## Appendix I

(*amphi ta eikosin etê*); so also Aristobulus, *FGrH* 139 F 6; cf. Plut.*Alex*.11.1; Just. 11.1.9; see discussion in Bosworth 1980, vol.1, 46; Heckel 1997, 78.

7. Plutarch, *Pericles* 1.5, gives a story, the gist of which is that Philip reproached Alexander at a symposium for playing the lyre so well, the moral being that kings should be too busy to play, and content themselves with appreciation; it is hard to believe that such attitudes would not have passed to the son too.

8. In Plato the reappearance of the *aulêtris* (212c) announces the arrival of Alcibiades, and his image of Socrates as a Marsyas involves further reference to the *aulos* (215b-c); in Xenophon the entertainment resumes at 9.2, but the *aulos* has featured almost as a theme, (2.1-2, 2.21-22, 3.1, 6.3-5, 7.5).

Appendix 2

# Report on the Working Vocabulary of the Doubtful Dialogues

Research carried out by Harold Tarrant and Terry Roberts

### 2a. The Working Vocabulary of the *Alcibiades*

*Early Operations*

At around the time when the original conference took place the preparation of special texts of Plato was underway, designed for the application of authorship tests successfully used on modern writers of English under the auspices of the University of Newcastle's Centre for Literary and Linguistic Computing.[1] There seemed no obvious reason why similar methods should not offer modest assistance with Greek authorship questions. Not just the *Alcibiades* was involved in our work, but also all other doubtful works in the Platonic Corpus. The fundamental assumption is that a given author will draw on a relatively consistent basic vocabulary while writing in the same genre, with comparatively small variations from work to work.[2] In order to draw more effectively on the experience of colleagues it was decided to produce non-inflected texts, so that the article, for instance, would appear as a single form throughout, as would any pronoun or demonstrative. Since the different philosophic topics treated by Plato mean that the vocabulary specific to certain problems is likely to prove quite unhelpful, we concentrated on what are known as 'function-words', defined here as those terms for which there will be obvious uses in virtually any Platonic dialogue. This definition privileges prepositions, particles, demonstratives, conjunctions, pronouns, and adverbs over verbs, nouns, and adjectives. Owing to the need to be able to compare dialogues whether in narrative or dramatic form, certain function-words for which there was much more opportunity in one form of dialogue than in the other were excluded. Those that did not appear in the top 200 words of our original sample were also excluded, leaving a total of 97 function-words as the maximum number of variables for our multivariate tests.

In general works were divided into 2000-word sections, which could in theory leave blocks of up to 3999 words undivided. Since all the 'doubtful' dialogues except the *Clitophon* exceeded 2000 words, to find a doubtful dialogue with peculiarities that exceeded those of any 2000-word block of an undisputed dialogue might reasonably be taken as an indication that it was by somebody other than Plato – at least if other plausible explanations

*Appendix 2*

were lacking. Undisputed works could contain considerable internal variation on all our tests, particularly where passages of monologic discourse were incorporated or where 'Socrates' imitated some inspired voice, told a myth, or adopted an overtly rhetorical tone. Trickier arguments, involving the kind of linguistic contortion that troubles translators, were also liable to produce rather more extreme results. Even so, some of the *spurious* dialogues, not included in the ancient corpus at all, could produce results that computer programs would place far beyond the ordinary range for any genuine dialogue of Plato. These included *Sisyphus*, *Axiochus*, and *Halcyon* (more commonly seen as pseudo-Lucianic), but not so much the *Eryxias*. The only genuine dialogue that would produce results that were in any way comparable was the *Parmenides*, where it is obvious to any reader that Plato adopts a completely different style, better suited to his Eleatic protagonist.

When the results were plotted using scattergrams the doubtful dialogues were usually placed marginally outside or well within the normal Platonic range, though there was considerable variation across tests. For instance, the *Amatores* was sometimes quite marginal, and at others mainstream, but when we also entered the third book of Xenophon's *Memorabilia*, that too could look surprisingly compatible with much of Plato, although it was not difficult to find criteria that would for the most part separate them.

We therefore considered a more select group of 25 function-words, words that Plato appears to employ more than is the norm for doubtful or non-Platonic works. In this case it became obvious that the spurious dialogues, *Axiochus*, *Halcyon*, *Sisyphus*, and *Eryxias* could easily be separated from the main body of Plato's works. Some of the *dubia* were also among the outriders, including (at one end of the scale) *Epinomis*, *Clitophon*, and *Epistle VII*, particularly the well known epistemological digression. The *Alcibiades*, however, was not placed by scattergrams at the edge of the main group, and the only observation of special note was its proximity to every other dialogue of the fourth tetralogy, *Alcibiades II*, *Hipparchus*, and *Amatores*. It was also close to Xenophon, but nevertheless kept the company of some impeccably Platonic material.

*The 47 function-word test*
The inconclusiveness of tests so far discussed led to the application of others. One of these involved those 47 function-words that appeared to be used *less* often in typical and uncontroversial examples of Plato's own 'Socratic' type of dialogue than in *either* the first three dialogues of the doubtful fourth tetralogy, *or* the first three dialogues of tetralogy seven. The test was applied to dialogues in dramatic form only in order to avoid anomalies that might arise from different methods of presentation. All dramatic *dubia* were included, with the *Hippias Major*, *Hippias Minor*, and *Ion* (the latter two modified by removal of the many poetic quotations),

*Report on the Working Vocabulary of the Doubtful Dialogues*

*Crito, Euthyphro,* and *Laches* to represent the 'early' dialogues, and *Philebus* (including an artificially separated ninth block of marginally fewer than 2000 words) to represent the later dialogues using Socrates as main speaker. When cluster-analysis was applied to the results for the 47 function-words alone, and then represented by a dendrogram (employing Ward's method, widely used for literary and linguistic computing) the resultant 'family-tree' placed most of the uncontroversial Platonic material (and much else) in one major group; of this group all blocks of *Philebus* were grouped with all blocks of the doubtful *Epinomis* and *Clitophon* in what looked like a 'late' family, punctuated only by a stray block of *Laches*; the other family included much that is regarded as early Plato and two blocks of the *dubia*, the second of *Alcibiades* II, and the only block of *Theages*. The other major group included (in one well separated family) all five blocks of the *Alcibiades* and (in the other family) block 1 of *Alcibiades II, Hipparchus, Minos*, blocks 2 to 4 of *Hippias Major*, and block 2 of *Euthyphro*. The presence of this last was a clear warning not to take membership of this group as evidence of spuriousness, particularly as evidence of the spuriousness of the *Hippias Major*.

The remarkable thing about these results was surely the ease with which they separated off all five blocks of the *Alcibiades*, placing them as a family at a substantial distance from the next closest. What this *proved* was simply that there was something distinctive about the regular working vocabulary of the dialogue that had hitherto been obscured. Being distinctive does not entail spuriousness, though in the next closest group *Euthyphro*2 was the one block from a dialogue about which doubts are virtually never raised. But besides confirming the internal coherence of the *Alcibiades*, the test discouraged us from thinking of it as *either* late Plato (since it seemed to have almost nothing in common with *Philebus*) *or* typical early Plato.

Keeping these provisional conclusions in mind, we examined corresponding results for the full range of 97 function-words across the same group of dialogues. This would help counter any misgivings about the manner of selection of the 47 words, bearing in mind that the *Alcibiades*' own peculiarities had already had an input into the choice of approximately half of the 47 variables. Now the *Philebus-Epinomis* family had lost *Clitophon* and *Laches* block 1, and had acquired only the second (final) block of the slightly incoherent *Alcibiades* II. It was loosely linked with another family that contained *Minos, Hipparchus, Clitophon, Hippias Major* blocks 2 and 3, and *Alcibiades* block 3 only. All other material was grouped at some distance into what one might think of as a more 'Socratic' group. One family within this group consisted of *Alcibiades* blocks 2, 4, and 5. These results still suggested a reasonable coherence of working vocabulary within the *Alcibiades*, while suggesting that blocks 1 and 3 were the least typical; still saw it as substantially different from that of Plato's later work; but continued to show it to be closer to other suspect dialogues than

## Appendix 2

| Group | Dialogue and block no. | Fac1 | Fac2 | Fac3 |
|---|---|---|---|---|
| T7 | Hippias Minor (2) | -0.46 | -0.48 | -1.58 |
| T4 Dubia | Alcibiades (4) | -0.12 | 0.22 | -1.48 |
| T4 Dubia | Hipparchus (1) | 0.02 | 0.71 | -1.25 |
| T7 | Hippias Major (3) | -0.22 | 0.64 | -1.22 |
| T9 Dubia | Minos (1) | -0.36 | -0.24 | -1.19 |
| T7 | Hippias Minor (1) | -0.77 | -0.34 | -0.99 |
| T7 | Ion (1) | -1.57 | -0.87 | -0.94 |
| T4 Dubia | Alcibiades (3) | -0.89 | 0.06 | -0.92 |
| T4 Dubia | Alcibiades II (2) | 0.28 | -0.50 | -0.88 |
| T4 Dubia | Alcibiades (5) | 0.44 | 1.65 | -0.78 |
| T4 Dubia | Alcibiades (2) | -0.59 | 0.70 | -0.76 |
| T4 Dubia | Alcibiades II (1) | 0.63 | 1.00 | -0.65 |
| T7 | Hippias Major (1) | -0.74 | -0.34 | -0.59 |
| T4 Dubia | Alcibiades (1) | -0.25 | 0.93 | -0.51 |
| T5 Dubia | Theages (1) | -0.82 | -0.04 | -0.10 |
| T7 | Hippias Major (4) | -0.49 | 0.69 | 0.04 |
| T7 | Hippias Major (2) | -0.63 | 1.29 | 0.17 |
| T1 Usual | Euthyphro (2) | -0.67 | 1.38 | 0.33 |
| T5 Usual | Laches (3) | -0.22 | 0.57 | 0.51 |
| T1 Usual | Crito (2) | -1.31 | -0.54 | 0.55 |
| T1 Usual | Crito (1) | -1.26 | -0.55 | 0.77 |
| T5 Usual | Laches (1) | -1.54 | -0.60 | 1.41 |
| T5 Usual | Laches (2) | -1.54 | 0.77 | 2.21 |
| T1 Usual | Euthyphro (1) | -0.76 | 1.07 | 2.22 |

Table 1. Factor analysis sorted according to factor 3.

to dialogues virtually always accepted as early Plato, since block 2 of *Laches* was the only block to which it showed any affinity.

We also applied factor analysis to the data. This has the effect of reducing the variance to a number of factors, the most significant variance becoming factor 1, the next significant factor 2, and so on. As expected the 47-word test placed all five blocks of the *Alcibiades* further to one end of the scale than any block of any other work in the test, showing a remarkable coherence. Though *Philebus* block 5, as well as *Hipparchus* and some other doubtful dialogues, was not far behind, it differed a great deal on factor 2. Factor analysis based on the 97-word test proved less revealing on the first two factors. However, factor analysis allows for a multitude of factors, even though it is usually only the first two that are charted. In this case there was interesting discrimination on factor 3. Tetralogy IV dialogues do not stand out from the Tetralogy VII dialogues, nor from *Minos*,

*Report on the Working Vocabulary of the Doubtful Dialogues*

but all these are given a lower score than any of the 'core' dramatic dialogues, here described as 'usual' because they generally display characteristics much closer to the norm for undisputed 'Socratic' dialogues of Plato, including those in narrative form. The *Theages* and the *Hippias Major* (excluding block 3) stand out least from the 'usual' group. Table 1 gives the figures concerned, sorted according to factor 3. The table illustrates the proximity of the *dubia*, in one significant respect, to the first three dialogues of Tetralogy VII (particularly *Hippias Minor* and *Ion*), and the substantial difference of both of them from the more highly regarded dialogues of a similarly 'Socratic' type.

*Separating Tetralogy VII dialogues*
We developed the working hypothesis that these Tetralogy VII dialogues had perhaps originated as sketches of a generic 'Socratic dialogue' type, with few distinctive Platonic features; and that they were only lightly revised – if at all – before taking their place in the corpus. Some tests suggested this because of a superficial similarity of the dialogues concerned with Xenophon. We took the average of 32 blocks of nine Platonic dialogues (*Apol., Chrm., Cr., Eud., Euphr., La., Ly., Meno, Rep.* I) and compared them with the averages of (a) *Alc., Alc.* II, *Hipprch.* (8 blocks); (b) *Hp. Ma., Hp. Mi., Ion* (7 blocks); and (c) Xenophon's *Memorabilia* (15 blocks). The typically Platonic group appeared to use some prepositions more (*meta, para, heneka*), and others less when compared with the other groups. We therefore looked at the favoured and non-favoured prepositions as a percentage of common vocabulary; all common prepositions as a percentage of total vocabulary; and favoured and non-favoured prepositions as percentages of total prepositions. The typically Platonic group also seemed rather richer in negatives, particularly those of *mê*-type, so we compared negatives as a percentage of total vocabulary, and *mê*-type as a percentage of total negatives. Finally, twenty or more function-words (other than prepositions or negatives) were selected that seemed to be somewhat commoner in (a) the main 'early Plato' group, (b) the Tetralogy IV group, or (c) the Tetralogy VII group. Averaging the blocks that made up each group we arrived at the following figures given in Table 2. The highest figures are in bold, and the lowest in italic.

On preposition use there is a general similarity between the Tetralogy IV and Tetralogy VII rates. On total negatives Tetralogy IV was even higher than Plato, with Tetralogy VII close to Xenophon, while both Tetralogies IV and VII fell well short of typical Plato on *mê*-type negatives as a percentage of the total. In function-word tests Xenophon seemed well short of the highest figures in all three groups, with a lower rate of function-words overall, and there seemed to be greater discrimination between the Tetralogy IV and Tetralogy VII dialogues here. While the tests on prepositions had suggested some similarities between Tetralogies IV and VII and Xenophon, the overall figures merely seem to indicate that

*Appendix 2*

| Test | E.Plato av. | T4.1-3 av. | T7.1-3 av. | X.*Mem.* av. |
|---|---|---|---|---|
| favoured prepositions | **0.40** | *0.18* | *0.15* | 0.32 |
| non-favoured prepositions | *1.01* | **1.60** | 1.34 | **1.66** |
| total prepositions | *3.12* | 3.51 | 3.59 | **3.64** |
| % favoured prepositions | **12.83** | 5.03 | *4.21* | 9.16 |
| % non-favoured prepositions | *32.35* | **45.45** | 37.30 | **44.99** |
| negatives | 4.05 | **4.37** | *3.23* | 3.45 |
| % *mê*-type negatives | 27.88 | *20.17* | 21.76 | **32.48** |
| Platonic Function words | **14.70** | 12.88 | *11.61* | 12.32 |
| T4 Function words | 10.11 | **14.73** | 10.46 | *6.71* |
| T7 Function words | 16.02 | *14.54* | **18.68** | *14.39* |

Table 2. Simple tests on prepositions, negatives and function-words.

*none of these groups show Plato's characteristic preferences* as determined by our main 'early' group. The reason for this in Xenophon's case is obvious, and in the Tetralogy IV group it is obvious *if* the dialogues concerned are spurious. One possible explanation of the oddities of the Tetralogy VII dialogues would be that Plato's preferences had at the time of writing not yet emerged – assuming their relative earliness. If this were the case, then one way of looking at factor 3 results on the 97-function-word test discussed above would be as an indication of the 'platonicity' of the vocabulary-mix. The further into negative territory a block's result is found, the less typically Platonic it is.

Our hypothesis concerning the Tetralogy VII dialogues must be of concern to anybody expecting to solve questions of authenticity by linguistic means. If there is a group of dialogues here, a group which have indeed been written by Plato but which do not, as yet, show the distinctive features of Plato's language, then the task becomes doubly difficult. The main hope of distinguishing between the uncharacteristic dialogues of Tetralogy VII and any inauthentic dialogues written by imitators of Plato's more 'Socratic' dialogues would be in the area of T4 and T7 function-words. Fortunately, the rate of T7 function-words was indeed found to diminish in time, so that they are less common in later Plato, especially after the *Republic*. Furthermore in regular Platonic dialogues the T4 function-words, at least as a percentage of the total function-words included in the tests, were found to increase over time. Table 3 documents this, using slightly modified function-word groups throughout (with marginally more rigorous selection criteria).

The figures for the change in rate between early and late Plato are particularly striking when one (a) confines oneself to Platonic works of a largely dialectical nature, ignoring the myth-like diction of *Timaeus-Critias* and the more expository *Laws* (whose vocabulary may in any case have been influenced by the hand of Philip of Opus).[5] The leap may even

*Report on the Working Vocabulary of the Doubtful Dialogues*

|         | Av.T7 | Av.X.Mem. | Av.Pl.E. | Av.Rep.(3). | Av.Pl.L(4) | Av. T4 |
|---------|-------|-----------|----------|-------------|------------|--------|
| Tot. FWs | 37.61 | 33.43 | 37.72 | 36.16 | 35.01 | 38.12 |
| Pl. FWs | 30.41 | 36.86 | 37.88 | 38.11 | 37.03 | 33.10 |
| T4 FWs | 21.30 | 20.08 | 20.54 | 20.65 | 23.07 | 29.67 |
| T7 FWs | 48.29 | 43.06 | 41.58 | 41.23 | 39.90 | 37.23 |

Table 3. Rates of various function-word groups as percentage of total.

be seen *within* a single dialogue, the *Theaetetus*, which had been split into sections, the crucial break between sections 4 and 5 falling at 184b. Table 4 offers some figures. All the *Protagoras* and *Philebus* had been processed for inclusion in this analysis, but only the first four blocks of *Sophist* and final three of *Statesman*:

| Dialogue | Av. Prot | av.Tht.1-4 | av.Tht.5-7 | Av.Phlb. | Av.Sph.&Plt. |
|----------|----------|------------|------------|----------|--------------|
| Pl. FWs | 37.94 | 37.29 | 33.49 | 34.68 | 35.47 |
| T4 FWs | 18.20 | 19.60 | 24.88 | 26.11 | 26.61 |
| T7 FWs | 43.86 | 43.10 | 41.63 | 39.21 | 37.92 |

Table 4. Rates as above, selected dialogues.

There are clear trends observable here as we move from early to late dialogues, though *Philebus* seems less stylometrically extreme than *Sophist* or *Statesman*. The trends are such that, were the *Alcibiades* a genuine Platonic dialogue, it would seem to be an extreme example of late style *on these criteria*. The most respected early dialogues offer a low rate of T4 function-words, increasing from around 18% to up to 26% by the late period, but *Alcibiades* rises to little short of 30%. A reverse trend is observable in T7 function-words, with *Alcibiades* below even the rates for *Sophist-Statesman*. On Plato's preferred function-words *Alcibiades* shows a low but far from unparalleled rate. That there are later features in the language of this dialogue has been generally recognised (cf. Denyer 2001, 22), but the results tabled above are probably more extreme than anything that would have been suspected. In a word, in terms of the combination of high T4 and low T7 function-words, we are unable to parallel *Alcibiades* blocks 2, 4 and 5 anywhere else in the corpus, while blocks 1 and 3 are not far behind, accurately reflecting the combined results of the 47-word and 97-word cluster analyses.

Unless there are special reasons for the *Alcibiades* to contain very high levels of T4 function-words, and very low levels of the T7 group, then it would have to be concluded that the dialogue is not early Plato.

*The characteristics of the central section*
It is natural to think of the structure of the *Alcibiades* as pedimental (A1, B, A2).[6] One might see Socrates' monologue (121a-124b) as the central B section, though Olympiodorus postulates a central *protreptic* section, run-

*Appendix 2*

ning from 119a to 124b. Stylometry suggests that a rather different voice is employed hereabouts, not confined to the monologue. This may perhaps explain why block 3 usually seems less extreme than blocks 2, 4, and 5, since the majority of this passage occurs in that block. Cluster analysis easily separated the protreptic passage as envisaged by Olympiodorus from the four remaining blocks of the work.

A dendrogram, using Ward's method and all the usual 97 function-words (except the article and four that had been lost from the commonest 300), grouped all the rest of the *Alcibiades* into a distinct family, while placing the 'protreptic' section separately, together with all blocks of *Memorabilia* II, the spurious *Axiochus*, the first block of the *Charmides* together with the last of the *Euthydemus*, then with the Diotima episode of the *Symposium* and both blocks of the *Menexenus*, and subsequently with Protagoras' myth in the dialogue named after him and both blocks of central palinode of the *Phaedrus*. These blocks were mostly characterised by a voice other than the normal voice of Plato's Socrates, some involving either him or another speaker as myth-teller, and others involving his adoption of a female voice — as occurs in the 'protreptic' passage.[7] The Myth of the Choice of Heracles, split between the first two blocks of *Memorabilia* II, involves both myth and female voices, while the blocks from *Charmides* and *Euthydemus* are a jumble, involving Socrates adopting the voice of the Thracian healer in the former, and a big contribution from the sophists and Crito in the latter. Much of it might be seen as protreptic in some sense, but for our purposes what mattered is (i) that the whole of this broader cluster offered us something other than Socrates' usual dialectical voice; and (ii) that within this cluster the 'protreptic' passage proved as close to Xenophon or the spurious *Axiochus* as to anything from genuine Plato.

What the separation of this central section had achieved was to further highlight the difference of the rest of the *Alcibiades* from comparable authentic texts, and to demonstrate that, though it is different, the central section is no more plausibly Platonic either.

This gave rise to one further important test. Factor analysis of a group of dialogues, including *Gorgias, Meno, Cratylus, Phaedo, Republic, Theaetetus, Phaedrus, Sophist,* and *Statesman*, had produced what appeared to be an approximate chronological order according to Factor 2 and a contrast between myth-like diction and intensive dialectical passages according to Factor 1. Into this group, but with some other slight variations, the *Alcibiades* was added. It was now Factor 1 that appeared to offer some chronological discrimination, and when averages of a dialogue's many blocks were calculated it would have given an order *Meno* (–1.13), *Gorgias* (1.07), *Republic* I –0.72), *Phaedo* (–0.54), *Alcibiades* (excluding protreptic, –0.49), *Cratylus* (0.46), *Republic* II-X (excluding Myth of Er, 0.007), *Theaetetus* (0.011), *Phaedrus* (0.20), *Statesman* (1.88), and *Sophist* (2.21). Obviously few will see the *States-*

*man* as preceding *Sophist*, but there is some plausibility in the rest of the order, given that the *Cratylus* is probably an early dialogue with modest later additions. Chart 1 reproduces this analysis, and includes the separate blocks of the *Alcibiades* but average values only for the other dialogues. If there were any substance in this, then the *Alcibiades*, if it were genuine, would seem to belong early in Plato's 'middle period'. The inclusion of the protreptic passage in the average would place it just before *Phaedo*.

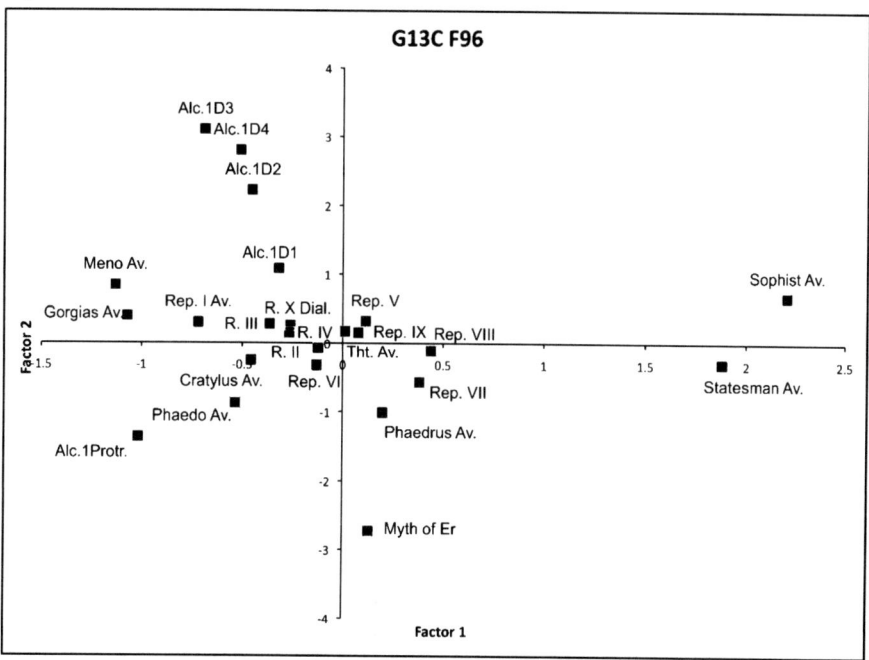

Chart 1. Analysis of 96 function-words, *Alcibiades* and selected dialogues.

Much more interesting is how the *Alcibiades* fared on Factor 2, which was interpreted as separating myth-like diction from whatever one should conceive as its opposite. In this case the 'protreptic' passage was the ninth most myth-like of the 117 blocks, behind the Myth of Er (analysed separately) and those blocks of *Phaedo*, *Phaedrus*, and *Statesman* that were influenced by mythic diction, and immediately before the block of the *Gorgias* that included the myth. This position is not easily explained purely in terms of the amount of monologue included, since not all monologue in Plato is particularly myth-like on our criteria. Rather one should postulate a plurality of non-standard registers, generally involving an assumption of seniority or privilege on the part of the main speaker. Here in the 'protreptic' passage Socrates speaks almost as if he were Alcibiades' mother. Three out of the four other blocks of the *Alcibiades* were the three *least* myth-like blocks of all, while the other (predictably the less anomalous first block) was the thirteenth least myth-like.

When running a factor analysis in SPSS one is able to deduce, from the component matrix, which individual words had tended to pull a block into an extreme position on a given factor. The words with the greatest tendency to draw the dialectical blocks of the *Alcibiades* into an extreme position were, in descending order, *pôs* (interrogative), *mên*, *kata*, *heteros*, *au*, *toinun*, *heis*, *nun* (temporal), *dê*, *pou* (indefinite), *ge*, *men*, *mêdeis*, *pote* (indefinite) *allêlous*, and *oun*. Hence it may be deduced that the *Alcibiades* is particularly rich in many of these terms, some (but by no means all) of which had been included in our list of T4 function words.

This test pointed towards three conclusions: (i) there is some reason for thinking that, *if Plato wrote this dialogue in his own natural language*, then it most probably belonged to the period of the *Phaedo*; (ii) its language was quite extreme in all its dialectical parts in a way that was obvious to computer analysis; and (iii) those dialectical parts differed radically in their basic vocabulary from the central 'protreptic' section.

*Conclusion*
There is one conclusion that is easy to draw: the *Alcibiades* is not regular 'early' Plato. That it is not regular 'late' Plato would be generally accepted as obvious, though Plato presumably remained able to revert to a largely forgotten style of his earlier years had he had sufficient motivation. In particular, if he ever turned to the revision of an earlier text he would presumably not have written any new material in a later style that was *obviously* different from the rest. Occasional features of a later style, at most, might creep in unintentionally. However, a late attempt to revert to a Socratic style of dialogue would presumably not have resulted in features that conflict with the Platonic Socrates' usual doctrines, and still less would it result in philosophical immaturity. We do not insist either that the work misunderstands the Platonic Socrates, nor that it is immature, but those who hold such views would surely find the theory of a late attempt to revert to a Socratic type of dialogue unconvincing. Nor is this what the current tests suggest. The basic working vocabulary appears to be more similar in some respects to that of dialogues such as the *Phaedo* that already introduce the Forms. None of our work had suggested that the *Alcibiades* differs from an early style in ways typical of a later one. In these circumstances the balance of probability is tipped in favour of this work being a spurious dialogue, written consciously in the tradition of Plato's 'Socratic' dialogues.

There are those who would assume that the work's very inclusion in the Platonic Corpus of Thrasyllus and others is a good argument in favour of authenticity. This is only the case if one can take a similar view of other works in the Corpus. Leaving aside the *Epistles*, which may be a special case, one should perhaps be able also to defend the authenticity of *Alci-*

*Report on the Working Vocabulary of the Doubtful Dialogues*

biades II, *Hipparchus*, *Amatores*, and *Epinomis*, about which some doubts were expressed even in antiquity. What the stylometry does show, however, is that the very position of this work in the Corpus counts against authenticity by revealing affinities with dialogues less often regarded as authentic, most notably *Alcibiades* II and *Hipparchus*. Whoever first grouped it with these two was either aware of or sensitive to the connections, just as they were aware of connections between the *Hippias*-dialogues and *Ion*. In the case of the *Alcibiades* one must doubt that this can mean that it is by the same author as its companions, but it may very well mean that it is from the same Academic environment.

Contributors to this volume have been encouraged to defend any date and any stance on the authorship that their research has made plausible. Only when the best traditional scholarship and stylometry are seen to be in agreement can one feel confident that one's opinion on these matters is established.

### Appendix 2b. Stylometry and the *Theages*

The *Theages* behaves in a totally different fashion from the *Alcibiades*. Initially it is much harder to find any means of separating it from the main body of undisputed early-to-middle Plato, but when it is divided at roughly the half way point it seems anything but unified.

Of our cluster analyses one places it close to the *Hippias*-dialogues, *Cratylus*, *Gorgias* part 1, and *Euthyphro*, as well as to *Alcibiades*, *Hipparchus*, and *Minos*. Another places it in the close company of irreproachable dialogues such as *Apology*, *Crito*, *Gorgias* part 2, *Laches*, and *Theaetetus*. Other dendrograms tend to place it with those dialogues of Socratic type that are least suspect. Typically dendrograms mapping otherwise genuine dialogues would place it in the close company of blocks from *Apology*, *Crito*, and *Meno*. The *Theages*, it seems, keeps respectable company, the only slight surprise being that neither *Apology*1 nor *Laches*1 is very dialogic.

Further investigation led us to divide the work approximately in half, and results were then stranger still. The first half bore the resemblance that we might have expected to most dialogues of Tetralogy IV before it, including the *Alcibiades*, showing the relatively high proportion of T4 function-words, and a low rate of T7 function-words, whereas the second half had an exceptionally high rate of Plato's preferred function-words, a very low rate of T4 function-words, and a modest rate of the T7 ones. In Table 5 we give all 2000-word blocks of the relevant doubtful works, and averages for some other unproblematic early-to-middle dialogues (sorted by Tetralogy IV words)

It will be observed here that *Theages* (block 2, words 1601-end) has both an exceptionally high proportion of typically Platonic function-words, and an exceptionally low rate of those associated with Tetralogy IV. It also has a particularly high incidence of those prepositions that tend to be common-

*Appendix 2*

| Dialogue/block | %PFws | %T4Fws | %T7Fws |
|---|---|---|---|
| *AlcibiadesI* (4) | 32.93 | 32.53 | 34.53 |
| *AlcibiadesI* (5) | 32.06 | 31.84 | 36.10 |
| *AlcibiadesI* (2) | 33.50 | 31.23 | 35.27 |
| *AlcibiadesII* (1) | 32.62 | 29.09 | 38.29 |
| *AlcibiadesI* (1) | 32.61 | 27.69 | 39.70 |
| *AlcibiadesI* (3) | 36.77 | 27.61 | 35.62 |
| **Theages (1)** | **36.64** | **26.42** | **36.95** |
| *Hipparchus* (1) | 32.80 | 25.22 | 41.99 |
| *AlcibiadesII* (2) | 34.96 | 24.84 | 40.20 |
| *Lysis* Av. | 35.63 | 22.14 | 42.23 |
| *Euthphr.*Av. | 36.27 | 21.33 | 42.40 |
| *Crat.* Av. | 36.89 | 21.08 | 42.03 |
| *Laches* Av. | 40.18 | 21.02 | 38.81 |
| *Meno* Av. | 39.25 | 20.96 | 39.80 |
| *Rep.I* Av. | 38.36 | 20.82 | 40.82 |
| *Euthd.* Av. | 37.13 | 20.71 | 42.16 |
| *Rep.5,7,&10* Av. | 38.11 | 20.65 | 41.23 |
| *Tht.pt.A* Av | 37.29 | 19.60 | 43.10 |
| *Prot.* Av | 37.94 | 18.20 | 43.86 |
| *Charm.* Av. | 39.66 | 17.08 | 43.25 |
| **Theages (2)** | **43.00** | **16.64** | **40.35** |
| *Apology* Av. | 40.01 | 16.58 | 43.41 |
| *Crito* Av. | 37.89 | 16.53 | 45.58 |

Table 5. Proportions of 65 selected function-words in various categories.

est in Plato (*heneka, meta, para*), a relatively normal rate of prepositions overall, and a more typical rate of *mê*-type negatives as a proportion of total negatives (Table 6).

Chart 2, based on 47 function-words, shows the Platonic works of doubtful authenticity in bold, and the acknowledged spuria in italic. It documents the proximity of the second half of *Theages* (= ThgB) to blocks of the *Apology* and also of *Xenophon* to the left of centre, while the first half (= TheagA) appears fairly far right, close to all 2000-word blocks of the *Alcibiades* as well as *Minos* and *Hipparchus*. The protreptic passage of the *Alcibiades* (= Alc.1Protr) and the long monologue included wholly within

*Report on the Working Vocabulary of the Doubtful Dialogues*

| Test type | Theages (1) | Theages (2) | Av. early Plato |
|---|---|---|---|
| Prepositions commonest in Plato, % of vocab. | 0.25 | 1.18* | 0.45 |
| Total common prepositions as % of vocab. | 2.69 | 3.58 | 3.36 |
| Mê-type negs. as proportion of negatives | 14.89 | 26.00 | 27.44 |

*The high figure is not a problem; of 1600-word blocks tested *Meno* (5) and *Protagoras* (2) both scored 1.19 on this test.

Table 6. Tests relating to prepositions and negatives.

it (= Alc.1Extr) appear in the upper left area, uncomfortably close to the *Epinomis*, *Epistle VII*, and *Clitophon*.

If one were to be guided by these results, it would perhaps be logical to think that some very Platonic material is to be found in the second half of the work, but that the first half is a later author's attempt to give that material a new setting. However, at less than 4000 words the *Theages* gives only a small sample, and one also has to bear in mind that the work is quite consciously made to resemble Plato, so that we find at 128a3-7, for instance, a very close reworking of *Apology* 19e5-20a2. Such imitation introduces additional problems for stylometry.

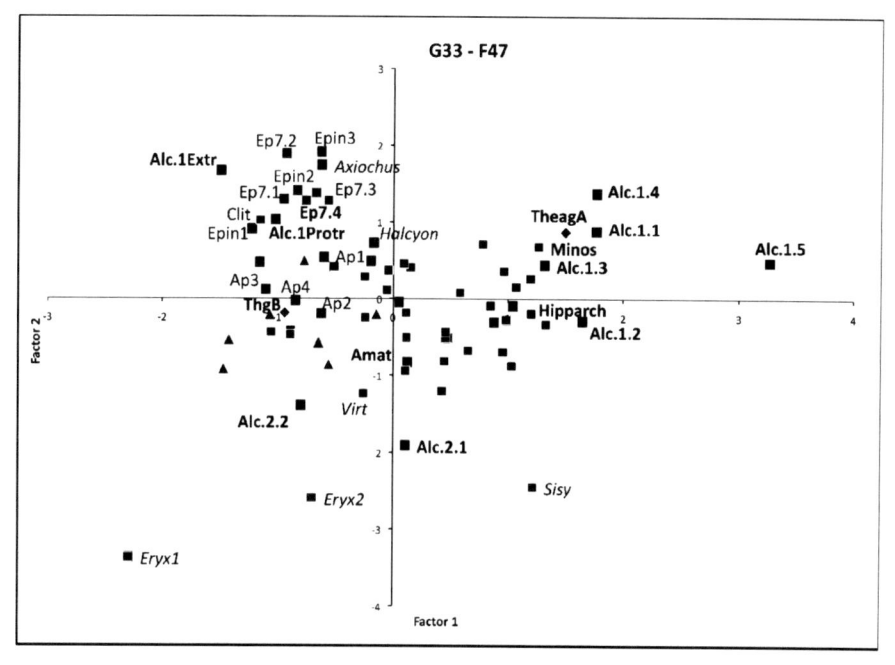

Chart 2. Chart based on 47 function-words (*dubia* in bold). Unmarked squares represent blocks of regular Plato; unmarked triangles represent blocks of Xenophon.

*Appendix 2*

**Notes**

1. My thanks to Professor Hugh Craig, the current Director, Em. Prof. John Burrows, the former Director, and Ms. Alexis Antonia for their support and assistance. Thanks are also due to the University of Newcastle for an internal grant, and to the Australian Research Council, whose funding of a wider project on the history of the Academy enabled the work to be extended.

2. Burrows 1987 had discovered in relation to Jane Austen that an author's most basic vocabulary varies within stable confines and thus acts almost like an authorial fingerprint.

3. The average of books V (5 blocks), VII (4 blocks), and X (3 blocks). The final block that is mostly myth has been excluded since monologic discourse, and myth in particular owing to its non-engagement with the auditor, has an effect on, function-word rates.

4. The blocks used were from *Laws* (26 blocks), *Sophist* (4 blocks), *Statesman* (4 blocks), *Philebus* (9 blocks), with the final block of *Republic*, but *Timaeus* and *Critias* are too atypical (being both monologic and in some sense mythical).

5. On Philip's revisions see Thesleff and Nails 2007. To judge from *Epinomis* Philip's rate of T4 and T7 function-words are around 18.45 and 42.24 respectively.

6. On pedimental structure see Thesleff 2009, 28 etc.

7. For further observations on the female voices here see Baynham and Tarrant, above p. 220.

# Bibliography

Allen, R.E. (1962) 'Note on *Alcibiades* I, 129b1', *American Journal of Philology* 83, 187-90.
Allen, R.E. (1967) *The Dialogues of Plato*, vol. 2: *The Symposium*. New Haven: Yale University Press.
Allen, T.W. (1893) 'A Group of Ninth-Century Greek Manuscripts', *Journal of Philology* 21, 48-55.
Annas, J. (1985) 'Self-Knowledge in Early Plato', in D.J. O'Meara (ed.), *Platonic Investigations*. Washington: Catholic University of America Press, 111-38.
Ast, F. (1816) *Platons Leben und Schriften*. Leipzig: Weidmann.
Bagg, R. (1964) 'Love, Ceremony and Daydream in Sappho's Lyrics', *Arion* 3.3, 44-82.
Bailey, D.S. (1975) *Homosexuality and the Western Christian Tradition*. Hamden: Archon Books.
Bailly, J.A. (2003) Review of M. Joyal, *The Platonic Theages: An Introduction, Commentary and Critical Edition* (Stuttgart, 2000), *Gnomon* 75, 102-7.
Bailly, J.A. (2004) *The Socratic Theages: Introduction, English Translation, Greek Text and Commentary*. Hildesheim: Georg Olms Verlag.
Balch, D.L. (2000) *Homosexuality, Science and the 'Plain Sense' of Scripture*. Grand Rapids: William B. Eerdmans.
Bartsch, S. (2006) *The Mirror of the Self: Sexuality, Self-knowledge, and the Gaze in the Early Roman Empire*. Chicago: University of Chicago Press.
Battistini, Y. (1995) *Sappho: La Dixième des Muses*. Paris.
Beavis, M.A. (2004) 'Philo's *Therapeutai*: Philosopher's Dream or Utopian Construction?', *Journal for the Study of the Pseudepigrapha* 14.1, 30-42.
Belfiore, E. (1980) 'Elenchus, Epode and Magic: Socrates as Silenus', *Phoenix* 34, 128-31.
Benardete, S. (tr.) (2001) *Plato's Symposium*. Chicago: University of Chicago Press.
Benitez, E.E. (1989) *Forms in Plato's* Philebus. Assen: Van Gorcum.
Beversluis, J. (2000) *Cross-Examining Socrates: A Defence of the Interlocutors in Plato's Early Dialogues*. New York: Cambridge University Press.
Bloch, M. (1946) *L'étrange Défaite*. Paris: Franc-Tireur.
Bloch, M. (1949) *The Strange Defeat* (tr. G. Hopkins). London: Oxford University Press.
Bloedow, E.F. (1973) *Alcibiades Reexamined*. Weisbaden: Steiner.
Blondell, R. (2006) 'Where is Socrates on the Ladder of Love?', in J.H. Lesher, D. Nails and S. Frisbee (eds), *Plato's Symposium: Issues in Interpretation and Reception*. Cambridge: Harvard University Press, 147-78.
Bloom, A. (2001) 'The Ladder of Love', in Plato's *Symposium* (tr. S. Benardete). Chicago: University of Chicago Press, 55-178.
Blundell, M.W. (1991) *Helping Friends and Harming Enemies: A Study in Sophocles and Greek Ethics*. Cambridge: Cambridge University Press.

# Bibliography

Boswell, J. (1991) 'Revolutions, Universals, and Sexual Categories', in G. Chauncey Jr., M.B. Duberman and M. Vicinus (eds), *Hidden from History: Reclaiming the Gay and Lesbian Past*. London: Greenwood, 17-36.

Boswell, J. (1996) *The Marriage of Likeness: Same-Sex Unions in Pre-Modern Europe*. London: HarperCollins.

Bosworth, A.B. (1980) *Historical Commentary on Arrian's History of Alexander* (2 vols). Oxford: Oxford University Press.

Bosworth, A.B. and Baynham, E.J. (eds) (2000) *Alexander the Great in Fact and Fiction*. Oxford: Oxford University Press.

Boyarin, D. (1994) *A Radical Jew: Paul and the Politics of Identity*, Berkeley: University of California Press.

Bradley, K.R. (1991) *Discovering the Roman Family: Studies in Roman Social History*. New York: Oxford University Press.

Brancacci, A. (2005) 'The Double Daimôn in Euclides the Socratic', in P. Destrée and N.D. Smith (eds), *Socrates' Divine Sign: Religion, Practice and Value in Socratic Philosophy*. Kelowna: Academic Printing and Publishing, 143-54.

Brandwood, L. (1990) *The Chronology of Plato's Dialogues*. Cambridge: Cambridge University Press.

Braun, W. (2004) *Philo, Feasts and Philosophy*: The Therapeutai 9 *(for Example) (A Summary)* [Online]. 28/01/2009. http://www.philipharland.com/meals/2004%20Braun%20Abstract.pdf

Brenkman, J. (1982) 'The Other and the One: Psychoanalysis, Reading, *The Symposium*', in S. Felman (ed.), *Literature and Psychoanalysis*. Baltimore: Johns Hopkins University Press, 396-456.

Brickhouse, T.C. and Smith, N.D. (1994) *Plato's Socrates*. Oxford: Oxford University Press.

Brooten, B.J. (1996) *Love between Women: Early Christian Responses to Female Homoeroticism*. Chicago: University of Chicago Press.

Bruell, C. (1999) *On the Socratic Education: An Introduction to the Shorter Platonic Dialogues*. Oxford: Oxford University Press.

Brunschwig, J. (1973) 'Sur quelques emplois d'ΟΨΙΣ', *Zetesis* (festschrift for Emil de Strycker). Antwerp and Utrecht, 24-39.

Burkert, W. (1983) *Homo Necans: The Anthropology of Ancient Greek Sacrificial Ritual and Myth*. Berkeley: University of California Press.

Burnet, J. (ed.) (1901-1907) *Platonis Opera* (5 vols), Oxford: Oxford University Press (repr. 1977).

Burnett, A.P. (1983) *Three Archaic Poets: Archilochus, Alcaeus, Sappho*. London: Duckworth.

Burrows, J.F. (1987) *Computation into Criticism: A Study of Jane Austen's Novels and an Experiment in Method*. Oxford: Clarendon Press.

Bury, R.G. (ed. and tr.) (1909) *The Symposium of Plato* (2nd edn. 1932). Cambridge: W. Heffer & Sons.

Bury, R.G. (tr.) (1967 and 1968) *Plato in Twelve Volumes*, Vols 10-11. Cambridge: Harvard University Press.

Butler, J. (1993) *Bodies that Matter: On the Discursive Limits of 'Sex'*. London: Routledge.

Calame, C. (1999) *The Poetics of Eros in Ancient Greece* (tr. Janet Lloyd). Princeton: Princeton University Press.

Calvo-Martínez, T. (2008) 'Le religiosité de Socrate chez Xénophon', in M. Narcy and A. Tordesillas (eds), *Xénophon et Socrate*. Paris: J. Vrin, 48-63.

# Bibliography

Cameron, A. (1939) 'Sappho's Prayer to Aphrodite', *Harvard Theological Review* 32.1, 1-17.

Chauncey Jr., G., Duberman, M.B., Vicinus, M. (1991) Introduction to Chauncey, Duberman, Vicinus (eds), *Hidden from History: Reclaiming the Gay and Lesbian Past*. London: Greenwood, 1-13.

Clark, P.M. (1955) 'The Greater *Alcibiades*', *Classical Quarterly*, new series 5, 231-40.

Colson, F.H. (1967) *Philo IX*. London: Harvard University Press.

Colson, F.H. (1979) 'Questions and Answers on *Genesis* 4:3-43', in R. Marcus, *Philo Supplement 1: Questions and Answers on Genesis*, London: Harvard University Press, 304-19.

Connor, W.R. (1971) *The New Politicians of Fifth-Century Athens*. Princeton: Princeton University Press.

Cooper, J.M. (ed.) (1997) *Plato: Complete Works*. Indianapolis: Hackett.

Couvreur, P. (ed.) (1901) *Hermeias, In Platonis* Phaedrum *Scholia*. Paris: É. Bouillon (repr. Hildesheim 1971).

Crompton, L. (2003) *Homosexuality and Civilisation*. Cambridge: The Belknap Press of Harvard University Press.

D'Ancona, C. (2005) 'Greek into Arabic', in P. Adamson and R. Taylor (eds), *The Cambridge Companion to Arabic Philosophy*. Cambridge: Cambridge University Press.

Daniels, N. (1979) 'Wide Reflective Equilibrium and Theory Acceptance in Ethics', *Journal of Philosophy* 76, 256-82.

Danzig, G. (2005) 'Apologetic Elements in Xenophon's *Symposium*', *Classica et Mediaevalia*,55, 17-48.

Davies, J.K. (1971) *Athenian Propertied Families: 600-300 BC*. Oxford: Clarendon Press.

Davis, P. J. (1979) 'The Four-Fold Classification in Plato's *Philebus*', *Apeiron* 13, 124-34.

Dawson, D. (1994) *Allegorical Readers and Cultural Revision in Ancient Alexandria*. Berkeley: University of California Press.

Denyer, N. (ed.) (2001) *Plato: Alcibiades*. Cambridge: Cambridge University Press.

Denyer, N. (ed.) (2008) *Plato: Protagoras*. Cambridge: Cambridge University Press.

Destrée, P. and Smith, N.D. (eds) (2005) *Socrates' Divine Sign: Religion, Practice and Value in Socratic Philosophy* (= *Apeiron: A Journal for Ancient Philosophy and Science* 38). Kelowna: Academic Printing and Publishing.

Dillon, J.M. (ed.) (1973) *Iamblichus Chalcidensis*. Leiden: Brill.

Dillon, J.M. (1994) 'A Platonist *Ars Amatoria*', *Classical Quarterly* 44, 387-92.

Dobson, W. (1836) *Schleiermacher's Introductions to the Dialogues of Plato*. London: J. & J.J. Deighton (repr. 1973).

Dockery, D.S. (1992) *Biblical Interpretation Then and Now: Contemporary Hermeneutics in the Light of the Early Church*. Grand Rapids: Baker Books.

Dorion, L.-A. (2003a) 'Akrasia et enkrateia dans les *Mémorables* de Xénophon', *Dialogue* 42, 645-72.

Dorion, L.-A. (2003b) Introduction to M. Bandini and L.-A. Dorion (eds), *Xénophon Mémorables*, vol. I. Paris: Les Belles Lettres, vii-cclii.

Douglas, M. (2002) *Purity and Danger: An Analysis of Concepts of Pollution and Taboo*. New York: Routledge.

Dover, K.J. (1989) *Greek Homosexuality*. Cambridge: Harvard University Press.

Dover, K.J. (ed.) (1992) *Perceptions of the Ancient Greeks*. Oxford: Blackwell.

## Bibliography

duBois, P. (1995) *Sappho is Burning*. Chicago: University of Chicago Press.
Duncan, R. (1977) 'Plato's *Symposium*: The Cloven Eros', *Southern Journal of Philosophy* 15, 277-92.
Dyck, J. (2002) 'Philo, Alexandria and Empire: The Politics of Allegorical Interpretation', in J.R. Bartlett (ed.), *Jews in the Hellenistic and Roman Cities*. New York: Routledge, 149-74.
Edelstein, L. (1966) *Plato's Seventh Letter*. Leiden: E.J. Brill.
Edmonds, R. (2000) 'Socrates the Beautiful: Role Reversal and Midwifery in Plato's *Symposium*', *Transactions of the American Philological Association* 130, 261-85.
Edwards, C. (1993) *The Politics of Immorality in Ancient Rome*. Cambridge: Cambridge University Press.
Ehrenberg, V. (1968) *From Solon to Socrates: Greek History and Civilization during the Sixth and Fifth Centuries BC*. London: Methuen & Co.
Elliot, N. (2008) *The Arrogance of Nations: Reading Romans in the Shadow of the Empire*. Minneapolis: Fortress.
Engberg-Pedersen, T. (1999) 'Philo's De Vita Contemplativa as a Philosopher's Dream', *Journal for the Study of Judaism* 30.1, 40-64.
Erler, M. (1987) 'Platons Schriftkritik und der Sinn der Aporien im *Parmenides* nach Platon und Proklos', in J. Pépin and H.D. Saffrey (eds), *Proclus: Lecteur et interprète des Anciens*. Paris: Editions du Centre National de la Recherche Scientifique, 153-63.
Fagles, R. (tr.) (1998) *Homer: The Iliad*. London: Penguin.
Farmer, D.H. (1987) *The Oxford Dictionary of Saints*. Oxford: Oxford University Press.
Ferrari, G.R.F. (1987) *Listening to the Cicadas: A Study of Plato's* Phaedrus. Cambridge: Cambridge University Press.
Fine, G. (2008) 'Does Socrates Claim to Know That He Knows Nothing?', *Oxford Studies in Ancient Philosophy* 35, 49-88.
Fink, C. (1989) *Marc Bloch: A Life in History*. Cambridge: Cambridge University Press.
Flower, M. (2000) 'Alexander the Great and Panhellenism', in A.B. Bosworth and E.J. Baynham (eds), *Alexander the Great in Fact and Fiction*. Oxford: Oxford University Press, 96-135.
Foley, H.P. (1998) '"The mother of the argument": *Eros* and the body in Sappho and Plato's *Phaedrus*', in M. Wyke (ed.), *Parchments of Gender: Deciphering the Bodies of Antiquity*. Oxford, Oxford University Press, 39-70.
Fortenbaugh, W.W. (1966) 'Plato *Phaedrus* 235c3', *Classical Philology* 61.2, 108-9.
Foster, G. (1965) 'Peasant Society and the Image of Limited Good', *American Anthropologist* 67, 293-315.
Foucault, M. (1986) *The History of Sexuality*, vol. 3: *The Care of the Self* (tr. R. Hurley). New York: Vintage Books.
Fowler, H.N. (ed. and tr.) (1914) *Plato: Euthyphro, Apology, Crito, Phaedo, Phaedrus* (intro. by W.R.M. Lamb). Cambridge: Harvard University Press.
Fränkel, H. (1962) *Early Greek Poetry and Philosophy: A History of Greek Epic, Lyric, and Prose to the Middle of the Fifth Century* (tr. M. Hadas and J. Willis). New York: Harcourt Brace Jovanovich.
Friedländer, P. (1945) 'Socrates Enters Rome: Georgio Lincoln Hendrickson Octogenario Feliciter', *American Journal of Philology* 66.4, 337-51.
Friedländer, P. (1964) *Plato* (tr. H. Meyerhoff.). Princeton: Princeton University Press.

## Bibliography

Frontisi-Ducroux, F. and Vernant, J.-P. (1997) *Dans l'Oeil du Miroir*. Paris: Editions Odile Jacob.

Gaca, K.L. (1999) 'Paul's Uncommon Declaration in Romans 1:18-32 and its Problematic Legacy for Pagan and Christian Relations', *Harvard Theological Review* 92.2, 165-98.

Gellrich, M. (1994) 'Socratic Magic: Enchantment, Irony, and Persuasion in Plato's Dialogues', *Classical World* 87.4, 275-307.

Giannantoni, G. (ed.) (1990) *Socratis et Socraticorum Reliquiae* (4 vols). Naples: Bibliopolis.

Gill, C. (1990) 'Platonic Love and Individuality', in A. Loizou and H. Lesser (eds), *Polis and Politics: Essays in Greek Moral and Political Philosophy*. Aldershot: Avebury, 69-88.

Gocer, A. (1999) review of M.J. Lutz, *Socrates' Education to Virtue: Learning the Love of the Noble* (Albany, 1998), *Review of Metaphysics* 52.3, 703-4.

Goldhill, S. (1998) 'The Seductions of the Gaze: Socrates and his Girlfriends', in P. Cartledge, P. Millett and S. von Reden (eds), *Kosmos: Essays in Order, Conflict and Community in Classical Athens*, Cambridge: Cambridge University Press, 105-24.

Goldhill, S. (2001) 'The Erotic Eye: Visual Stimulation and Cultural Conflict', in S. Goldhill (ed.), *Being Greek under Rome: Cultural Identity, the Second Sophistic and the Development of Empire*. Cambridge: Cambridge University Press, 154-94.

Goldin, O. (1993) 'Self, Sameness, and Soul in *Alcibiades* I and the *Timaeus*', *Freiburger Zeitschrift für Philosophie und Theologie* 40, 5-19.

Gooch, P. (1992) 'Has Plato Changed Socrates' Heart in the Phaedrus?', in L. Rossetti (ed.), *Understanding the Phaedrus: Proceedings of the II Symposium Platonicum*. Sankt Augustin: Academia Verlag, 309-12.

Goodenough, E.R. (1940) *An Introduction to Philo Judaeus*. New Haven: Yale University Press.

Gordon, J. (2003) '*Eros* and Philosophical Seduction in *Alcibiades* I', *Ancient Philosophy* 23, 11-30.

Gosling, J.C.B. (tr.) (1975) *Plato: Philebus*. Oxford: Clarendon Press.

Gould, T. (1963) *Platonic Love*. London: Routledge & Kegan Paul.

Gouldner, A.W. (1965) *Enter Plato: Classical Greece and the Origins of Social Theory*. New York: Basic Books.

Gray, V. J. (1998) 'The Framing of Socrates: The Literary Interpretation of Xenophon's Memorabilia', *Hermes Einzelschriften* 79, Stuttgart: Franz Steiner Verlag.

Greene, E. (2009) 'Sappho 58: Philosophical Reflections on Death and Aging', in E. Greene and M.B. Skinner (eds) *The New Sappho on Old Age: Textual and Philosophical Issues*. Cambridge: Harvard University Press, 147-61.

Greene, W.C. (1938) *Scholia Platonica*. Haverford: American Philological Association.

Gribble, D. (1999) *Alcibiades and Athens*. Oxford: Oxford University Press.

Griswold, C.L. (1986) *Self-Knowledge in Plato's Phaedrus*. New Haven: Yale University Press.

Grote, G. (1865) *Plato and the Other Companions of Socrates* (3 vols). London: W. Clowes and Sons.

Guthrie, W.K.C. (1971) *The Sophists*. Cambridge: Cambridge University Press.

Hackforth, R. (1945) *Plato's Examination of Pleasure*. Cambridge: Cambridge University Press.

# Bibliography

Hadas, M. (ed.) (1967) *The Complete Plays of Aristophanes*. London: Bantam Books.
Hadot, P. (1995) *Philosophy as a Way of Life: Spiritual Exercises from Socrates to Foucault* (ed. A.I. Davidson; tr. M. Chase). Oxford: Blackwell.
Hallett, J.P. (1989) 'Female Homoeroticism and the Denial of Roman Reality in Latin Literature', *Yale Journal of Criticism* 3, 209-27.
Halliwell, S. (tr.) (1987) *The Poetics of Aristotle*. London: Duckworth.
Halperin, D.M. (1985) 'Platonic Erôs and What Men Call Love', *Ancient Philosophy* 5, 161-204.
Halperin, D.M. (1986) 'Plato and Erotic Reciprocity', *Classical Antiquity* 5, 60-80.
Halperin, D.M. (1991) 'Sex Before Sexuality: Pederasty, Politics and Power in Classical Athens', in G. Chauncey Jr., M.B. Duberman, M. Vicinus (eds), *Hidden from History: Reclaiming the Gay and Lesbian Past*. London: Greenwood, 37-53.
Halperin, D.M. (1992) 'Plato and the Erotics of Narrativity', in J.C. Klagge and N.D. Smith (eds), *Oxford Studies in Ancient Philosophy Supplementary Volume: Methods of Interpreting Plato and his Dialogues*. Oxford: Clarendon Press, 93-129.
Halperin, D.M. (2005) 'Erotic Irony: Six Remarks on Platonic Eros', in S. Barsch and T. Bartscherer (eds), *Erotikon: Essays on Eros, Ancient and Modern*. Chicago: University of Chicago Press, 48-58.
Hamerton-Kelly, R. (ed.) (1987) *Violent Origins: Ritual Killing and Cultural Formation*. Stanford: Stanford University Press.
Hampshire, S. (1989) 'Morality and Conflict', in S.G. Clarke and E. Simpson (eds), *Anti-Theory in Ethics and Moral Conservativism*. Albany: State University of New York Press, 135-63.
Hardie, A. (2005) 'Sappho, the Muses, and Life after Death', *Zeitschrift für Papyrologie und Epigraphik* 154: 13-32.
Harris, W.V. (ed.) (2006) *Rethinking the Mediterranean*. Oxford: Oxford University Press.
Heckel, W. (1997) *Justin: Epitome of the Philippic History of Pompeius Trogus*. Oxford: Clarendon Press.
Hengel, M. (1991) *Judaism and Hellenism: Studies in their Encounter in Palestine during the Early Hellenistic Period*. London: SCM Press.
Hermann, C.F. (1853) *Platonis Dialogi*, vol. 6. Leipzig.
Hodkinson, S. (2000) *Property and Wealth in Classical Sparta*. London: Duckworth and the Classical Press of Wales.
Hoffmann, P. (1985) 'Le sage et son démon: La figure de Socrate dans la tradition philosophique et littéraire', *Annuaire, École pratique des hautes études, V. Section, Sciences Religieuses* 94, 417-35.
Holden, H. (ed.) (1868) *Aristophanis Comoediae* (2 vols). Cambridge: Cambridge University Press.
Hornblower, S. (2000) *Who's Who in the Classical World*. Oxford: Oxford University Press.
Hornblower, S. (2000b) 'The Old Oligarch and Thucydides: a Fourth-century Date for the Old Oligarch?', in P. Flensted-Jensen, T.H. Nielsen and L. Rubinstein (eds), *Polis and Politics: Studies in Ancient Greek History Presented to M.H. Hansen*. Copenhagen: Museum Tusculanum Press, 363-84.
Horner, T.M. (1978) *Jonathan Loved David: Homosexuality in Biblical Times*. Philadelphia: Westminster Press.
Horsley, R. (1994) 'Innovation in Search of Re-orientation: New Testament Studies

## Bibliography

Rediscovering its Subject Matter', *Journal of the American Academy of Religion* 62.4, 1127-66.

Howland, J.A. (1990) 'Socrates and Alkibaides: Eros, Piety, and Politics', *Interpretation* 18.1, 63-90.

Hutchinson, D.S. (1997a) *Alcibiades*, in J.M. Cooper (ed.), *Plato: Complete Works*. Indianapolis: Hackett, 557-95.

Hutchinson, D.S. (1997b) 'On Alcibiades Minor', in J.M. Cooper (ed.), *Plato: Complete Works*. Indianapolis: Hackett, 596-7.

Huss, B. (1999) 'The Dancing Socrates and the Laughing Xenophon, or: the Other Symposium', *American Journal of Philology* 120, 381-409.

Hyland, D. (1968) '*Erôs, Epithumia* and *Philia* in Plato', *Phronesis* 13, 32-56.

Irigaray, L. (1989) 'Sorcerer Love: A Reading of Plato's Symposium, Diotima's Speech' (tr. Eleanor H. Kuykendall), *Hypatia* 3.3, 32-44.

Irwin, D. (ed.) (1972) *Winckelmann: Writings on Art*. London: Phaidon.

Irwin, T. (1995) *Plato's Ethics*. Oxford: Oxford University Press.

Ivarrson, F. (2008) 'A Man has to Do What a Man has to Do: Protocols of Masculine Sexual Behaviour and *1 Corinthians 5-7*', in B. Holmberg and M. Winninge (eds), *Identity Formation in the New Testament*. Tübingen: Mohr Siebeck, 183-98.

Jenks, R. (2005) 'Varieties of *Philia* in Plato's *Lysis*', *Ancient Philosophy* 25, 65-80.

Johansen, T.K. (1998) *Aristotle on the Sense-Organs*. Cambridge: Cambridge University Press.

Johnson, D.M. (1999) 'God as the True Self: Plato's *Alcibiades I*', *Ancient Philosophy* 19, 1-19.

Johnson, D.M. (2003) *Socrates and Alcibiades: Four Texts*. Newburyport: Focus Publishing.

Johnson, M. (1999) 'Catullus 37 and the Theme of Magna Bella'. *Helios* 26, 85-96.

Jones, H.S. and Powell, J.E. (eds) (1955) *Thucydidis Libri*. Oxford: Oxford University Press.

Jowett, B. (1892) *The Dialogues of Plato Translated into English* (3rd edn). Oxford: Oxford University Press.

Joyal, M. (1995) 'Tradition and Innovation in the Transformation of Socrates' Divine Sign', in L. Ayres (ed.), *The Passionate Intellect. Essays on the Transformation of Classical Traditions, Presented to Professor I.G. Kidd*. New Brunswick: Transaction Publishers, 39-58.

Joyal, M. (2000) *The Platonic* Theages: *An Introduction, Commentary and Critical Edition*. Stuttgart: Franz Steiner Verlag.

Joyal, M. (ed.) (2001) *In Altum: Seventy-five Years of Classical Studies in Newfoundland*. St. John's: Memorial University of Newfoundland.

Joyal, M. (2001) 'Socrates, DAIMONIOS ANER: Some textual and interpretative problems in Plato', in M. Joyal (ed.), 343-57.

Joyal, M. (2003) Review of N. Denyer, *Plato: Alcibiades,* in *Bryn Mawr Classical Review*, 2003.01.28.

Kahn, C.H. (1996) *Plato and the Socratic Dialogue: the Philosophical Use of A Literary Form*. Cambridge: Cambridge University Press.

Kendeck, M. (2000) 'Xenophon, *Hiero* or *Tyrannicus*', in V. Gourevitch and M.S. Roth (eds), *Leo Strauss: On Tyranny*, Chicago: University of Chicago Press, 3-21.

King, F.J. (2007) *More Than a Passover: Inculturation in the Supper Narratives of the New Testament*, Frankfurt: Lang.

# Bibliography

Kittel, G. (1932) *Theologisches Wörterbuch zum Neuen Testamentum.* Stuttgart: Kohlhammer.

Klawans, J. (2001) 'Pure Violence: Sacrifice and Defilement in Ancient Israel', *Harvard Theological Review* 94.2, 135-57.

de Lacy, P. and Einarsen, B. (ed. and tr.) (1959) *Plutarch: Moralia*, vol.7. Cambridge: Harvard University Press.

Lear, J. (1999) *Open Minded: Working Out the Logic of the Soul.* Cambridge: Harvard University Press.

Ledbetter, G.M. (2003) *Poetics before Plato: Interpretation and Authority in Early Greek Theories of Poetry.* Princeton: Princeton University Press.

Ledger, G. R. (1989) *Re-counting Plato.* Oxford: Clarendon Press.

Levine, A-J. (2007) 'Theory, Apologetic, History: Reviewing Jesus' Jewish Context', *Australian Biblical Review* 55, 57-78.

Liddell, H.G., Scott, R. and Jones, S. (1996) *Greek-English Lexicon* (10th edn), Oxford: Oxford University Press.

Littman, R.J. (1970) 'The loves of Alcibiades', *Transactions and Proceedings of the American Philological Association* 101, 263-76.

Lowenthal, D. (1985) *The Past is a Foreign Country.* Cambridge: Cambridge University Press.

Ludwig, P. (2002) *Eros and Polis: Desire and Community in Greek Political Theory.* Cambridge: Cambridge University Press.

Lukinovich, A. (1990) 'The Play of Reflections between Literary Form and the Sympotic Theme in the *Deipnosophistae* of Athenaeus', in O. Murray (ed.), *Sympotica: A Symposium on the Symposium.* Oxford: Oxford University Press, 263-71.

Mack, B. (1987) 'Introduction: Religion and Ritual', in R. Hamerton-Kelly (ed.), *Violent Origins: Ritual Killing and Cultural Formation*, Stanford: Stanford University Press, 1-74.

Mackenzie, M.M. (1988) 'The Virtues of Socratic Ignorance', *Classical Quarterly*, new series 38, 331-50.

Makowski, J.F. (1996) 'Bisexual Orpheus: Pederasty and Parody in Ovid', *Classical Journal* 92.1, 25-38.

Marchant, E.C. (ed.) (1921) *Xenophontis opera omnia: tomus II: Commentarii, Oeconomicus, Convivium, Apologia Socratis* (2nd edn). Oxford: Clarendon Press.

McCarty, W. (1989) 'The Shape of the Mirror: Metaphorical Catoptrics in Classical Literature', *Arethusa* 22, 161-95.

McCabe, M. (2000) *Plato and His Predecessors.* Cambridge: Cambridge University Press.

McConnell, T C. (1984) 'Objectivity and Moral Expertise', *Canadian Journal of Philosophy* 14, 193-216.

McDowell, J. (1985) 'Values and Secondary Qualities', in T. Honderich (ed.), *Morality and Objectivity.* London: Routledge, 110-29.

McNeill, D.N. (2001) 'Human Discourse, Eros, and Madness in Plato's *Republic*', *Review of Metaphysics* 55.2, 235-68.

Merlan, P. (1975) *From Platonism to Neoplatonism.* The Hague: Martinus Nijhoff.

Mettauer, T. (1880) *De Platonis Scoliorum Fontibus.* Turici.

Millar, J.E. (1997) 'Response: Pederasty and Romans 1:27: A Response to Mark Smith', *Journal of the American Academy of Religion* 65.4, 861-6.

Minnich, N.F. (1996) 'An Enigma: Montaigne, Admirer of Alcibiades', *South Atlantic Review* 61.2, 9-26.

# Bibliography

Moore, S.D. and Anderson, J.C. (1998) 'Taking It Like a Man: Masculinity in 4 Maccabees', *Journal of Biblical Literature* 117.2, 249-73.
Morrison, D. (1995) 'Xenophon's Socrates as Teacher', in P. Vander Waerdt (ed.), *The Socratic Movement*, Ithaca: Cornell University Press, 181-208.
Morrison, D. (2008) 'Remarques sur la psychologie morale de Xénophon', in Narcy and Tordesillas (eds), *Xénophon et Socrate*, Paris: J. Vrin, 11-28.
Motte, A. (1989) 'La catégorie platonicienne du démonique', in J. Ries (ed.), *Anges et démons: Actes du colloque de Liège et de Louvain-la-neuve 25-26 novembre 1987*, Louvain-la-neuve, 205-21.
Mühl, M. (1966) 'Die traditionsgeschichtlichen Grundlagen in Platons Lehre von den Dämonen (*Phaidon* 107d, *Symposion* 202e)', *Archiv für Begriffsgeschichte* 10, 241-70.
Nails, D. (1994) 'Plato's "Middle" Cluster', *Phoenix* 48, 62-7.
Nails, D. (2002) *The People of Plato: A Prosopography of Plato and Other Socratics*. Indianapolis: Hackett Publishing Company.
Nehamas, A. (1992) 'What Did Socrates Teach and to Whom Did He Teach It?', *Review of Metaphysics* 46.2, 279-306.
Nehamas, A. (1998) *The Art of Living: Socratic Reflections from Plato to Foucault*. Berkeley: University of California Press.
Neyrey, J.H. (1998) *Honor and Shame in the Gospel of Matthew*. Louisville: John Knox Press.
Nichols, M. (2004) 'Socrates' Contest with the Poets in Plato's Symposium', *Political Theory* 32, 186-206.
Nightingale, A.W. (1995) *Genres in Dialogue: Plato and the Construct of Philosophy*. Cambridge: Cambridge University Press.
Nightingale, A.W. (2004) *Spectacles of Truth in Classical Greek Philosophy*. Cambridge: Cambridge University Press.
Nussbaum, M. (1986) *The Fragility of Goodness: Luck and Ethics in Greek Tragedy and Philosophy* (rev. edn, 2001). Cambridge: Cambridge University Press.
Nussbaum, M. (2001) *Upheavals of Thought: The Intelligence of Emotions*. Cambridge: Cambridge University Press.
Nye, A. (1990) 'The Subject of Love: Diotima and her Critics', *Journal of Value Inquiry* 24, 135-53.
O'Connor, D. K. (1994) 'The Erotic Self-sufficiency of Socrates: a Reading of Xenophon's *Memorabilia*', in P. Vander Waerdt (ed.), *The Socratic Movement*. Ithaca: Cornell University Press, 151-80.
Oden, T.C. (2008) *How Africa Shaped the Modern Christian Mind: Rediscovering the African Seedbed of Western Christianity*. Downers Grove: Inter Varsity Press.
O'Neill, W. (1965) *Proclus: Alcibiades* I. The Hague: Martinus Nijhoff.
Olyan, S.M. (1994) '"And with a Male You Shall Not Lie the Lying down of a Woman": On the Meaning and Significance of Leviticus 18:22 and 20:13', *Journal of the History of Sexuality* 5.2, 179-206.
Opsomer, J. (1997) 'Plutarch's defence of the *Theages*: in defence of Socratic philosophy?', *Philologus* 141, 114-36.
Osborn, E. (2001) *Irenaeus of Lyons*. Cambridge: Cambridge University Press.
Osborne, C. (1996) *Eros Unveiled: Plato and the God of Love*. Oxford: Oxford University Press.
Padgug, R. (1991) 'Sexual Matters: Rethinking Sexuality in History' in G. Chauncey Jr., M.B. Duberman, M. Vicinus (eds), *Hidden from History: Reclaiming the Gay and Lesbian Past*. London: Greenwood, 54-64.

## Bibliography

Paglia, C. (1992) *Sex, Art, and American Culture*. London: Penguin.
Pangle, T. (1994) 'Socrates in the Context of Xenophon's Political Writings', in P. Vander Waerdt (ed.), *The Socratic Movement*. Ithaca: Cornell University Press, 127-50.
Parker, H.N. (1993; 1996) 'Sappho Schoolmistress' in E. Greene (ed.), *Re-Reading Sappho: Reception and Transmission*. Berkeley: University of California Press, 146-86.
Parker, H.N. (2006) 'What Lobel Hath Joined Together: Sappho 49 LP', *Classical Quarterly* 56.2, 374-92.
Pauly, A., Wissova, G. and Kroll, W. (1894-) *Realencyclopädie der Classischen Altertumswissenschaft*, Stuttgart: J.B. Metzler.
Pelling, C. (2002) *Plutarch and History: Eighteen Studies*. London: Duckworth and The Classical Press of Wales.
Pender, E. (2007) 'Sappho and Anacreon in Plato's *Phaedrus*', *Leeds International Studies* 6.4, 1-57.
Penner, T. and Rowe, C. (2005) *Plato's Lysis*. Cambridge: Cambridge University Press.
Perrin, B. (ed. and tr.) (1916) *Plutarch: Parallel Lives*, vol. IV (repr. 2000). Cambridge: Harvard University Press.
Petropoulos, J.C.B. (1993) 'Sappho the Sorceress: Another Look at fr. 1 (LP)', *Zeitschrift für Papyrologie und Epigraphik* 97, 43-56.
Pradeau, J.-F. (1999) *Introduction* to C. Marboeuf and J.-F. Pradeau (eds), *Platon: Alcibiade*. Paris: Flammarion, 9-81.
Price, A.W. (1989) *Love and Friendship in Plato and Aristotle*. Oxford: Oxford University Press.
Provencal, V. (2005) '*Glukus Himeros*: Pederastic Influence on the Myth of Ganymede', *Journal of Homosexuality* 49, 87-136.
Purcell, N. and Horden, P. (2000) *The Corrupting Sea*. Oxford: John Wiley & Sons.
Race, W.H. (1989-90) 'Sappho, fr. 16 L-P and Alkaios, fr. 42 L-P: Romantic and Classical Strains in Lesbian Lyric', *Classical Journal* 85, 16-33.
Rawls, J. (1951) 'Outline of a Decision Procedure for Ethics', *Philosophical Review* 60, 177-97.
Rawls, J. (1972) *A Theory of Justice*. Cambridge: Harvard University Press.
Reeve, C.D.C. (2006) 'A Study in Violets: Alcibiades in the *Symposium*', in J.H. Lesher, D. Nails and S. Frisbee (eds), *Plato's Symposium: Issues in Interpretation and Reception*. Cambridge: Harvard University Press, 124-46.
Reeve, C.D.C. (2009) 'Plato on Eros and Friendship', in H. Benson (ed.), *A Companion to Plato*. Oxford: Blackwell Publishing, 294-307.
Renaud, F. (2007) 'La conoscenza di sé nell'Alcibiade I e nel commento di Olimpiodoro', in M. Migliori, L. Napolitano Valditara, A. Fermani (eds), *Interiorità e Anima. Psychè in Platone: Vita & Pensiero*, Milan, 225-44.
Renaud, F. (2008) 'Tradition et critique: lecture jumelée de Platon et Aristote chez Olympiodore', *Laval théologique et philosophique* 64 [= special issue: *Le commentaire philosophique dans l'Antiquité et ses prolongements: Méthodes exégétiques I*], 89-104.
Ricoeur, P. (2004; 2006) *Memory, History, Forgetting* (tr. K. Blamey and D. Pellauer). Chicago: University of Chicago Press.
Rist, J.M. (1963) 'Plotinus and the DAIMONION of Socrates', *Phoenix* 17, 13-24.
de Romilly, J. (1992) *The Great Sophists in Periclean Athens* (tr. J. Lloyd). Oxford: Clarendon Press.
Roochnik, D. (1987) 'The Erotics of Philosophical Discourse', *History of Philosophy Quarterly* 4, 117-29.

# Bibliography

Rosen, S. (1999) *Plato's Symposium*. South Bend: St Augustine's Press.
Rossetti, L. (2008) 'Savoir imiter c'est connaître: le cas de Mémorables, III, 8', in Narcy and Tordesillas (eds), *Xénophon et Socrate*, Paris: J. Vrin, 111-27.
Rowe C. (ed.) (1986) *Plato: Phaedrus*. Warminster: Aris and Philips.
Rowe C. (ed.) (1998) *Plato: Symposium*. Warminster: Aris and Philips.
Rowe C. (2005) Introduction to *Plato: Phaedrus*. London: Penguin, ix-xxix.
Runia, D.T. (1994) 'Philonic Nomenclature', *Studia Philonica Annual* 6, 1-27.
Santas, G. (1988) *Plato and Freud: Two Theories of Love*. Oxford: Basil Blackwell.
Satlow, M. (1994) '"They Abused Him Like A Woman": Homoeroticism, Gender Blurring and Homoeroticism in Late Antiquity', *Journal of the History of Sexuality* 5.1, 1-25.
Sayre, K. (1983) *Plato's Late Ontology: A Riddle Resolved*. Princeton: Princeton University Press.
Schleiermacher, F.D.E. (1996) *Über die Philosophie Platons*. Hamburg: F. Meiner.
Schwartz, M.B. (2000) 'Greek and Jew: Philo and the Alexandrian Riots of 38-41 CE', *Judaism*. http://findarticles.com/p/articles/mi_m0411/is_2_49/ai_64332273 (21/10/08).
Scott, D. (2000) 'Socrates and Alcibiades in the *Symposium*', *Hermathena* 168, 25-38.
Scott, G. (2000) *Plato's Socrates as Educator*. Albany: State University of New York Press.
Scott-Kilvert, S. (tr.) (1960) *Plutarch: The Rise and Fall of Athens: Nine Greek Lives*. Harmondsworth: Penguin.
Sedley, D. (2003) *Plato's Cratylus*. Cambridge: Cambridge University Press.
Segal, C. (1974; 1996) 'Eros and Incantation: Sappho and Oral Poetry', in E. Greene (ed.) *Re-Reading Sappho: Reception and Transmission*. Berkeley: University of California Press, 58-75.
Segonds, A.-Ph. (1985) *In Alcibiadem (Proclus, Sur le premier Alcibiade de Platon)* (2 vols). Paris: Les Belles Lettres.
Sheffield, F. (2006) *Plato's* Symposium: *The Ethics of Desire*. Oxford: Oxford University Press.
Shiner, Roger (1974) *Knowledge and Reality in Plato's Philebus*. Assen: Van Gorcum.
Silverman, K. (1996) *The Threshold of the Visible World*. New York: Routledge.
Sinclair, T.A. (1981) *Aristotle: Politics* (revised by T.J. Saunders). Harmondsworth: Penguin.
Smith, A.N.D. (2004) 'Did Plato Write the *Alcibiades* I?', *Apeiron* 37, 93-108.
Smith, A.N.D. and Woodruff P.B. (eds) (2000) *Reason and Religion in Socratic Philosophy*. Oxford: Oxford University Press.
Smith, M.D. (1996) 'Ancient Bisexuality and the Interpretation of *Romans* 1:26-7', *Journal of the American Academy of Religion* 64.2, 223-56.
Solmsen, F., Merkelbach, R. and West, M.L. (eds) (1990) *Hesiodi Opera* (3rd edn). Oxford: Oxford University Press.
Sorabji, R, (2006) 'The transformation of Plato and Aristotle', in H. Tarrant and D. Baltzly (eds), *Reading Plato in Antiquity*. London: Duckworth, 185-93.
Stallbaum, G. (1839) *Platonis Parmenides cum quattuor libris prolegomenorum et commentario perpetuo; accedunt Procli In Parmenidem Commentarii nunc emendatius editi* Frankfurt: Lipsiae (repr. 1976)
Stallbaum, G. (1857) *Platonis opera omnia*, vol.1. Leipzig: Franz Steiner Verlag.
de Ste. Croix, G.E.M. (1975) 'Aristotle on History and Poetry (*Poetics* 9, 1451a36-

# Bibliography

b11)', in B. Levick (ed.), *The Ancient Historian and His Materials*. Farnborough: Gregg, 45-58.
Steel, C. (1987) 'L'anagogie par les apories', in G. Boss and C. Steel (eds), *Proclus et son Influence*. Zürich: Grand Midi, 101-28.
Steel, C. (2007-2008) *In Parmenidem: Procli In Platonis Parmenidem Commentaria* (2 vols). Oxford: Clarendon Press.
Steiner, D.T. (2001) *Images in Mind: Statues in Archaic and Classical Greek Literature and Thought*. Princeton: Princeton University Press.
Stenström, H. (2008) 'Masculine or Feminine? Male Virgins in Joseph and Aseneth and the Book of Revelation', in B. Holberg and M. Winninge (eds), *Identity Formation in the New Testament*. Tubingen: Mohr Siebeck, 199-222.
Stewart, R.S. (1989) 'The Epistemological Function of Platonic Myth', *Philosophy and Rhetoric* 22, 260-80.
Szesnat, H. (1998) '"Pretty Boys" in Philo's *De Vita Contemplativa*', *Studia Philonica Annual* 10, 87-107.
Szesnat, H. (1999) 'Philo and Female Homoeroticism: Philo's Use of *GYNANDROS* and Recent Work on *Tribades*', *Journal for the Study of Judaism* 30, 140-7.
Taki, A. (2008) 'A Chasm Underneath the Smoothed Consensus: A Note on Plato's Idiosyncratic Use of *alethe legeis*', *Tokyo Daigaku Seiyo-Koten-Gaku Kenkyushitsu Kiyo (Bulletin of the Department of Classics, University of Tokyo)* 4, 83-93.
Taki, A. (2010) 'Proclus' Interpretative Method of Plato: a Problem in his Identification of Inferences in a Dialogue in his *Commentary on the Alcibiades* I', in Y. Oshiba and N. Koike (eds), *Seiyo-Koten-Gaku no Ashita e (Toward Tomorrow of Western Classics: Essays Presented to Kiichiro Itsumi)*. Tokyo, 201-14.
Taplin, O. (2001) *Literature in the Greek World*. Oxford: Oxford University Press.
Tarán, L. (1985) 'Platonism and Socratic Ignorance', in D.J. O'Meara (ed.), *Platonic Investigations*. Washington: Catholic University of America Press, 85-109.
Tarrant, H. (1993) *Thrasyllan Platonism*. Ithaca: Cornell University Press.
Tarrant, H. (2000) *Plato's First Interpreters*. London: Duckworth.
Tarrant, H. (2001) 'Naming Socratic Interrogation in the Charmides', in L. Brisson and T.M. Robinson (eds), *Plato:* Euthydemus, Lysis, Charmides: *Proceedings of the V Symposium Platonicum (Selected Papers)*. Sankt Augustin: Academia Verlag, 251-8.
Tarrant, H. (2005) 'Socratic Synousia?', *Journal of the History of Philosophy* 43, 131-55.
Tarrant, H. (2006/7) 'Piecing Together Polemo', *Mediterranean Archaeology* 19.20, 225-32.
Tarrant, H. (2007) 'Olympiodorus and Proclus on the Climax of the *Alcibiades*', *International Journal of Platonic Theology* 1, 3-29.
Tarrant, H. (2009) 'The Object of Alcibiades' Love', *Literature and Aesthetics* 19, 74-87.
Tarrant H. (2010) 'The Theaetetus as a Narrative Dialogue?', in N. O'Sullivan (ed.) *ASCS 31 Proceedings*. http://classics.uwa.edu.au/ascs31.
Tarrant H. (forthcoming) 'L'importance du Théétète avant Thrasylle', in D. el Murr (ed.).
Taylor, A E. (1926) *Plato: The Man and His Work*. London: Methuen & Co.
Taylor, C.C.W. (1991) *Plato: Protagoras*. Oxford: Clarendon Press.
Taylor, C.C.W. (2006) 'Socrates the Sophist', in L. Judson and V. Karasmanis (eds), *Remembering Socrates: Philosophical Essays*. Oxford: Oxford University Press, 57-68.

## Bibliography

Teloh, H. (1986) 'The Importance of the Interlocutors' Characters in Plato's Early Dialogues', in J. Cleary (ed.), *Proceedings of the Boston Area Colloquium for Ancient Philosophy* 2, 25-38.
Thesleff, H. (1967) 'Studies in the Styles of Plato', *Acta Philosophica Fennica* 20. Helsinki: Societas Philosophica Fennica [= Thesleff 2009].
Thesleff, H. (1982) 'Studies in Platonic Chronology', *Commentationes Humanarum Litterarum* 70. Helsinki: Societas Scientiarum Fennica.
Thesleff, H. (2003) 'A Symptomatic Text Corruption: Plato Gorgias 448a5', *Arctos* 37, 251-7.
Thesleff, H. (2007) 'The Gorgias re-written – why?' in L. Brisson and M. Erler (eds), *Plato: Gorgias and Meno: Proceedings of the VII Symposium Platonicum* (Selected Papers). Sankt Augustin, Academia Verlag, 78-83.
Thesleff, H. (2009) *Platonic Patterns: A Collection of Studies by Holger Thesleff*. Las Vegas: Parmenides Publishing.
Thesleff, H. and Nails, D. (2003) 'Early Academic Editing: Plato's *Laws*', in S. Scolnicov and L. Brisson (eds), *Plato's Laws: From Theory into Practice*. Sankt Augustin: Academia Verlag, 14-29.
Thompson, J.A.K. (tr.) (1953) *Aristotle: Nichomachean Ethics*. London: Penguin.
Trapp, M.B. (1994) *Maximus Tyrius: Dissertationes*. Leipzig: Teubner.
Trapp, M.B. (1997) *Maximus of Tyre: The Philosophical Orations*. Oxford: Clarendon Press.
Tuckey, T.G. (1968) *Plato's Charmides*. Amsterdam: Hakkert.
Vernant, J.-P. (1991) *Mortals and Immortals: Collected Essays*, ed. F. Zeitlin. Princeton: Princeton University Press.
Vernant, J.-P. and Doueihi, A. (1986) 'Feminine Figures of Death in Greece', *Diacritics* 16.2, 54-64.
Vlastos, G. (1973) *Platonic Studies*. Princeton: Princeton University Press (2nd edn 1981).
Vlastos, G. (1991) *Socrates: Ironist and Moral Philosopher*. Ithaca: Cornell University Press.
Vlastos, G. (1994) *Socratic Studies*. Cambridge: Cambridge University Press.
Ward, R.B. (1997) 'Why Unnatural? The Tradition behind Romans 1:26-7', *Harvard Theological Review* 90.3, 263-84.
Warner, R. (tr.) (1972) *Thucydides: History of the Peloponnesian War*. London: Penguin.
Warner, R. (tr.) (1965) *Xenophon: Memorabilia*. London: Penguin.
Weil, R. (1977) 'Aristotle's View of History', in J. Barnes, M. Schofield and R. Sorabji (eds), *Articles on Aristotle 2: Ethics and Politics*, London: Duckworth, 202-17.
Wellman, R.R. (1966) 'Socrates and Alcibiades: The *Alcibiades Major*', *History of Education Quarterly* 6.4, 3-21.
Westerink, L.G. (ed.) (1954) *Olympiodorus, Commentary on the first Alcibiades of Plato*. Amsterdam: North Holland Publishing Company (repr. 1982).
Westerink, L.G., Trouillard, J. and Segonds, A.-Ph. (2003) *Prolégomènes à la philosophie de Platon*, Paris: Les Belles Lettres.
Von Wilamowitz-Moellendorff, U. (1908) *Greek Historical Writing and Apollo: Two Lectures Delivered Before the University of Oxford* (tr. G. Murray), Oxford: Oxford University Press.
Wills, J. (1967) 'The Sapphic Umwertung aller Werte', *American Journal of Philology* 88, 434-42.

## Bibliography

Whittaker, C.R. (1997) 'Moses Finley: 1912-1986', *Proceedings of the British Academy* 94, 459-72.

Whittaker J. (1990) *Alcinoos: Enseignement des doctrines de Platon* (French tr. by P. Louis). Paris: Les Belles Lettres.

Winston, D. (1998) 'Philo and the Rabbis on Sex and the Body', *Poetics Today* 19.1, 41-62.

Wohl, V. (1999) 'The Eros of Alcibiades', *Classical Antiquity* 18.2, 349-85.

Wohl, V. (2002) *Love Among the Ruins: The Erotics of Democracy in Classical Athens*. Princeton: Princeton University Press.

Wohl, V. (2004) 'Dirty Dancing: Xenophon's *Symposium*', in P. Murray and P. Wilson (eds), *Music and the Muses: The Culture of Mousike in the Classical Athenian City*. Oxford: Oxford University Press, 337-63.

Wright, D.F. (1984) 'Homosexuals or Prostitutes? The Meaning of Arsenokoitai (1 Cor. 6:9; 1 Tim.1:10)', *Vigiliae Christianae* 38.2, 125-53.

Young, G. (tr.) (1957) *Sophocles: Oedipus Tyrannus*. London.

de Young J.B. (2000) *Homosexuality: Contemporary Claims Examined in Light of the Bible and other Ancient Literature and Laws*. Grand Rapids: Kregel Publications.

Zaslavsky, R. (1981) *Platonic Myth and Platonic Writing*. Lanham: University Press of America.

# Index to Platonic Works

*Alcibiades I*: *passim*, chiefly 1-29 (especially 13, 21-2), 35, 41, 45-8, 74, 77-89 (especially 77-8, 82-5, 86), 90-106, 107-18 (especially 116), 119-33, 149-54, 160-2, 180-9, 190-5, 200-4, 215-21, 223-33
    103a-4a: 86, 90-106, 133, 143, 149, 154
    105a-6a: 59, 142, 152-3, 192, 201
    109a-d: 201-3
    112d-114e: 184-6, 201-3
    115a-116d: 21, 112, 185
    116d-e: 216-19
    116d-118c: 77, 82-5, 203-4
    121b-4b: 219-20
    124b-c: 107, 112, 149, 152, 203
    126b-127d: 89
    128e-134e: 45-6, 113, 118, 127, 151-3
    132d-133c: 45-7, 136, 149-50, 191-2
    135d-e: 48, 150-3, 195
*Alcibiades II*: 134-46, 224-5
    138a-e: 137
    140c-d: 140
    143e-4e: 138, 143
    150c-51c: 135-6, 138, 141
*Apology*: 78-9, 83-5
    20c-23c: 78-9, 85
*Charmides*: 25, 79-82, 87, 124
*Cratylus*: 121, 156, 163, 240-1.
*Crito*: 119, 122-3
*Epistles*
    VII & VIII: 213
    VII 342c-e: 139
*Euthydemus*: 230
*Euthyphro*: 99, 141, 163, 225
*Gorgias*: 61-3, 94, 123, 142
    447b: 70
    481d-519e: 71-4, 76
*Hippias Major*: 155
*Hippias Minor*: 88, 227
*Ion*
    535e-6d: 157
*Laws*
    Book I: 126
    Book VIII: 171
    Book X: 110-11, 116
*Lysis*: 30-6, 42-3, 86

*Meno*: 123, 125, 138
    80d-86c: 80-1, 96-7
*Menexenus*: 145
*Parmenides*: 181-2, 185-7
*Phaedo*
    68ec-69e: 125
*Phaedrus*: 18-21, 36-41, 44, 111, 116-17, 127, 150, 192-6
    229e: 18
    235b-d: 20
    244a-245c: 20, 137, 150
    248a-257a: 14, 48-9, 57, 59, 107-9, 150, 198, 230
*Philebus*: 123, 225-6, 229
    23b-31b: 121
*Politicus*, see *Statesman*
*Protagoras*: 61-70; 122, 124, 129
    309a-d: 35, 62-4
    316a: 70
    318a-d: 155
    320a-b: 65
    320c-8b: 66, 97, 102, 104
    336b-e: 70
    339b-347a: 66-8
*Republic*: 139, 141
    Book I: 117-18, 191
    Book IV: 125-6
    Book VI: 108, 118, 194-5
    Book VII: 48, 117-18
    Book IX: 20, 142
    Book X: 27, 142
*Statesman*: 229-31
    306a-309b: 125-6
*Symposium*: 30, 34-5, 40-4, 56-8, 62, 75-6, 116, 151-2, 193-6, 198-9, 220-1
    174e-5e: 34-5, 55, 157, 163, 199
    180c-5c: 27, 148, 161
    201d-12b: 9-17, 20, 36-7, 47-8, 117, 149, 193-5, 220
    212d-22b: 25, 27, 28, 34-6, 45, 114-15, 137, 141, 159, 162, 201, 213
*Theaetetus*: 156, 159-60, 163, 192, 229
*Theages*: 154-60, 233-6
*Timaeus*: 193, 228

# General Index

Aeschines Socraticus: 61-2, 147-54, 161, 196
Alcibiades: 11, 54, 61-76 (especially 61, 65, 70, 73-4), 114-15, 134, 200-13, 215-21
    and Socrates: 8, 11, 13, 14, 25, 35-6, 46, 54-5, 56-7, 62, 63-4, 71, 107, 111-12, 114-15, 140-1
    death of: 134
    literary tradition: 57-8, 61-2, 147-9, 200-4
    in *Alcibiades II*: 134-46
    in Aristophanes: 72, 147
    in Plato: 57-8, 62, 65-6, 71-2, 74-5
    in Plutarch: 61, 72, 163, 197, 199, 215-16, 218
    in Thucydides: 67-9, 71-2, 140, 216-18
Alexandria: 164-79
Ammon: 151
Aphrodite: 8, 10, 20, 22, 24
Archelaus of Athens: 1, 36
Archelaus of Macedon: 138, 145
arguments:
    in the *Alcibiades I*: 83-5, 90-106, 119-20, 126, 128-9, 172, 183-6
    in the *Alcibiades II*: 134, 138
Aristides (pupil of Socrates): 55, 154-60
Aristophanes
    *Clouds*: 107, 147
    *Frogs*: 72, 107
    *Wasps*: 72
Aristotle: 134, 207-9
    *Magna Moralia*: 47
    *Nicomachean Ethics*: 140, 142-5
    *Poetics*: 208-9
    *Politics*: 104

Bloch, M.: 204-10
Blundell, M.: 11
Butler, J.: 12

Callicles: 61-3, 70-1, 73-4, 76
Charmides: 24-6, 40-1, 140
consensus: 90-106
courage: 123-30, 171, 173, 210
Crantor: 158-9
Crates: 158-9

Critias: 2, 54-5, 61-2, 70 with n.15, 75-6, 81-2, 140
Critoboulus: 49-50, 52-4
Cynics: 137, 139-40

*daimôn*: for Socrates' *daimôn*, see Socrates: his divine sign
Denyer, N.: 4, 46, 63, 104-6, 130-2, 180, 216-17
Diotima: 8-13, 17, 26, 36, 57, 196, 220
divine sign: see Socrates: his divine sign
Douglas, M.: 170-1
Dyck, J.: 174

Edmonds, R.: 110
Egypt: 141, 167-8
*epistrophê*: see turning
Erler, M.: 182
*eros* (*Eros*): 7-29, 30-44, 45-60, 108, 147-63
    as *daimôn*: 15, 194-7, 149-50, 157, 193, 194-5
    *erastês/erômenos*: 13-15, 31, 33, 35, 38, 40, 47-8, 52, 107-18
    as madness: 19-21, 49-50, 137, 150
    as pedagogy: 13-15, 22, 25, 45-60, 147-63, 164-79, 195-8
Euthyphro: 99, 163, 190
expertise: 2, 5, 30-1, 36-41, 78, 84-5, 100-3, 126, 151, 155, 160-2, 196, 201

Foley, H.: 16
Fränkel, H.: 16-17
friendship: see *philia*

Galen: 22
Goldhill, S.: 50-1
Good, the: 21-2, 32, 66-7, 72, 108-15, 144-5, 194-5
Gorgias: 17-18
Greek language: 92-8
Gribble, D.: 216, 221
Griswold, C.: 37-8

Hadot, P.: 12-13
Halperin, D.: 13, 58-60, 109, 111, 116, 172

## General Index

Hermeias: 6, 199
homosexuality: see relationships
Hornblower, S.: 220
Howland, J.: 134-5, 138, 143-4
Hutchinson, D.: 140

Iamblichus: 180-1, 184
Irwin, T.: 124-5
Isocrates: 2, 162, 219

Jewish Culture and Religion: 164-79
Jowett, B.: 127-8, 131-5
Joyal, M.: 119, 154, 196
justice: 73, 90-106, 124-7, 144-5, 201-2, 227-9

Klawans, J.: 169
knowledge: 33-9, 45-9, 69, 77-88, 90, 94-106, 108, 110, 112-15, 124-7, 147-8, 150-1, 183, 185-6, 196
 self-knowledge: 14-15, 18, 22, 37, 39, 45-8, 77-8, 113, 127, 136-7, 140, 142-3, 150-3, 186, 191, 196-7

liberal society: 103

Macedonia: 1, 138, 217
McConnell, T.: 100
McNeill, D.: 20
Maximus of Tyre: 8-11, 25-8
*megalopsuchia*: 134-46
mirror-images: 45-51, 54, 58, 131, 140, 161

Neoplatonism: see under Proclus and Olympiodorus
Nietzsche, F.: 139
Nightingale, A.: 21, 47, 58-9
Nussbaum, M.: 117, 139
Nye, A.: 109, 111, 117

Oedipus: 137-8, 142-4
Olympiodorus: 152-3, 181, 190-9
Osborne, C.: 13
Ovid: 19, 24, 172

Parker, H.: 18-20
Parmenides: 1, 181-2, 185-6
Pausanias: 35, 148, 151
pedagogy: 7, 11-15, 22, 24-6, 45-60, 135-6, 147, 151-7, 164-79, 196-8; see also teaching
Pender, E.: 19-21
Penia: see Poros

Peparethos: 216-19
Pericles: 65, 73, 76, 138, 142-3, 203-4, 211, 216
Persia: 13, 140, 144, 216, 219-20
*philia*: 23, 40-4, 52-3, 86, 89, 176, 201-3
Philip II: 217-19
Philo of Alexandria: 164-79
Plato: see Index to Platonic Works
Platonism and the Platonic tradition: 21, 46, 147-63, 180-98
Polemo of Athens: 158-63, 197
Poros and Penia: 10-12, 194, 220
Proclus: 90-1, 94-5, 98-9, 104-5, 180-9, 199
Protagoras: 8, 16, 155-6

relationships:
 dual-role: 107-18
 homosexual: 165-79
 pederastic: 14, 30, 33, 41, 46, 49-52, 69, 172-3, 177-9
 reciprocal: 33, 58, 109, 111, 117, 150-1, 197
religion, traditional: 95, 134-6, 141, 145, 167-9, 174

Sappho: 7-11, 14-29
Schleierlacher, F.: 120, 161, 180
Smith, N.: 120-3, 130-3
Socrates: *passim*
 and Alcibiades: 7-29 (especially 8, 11, 14), 35-6, 56-7, 61-76 (especially 63-4, 71), 107, 111-12, 114-15, 147-63
 defence of: 50-1, 54-5, 61, 63, 69-70, 73-4
 divine sign: 18, 23, 149, 190-9 (with reference to the authenticity of *Alcibiades I*: 120, 123)
 *elenchus*: 80, 82, 95, 151, 153, 159, 182-4, 196
 *enkrateia*: 50-3, 57
 influence on young: 2, 30, 55, 66-9, 72-3; (failure of): 14-15, 62, 73, 107-18, 134-46
 and Sappho: 7-29
 Socratic ignorance: 36 37, 39, 77-89, 108, 161, 186
 Socratic irony: 21-2 with n.32, 35-6, 37 with n.32, 41, 64, 107
 *Sôkratikoi Logoi*: 61-2, 180-9
Sophists: 64, 65
 Eros as sophist: 8, 10, 12-13, 24, 27
 language of: 155-6
 The Many as sophist: 143

253

## General Index

Sappho as precursor: 16
Sophistic interpretation of myth: 37
Sophistic pedagogy and thought: 54, 62-5, 69-71, 151
soul, tripartite: 123, 130
Sparta: 67-9, 126, 135, 140, 200, 226, 229
Stenström, H.: 172-3
stylistic analysis (stylometry): 119-20, 123, 130, 134, 157, 223-36

Taplin, O.: 12-13
Taylor, A.: 120-1
teaching and learning: 64-9, 74-5, 90-106, 133, 135-6, 149, 151, 154, 196, 201 (and see pedagogy)
Teiresias: 138
Thucydides (historian): 77-84, 140, 207-12, 216-17, 221
tragedy: 137-45
turning (return, *epistrophê*): 196, 206
tyranny: 11, 20, 132, 136-44, 192

Vernant, J.-P.: 10, 14, 53-4
virtue: 36, 55, 64-7, 90-106, 124-33, 140, 152, 172
Vlastos, G.: 48, 105

Wellmann, R.: 22
Wohl, V.: 13-14

Xenocrates: 158-9
Xenophon: 45-60, 61, 62-3, 134, 138, 192
 *Hiero*: 144
 *Memorabilia*: 49-50, 54-6, 61-2, 70, 148, 190
 *Symposium*: 7, 52-3, 54, 57, 222
 influence on *Alcibiades II*: 141
 Ps.-Xenophon, 'Old Oligarch': 220-1

Zeno (of Citium): 163
Zeno (of Elea): 133, 181